SOLDIERS OF THE NATION

Studies in War, Society, and the Military

GENERAL EDITORS

Kara Dixon Vuic
Texas Christian University

Richard S. Fogarty
University at Albany, State University of New York

EDITORIAL BOARD

Peter Maslowski
University of Nebraska–Lincoln

David Graff
Kansas State University

Reina Pennington
Norwich University

SOLDIERS OF THE NATION

Military Service and Modern Puerto Rico, 1868–1952

HARRY FRANQUI-RIVERA

UNIVERSITY OF NEBRASKA PRESS | LINCOLN

© 2018 by the Board of Regents of the University of Nebraska

Parts of chapter 3 were previously published in "'So a New Day Has Dawned for Porto Rico's Jíbaro': Military Service, Manhood and Self-Government during World War I," *Latino Studies* 13, no. 2 (2015): 185–206.

All rights reserved

Library of Congress Cataloging-in-Publication Data

Title: Soldiers of the nation: military service and modern Puerto Rico, 1868–1952 / Harry Franqui-Rivera.
Other titles: Military service and modern Puerto Rico, 1868–1952
Description: Lincoln NE: University of Nebraska Press, [2018] | Series: Studies in war, society, and the military
Identifiers: LCCN 2017052571
ISBN 9780803278677 (cloth: alk. paper)
ISBN 9781496222343 (paperback)
ISBN 9781496205445 (epub)
ISBN 9781496205452 (mobi)
ISBN 9781496205469 (pdf)
Subjects: LCSH: Puerto Rico—Military relations—United States. | United States—Military relations—Puerto Rico. | Puerto Rico—History—1898–1952. | Soldiers—Puerto Rico—History. | Puerto Rico—History, Military.
Classification: LCC E183.8.P9 S67 2018 | DDC 355/.0310973097295—dc23 LC record available at https://lccn.loc.gov/2017052571

Set in Janson Text LT Pro by E. Cuddy.

To all Puerto Rican soldiers and veterans, whose contribution to Puerto Rican history and the American experience has been largely ignored.

CONTENTS

List of Illustrations | ix
Acknowledgments | xi
Introduction | xiii

1. Birth of a Nation: A Labor of Thirty Years, 1868–1898 | 1
2. Puerto Rican a la Americana: A Hearts and Minds Campaign, 1898–1914 | 35
3. A New Day Has Dawned: World War I and Mobilization of the Peasant | 63
4. War against the Yankees! Prelude to the Battle over Modern Puerto Rico | 97
5. Education, Industrialization, and Decolonization: The Battlefields of World War II | 127
6. Fighting for the "Nation"? War at Home and Abroad | 169

Conclusion | 199

Notes | 215
Bibliography | 283
Index | 295

ILLUSTRATIONS

1. "Porto Ricans" in American Colonial Army on El Morro Castle's parade field, 1899 | 48
2. Porto Rico Provisional Regiment of Infantry parades before the Teatro Tapia in San Juan, ca. 1903 | 56
3. Soldiers of the 65th Infantry repair phone lines in Caguas, P.R. | 144
4. Club Damas de Puerto Rico supports the war effort | 147
5. Vocational training for Puerto Rican soldiers during World War II | 154
6. "Industrialization needs us." "Puerto Rico needs electricians." | 159
7. Puerto Rico National Guardsman and Insular Police officer during Nationalist uprising | 176
8. Chaplain blesses a Puerto Rican flag in Korea | 191
9. Flag of the Commonwealth of Puerto Rico presented to the 65th Infantry Regiment, 3rd U.S. Infantry Division, in Korea | 192
10. Puerto Rican soldiers serving with the 65th Infantry in Korea hold the Puerto Rican flag, fall 1952 | 193

ACKNOWLEDGMENTS

The research for this book began some fifteen years ago. During that time, I earned a master's degree in military history and a PhD in Latin American and Caribbean history. The process was not an easy one, and many times it seemed unmanageable.

As a graduate student, it was difficult to find scholars who would guide my research. In my field, Latin American and Caribbean history, there seems to be a knee-jerk reaction to all matters related to the military in general and to the U.S. military in particular. So it was hard to get scholars to take a serious look at my thesis. Moreover, I found that several truisms in Puerto Rican history, which have made their way into academic discourse, were based not on facts but on what I have come to understand as a national mythology.

In these skewed narratives, Puerto Ricans have been but peons in an imperial-colonial game, used as cannon fodder and disposable labor for the metropolis. The list goes on. As life has taught me, and my research confirmed, history is more complicated than that. So I could see former Puerto Rican peasants gaining agency through military service without having to engage in mental gymnastics to find a colonial complex that might have explained this supposed agency. This position didn't win me any friends, and in fact it closed many doors. When I was still a graduate student, senior scholars advised me that I would never get a position as a professor because of my topic and analysis. I was advised to change my topic and not publish my findings. I decided that it was a matter of ethics that my research should be published.

One of the first scholars to read my work and understand that there wasn't an ounce of imperial apologia in it was José A. Hernández. His support, thorough readings of my many drafts, and recommendations were invaluable. I would also like to acknowledge the support my dissertation committee gave me. Lowell Gudmundson, Jane Rausch, John Higginson, Guillermo Irizarry, and Agustin Lao-Montes were instrumental in shaping my work. I owe much to the support and friendship that Alice Nash, Laura Lovett, Gloria Bernabe Ramos, Jose Ornelas, Julie de Chantal, and Brian Bixby, among many others, showed me since my very first days at the University of Massachusetts, Amherst.

I would like to recognize the Temple University history faculty, in particular Mary Procida, Russell F. Wrigley, Gregory Urwin, Jay Lokenhour, and Richard Immerman, who showed me how to be a historian and suffered through my many grammar mistakes as I learned to write in English. The same goes for my Temple classmates Bob Wintermute, Uta Raina, and Ginger Davis.

I spent time at the Center for Puerto Rican Studies, Hunter College, CUNY, where the staff provided me with the space, time, and resources to focus on research and writing. I'm indebted to Edwin Meléndez for his unconditional support. I'm humbled by the friendship the staff and scholars provided me. Marilisa Jiménez, Consuelo Martínez-Reyes, José de Jesus, Xavier Totti, Monique Aviles, Lorena García Barroso, Carlos Vargas-Ramos—thank you!

Aldo Lauria-Santiago, Ana Y. Ramos-Sayas, Teresita Levy, Rosa Carrasquillo, Arlene Torres, Milago Denis-Rosario, Lara Putnam, and the blind reviewers involved in this process, thank you for reading parts of what became my manuscript at different stages and for your precious comments and recommendations. Any shortcomings are all mine.

Finally, I would like to acknowledge my family. They have given me time and space during nights and weekends and one too many family nights. To my wife, Patricia, my son, Galli, and my daughter, Olivia: you are my rock. Thank you!

INTRODUCTION

During the summer of 2001 I interviewed several Korean War veterans in Puerto Rico. Those interviews were part of my research on the renowned 65th Infantry Regiment, also known as the Borinqueneers. I hoped the interviews would bring a more personal feeling to my project. But those veterans did more than that. They opened my eyes to larger historical processes. Many described themselves as *jíbaros*, as humble Puerto Rican rural folks. When I met them, they no longer lived off the land. In fact, after the war many finished high school and attended vocational schools and colleges. They set up small and medium-sized businesses, from the local *colmado* and *barra* to an engineering contracting firm and everything in between. Some became local leaders or assemblymen or joined the army of technicians and technocrats in charge of carrying out the socioeconomic restructuring of the island as envisioned by the creators of the political experiment we know as the Estado Libre Asociado de Puerto Rico (ELA), or the Commonwealth.

They had been transformed by their military service. Their professions had little to do with the romanticized figure of the Puerto Rican rural folk. However, they proudly claimed that they continued to be jíbaros.[1] And true to form, they showed me the hospitality for which the rural folk are famous. I was invited into their houses and to their tables. I quickly figured I was going through a vetting process. At their tables I was offered a mix of imported goods and the fresh plantains, green bananas, tubers, avocados, mangoes, and oranges that they continue to grow in small plots of land (*el patio*) behind their cement houses. The generous meals they offered me were representative of two worlds. There was the modern world exemplified by the processed, imported food bought at the supermarket, Sam's Club, or Costco. But there also was a world that had supposedly disappeared during the march toward a modern industrialized Puerto Rico. That world was represented by the *viandas* (tubers) and other products they offered me from their gardens. As I enjoyed their hospitality and broke bread with them, I realized that these veterans had not just negotiated these two worlds. They had fused them. Military service had transformed them in many ways, but it had also allowed them to subsidize that jíbaro way of living. And in that sense, they had made their colonial encounter with the military a collaborative experience in which, to borrow Michael C. Hawkins's description of the clash between the Moros of the Southern Philippines and the U.S. military, they "established the parameters of their own modern selves."[2]

These soldiers did more than negotiate and establish their own identities. They were instrumental in redefining Puertoricaness and modern Puerto Rico during the transformative 1940s and 1950s. In 1952 a military news release from Korea announced that

> a can full of Korean earth, hallowed by the sacrifices of Puerto Rican American soldiers, is on its way to Corozal, Puerto Rico, where it will become part of a monument to Puerto Ricans who gave their lives in Korea. The frozen, snow-covered soil was taken from ground over which the Puerto Rican Regiment has battled, and from an area where men have died. It will be placed in the cornerstone of the Corozal monument.[3]

Corozal, a mountain town in Puerto Rico, was but one of numerous towns that erected monuments and plaques commemorating the fallen in Korea. Far from being a sad reminder of the lives lost in combat or of the disappearance of the jíbaro before the juggernaut of industrialization and modernization, these monuments recognize the role of the island's common folk in the creation of modern Puerto Rico.[4]

The political entity we know as the Estado Libre Asociado de

Puerto Rico came into existence during the Korean War. Tens of thousands of Puerto Ricans participated in this conflict. Political figures and the press portrayed the war as a battle for the decolonization of Puerto Rico and the soldiers as the embodiment of the philosophy behind commonwealth status. Calls for more autonomy and support for the commonwealth formula appeared in mainstream local newspapers alongside articles lauding the men of the 65th as a possible catalyst in forging a new national identity.[5] The rationale behind these articles was that the Borinqueneers' commitment to Korea as first-line troops "will help Puerto Ricans to come out of their complexes of insularism, and erase the marks of inferiority, which are the by-product of hundreds of years of colonial type regimes."[6] The local press and politicians saw service as a regenerative process that would prepare the Puerto Ricans for self-government. The men of the 65th were praised as the quintessential example of what it meant to be a Puerto Rican: modern, manly, and hence deserving of self-rule and self-determination by virtue of his military training, service, and sacrifice. As local leaders equated mass participation in the Korean War with a new national identity anchored on modernity and manhood and the promise of decolonization, *el sesenta y cinco*, as the 65th was popularly called, became a national icon.[7] In this sense, the foundation of the monuments symbolizes the foundation of the modern Puerto Rican state and of modern Puerto Rican national identities—at least as imagined by the new colonial entity's ideologues.

The active participation of Puerto Rican troops in the Korean War, however, was just the climax of a long process in which Puerto Ricans, like many colonial and subaltern groups, sought to prove their manhood and right to self-determination and decolonization through military service. In this study, I analyze the impact of military service on the converging sociocultural and political histories of Puerto Rico. In particular, I explore the military mobilization and demobilization of rural and urban working-class sectors from the 1860s to the 1950s. The analysis centers on patterns of inclusion/exclusion within the military and how they transformed into socioeconomic and political disenfranchisement or enfranchisement. It is of paramount importance to analyze these processes from three perspectives. First, what compelled the metropolis to either mobilize or demobilize the Puerto Ricans? Second, what roles did the Puerto Rican elites play in these projects? Third, how did these processes affect and in turn become altered by the colonial subjects going through them? To answer these questions, I rely on an intersectional analysis of gender, race, and class to understand modernity projects driving nation-state building and identity formation processes via military service taking place in a colonial setting under two empires.

Manhood, Race, and Military Service

Puerto Rican leaders who thought that participation in the Korean War would lead to political equality, self-determination, and self-government were not breaking new ground. Members from minority groups and colonial subjects have joined the military of their respective countries or empires as a means to improve their socioeconomic standing and to gain acceptance from mainstream dominant groups as well as for patriotism and even the thrill of adventure.[8] In turn, leaders from these communities have tried to transform their service into political gains, from obtaining full citizenship to ending or ameliorating colonial relations by proving their community's collective worth. Military service may work as a vehicle for enfranchisement, but it is also used as a tool for denying full citizenship and self-government to entire groups. Subordinated roles in or outright exclusion from the military are used to rationalize limited citizenship as well as the construction of colonial subjects. This is done by linking military service and martial prowess with fitness for self-government in gendered and racialized terms.

As soon as the United States took over the island in 1898, prominent Puerto Ricans requested the creation of local militias. They did so because they understood the links between service, manhood, and political enfranchisement. The yellow press in the United States had portrayed Cuba and Puerto Rico as damsels in distress, abused by Spain and in need of rescue by a virile Uncle Sam to sell the idea of intervening in the Cuban War of Independence. The cartoons soon changed after U.S. intervention to portray both islands as unruly black children.[9] These gendered and racial narratives were dominant by *fin de siècle*. In a study of U.S. culture at the turn of the nineteenth century, Gail Bederman discusses several noteworthy instances in which men used "ideas about white supremacy to produce a racially based ideology of male power." She explains that "between 1890 and 1917, as white middle-class men actively worked to reinforce male power, their race became a factor which was crucial to their gender."[10] Race was instrumental in the imagining of American manhood. Bederman asks us to understand manhood or masculinity as the "cultural process whereby concrete individuals are constituted as members of a preexisting social category—as men," a process that "produces a set of truths about who an individual is and what he or she can do."[11] Within this context, nonwhites could never be true men, and their position in society must be subordinated to white men and women. Hence it was important to deny nonwhite men access to symbols of manhood.

Disagreement about what attributes were considered "manly" at different places and historical junctures is inevitable. However, few would argue against military service being an almost universal rite of passage into manhood.[12] Preventing nonwhite males from serving in the military, limiting them to support roles, or questioning their martial prowess denied them this rite of passage and helped to create and perpetuate the myth that nonwhites are unworthy of full citizenship and unfit for self-determination and government.

Kristin L. Hoganson has argued that in the United States, gender served as a "coalition building political method" that helped to consolidate contradictory arguments while unifying peoples from different walks of life in favor of war with Spain in 1898. It was widely accepted that combat "would bolster American manhood." Mainstream narratives glorified military action because it was supposed to provide the grounds for the making of better men vested in complete manliness "a prerequisite for full citizenship and political leadership."[13] Not all men were to be given the same opportunity to prove their manhood. In her seminal work,

"Black and Blue on San Juan Hill," Amy Kaplan has explained how black soldiers were portrayed as inferior to their white counterparts, prone to panic and cowardice, and only able to perform acceptably when firmly and often brutally led by white officers. From Theodore Roosevelt's account of the war to yellow press reports, the contribution of blacks was constructed in a way that portrayed them as unfit for leadership roles, if not outright service. Such characterizations were used to reinforce racial hierarchies at home and to ease racial anxieties and the fear of racial contamination as the United States expanded.[14] It is not coincidental that the U.S. military began to restrict the role of blacks in the military after the Spanish-American War and the subsequent Filipino insurrection against American rule ended.[15] Precluding blacks from combat positions and denying them officers' commissions was the local manifestation of an imperial ideology justified on the grounds of the incapability of darker races to achieve full manhood and self-government.

The gendered and racialized discourses used in support of the war in 1898 traveled with the American armies. As military service became definitive proof of manhood and a prerequisite for full citizenship and self-rule, calling into question the military competency of Cuban and Filipino rebels became an expeditious rationalization for empire. Cuban rebels, instrumental in securing a U.S. victory in Cuba, were portrayed as being even more lacking in martial prowess and manliness than African American troops.[16] The implications are clear. The African American soldier performed slightly better and was somewhat manlier than his Cuban counterpart because the former was led and controlled by white officers. In these skewed narratives, African Americans and Cubans evidenced their innate inability for martial prowess, which rendered them as incomplete men. These narratives then worked domestically and internationally, serving both to strengthen racial hierarchies at home and abroad. This logic was promptly extended to Puerto Ricans who were active participants in the Puerto Rican campaign, but did not have a rebel army waiting to greet the invading American forces. The ethnoracial assignments of the new colonial subjects under the American imperial umbrella were built upon the premise of their men's compromised manhood as evidenced by their supposedly inadequate or nonexistent martial spirit.

Accepting martial aptitude as a definer of manliness and fitness for self-rule was not the exclusive prerogative of the American empire. Most of the western world, and by addition its colonies, operated under similar assumptions.[17] Ada Ferrer has argued that as Cuban independence seemed reachable, sectors within the rebel army were preoccupied with the kind of leaders who would emerge from what had become a multiracial society and rebel army. White Cuban rebels used a "masculine discourse of insurgency and nationalism" as early as 1868 by making a call to arms that exhorted the Cuban men to fight and regain their rights as men. They worried that men they deemed unfit for political leadership might attain it due to their military service.[18] Afro-Cubans were to be accepted into the Cuban nation but not exactly as equals. For that matter the combat record, loyalty, and dedication to the struggle for independence of Afro-Cuban officers, as exemplified by the court-martial of black rebel Quintín Bandera, were called into question as the war neared its end.[19] A rebel military tribunal regarded Bandera's persona, culture, and his supposedly voracious sexual appetite as evidence of his "rustic" nature and incapacity to achieve modern manhood. Afro-Cubans could not be denied citizenship and some access to the Cuban nation, as they had mobilized en masse in the struggle for independence. But inclusion and their role within the emergent Cuban nation could be limited, which in this case was done by misconstruing the role of black rebel officers on the basis of cultural and racial inferiority as shown by their "rustic" manhood. Both within the crumbling Spanish empire and the emerging American imperium, gender and racial narratives served to construct nonwhite men as inferior, incapable of achieving full and modern manhood and utterly unfit for self-rule.

Puerto Ricans were not exempt from the belief that military service created better and manlier men, and neither were they oblivious to the link between military service and politics. The local elites had witnessed the gradual demobilization of the Puerto

Rican militias throughout the eighteenth century as the Spanish colonial administration tightened its control over the island. Before the U.S. invasion, Puerto Rican revolutionary Ramón Emeterio Betances had warned that if the Puerto Ricans did not overthrow the Spaniards, the island would become an American colony.[20] Eugenio María de Hostos, another champion of independence, believed that centuries of oppression had weakened the Puerto Ricans to the point where they might not even constitute a people. Hostos, who lamented not having any military skills to contribute to the liberation of the island, thought that military training and schooling would put the Puerto Ricans onto the path to modernity and self-determination. Understanding these links, political leaders and opinion makers sought access to military service and argued for the military schooling of Puerto Ricans as soon as the United States took over the island.[21]

Military service itself was not enough for an individual's "manhood" and modernity to be recognized. A group's assignment and behavior during war was the ultimate test. Parties of scouts assisted in the U.S. invasion, and hundreds of Puerto Ricans rose against the Spanish establishment on their own while others fought alongside the Cuban rebels. However, the new metropolis was quick to elevate the supposedly nonmartial and docile nature of the Puerto Ricans into an enduring myth, even as it mobilized them.[22] Hence, even though Puerto Ricans started to serve in the U.S. military in 1899, when the Porto Rican Battalion of Volunteers was instituted, and Puerto Ricans served during the two world wars, the military authorities did not trust Puerto Rican units in combat. The Puerto Ricans were remobilized under the American flag, but the service of local units would be limited, conditioned, and colonial in nature until the Korean War.

The military experience of the Puerto Ricans under the United States (and under Spain) may have been colonial in nature, but that does not mean that negotiation did not occur. As Laura Briggs has argued, "Internal power relations of gender, race, class, age, and so on, can be worked out through the structures of colonialism (what structures are untouched by it) without being in any meaningful sense determined by them."[23] Power relations are inevitably influenced by the metropolitan structures, but the colonial subjects have a say in shaping the nature of these institutions and the outcome of colonial projects.[24]

The military plays a relevant role in nation-building projects and in the development of national identities. Florencia Mallon has argued that the degree of military, paramilitary, and political mobilization of subaltern subjects contributes to the depth of the liberal spirit of a country's polity. She argues that subaltern groups not only sense a stake in nation-state formation but also seek to participate in its design. Participation is contested at the local level and filtered through regional politics until it moves to the national level where negotiation continues and a consensus is reached. Mallon calls this stage hegemony, a process that will continue endlessly as counter hegemonic forces keep challenging the dominant entity. During periods of crisis, these groups get the opportunity to strengthen their political stand and gain more inclusion and participation in developing or redefining the nation (and national identities) and its institutions, either by being included in political coalitions or by being mobilized for war.[25]

As Eileen Suárez Findlay has argued, "Spanish and U.S. imperialism have obviously profoundly shaped Puerto Rican history, as have a variety of attempts to forge a coherent national identity," while both empires have tried to create colonial "national" identities for its subjects.[26] Spanish and U.S. imperialists tried to implement different colonial state/nation-building and colonial state/nation-formation projects in Puerto Rico (and elsewhere) in which controlling the identity of the colonial subjects was of paramount importance. These projects, as Julian Go argues, "were rarely if ever realized in full." Moreover, those projects were aided, challenged, and altered by the local elites and popular sectors.[27] Both counter the metropoles with their own projects.

Benedict Anderson has argued that the nation is an imagined political community "and imagined both inherently limited and sovereign."[28] Nancy Morris, however, contends that a group's self-recognition as a nation is usually based on "some combination of objective characteristics of history, language, culture, and territory," which may lead to a desire for self-determination but which is not necessarily "equal to a desire for political independence."[29] It is important to understand that national sovereignty has several meanings in the case of Puerto Rico and that the island's double colonial experience led to the creation of very flexible national identities and political communities in which a case for *autonomismo* (political autonomy without outright separation from the metropolis) and even for full annexation could be made using the same symbols usually identified with independence.[30] The empowerment of the popular sectors accounts for these broad and inclusive definitions of national identities and decolonization projects in Puerto Rico, and military service was essential for the enfranchisement of these sectors. Access to military service was one of those areas in which the construction of identities and competing colonial and nation-building projects was contested and defined. In Puerto Rico, military service became an arena where coloniality was always in contestation and negotiated.

Nation-Building Projects via Military Service

Studying military mobilization as political enfranchisement requires us to answer the question of who controls the military and mobilization? The contrast between the Spanish and American empires with regard to the military service of those born on the island is striking. In the case of Puerto Rico, Spain sought and mostly succeeded in controlling the military on the island and in exercising tight control over the colonial political apparatus. Under American rule thirty years later, the military became a tool for the "Americanization" of the island as part of a broader nation-building project in the circum-Caribbean. The United States relied on a nation-building project via limited inclusion (both politically and militarily) and cultural assimilation to cement its control over Puerto Rico. In this regard, understanding the armed forces as a culture-homogenizing agent and as a tool for socioeconomic and political empowerment helps to explain the formation and evolution of Puerto Rican national identities from the 1860s to the 1950s. Studying the mass participation of popular sectors in military institutions should add to our understanding of the development of Puerto Rico's national identities and how these evolving identities influenced the political choices of the island.

Spain relied for centuries on local militia to keep Puerto Rico within its fold. The island also provided a manpower pool and a staging area from which to quench revolts in other parts of the empire. However, after the failed insurrection against Spanish rule, known as el Grito de Lares de 1868, Spanish colonial authorities moved swiftly to dismantle the remaining militias manned by *"los hijos de este país."* The Spanish authorities' response to growing discontent against their rule in the island took shape as a colonial project that relied on exclusion to prevent the people born on the island from developing strong national identities that could be used to challenge Spanish sovereignty. These policies can be aptly called an anti–nation-building project in which the creation of colonial identities by suppression and exclusion was a priority.

The demobilization of the Puerto Ricans, a very restrictive polity, and the dearth of a common education were some of the patterns of repression and exclusion that led to the slow and ambivalent development of distinct national identities in the island. The late Spanish colonial project, especially after el Grito de Lares, was marked by increased political and military exclusion. The island-born elites' (*criollos*) lack of political power and their economic subordination to the elites born in Spain, the *peninsulares*, have been accepted in Puerto Rican historiography as a source of grievance that ultimately moved the *criollos* to embrace independence, or *autonomismo*.[31] Political exclusion and economic subordination were real but affected a relatively small sector of the population which still saw in Spain a warrantor of their position on the island. Demobilizing the local militias, on the other hand, affected far more people.[32] Demobilization allowed Puerto Ricans to see the Spaniards as a foreign "Other." However, four centuries of history are hard to erase. Even as Spanish control over Puerto Rico was coming to an end, the *criollo* elites continued to pride themselves on the cultural legacy and affinity, such as blood, race, traditions, language, religion, and history, they felt they shared with their Iberian counterparts. The development of distinct national identities under Spanish sovereignty was a slow, confusing, and ambivalent process partially due to the Puerto Rican elites' real or imagined cultural affinity with Spain.

The historical juncture of 1898 left a mark in the developing of Puerto Rican national identities. Although cultural affinity may have been absent between Puerto Ricans and Americans in 1898, the fact that military institutions, the political arena, and the public school system were opened to the masses profoundly altered the islanders' identities.[33] Modern Puerto Rican national identities are influenced by the clash of two colonial projects and experiences.

Americanization via Mobilization

Establishing local military units in Puerto Rico served the American administrators to consolidate power in the new American colony. But more important, the mobilization of the Puerto Ricans was also intended to remake them. This is not surprising, as in the early twentieth century the military prided itself on being scientific. After 1898 the U.S. military was interested in shaping colonial subjects within the American empire.[34] The United States also embarked on a comprehensive buildup of the public education system, which was intended to Americanize the inhabitants of the island, just like military service.[35] Colonial administrators, as well as local elites, believed that military training and experience would transform Puerto Rican individuals, who would then transmit their modern military values to the rest of the population.[36]

The United States exercised direct control of the armed forces on the island, but relied on local elites to run the rest of the colonial apparatus. Thus, from very early on, Puerto Rican politicians and local leaders wielded a degree of indirect control over the military, even if they responded directly to Washington. This situation allowed for local elites to gradually claim control over the military establishment on the island (most notably after the creation of the Puerto Rico National Guard in the aftermath of World War I) and over the projects of modernization via military service in a process I call "criollization."

Criollization is similar to the creolization that originated in the French Caribbean. Like its antecedent, criollization considers trans- and multiculturalism and the hybridity of the people's institutions and systems. But while creolization is used more commonly to explain the "new world" experience, and it addresses mostly early colonization, slavery, and migration, criollization explains how a mostly white colonial elite regains power under a new metropolis by controlling some of the colonial institutions.

Criollization created the opportunity for the popularization of military institutions. The military is "popularized" when it is opened to popular sectors of society. This happened between World War II and the Korean War. The local administrators of the reformed colony grew dependent on the military service of tens of thousands of Puerto Ricans and had to respond to their socioeconomic and political needs.

In the early 1940s, Luis Muñoz Marín, the first elected governor of the island and main architect of the final commonwealth formula, galvanized the electoral power of the masses behind a populist project initially based on social justice. Moreover, he used the participation of Puerto Ricans in the U.S. military as a bargaining tool to advance the decolonization project and finally to sell the concept of the commonwealth formula to the electorate. But this is not a story of the manipulation of the popular sectors. Muñoz Marín's decision to renounce independence was not simply the logical development of criollo *autonomismo* or a symptom of the growing dependence of the island on federal programs and monies, or due simply to political fragmentation in the island and staunch opposition to independence from Washington. The mobilization of popular sectors and the PPD's reliance on military service to advance its projects are key to understanding Muñoz Marín's change of heart.

The role played by the tens of thousands of Puerto Ricans in the metropolitan military was threefold. First, these soldiers served as political leverage during World War II to speed up the decolonization process as envisioned by Muñoz Marín. Second, they incarnated the commonwealth ideology by fighting and dying in the Korean War. And third, the Puerto Rican soldiers would thereafter join the army of technicians and technocrats attempting to fulfill the promises of a modern industrial Puerto Rico. The Puerto Rican soldier was neither cannon fodder for the United States nor the pawn of the local political elites. Regaining their masculinity, upward mobility, and political enfranchisement were incentives enticing the Puerto Ricans into military service.

The empowerment of popular sectors by enfranchisement and participation in the political and military institutions ultimately created a very liberal, popular, and broad definition of Puerto Ricans' national identities. It is important to stress the point that if these soldiers were used to complete a project centered on reforming the colonial state, industrial modernization, and a new modern national identity, they were not mere puppets. When the Puerto Rican jíbaro soldier became the embodiment of the commonwealth formula, the political leaders involved in its design were responding to the open and flexible identities evident among popular sectors of Puerto Rican society, which compelled them to defend the "American nation" to show their *puertorriqueñidad*. The men exalted as Puerto Rican heroes, an integral part of the foundational mythology of the reformed colonial state, wore U.S. Army uniforms. They had a say in the conceptualization of Puertoricaness in a never-ending contest for control of Puerto Rico's national identities, and this phenomenon translated into the political arena and contributed to the creation of the Estado Libre Asociado in 1952. Military mobilization and demobilization and inclusion/exclusion patterns of popular sectors in Puerto Rico under both metropoles altered the character of Puerto Rican national identities and thus the island's political history.

The structures and processes I have chosen to study require me to take a *longue durée* approach. I do not follow a perfectly linear narrative but an exponential one. Times of crisis, such as wars, famines, and economic depressions, have served as accelerators of historical processes. Periods of crisis tend to lead to the rise or fall of empires and political systems, to the cyclical realignment of the world, or the inclusion or exclusion of disenfranchised groups within a state's or empire's polity. The focus is on critical historical junctures under Spain and the United States and the policies followed by both metropolitan powers and local leaders, in an attempt to map the intersection of local, national, and international histories and their effect on the structures and processes under study

Chapter 1 begins by analyzing the scholarly and popular debate about the significance of the Lares revolt of 1868 and the policies followed by Spain before and after the event. I argue that the revolt may not have been a national revolution, but the policies followed by the Spanish colonial authorities after the event fueled the emergence of national Puerto Rican identities. Furthermore, I trace the importance of military institutions under Spanish sovereignty and how the metropolis, seeking to limit local participation in the military to both forestall insurrection and the development of national identities, accomplished the opposite.

Chapter 2 looks at the transfer of sovereignty over Puerto Rico from Spain to the United States in 1898 and examines the factors that facilitated or hindered the transition. The transfer of sovereignty was facilitated by several factors: The war in Puerto Rico was relatively bloodless; Spain officially relinquished control over the island; the United States slowly increased access to political power, and Puerto Rican elites and the popular sector participated actively in the institutions of the new metropolis. The United States set up a tutelary colonial state intended to "modernize" the island and its inhabitants through a nation-building project supposedly guided by "benevolent assimilation" and "compassionate uplifting"—a comprehensive plan to "Americanize" the island and its inhabitants. This nation-building project, which for the first two decades of U.S. control over the island was firmly in the hands of the metropolis, relied heavily, both directly and indirectly, on the military and on military service.

Chapter 3 addresses the debate for vesting Puerto Ricans with U.S. citizenship in 1917, just as the United States prepared to enter World War I. I argue that the unwillingness of the vast majority to resist becoming American citizens reflects the impact that the U.S. institutions already had on Puerto Ricans. Moreover, the first mass participation of Puerto Ricans in the U.S. military, and the support of the newly elected Puerto Rican legislature, local leaders, and the press for the war effort, momentarily cemented U.S. control over the island. However, during World War I, overreliance on the local elites to mobilize and control the peasantry and urban working classes started to undermine U.S. control over the military apparatus, the political structures in the island, and the nation-building project via military service.

Chapter 4 addresses the socioeconomic and political situation in Puerto Rico during the Great Depression and on the eve of World War II. During this period, mostly due to economic hardship, but also because of the emergence of the Nationalist Party led by Pedro Albizu Campos and the violent response of the U.S. colonial authorities to the nationalist challenge, the island experienced political instability and violence. This chapter analyzes how the economic distress afflicting the island fueled political discontent and how such discontent was in turn used by two emerging political leaders, Pedro Albizu Campos and Luis Muñoz Marín, to further different political projects. I argue that what transpired during these years of political violence, especially the shooting war between Nacionalistas and the Insular Police, was also a war over control of Puerto Rican identities.

Chapter 5 explores how once again war brought the promise of political and economic advancement by rekindling Puerto Rico's strategic position. Puerto Ricans were called to arms. Different projects of decolonization and modernization, which included the revitalization of the economy and of the Puerto Rican's self-esteem, rested on the roles these soldiers were about to play. The metropolis sought to secure the loyalty of natives of the island by allowing their mass entry into the U.S. military and by conferring upon them the same benefits as Continental soldiers and veterans. A return to the idea of Americanization through military service (and public education) made a comeback as war engulfed Europe. The metropolis was also more inclined to granting a higher degree of self-government to Puerto Rico, since it would enhance its standing in the international arena and could very well quench political unrest on the island.

Aware of Puerto Rico's military and diplomatic relevance, Luis Muñoz Marín, leading the Popular Democratic Party, followed a strategy that supported the war effort and placed the socioeconomic restructuration of the island above everything else while using the participation of Puerto Rican soldiers in the war and the island's strategic position as leverage to extract political concessions. Muñoz Marín and the Populares secured veterans' benefits so that these men and women could attempt to change the dire socioeconomic condition of the island. A march toward a "modern" Puerto Rico had started, and these jíbaro soldiers would lead it. That Muñoz Marín came to depend on the votes of the peasantry and rural working classes to attain political power and on their military mobilization to advance the socioeconomic restructuration of the island would influence his decision to change his political goals, first tactically and later definitively.

Chapter 6 analyzes the state of political forces in the island at the end of World War II. This chapter addresses political and diplomatic factors and how they affected the process of decolonization in Puerto Rico. I will argue that faced by the indifference of Congress, growing dependence on federal programs, and increasingly complex Puerto Rican national identities, Luis Muñoz Marín opted for the path of autonomismo, leading to the creation of the Commonwealth of Puerto Rico. The viability of the Estado Libre Asociado would be proved in the local confrontation with the Nacionalistas in 1950. The free association pact would be sealed in blood on the battlefields of Korea as the Puerto Rican soldier became the incarnation of the ideals of the commonwealth: the coexistence of "the two great cultures of the hemisphere" in one space. In the process, new modern Puerto Rican identities emerged and briefly became hegemonic.

1

Birth of a Nation

A Labor of Thirty Years, 1868–1898

> Puerto Rico needs to reform its public education, conveniently Hispanicizing it, and to this end it is necessary to get rid of the professors born in this country . . . [and] to ban the people of this country from certain positions. Those born in this province should only be allowed to occupy the most subaltern positions, and only after unequivocally proving their unyielding *españolismo*.
> —José A. Gautier Dapena, *Trayectoria del pensamiento liberal*[1]

For more than three centuries Spain relied on local militia to keep Puerto Rico within its fold and to provide a manpower pool and a staging area from which to quench revolts in other parts of the empire. However, after the failed insurrection against Spanish rule, known as el Grito de Lares of 1868, Spanish colonial authorities moved swiftly to dismantle the local militias manned by *los hijos de este país* (natives of the land). The late Spanish colonial project in Puerto Rico, especially after el Grito de Lares, was marked by increased political repression and military exclusion.[2] Banning thousands of Puerto Ricans from the military and politically subjugating the island-born elites were self-supporting strategies aimed at keeping the island under Spanish control.

The demobilization of the Puerto Ricans following the Lares revolt is of paramount significance. Historian Florencia Mallon has argued that during periods of crisis, subaltern groups get the opportunity to strengthen their political stand and gain more inclusion and participation in developing or redefining the nation and its institutions, either by being included in political coalitions or by being mobilized for war.[3] Focusing on the creation of national discourses and identities and how they alter state formation, Fernando López-Alves argues that political and military mass mobilization of peasants and lower classes, the type, duration, time frame, purpose, and who leads such mobilization affect the creation of a region's polity and lead to a higher or lower degree of democracy within a given state.[4] Both scholars agree that as marginalized groups participate in political and military mobilization, they have a better chance of becoming part of the hegemonic group in a given society.

In the case of Puerto Rico, we have a peculiar situation due to its colonial situation and the preponderantly military nature of the colony. On the one hand, we have a major nation seeking to demobilize those born on the island while also engaging in the political repression of the local *criollo* elites. The nation and its colonial bureaucracy had a mutually supportive relationship with the *peninsulares* (the Spaniards born in the Iberian Peninsula). On the other hand, the criollo elites, even as they organized politically, had but a tenuous command of the lower classes and the peasantry's loyalties. In nineteenth-century Puerto Rico, most notably after the 1860s, instead of mobilization we are presented with the demobilization of the local population while the political arena plays out more like a contest between liberal reform-oriented (and separatist) criollos in one camp and the colonial administration and peninsulares in the other. Little opportunity for broad political mobilization and the demobilization of the local population are prominent features of mid- to late nineteenth-century Puerto Rico.

In this chapter I analyze the policies followed by Spain and its colonial apparatus in Puerto Rico with regard to military mobilization during periods of crises, and how those policies affected those born on the island. What did Spain seek to gain from excluding the island-born from military service? Did military participation transform into political enfranchisement? Is the opposite true? Did the demobilization of the inhabitants of Puerto Rico mean political and socioeconomic disenfranchisement? Did disenfranchisement and displacement encourage the development of distinctive Puerto Rican national identities?

Spanish colonial policies in Puerto Rico curtailed the emergence of broad political coalitions that could seriously challenge the metropolis, but those same policies negatively impacted Spain's control over the island as well. Clearly Spanish policies aimed at demobilizing the Puerto Ricans can be seen as an effort to destroy the basis of a potential rebel army while also providing cheap labor for the incipient export-oriented capitalist agricultural enterprises. However, the demobilization of the Puerto Ricans was also intended to impede the emergence of distinct national identities that might be used as a battle cry against Spanish sovereignty. The combination of these policies of exclusion and demobilization weakened the criollos and liberals politically as the colonial administration intended. But these policies also highlighted the differences between peninsulares and those born on the island, and eventually they stimulated the emergence of Puerto Rican national identities and the anti-Spanish feelings so feared by Spain.

Prelude to Revolution

In 1808 the Spanish Empire in the Americas extended from California to Cape Horn and from the Caribbean Sea to the Pacific Ocean. Roughly two decades later, Cuba and Puerto Rico were all that was left of this vast empire. Cuba had long been a profitable colony. In contrast, Puerto Rico had been relegated to the role of a military station since the mid-1500s. Although Spain had long wanted Puerto Rico to become an agriculturally productive colony, by the late 1700s its economy was still stagnant. The collapse of the Spanish Empire had consequences for its last two American colonies. First, Cuba and Puerto Rico became the destination for thousands of *peninsulares* and criollo loyalists from the empire's mainland. Many were former colonial administrators and members of a defeated military. These newcomers brought a conservative and pro-Spain element to these islands.[5] Second, with its international standing and prestige severely diminished, Spain sought to strengthen its hold over its remaining American colonies. Moreover, throughout the 1800s, but especially after losing its continental empire, Spain would seek to exploit its last colonies more efficiently. In the case of Puerto Rico, the crown also sought to make it self-sufficient, as its colonial administration could no longer rely on the centuries-old yearly stipend known as the Situado Mexicano.[6] Eventually the combination of these factors would put the local elites and peasants at odds with Spain. But for the time being, with the exception of slave revolts, minor civilian riots, and pay-related mutinies among garrisoned troops, both islands appeared to be firmly in the hands of the Iberian metropolis.[7]

The relative calm that seemed to prevail gave way to political turmoil in the 1860s. Economic development and changing demographics influenced the political arena. Puerto Rico experienced a sixfold population increase accompanied by marked economic expansion.[8] From the 1820s to the 1850s, sugar cane cultivation expanded dramatically mostly in the island's coastal valleys. Coffee cultivation in the mountain regions began to expand in the 1850s and by the 1880s had overtaken the sugar sector.[9] The expansion of these sectors was cyclically curtailed by global market conditions and by limited and expensive credit. Credit was mostly controlled by immigrant *peninsulares* merchants, a fact that highlighted a clear class distinction between them and the local criollo elites under them.[10] As both economic sectors expanded, the *hacendado*, small merchants, and professional criollo elites also grew and became increasingly interested in self-rule.[11] Economic needs were paramount behind the criollo elites' interest in political power.[12] Puerto Rican historiography has identified the criollos' lack of political power and their economic subordination and indebtedness to the peninsulares as a source of grievance that ultimately put them at odds with Spain.[13] The criollos sought political power to rectify the inequalities they perceived between themselves and peninsulares. By the 1860s the criollos were mostly represented by two main political factions. There were the liberals who sought to reform, modernize, and democratize the colony, and there were the radical separatists. Both factions were persecuted by the colonial administrators.

On December 21, 1865, a new liberal government in Madrid attempted to appease the growing discontent in all its overseas provinces by setting up a board of review to hear formal grievances from provincial representatives. Elected representatives from each overseas province would present their petitions to this entity, the Junta Informativa de Reformas de Ultramar (Informative Board on Overseas Reforms), which would then advise the Spanish Cortes on how to address the colonies' demands. Cuba and Puerto Rico had not been allowed to send representatives to the Cortes since 1837. In Puerto Rico, the announcement was well received by criollo liberals and with cautious optimism by separatists.[14] Liberal reformists and separatists made common cause against the conservatives to secure representation in the Puerto Rican delegation. The Junta began its meetings on December 1866. Only four of the Puerto Rican delegates—three liberals and a conservative—reached Madrid in time to present their petitions. The Puerto Rican delegation, in opposition to the Cubans, recommended the abolition of slavery. Decentralizing the colonial government, more criollo participation in the colonial administration, full representation in the Cortes, and expansion of suffrage were some of the requests presented by the Cuban delegate José Morales Lemus. The Puerto Rican delegates seconded the Cuban delegation's petition. On April 27, 1867, the Junta's hearings came to an end. Spain did not agree to a single reform. Instead of liberalizing trade with the colonies, as both Cubans and Puerto Ricans had recommended, Spain saw fit to increase their already heavy tax burden. Local authorities in Puerto Rico increased their persecution of the abolitionists, culminating with the exile of the most prominent liberals.[15] The failure of the Junta Informativa and the subsequent political repression convinced separatists and many liberals that there could not be a negotiated solution with Spain.

Liberals and separatists from the criollo elites were not alone in their resentment. On June 11, 1849, Juan de la Pezuela y Ceballos, Puerto Rico's gobernador y capitán general, had instituted a passbook system, known as *libreta de jornaleros*. The passbook system affected thousands of Puerto Rican peasants. As Laird W. Bergard explains, since the 1850s the "landless population" had been subjected to "more organized and systematic methods of exploitation."[16] The system was intended to provide a cheap and reliable labor force for the plantations and other enterprises. Free blacks, people of mixed race, and poor whites ages sixteen and older were subjected to the *reglamento*, which forced them to work for others. Even those who owned some land but could not provide for all their needs were forced to work for others, either for wages or for goods. The *jornaleros* were forced to carry a notebook at all times in which their daily activities were to be logged. Although the *reglamento* included penalties for employers' abusive behavior, all kinds of exploitations were frequent.[17] Both criollos and peninsulares benefited from the exploitation of the peasantry, but the indebted criollo landowners were able to portray the peninsulares as foreign and as the real cause for the impoverishment and exploitation of the peasantry.[18]

During the 1860s a criollo elite who could not extract political concessions from a seemingly intractable metropolis grew increasingly discontent. Spain's reluctance to implement liberal reforms exacerbated what was basically a class struggle between peninsulares and criollos. Criollo hacendados in general, but coffee growers and small merchants in particular, found themselves heavily indebted to peninsulares and larger merchants.[19] The situation of coffee growers further deteriorated when Hurricane San Narciso hit Puerto Rico on October 29, 1867, devastating the coffee region. As 1867 ended, coercive policies seeking to control labor, a peninsular-criollo class dichotomy, and an increasingly repressive, intrusive, and assertive metropolis and colonial administration were some of the factors leading to Lares. Ironically, the metropolis was repeating policies and re-creating the patterns that had cost it its empire on the American mainland. Counting on the support of thousands of aggrieved peasants forced into the passbook system, radical abolitionists in exile, and small merchants and coffee growers on the island made common cause to free Puerto Rico from Spain.

The Lares Revolt

The sine qua non in discussions about nationalism and national identities in Puerto Rico is without doubt el Grito de Lares of

September 23, 1868, the biggest revolt against Spanish rule ever staged on the island.[20] This revolt occurred almost in unison with the Glorious Revolution in Spain (September 19–27, 1868) and el Grito de Yara (October 10, 1868), which started the Ten Years' War and thirty years of struggle for independence in Cuba. On January 6, 1868, prominent Puerto Rican separatists exiled in New York, under the guidance of Ramón Emeterio Betances, founded the Comité Revolucionario de Puerto Rico. They aimed to overthrow the Spanish regime on the island and to create a democratic republic. The revolutionary committee proceeded to organize cells on the island for this purpose and to secure weaponry for the rebel army.[21] A series of setbacks doomed the plans of the *revolucionarios*. They managed to secure five hundred rifles, six canons, ammunition, and the small transport ship *El Telegrafo* to arm the revolutionary army; however, their ship was confiscated in Saint Thomas.[22] Betances, who had planned to land in Puerto Rico with men and weapons on the first day of the revolution, set originally for September 29, was detained in Santo Domingo and never made it to the island.[23]

Meanwhile, the leaders in Puerto Rico faced problems of their own. On September 19, a rebel agent was apprehended in the western city of Mayagüez, and the next day a *miliciano* in the northwestern town of Quebradillas informed his commander of rebel plans in Camuy. Capitán General Julián Juan Pavía ordered Spanish troops to full alert. In the first hours of the morning of the 21st, Spanish authorities detained the rebel leader Manuel María González and searched his house. The Spanish authorities found a list of members of the rebel cell and a copy of their *reglamento*. The Camuy rebels who were not arrested fled to Lares and warned the rebel cell in that town. From Lares, messengers were sent to alert the rebel cell in Mayagüez that their plans had been compromised and of the need to launch the rebellion as soon as possible. They also wanted the Mayagüez cell to alert other cells throughout the island. Reckoning that speed was of the essence, the leadership of the rebel cells in Camuy, Lares, and Mayagüez decided to launch their revolt six days early.[24]

On September 23, 1868, hundreds of rebels started to converge on the farm of Manuel Rojas, a rebel leader and coffee grower in the mountain town of Lares. On their way to Lares, the rebels exhorted slaves and jornaleros to join them, in some cases threatening to kill them if they did not do so.[25] That evening the rebels marched into the town itself and took it without resistance. They proceeded to form a provisional government of republican character. The Republic of Puerto Rico, with a president and a cabinet appointed by the chief military leaders present in Lares, was officially established on the morning of September 24.[26] Manuel Rojas and Juan de Mata Torreforte instructed the new government to recruit and organize more rebel soldiers and to secure funding by forcing the merchants to loan money to the republic.[27] By decree, the rebel government declared null the hated jornalero (passbook) system that forced landless peasants to work as peons and promised freedom to those slaves who joined them in the fight against the Spaniards. The rebels also welcomed foreigners to join their ranks and become patriots of the republic. Another decree gave Spaniards in Puerto Rico three days to swear allegiance to the new republic or to leave the island if they did not. The decree also warned of extreme repercussions if the Spaniards decided to stay and did not support the rebels and the republic.[28]

The chief rebel commanders, Rojas and Torreforte, named the officers of the Ejército Revolucionario, which at that point consisted of roughly six hundred men. They named eight brigadier generals plus colonels for the infantry, artillery, and cavalry. Apparently these colonels were quickly promoted to generals. That the rebel leadership appointed so many generals and colonels for such a small number of rebels suggests that the leaders believed they would be able to gain popular support. Late in the morning of the 24th, the rebels proceeded to the town of San Sebastian del Pepino. The commanders of the *milicias disciplinadas* (local militias) in Pepino, Lieutenant Manuel Cebollero and Alférez Eusebio Ibarra, had spent the previous night organizing slaves and jornaleros into a fighting force to join the rebel column coming from Lares. They had also promised the rebel leadership that their milicianos would join the rebellion. Later that morning, roughly forty rebels on horseback entered Pepino's plaza shooting and chanting, "Death to the Spaniards and the Queen," while exhorting the milicianos to join them. To their surprise, the milicianos responded to the rebels with intense fire, ignoring the calls of Cebollero and Ibarra. More rebels continued to pour into Pepino, but their efforts bore no fruits against the effective fire of the milicianos and the town's civilians, who fired rifles and threw dynamite from the rooftops. The battle lasted more than an hour before the rebels, repulsed twice and driven off the Plaza by the *milicianos*, decided to head back to Lares. The confrontation left eight rebels dead and two *milicianos* wounded. Fighting against *milicianos* and civilians, the rebels lost the only engagement of the revolt. Disconcerted by the unwillingness of the *milicianos* to join them, and recognizing that without them on their side they could not possibly defeat the peninsular troops on the island, the rebel army quickly melted away. Scattered in the mountains and with no hope of a general uprising or aid coming from the exterior, the rebels eventually surrendered. More than five hundred rebels found themselves imprisoned. Eighty died while in custody due to poor sanitary conditions. Seven were sentenced to death, but by virtue of a general amnesty, all rebels were set free by January 1869.[29]

The Lares Uprising's Significance

From a strictly military standpoint, the revolt was a fiasco. Lares was the only town taken by the rebels, and the Spanish authorities crushed the revolt in roughly twenty-four hours. The brevity of the uprising is even more damning when taking into account that the rebel army was defeated by milicianos, who were an auxiliary corps manned almost exclusively by Puerto Ricans. Furthermore, the rebels did not enjoy broad support from the island's inhabitants, who were either unaware of the events or chose to remain neutral or loyal to Spain. Lack of communication and coordination and poor leadership just accentuated the absence of support from the island's community in general. More than 60 percent of the participants were jornaleros, peasants, or slaves, many of whom declared that they were forced to join the rebels under pain of death.[30] Though a failure from a military point of view, some view the Lares uprising as a defining moment for Puerto Rican nationality, a moment when the island's people ceased to see themselves as Spaniards. And to this day, el Grito de Lares remains an integral part of Puerto Rico's foundational mythology.

One school of thought regards this revolt as the birth of national consciousness in Puerto Rico and as a true national uprising.[31] However, agrarian and economic historians tend to highlight class conflict as the revolt's trigger. Criollos were seeking to correct what they perceived as economic and political injustices perpetrated by peninsular merchants and creditors.[32] Economic historian James L. Dietz sees the revolt as the moment when "Spanish domination, and in particular peninsular control over the largest commercial establishment and credit, became an obstacle rather than an ally to the members of this class, as well as to educated professionals, just as it had in the rest of the New World."[33] Dietz agrees with Bergard that "Lares was a concrete manifestation of the attempt by members of the more powerful creole class to end the dominance of the hated Spanish merchants."[34] The 1860s and the Lares revolt marked "the point at which the development of Puerto Rico's productive forces came into fundamental conflict with Spain's sociopolitical domination."[35] Bergard goes even further and concludes that the "revolution's principal causes were local, not national in scope." For the men who marched chanting, "Viva Puerto Rico libre," freedom meant "depriving Spanish merchants of the control over the coffee export economy in Puerto Rico's *cordillera central*."[36]

In fact, despite its brevity, el Grito de Lares has inspired many politicians and poets. Writing for the *San Juan Star* in celebration of the first centenary of the revolt, Juan Antonio Corretjer (1908–85), one of Puerto Rico's greatest poets and untamable fighter for Puerto Rico's independence, described the revolt as the day Puerto Rico became a nation.[37] Of course, that vision is possible in hindsight, which also allows for the reformulation of Puerto Rico's national mythology, its stories and histories, and of Puertoricaness itself. The failed revolt had become an obscure footnote on the island's history until the 1930s, when the

Partido Nacionalista Puertorriqueño (Nationalist Puerto Rican Party) adopted the Lares revolt as a national icon. In 1969 Luis A. Ferré, the first governor of the island presiding over a party seeking federated statehood, declared the event a national holiday. At first glance it may look contradictory that such diametrically opposed political camps embraced the same event as part of the island's national iconography. However, Puerto Ricans from different sides of the political spectrum understood that control of the national symbols has long played an important role in Puerto Rican politics. As argued by Arlene Dávila, command of the national mythology and its icons and appealing to national identities and feelings wield significant political power in Puerto Rico.[38] This point was not lost to the Spanish authorities in 1868. Just about 7 percent (39 out of 551 detainees) of the Lares rebels were born outside the island. However, foreigners occupied important positions within the rebel cells, a fact that became the basis for the Spanish colonial government's portrayal of the revolt as being foreign-inspired and led.[39]

The criollos leading the Lares revolt were not able to mobilize the masses to support their cause even after appealing to the national spirit of Puerto Ricans.[40] The demographics of the island in 1868 were less than ideal for promoting a sense of national unity. During the early nineteenth century, the island's population had quadrupled.[41] In her classic work on foreign immigration to Puerto Rico, Estela Cifre de Loubriel identified three distinct immigration waves, 1800–1850, 1850–80, and 1880–98. The first stage was characterized by an influx of immigrants from Santo Domingo, as well as French elements from Haiti and political émigrés from Venezuela. Cifre de Loubriel argues that foreign immigration, triggered by the Real Cédula de Gracias of August 10, 1815, accounted for much of the immigration to Puerto Rico during this first period which she considers essential in the formation of Puerto Rico as a *pueblo*. She identifies this stage as the moment when Puerto Ricans began to emerge as a distinctive people.[42] Such appraisal ignores pervasive racial divisions on the island and the contribution of nonwhite peoples to the Puerto Rican pueblo.

More recent scholarship has focused on non-European migration to Puerto Rico during the first half of the nineteenth century and challenged the assumption that the Real Cédula served to whiten Puerto Rico. Joseph C. Dorsey has shown that especially after 1815, thousands of African and Caribbean slaves came to Puerto Rico from the non-Hispanic Caribbean.[43] The influx of nonwhites to Puerto Rico was not restricted to slaves. Free men of color, both black and mulattoes from the non-Hispanic Caribbean, joined waves of immigrants from the Spanish American mainland and Europe. Jorge Luis Chinea has shown how these nonwhite immigrants were instrumental in providing labor, capital, and the technical skills that nurtured the incipient cash-crop economy on the island, and by the middle of the nineteenth century a third of landowners in Puerto Rico were free men of color.[44] Nonwhite immigration was tolerated because of the island's economic needs, but it was not welcome, and both slaves and free people of color were actively policed and suppressed.[45] After the sugar crisis of 1848, the colonial administration virtually closed nonwhite immigration to Puerto Rico while encouraging white migration.[46]

Because of the massive and varied immigration, several European and African languages and their creolized versions could be heard in Puerto Rican barrios. Slaves and freedmen from the Dutch, Danish, and French Caribbean, Corsicans, Italians, French, Germans, and others had settled in and created small enclaves virtually isolated from the rest of the island. With few roads connecting the different towns, and with no common experience or common education to share beyond their immediate community, it was difficult if not impossible to appeal to national identity feelings. Further, racial division was a big obstacle for the emergence of a strong national spirit that could fuel the anticolonial struggle in Puerto Rico. The population in 1860 was almost equally divided between whites and blacks. The colonial authorities and their conservative allies used the ever-present fears of racial war after the Haitian Revolution to instill fear in liberals and separatists alike.[47] As late as 1872, conservatives argued that upon becoming independent, Puerto Rico would lose close to 100,000 whites, which would make the nonwhite population the majority. This nonwhite population would then try to take control of the government by any means, including racial war against the white population. Conservatives based their claims on the number of free people of color and slaves who joined the Lares uprising and on the fact that many rebels were known abolitionists.[48]

This colonial narrative, which had worked for the Spaniards in Cuba to end the Ten Years' War and the "Little War" of 1879–80, was intended to deny the existence and viability of a Cuban and a Puerto Rican nation.[49] On both islands the colonial narratives of racial war served to impede the emergence of strong separatist movements by dividing blacks, mulattos, and whites. In Cuba, however, the rebels found an effective counternarrative by the 1890s.[50] Puerto Rico was another story, and as we will see, as late as 1898 local leaders (with the exception of exiled separatists and radicals) still clung to Spain.

Lares's Aftermath

While the Lares uprising may not have been a national movement, the policies followed by the Spanish colonial authorities in its aftermath promoted the emergence of Puerto Rican national identities. From this standpoint Lares had undeniably important consequences. If the revolt itself did not separate Puerto Ricans from Spaniards, Spanish colonial policies would make the differences between them all too clear. Following the insurrection, the newly appointed governor y capitán general of Puerto Rico, Gen. Laureano Sanz, moved to exclude natives of the island from teaching positions while promoting the *españolización* of public and private instruction. Sanz also sought to ban Puerto Ricans from the clergy and from all administrative posts except the most "subaltern ones" and only after having "unequivocally proved their unblemished" loyalty to Spain.[51] These measures created even more friction between peninsulares and the criollos, for they closed traditional routes to socioeconomic and political improvement. As discussed above, there is a vast historiography highlighting the dichotomy between peninsulares and criollos and their political and class struggles. Then again, such struggles affected a relatively small elite that depended on Spain to ensure their status on the island.

Spain's exclusionary policies, however, were not restricted to the political realm and the colonial administration. Los hijos de este país, who not only had served faithfully for more than three hundred years but who had also suppressed the Lares revolt, found themselves excluded from the military. Soon after the revolt, the colonial administration banned Puerto Ricans from its armed forces in an attempt to forestall other insurrections. Unlike the political suppression of the criollo elites, the demobilization of the local population directly affected a large sector of the population. As part of a larger colonial project, after 1868, and especially under Sanz's leadership, the Iberian metropolis was invested in preventing the emergence of strong nationalist feelings. In essence, Spain embarked on what can be described as an anti-nation-building project. Political repression, demobilization of the population, and the españolización of the island were some of the tools with which to avoid the emergence of strong Puerto Rican national identities that could be used to rally natives against Spanish domination.

Sanz's plans had the opposite effect. By closing the military to natives of Puerto Rico, the Spaniards created a common denominator for those born on the island: exclusion by birthplace. Barring los hijos de este país from the military was more damaging than any other form of exclusion by the colonial administration, since it affected most of the population, not just a small criollo elite. By following exclusionary policies, the Spanish colonial authorities made more obvious the differences between peninsulares and Puerto Ricans, lost the opportunity to co-opt Puerto Ricans into serving Spain, and ultimately promoted the development of Puerto Rican national identities. The combined exclusion of Puerto Ricans from the colonial administration and the military undermined the loyalty of the island's inhabitants and kindled a sense of national unity vis-à-vis the Spaniards.

Under Spanish control, the development of national identities was a slow, confusing, and ambivalent process because of socioeconomic and demographic factors above mentioned and because of the Puerto Rican elites' real or imagined cultural affinity with Spain. Up to the very last days of Spanish domination over Puerto Rico, the criollo elites continued to pride themselves on the cultural legacy and affinity, such as blood, race, traditions, language, religion, and history, they believed to have in common with their European cousins.[52] Moreover, most of the criollo elite saw Spain as "indispensable for their survival."[53] Soon after el Grito de Lares, most of the liberal criollo leadership opted for a policy of *autonomismo* or a higher degree of political freedom as opposed to independence from Spain.[54] The reluctance of the criollo leadership to sever its ties to Spain, and degrees of cultural affinity with Spain that the elite seemed to embrace, may have slowed the development of Puerto Rican national identities. This is not to say that the criollos that stayed on the island had many other options. The demobilization of the Puerto Ricans hindered the political choices of the criollo leadership. In fact, the criollos' position was weakened by the absence of Puerto Rican militias. Military exclusion provided Puerto Ricans with a common experience that may have moved them toward a shared identity, a shared sense of grievance. But it also weakened the criollos and liberals for the simple fact that by disarming the local population, the colonial authorities suppressed the threat of armed rebellion and could focus on the surveillance and repression of the criollos.

Controlling access to the military and paramilitary apparatus and seeking to curtail the power of the liberals and criollos on the island were not new colonial strategies. Nor was military service a marginal issue for the inhabitants of the island. A review of the political trajectory and of the development of the Puerto Rican militias during the nineteenth century will illustrate the military character of the colony and of those who made it their home and how Spain sought to neutralize the liberals and the criollo elite by disarming the population.

The Military Colony

Puerto Rico has an intimate history with military institutions. From 1582 to 1897, the island was ruled either as a presidio, a camp, or a military plaza, and it was not until 1898 that Puerto

Rico briefly enjoyed a civil government.⁵⁵ In 1582 the first garrison of regular Spanish troops was assigned to the island, and the functions of governor and alcaide (keeper) del morro were fused, effectively making the island a capitanía general.⁵⁶ The duties of the capitán general included the command, organization, and jurisdiction of the army and militias. Within the Spanish Empire these administrative positions were separated from, and subordinated to, the offices of the viceroys or governors. In the case of Puerto Rico, however, this office also entailed the administration of all affairs of the island. In the late eighteenth century, as part of the Bourbon reforms, Intendentes de Ejército y Provincia were added to the imperial bureaucracy and existed alongside the positions of governor, viceroy, or captain general throughout the Spanish Empire, but not in Puerto Rico, where the capitán general remained as absolute ruler.⁵⁷ For most of its history, Puerto Rico was a military bastion, and everything else was secondary.

Héctor Andrés Negroni has argued that since the island was but a military camp, the islander could be nothing but a soldier or at least be influenced by Puerto Rico's military baggage.⁵⁸ In 1887, in a study of the Puerto Rican jíbaro, Francisco del Valle Atiles declared: "Since those remote days when Spain fought wars with England and the Netherlands [he refers to the sixteenth, seventeenth and eighteenth centuries, a period during which no less than fifty-six invasions took place] until this very day, the jíbaro has been a good Spanish soldier, willing to die for the motherland (*patria*); called by the government or volunteering, he has heeded the call of duty."⁵⁹ The military nature of the island can also be illustrated by its budget. In 1842, when the population had increased from roughly 80,000 inhabitants in 1783 to almost half a million, and with coffee, sugar, and tobacco production rising to unseen levels and enjoying a favorable trade balance, military expenditures still accounted for 50 percent of the island's budget, rapidly rising to 69 percent in 1846, and finally leveling off at 50 percent by 1865.⁶⁰ Even though Puerto Rico prospered economically, and its population grew exponentially during the nineteenth century, the military nature of the colony remained mostly unchanged.

Organization of Militias

As Spain strengthened its hold over the territories in the Americas, it sought to regulate the administration of its possessions. *Milicias irregulares* (irregular militia) had existed in Puerto Rico from the Spanish colonization and conquest in 1508 until 1692, when they were replaced by the Milicia Irregular Urbana.[61] The milicias were composed of free males between the ages of twelve and sixty.[62] Their mission included safeguarding public order and territorial defense.[63] The milicia was the only military body opened to those born on the island until 1741, when they were permitted to join two of the units of the permanent garrison. In 1700 there were 1,000 men in the Milicia Irregular Urbana. As Negroni suggests, since the permanent garrison on the island during this period never exceeded 400 men, the militia was the core of Puerto Rico's defenses.[64] By 1763, the militias counted 5,611 men out of a total population of only 46,197, including women and children.[65] One out of every nine inhabitants was directly involved in the militias. Furthermore these militia men, unlike the regular army garrison troops, had settled on the island, were part of communities, and were part of families. Spanish soldiers rotated in and out, but the militia was organic to the island and had grown roots in it.

Reforming the Militias

In 1765 the Milicia Irregular Urbana was replaced by the Milicia Urbana and the Milicia Disciplinada (urban and disciplined militia, respectively), by virtue of the reforms launched by Field Marshal Alejandro O'Reilly.[66] O'Reilly arrived in Puerto Rico on April 8, 1765, entrusted by Carlos III de Borbón to inspect the defenses and garrisons of the Spanish Antilles. In his report on the conditions of the island, O'Reilly dedicated only eleven sections to the political and economic situation of the island while writing fifty-three on military matters.[67] Finding the defenses in poor state, the troops demoralized, and the lack of relevant data regarding the milicias irregulares, he recommended their dissolution and the creation of a disciplined entity divided into two corps using the reglamento of the Cuban militias.⁶⁸ Out of O'Reilly's recommendations emerged the Milicia Urbana as a type of police force and the Milicia Disciplinada as the equivalent of a military reserve and the main auxiliary corps for the regular troops stationed on the island. The Milicias Urbanas was created as a reserve or auxiliary corps and replacement pool for the Milicias Disciplinadas and in charge of police duties and coastal watch. It came to consist of roughly 38,000 men by 1832, or 11 percent of the island population.⁶⁹ This figure is impressive by itself, but more so when taking into consideration that it does not include those serving in the Milicias Disciplinadas, which had roughly 7,000 men under arms, or those serving in the *battallones fijos* (battalions of the Spanish army assigned permanently to the island).⁷⁰

Manning the regular garrison of the island with hijos de este país, or those born in the Americas, was not an accepted practice within the Spanish Empire. Nonetheless, more often than not, reality superseded legislation in the Spanish Empire. By the 1640s, hijos de este país were being used to guard the fortifications in San Juan. Reprimanded for this practice, Capitán General Fernando de la Riva Agüero (1643–48) responded that without those born on the island, there would be no one to guard the walls.⁷¹ It was not until 1741 that those born in Puerto Rico were legally accepted into the regular forces assigned to Puerto Rico. By royal decree the island-born were allowed to fill up to half the allotted military positions for the garrison in Puerto Rico. As a force of four hundred men, this troop came to be known as the Batallón de Veteranos, or Fijo.⁷² The Fijo was to be reinforced by peninsular troops attached to it and supported initially by the milicias irregulares and later by the urbanos and disciplinados. After his inspection of the island's defenses, O'Reilly discharged half the soldiers of the Fijo and recommended augmenting the garrison on the island with peninsular troops, which started to rotate in regimental strength in 1795.⁷³

Puerto Rico during the Age of Revolution

The expansion in size and role of the militias and regular troops in Puerto Rico did not occur in a political vacuum, nor was this phenomenon just the result of O'Reilly's report and recommendations. Events in Europe and in the Spanish Empire in the Americas precipitated the growth and relevance of the Puerto Rican militias. The French Revolution and subsequent revolutionary and Napoleonic wars propelled the wheels of change in the Americas as much as it did in Europe. The Napoleonic invasion of Spain provided for the brief rise of liberalism in the peninsula and on the island. By the decree of January 22, 1809, after three centuries of absolutist rule, the Junta Suprema y Gubernativa de España e Indias provided for the election on the island of one *diputado a cortes* (representative to the courts). The decree also recognized the American colonies as Spanish provinces.[74] It is at this point that political tendencies on the island became more contrasting, and not surprisingly this is also the beginning of a long campaign to demobilize those born in Puerto Rico. Criollos and some reform-minded peninsulares grouped under liberal and reformist ideas while the merchant class and the colonial administration became markedly conservative.[75] The liberals and reformists won the general elections held between 1809 and 1813, and during this period Puerto Ricans earned Spanish citizenship.

The rapid growth of the militias and the political power gained by the liberals on the island alarmed the Spanish authorities. In 1810 Capitán General Salvador Meléndez (1809–20) tried but failed to dissolve the Milicias Urbana. In effect the Milicia Urbana expanded from roughly 17,000 men in 1810 to 33,000 in 1813. Furthermore, the militias in Aguadilla and Mayagüez (northwestern and western parts of the island, respectively) came to include batteries with more than forty pieces of artillery.[76] The urbanos, composed entirely of hijos de este país, had become a formidable force. With the peninsula in despair due to the French invasion, the perennial fear of a Haitian-led invasion, and a possible insurrection elsewhere, Melendez could not push too hard and risk alienating the island's population, nor could he really rescind of the urbanos' manpower.

The French invasion of the Iberian Peninsula and the wars of independence in the Spanish Empire compelled political fluctuations and created military needs that initially benefited the island.

The milicias' expansion and the weakness of the crown and the Cortes allowed the liberals briefly to gain the upper hand, both on the peninsula and on the island. However, after France's defeat and the restoration of the absolutist monarch Fernando VII, the militias and the liberals came under attack.

Return of the Absolutist King

Fernando VII moved quickly to reduce the power of liberals and the role of the militia on the island. On May 4, 1814, he returned Puerto Rico to colonial status. Those born in Puerto Rico lost political representation and their Spanish citizenship. The return of the king also doomed regular military units on the island. The Fijo, which had participated in the Haitian Revolution in 1792 and 1793 and was again sent to Sainte Domingue between 1809 and 1812, came under suspicion when it was dispatched to Venezuela. Sending the Fijo to Venezuela to aid the royalist armies drew criticism from criollos in Puerto Rico, which prompted Fernando to suppress the body in 1815.[77] Despite the protest of prominent criollos and even the secretary of government on the island, the Fijo was not to be reinstated. Even the colonial administration recognized that dissolving the body was not just unnecessary but also counterproductive, since it offended the sensibility of loyal Puerto Ricans.[78] Seven decades would pass before the hijos de este país were again accepted into the Spanish army units serving on the island.

Emboldened by the return of the absolutist king, Melendez sought to neutralize the Milicia Urbana and in 1817 created a new reglamento that stripped the urbanos of firearms, restricting them to the use of machetes and spears. Moreover, he sought to put the urbanos under the direct control of the capitán general, circumventing local authorities. The reglamento also established the separation of whites and *morenos* who until then had fought in the same units.[79] Thus the only regular military unit on the island that accepted Puerto Ricans, the Fijo, had been suppressed, and the all-Puerto Rican Milicia Urbana was seriously weakened by removing its firearms. As if these measures were not enough, Melendez proceeded to create a force mirroring the milicias.

The Instituto de Voluntarios existed on the island between 1812 and 1898 as a paramilitary corps made of mostly peninsular volunteers. The origin of this corps lay in the fear of the colonial authorities that sooner or later both the milicias urbanas and disicplinadas would become the nucleus of a rebel army. Hence the instituto was intended to counterbalance and eventually replace the militias. In its inception this volunteer corps was exclusively for civilians born in Spain. Later it was divided into two battalions of voluntarios distinguidos, one for those born on the island and another for peninsulares. Merchants and landowners from San Juan made up the bulk of these corps.[80] In 1813 Capitán General Melendez dissolved the battalions and reorganized them into the Cuerpo de Voluntarios Distinguidos. Melendez also decreed that the new corps was to be integrated by those born in Spain or their first generation born on the island, and he authorized the use of weaponry, including firearms, and uniforms similar to that of the regular Spanish army while simultaneously banning the use of firearms among the urbanos. The voluntarios, who hailed from the most conservative families, served as a counterbalance to the urbanos.

The other militia corps, the disiciplinado, was probably saved by the fact that it was essential for the defense of the island and there was insufficient peninsular manpower to replace it. Although the disciplinados survived Melendez's purge of Puerto Rican elements from the Spanish military, the demobilization of the island inhabitants would continue until the whole military and paramilitary apparatus was firmly controlled by peninsulares and their offspring. The urbanos, weakened as they were in 1817, continued to fulfill their duties until 1853, when the capitán general, Lt. Gen. Fernando de Norzagaray, ordered the suppression of the urbanos in several towns. In 1855 the official order came to disband the rest of the corps, and this was finalized in 1860.[81] Eventually Puerto Rican militias would be replaced by the Instituto de Voluntarios and the Guardia Civil.

In 1820 there was yet another brief wave of liberalism and constitutional government. With the triumph of the *constitucionalistas* in Spain that year, the Constitution of Cadiz of 1812 once more ruled the island, and the *liberales*, who continued to dominate the elections, actively sought to curtail the power of the capitán general by separating military matters from civilian affairs.[82] The Spanish Cortes passed a law presented by the Puerto Rican representative, Demetrio O'Daly, providing for the separation of civil and military commands in Puerto Rico, and Francisco González de Linares became the first civil governor of the island in 1822. This separation of powers, however, was short-lived; it was annulled in December 1823 after the return of Fernando VII.[83] After Fernando's death in September 1833, María Cristina de Borbón became regent queen on behalf of Isabel II, and she named Francisco Martínez de la Rosa as prime minister. The new peninsular regime reestablished the Cortes and called for new elections to be held in July 1834.[84] The liberals continued to dominate the elections until 1836 when for the first time conservative representatives were elected, mostly due to the restrictive system of *"electores pudientes"* or well-to-do voters, who favored the conservatives.[85] Even after the triumph of the conservatives in 1836, Spain saw fit to end American representation in the Cortes and to vest the military governor of the island with dictatorial powers known as *facultades omnimodas*.[86] This absolutist period lasted until the Revolución Gloriosa of 1868, which resulted in the overthrow of Isabel II and her eventual abdication on June 25, 1870. The return of a semiconstitutional period occurred as the result of a combination of revolts that shocked the Spanish Empire in 1868. In Puerto Rico, constitutionalism was severely limited by the weakness of the liberals who had seen the military and paramilitary apparatus on the island gradually fall into the hands of the peninsulares and their conservative allies.

In 1864 the Cuerpo de Voluntarios Distinguidos, which since 1812 had acted as a counterbalance for the Puerto Rican militias, was reorganized and expanded with the name of Instituto de Voluntarios. Negroni argues that the expansion was necessary to replace the permanent garrison on the island, much of which had been sent to La Española to suffocate the Dominican rebellion that followed that island's reincorporation to the Spanish Empire on March 17, 1861.⁸⁷ The need to replace the troops was indeed real. However, nothing but the peninsulares' mistrust of those born on the island and the colonial authorities' commitment to strengthening the conservatives' position justified the replacement of regular troops with the voluntarios.

On June 7, 1867, an event known as the Tercer alzamiento de artilleros occurred in San Juan. Upset for not enjoying the same privileges as the artillery men serving on the peninsula, a group of soldiers from the artillery regiment rioted. Although the uprising was triggered by the economic inequalities between peninsular soldiers serving on the island and those on the peninsula, the governor, Lt. Gen. José María Marchessi (1865–67), ordered the execution by firing squad of a corporal and took the opportunity to exile several separatists, including Ramón Emeterio Betances and Segundo Ruiz Belvis.⁸⁸ Ironically, exile put these separatist leaders directly in touch with Cuban revolutionaries in New York and may have triggered the events that led to the Lares revolt of 1868.

The End of Puerto Rican Militias

It is noteworthy that the Spanish Glorious Revolution of September 18, 1868, on the peninsula combined with el Grito de Lares on September 23 in Puerto Rico and the Grito de Yara on October 10 in Cuba to bring a liberal government to Spain. However, even though Spain was flirting with liberalism, the governor of the island, Gen. José Laureano Sanz (1868–70, 1875), was markedly reactionary. Sanz engaged in political persecution and banishment to quiet the liberals. Furthermore, when the Spanish Cortes approved a new constitution on June 6, 1869, it was not extended to Puerto Rico. At this point, the Cortes intended to follow a colonial policy of assimilation regarding insular possessions.⁸⁹

After the Lares insurrection, the Instituto de Voluntarios began to expand while the milicias were being extinguished. Between 1868 and 1870, Sanz reorganized the instituto into nine battalions roughly divided by districts. On July 27, 1869, at Sanz's insistence, the Reglamento de Voluntarios was published. Among other things it allowed its members to be protected under the *fuero activo de Guerra* during time of war and the *fuero criminal* after fifteen years of service.⁹⁰ These protections effectively awarded legal impunity to the voluntarios. Furthermore, on November 1, 1868, the Spanish minister of overseas possessions authorized the creation of the Guardia Civil in Puerto Rico.⁹¹ The mission of the Guardia Civil was to control the population and guarantee civil order. Sanz immediately moved to make it a loyal and effective repressive tool. Since its inception, its members were from the conservative faction on the island who proceeded to persecute the liberals. In its first years, the guardia was composed of roughly three hundred men, all of them peninsulares. Like the voluntarios, the Guardia Civil soon came to be protected by all the *fueros* protecting the military.⁹²

Immediately before the Lares revolt, the milicias disciplinadas were composed of 7,900 men, which as Negroni points out was about the same strength as the Puerto Rico U.S. National Guard in 1992 when the island's population approached four million inhabitants. Since a lieutenant, an *alférez* (second lieutenant in the Spanish military), and a few milicianos participated in the revolt, the loyalty of the whole corps was put in doubt. On February 12, 1870, Sanz ordered the suppression of the milicias disciplinadas' active service effective March 1870. The troop was disbanded. The cadre of officers was allowed to continue wearing their uniforms and to receive monthly payments for service and pension, but they had no raison d'être.⁹³

Military education also came to be reserved for peninsulares and their conservative allies. Out of O'Reilly's recommendations, a military academy had been founded on the island in 1765.⁹⁴ In 1874 the Academia was reorganized and renamed the Academia de Infantería with room for sixteen cadets. Although in theory anyone between the ages of sixteen and twenty-five could apply for admission (age fourteen if the applicant was a member of a military family), the acceptance requirements effectively banned those not belonging to the elite.⁹⁵ Moreover, two-thirds of the positions were to be filled by the children of military personnel, leaving the remaining spaces for the children of civilians. Since Puerto Ricans were effectively banned from the military (until

1884), two-thirds of the cadets were actually the children of peninsular officers, and given the rigorous requirement for admittance, only those in a position to secure an extraordinary education for their children could hope to send them to the Academia. This elite academy, which provided the best education on the island until the change of sovereignty in 1898, was in effect reserved for peninsulares, their offspring, and the elite.[96] In 1880 the island was allowed to send students directly to the military academies in Spain, but being that the admittance process was as rigorous and with the added economic constraint, the military schools were for all purposes reserved for the island's elites.

The elimination of the Fijo in 1815, the urbanos between 1855 and 1860, and the disciplinados in 1870, coupled with the strict requirements and exclusionary policies of the military academy, combined to demobilize the inhabitants of Puerto Rico with the exception of the peninsulares and their conservative allies. Moreover, as Puerto Ricans were being excluded from traditional military and paramilitary institutions, the colonial administration used every opportunity to strengthen the Guardia Civil and the voluntarios. The dearth of a military force that could counterbalance the military institutions in the hands of peninsulares weakened the liberals, who had to be content with whatever liberal reforms emerged from the political crises that periodically visited the peninsula.

The Political Arena

Political exclusion intertwined with short-lived political reforms after 1868 and continued until the end of Spanish domination. Out of the reforms that followed the critical period of September 1868 emerged the first political parties on the island. On November 20, 1870, the Partido Liberal Reformista (PLR) was founded in Puerto Rico. Farmers, cattle ranchers, industrialists, storekeepers, professionals, and the middle class made the bulk of the party.[97] The liberal reformists were divided between two philosophies: autonomy and assimilation. The latter became dominant, breaking with a long tradition of liberals seeking autonomy dating back to the first Puerto Rican *delegado a las cortes*,

Ramón Power y Giralt. The quick suppression of the Lares rebels and the political persecution and banishment of separatists and liberals alike provided the ground for this apparent rupture with autonomist ideals.

A few days after the establishment of the PLR, the conservatives followed suit and created their own party. Elections were held in 1871 and were dominated by the liberals. Sanz, who had been replaced by the liberal governor, Lt. Gen. Gabriel Baldrich (1870–71), on May 20, 1870, was the only conservative elected, running for the district of San Juan where most conservatives lived.[98] The conservatives responded, promoting instability by causing riots and accusing Baldrich of harboring liberals. Their efforts bore fruit, and Baldrich was relieved of his charge on September 13, 1871, and replaced by yet another conservative, Ramón Gómez Pulido.[99] New elections were held on April 1872 under a decree recognizing the voting rights of only free Spaniards who were at least twenty-five years old and who were literate or could pay eight pesos to the colonial authorities. Nine of the fifteen delegates elected were peninsulares, and eight were from the conservative faction. This phenomenon was known as *cunerismo*, or election by birthplace.[100]

The liberal delegates elected succeeded in presenting the irregularities of the 1872 elections before the Cortes, paving the way for new elections to be held in August. The liberals won every district except that of San Juan, where the conservatives reelected Sanz. This was followed by a series of reforms including the final abolition of slavery, more extensive male suffrage, freedom of the press and association, and elimination of the governor's *facultades omnímodas*. In 1873 the liberals controlled every district as the conservatives abstained from participating.[101] None of these reforms would have been possible without Amadeo I de Saboya's abdication, which prompted the Spanish Cortes to declare the first Spanish republic on February 11, 1873.[102] The government of the new republic moved to make Puerto Rico one of the eighteen states included in the Spanish federal republic and extended all the protections of the Spanish constitution of 1869 to those born in Puerto Rico.[103] These measures were short-lived.

The fall of the Spanish republic on January 3, 1874, brought the accession of Alfonso XII and a parliamentary monarchy to the peninsula, but the island regressed to a more absolutist reality. Once more, Laureano Sanz was sent to Puerto Rico as governor with restored facultades omnimodas. He immediately eliminated constitutional guarantees as well as freedom of the press and association. Sanz also imposed a new decree banning vagrancy, and he expelled liberals from government and teaching positions. Moreover, following Sanz's steps, on March 4, 1873, Capitán General Juan Martínez Plowes promoted the Instituto de Voluntarios to "active reserve of the Army" and expanded the corps to thirteen battalions with four companies of one hundred men each. The voluntarios were composed of the most pro-Spanish elements on the island, and since its members belonged to the conservative party (later Incondicional Español), they effectively became a political party in arms.[104] After his return to power in 1875, Sanz obtained permission to double the Guardia Civil. He used both corps to persecute the liberals.[105] Even though Sanz was removed in 1875, mostly due to international pressure, his successor, Gen. Segundo de la Portilla (1875–77), was able to help elect *cuneros* from the conservative families. Without the participation of the liberals, the conservatives (*incondicionales* after 1880) won all the seats in the general elections of 1876 and dominated all six general elections between 1879 and 1896.[106] In just eight years after the Lares revolt, the liberals on the island had been weakened to the point that participating in general elections became pointless.

In 1887, out of the havoc created by the colonial administration's persecution emerged the introduction of *compontes*, or corporal punishment, and imprisonment of hundreds of liberals under the governorship of Romualdo Palacios, the Partido Autonomista Puertorriqueño (PAP). Although Román Baldorioty de Castro, founder of the party and arguably one of the most influential Puerto Rican political figures of the nineteenth century, desired a more flexible and autonomous relationship with Spain, the autonomistas' assembly chose the views of Rafael María de Labra. Thus the goals of this new party were to obtain the same political and legal identity and protections as those living on the peninsula and to seek the greatest degree of decentralization within the framework of national unity.[107] Even Luis Muñoz Rivera, soon to emerge as one of the dominant political figures on the island and faithful friend of Baldorioty de Castro, did not believe that full autonomy was an attainable goal and urged instead for decentralization. Weighing the options of the liberals, Muñoz Rivera rejected annexation to the United States on the grounds that "all Puerto Ricans feel proud of their Latin blood." He also rejected the "separatist rebellion which no one amongst us defends, and, given the people's circumstances is an impossible utopia."[108]

The Carta Autonómica of 1897

The autonomistas did not participate in the general elections of 1893–96. The whole period was marked by constant dissension among the autonomist leadership and by electoral boycotting in protest of what they perceived as unfair electoral laws that severely limited the number of voters. However, on August 8, 1897, an anarchist assassinated the Spanish prime minister, Antonio Cánovas del Castillo, setting the stage for Práxedes Mateo Sagasta to assume the presidency of Spain. As leader of the Partido Liberal Fusionista Español, Sagasta had agreed with Muñoz Rivera to grant an autonomous government (*régimen autonómico*) to Puerto Rico in exchange for the autonomistas' support of his party.[109] To reflect the nature of the new alliance with Sagasta, the autonomist party changed its name to Partido Liberal Fusionista Puertorriqueño. The republican faction within the autonomist party, led by José Celso Barbosa, abandoned the party and created the Partido Autonomista Histórico (Ortodoxo).[110] Soon after coming to power, Sagasta made good on his promise to the autonomistas by securing the Carta Autonómica (Autonomous Charter) on November 25, 1897.

The Carta Autonómica of 1897 was liberal indeed. Sixteen Puerto Rican delegates were to be elected by popular vote to represent the island in the Spanish Cortes while three senators were to be chosen by an assembly of elected officials to serve in the Peninsular Congress. The assembly also elected the eight members of the Consejo de Administración (Administrative Council), who together with the thirty-two members of the popularly elected Cámara de Representantes (Chamber of Representatives) constituted the Puerto Rican Parliament. Title VII, Article 43 of the charter guaranteed veto power to the Puerto Rican Parliament over decisions reached by the Peninsular Congress, while Article 2 declared that the "present constitution shall not be amended except by virtue of a special law and upon petition of the insular parliament."[111] The charter also provided for the creation of a cabinet by the winning coalition or party. The ministries of the new cabinet were of extreme importance and included Treasury; Agriculture, Industry, and Commerce; Public Works, Communication, and Transportation; Public Education; and Justice and Government, plus a presiding cabinet member.[112] However, as established by Article 41, the governor retained command of all the armed forces on the island, and all authorities and offices remained subordinated to his office.[113] Moreover, the charter was declared by royal decree and not by a law passed by the Cortes. Thus while seeking liberal reforms, Sagasta and the liberals circumvented the most republican of Spanish institutions.

The new regime was inaugurated on February 8, 1898, and general elections were held on March 27. Of roughly 120,000 votes, the autonomistas obtained more than 97,000 and the conservatives 3,729 votes.[114] Sixteen autonomistas, ten from the liberal faction and six from the orthodox, were elected as *diputados a cortes*. On April 10, the first cabinet was formed and three senators were chosen.[115] On April 21, 1898, scarcely two months after the inauguration of the autonomic government, the governor general of the island declared martial law. On July 17, 1898, constitutional guarantees were reinstated and the insular parliament was inaugurated. Eight days later, the United States invaded Puerto Rico.

La Carta Autonómica in a Global Context

The Carta Autonómica and the subsequent electoral victory represent the triumph of the autonomistas, and throughout the following century it would capture the imagination of political groups seeking autonomy or other decolonization formulas. However, the circumstances of such success must be examined. The granting of the Autonomous Charter had as much to do with chance (the assassination of Cánovas del Castillo) as it had to do with international and colonial problems plaguing Spain. By 1897 the Cuban war of independence was in full swing, and diplomatic relations between the United States and Spain had reached a historic low. In 1895, when the Cuban rebellion reignited with the Grito de Baire, the United States followed a path of neutrality that actually favored the Spaniards.[116] American neutrality and recognition of Spanish sovereignty over Cuba, however, were conditional. The Spaniards had to facilitate Cuban trade with the United States and were not to relinquish control over Cuba to any third party. Moreover, as Louis Pérez has argued, any modification of sovereignty that "did not result in U.S. acquisition of the island was unacceptable."[117]

When it became evident that the Spaniards could not bring an end to the war, the Cleveland administration took a firmer stand, seeking to gain concessions for the Cubans, hoping that such measures would stop the conflict and prevent the independence of the island. The Cuban rebels themselves had become an unwanted third party.[118] By 1897 it was clear that sooner or later the Cuban rebels would win the war. For three years, the Cubans had been destroying the infrastructure of the island, rendering the Spanish army incapable of launching major military actions. According to Valeriano Weyler, supreme commander of the Spanish forces in Cuba, the rebels "had brought the Spanish army to the brink of defeat."[119] The rebels were so certain of their imminent victory that they rejected Spain's offering of autonomy.[120] Unlike their counterparts in Puerto Rico, the Cuban leaders had the military means to obtain independence. This situation left the McKinley administration with two choices: to accept Cuban independence or to sanction military intervention. McKinley followed Cleveland's latest approach. In his inaugural address, he referred to the unrest in Cuba and stated that a "firm and dignified policy that would protect the rights of Americans everywhere was needed."[121] The increasingly aggressive posture of the U.S. government put Spain in a precarious position and made the ceasing of hostilities imperative. It is within this context that the autonomic charter of 1897 came into existence.

Soon after the battleship *Maine* exploded in Havana harbor on February 15, 1898, the United States entered the war and quickly beat Spanish forces weakened by years of fighting in Cuba and the Philippines. As a result of its victory over Spain, and by virtue of the Treaty of Paris of December 10, 1898, the United States gained full control over Puerto Rico, Guam, Wake Island, and the Philippines, and gained limited control over Cuba by the Teller Amendment.[122] As it had been with the short-lived political reforms obtained throughout the nineteenth century, the lifespan of the Carta Autonómica was at the whim of the military and political rulers from the peninsular metropolis. The Puerto Rican delegates were excluded from the peace negotiations, even though the future of the island was at stake, and according to the island's legal political relations with Spain, as stated in the charter of 1897, they had veto power over such decisions. That they did not have a voice in the Paris protocols evidenced the ephemeral and capricious nature of liberal overtures within the Spanish political establishment.

The failure of the liberales and later of the autonomistas to secure a stronger presence within the Spanish military on the island or to restore the Puerto Rican militias left them in a very weak position from which to negotiate with both Spain and the United States. The autonomistas were also undermined for reasons beyond their control. Throughout the nineteenth century the separatists consistently failed to become a significant threat to the colonial authorities in Puerto Rico. Their failed and sometimes stillborn attempts to overthrow the Spanish authorities served as an excuse to demobilize the inhabitants of the island, to arm the most loyalist and conservative elements of Puerto Rican society, to curtail civil rights, and to persecute those liberals who stayed on the island. Thus separatists' attempts served to erode the position of the liberals who had to prove their loyalty and endure cyclical waves of political persecution.

During the crises that periodically visited the peninsula and the rest of the Spanish Empire, especially between 1808 and 1824 and in 1868, Puerto Rico did not obtain its independence. Instead of more inclusion, these periods of crisis provided opportunities for the metropolis to exclude the island's polity groups, which had previously enjoyed limited inclusion, while giving bureaucratic positions and putting the military into the hands of newly arrived peninsulares and royalists from the U.S. mainland. With the exception of some short-lived liberal openings, those born on the island were gradually demobilized and the popular sectors coerced into working for agro-capitalist enterprises. The demobilization and *peonización* of those born on the island were but two sides of the same coin. Not surprisingly, demobilization occurred while new policies, such as the reglamento de jornaleros, were established to provide cheap and, in some cases, free labor for the developing agro-capitalist industry.

With the suppression of the disciplinados in 1870, the popular sectors' participation in the defense of the island came to an end and would not be fully restored until the creation of the U.S. Puerto Rico National Guard in 1919. The hijos de este país, with the exception of the most unconditional loyalists, were excluded from this vital access to socioeconomic and political power. Captaincies had been passed down from father to son to grandson, and the capitán de milicias was a respected community member. Moreover, even though conservative well-to-do volunteers replaced the milicias, they did not capture the imagination of the Puerto Ricans, nor did they instill the pride the milicias once did. For if the milicias had existed to protect the island, the entities that replaced them were intended for the suppression of the local population and the persecution of the liberals. As a matter of fact, works on Puerto Rican military history, including the first official Puerto Rican National Guard history, trace the creation of the U.S. Puerto Rico National Guard units to those militias which came to be known as milicias puertorriqueñas and purposely exclude the Guardia Civil guard and the Instituto de Voluntarios from their lineage.[123]

In 1870, with the dissolution of the disciplinados, Puerto Rico's military and paramilitary apparatus came to be completely in the hands of peninsulares and later shared with their offspring. It has been pointed out that displacement and the economic subordination of those born on the island to the peninsulares precipitated the Lares revolt and subsequent attempts to overthrow the Spanish colonial regime, as well as the emergence of distinguishable Puerto Rican identities. Exclusion from the military played a major role in the displacement and disenfranchisement of the Puerto Ricans.[124]

The exclusionary policies of the Spanish colonial administration, as early as the 1810s, when the rest of the empire except Cuba and Puerto Rico revolted and finally won independence, created tensions between criollos and peninsulares at the highest levels of power. The emergence of the instituto and the final suppression of the milicias sent a message to those born on the island; they were not to be trusted for they were not really Spaniards. More important, the male population that did not belong to the elite found itself ever more excluded from access to socioeconomic power, and even adulthood and manhood, for if they could not defend their land, they remained in a childlike state, especially given the colony's military character and tradition. Removing the natives of Puerto Rico from the colonial armed forces, a very restrictive policy, and dearth of a common education were some of the patterns of exclusion that led to the slow development of a distinct national identity on the island. Thus it was not the Lares revolt itself, but the policies followed by the colonial authorities afterward that fueled the developing of distinctive Puerto Rican national identities. However, this was embryonic, greatly in part to the Puerto Rican elites' need of a state to guarantee their commanding position in society and because of their perceived cultural affinities vis-à-vis Spain such as language and religion. The developing of a separate identity was also slowed by the criollo elite's reluctance to move toward independence, which was itself a consequence of the weakening of the criollo elite by the demobilization of the inhabitants of the island. Nonetheless, the landslide victory of the autonomistas in 1898 shows that the majority of the inhabitants rejected the *incondicionalismo español*. This is even more important when considering that the autonomistas of 1898 were not sponsoring the watered-down version defended by the liberals right after the Lares revolt, but a more radical stance which among other things declared the right of the Puerto Ricans to govern their island as they saw fit.

When the first U.S. soldiers landed on the island, most Puerto Ricans had no reason to support the colonial administration. Initially the majority openly embraced the invaders. Soon afterward, resistance against the American occupation materialized. Resistance and support would come from both the elites and popular sectors. The criollo elites, who had played the power game with the Spanish metropolis, would continue to do so with the United States. This time, however, separatistas, autonomistas, and anexionistas had learned their lesson. There would be neither independence, autonomy, nor inclusion into the Union if the Puerto Ricans did not bear arms either as part of the armies of the new metropolis or as native militia. Under the new regime, enfranchisement and decolonization, and reclaiming the masculinity of the Puerto Ricans were to be sought by all means, including and in fact emphasizing military service.

2

Puerto Rican a la Americana

A Hearts and Minds Campaign, 1898–1914

> The native soldiers [had become] an object lesson to the communities in the neighborhoods of their posts . . . and from that standpoint, as from many others has undoubtedly been a very potent education influence. Each man of the battalion will be a committee in himself to spread among the natives, stories of American prestige. . . . The soldiers feel a pride in their service and there is an undoubted stimulant by it toward general loyalty.
> —Charles H. Allen to Elihu Root[1]

In the aftermath of the Spanish-Cuban-Filipino-American War of 1898, the United States engaged in its first extracontinental nation-building projects. As de facto ruler of the Philippines, Cuba, and Puerto Rico, the United States sought to transform the socioeconomic and political structures of these countries into something more in tune with mainstream American tenets. In few places were these efforts as intense and prolonged as in Puerto Rico. As the United States took over Puerto Rico, it immediately began sanitary and relief efforts while building a public education system in the image of New England's system. The transformation of the island was not limited to humanitarian and educational projects. The American colonial administration sought to change the socioeconomic and political structures in Puerto Rico, too. In essence, colonial authorities intended to mold the Puerto Ricans in the image of Americans. Indeed, the early attempts to "modernize" the island and its inhabitants through a nation-state building project were supposedly guided by "benevolent assimilation" and "compassionate uplifting."[2] These projects relied heavily, both directly and indirectly, on the military.

The American colonial administrators, however, were not the only actors in this play. The island's elites (both criollos and peninsulares) initially welcomed the Americans and participated actively. They also developed and championed their own versions of Americanization.[3] Furthermore, they pushed for the acceptance of Puerto Ricans into the U.S. military as well as the creation of a native militia to garrison the island.

This chapter explores the role of the U.S. military as part of the metropolis's colonial project of nation-building and the motivations of the island's elites for supporting Puerto Rican military service. How did the combination of an American nation-building project and local participation influence Puerto Rican politics and identities? Was the American metropolis successful in reversing perceived patterns of political exclusion among the island's population? By answering these questions this chapter seeks to underline the links between the military remobilization of the Puerto Ricans, political enfranchisement, and the development of cultural and political identities in the early years of American dominance over Puerto Rico.

The 1898 U.S. Military Campaign

Several factors facilitated the transfer of sovereignty over Puerto Rico from Spain to the United States in 1898 and eased the nation-building project as envisioned by U.S. officials. The war in Puerto Rico was relatively bloodless, which eliminated much of the trauma usually associated with this kind of event. American troops landed in Puerto Rico on July 25, 1898. Their campaign extended until August 12 when Spain and the United States signed an armistice. During this period the U.S. forces engaged the Spaniards on six occasions, suffering thirty-six wounded and seven killed in action, while the Spaniards suffered eighty-eight wounded and seventeen killed in action.[4] In addition, Maj. Gen. Nelson Miles, commander of U.S. troops in Puerto Rico, took great pains not to alienate the local population.[5] He went as far as to try to obtain the release of political prisoners in Spain and Africa in an attempt to win the goodwill of the Puerto Ricans.[6]

General Miles considered the support, or at least the neutrality, of the local population when designing his plan of action. Surprising even his closest aides, he changed the initial landings, scheduled to take place in Fajardo on the northeastern tip of the island, to Guánica, located in the southwest. Military historians have emphasized interservice rivalry and Miles's obsession with relegating the Navy to a secondary role in this campaign to explain the landing at Guánica. It is more likely, however, that military and political matters influenced Miles's decision. As he informed the naval commander of the expedition, the population of the southern part of the island was more inclined to side with the Americans than those near the capital and that landing in the south would take the Spaniards by surprise, tipping their defenses off balance.[7]

After landing at multiple sites along the southern coast, the invading force moved west and north in four columns advancing without naval cover. It was part of Miles's plan that the army receive the most exposure during the campaign. He had informed Secretary of War Russell A. Alger of the benefits of marching across the country as opposed to marching under the protection of the fleet's guns along the coast. He insisted that his troops' visibility would attract the support of the Puerto Ricans. In this regard, he even opposed the naval bombardment of San Juan on the grounds that it would cause unnecessary harm to civilians and needlessly alienate a population willing to assist the Americans.[8] In effect, Miles undertook a campaign for the hearts and minds of the islanders.

The McKinley administration enlisted the help of Puerto Ricans. Before and during the invasion of Puerto Rico, U.S. forces organized three Puerto Rican corps charged with facilitating the invasion and the war effort on the island. The first group, the Porto Rican Commission, was composed of a dozen Puerto Ricans and presided over by an American. The PRC mediated between the population and soldiers, explained the aims of the war, and tried to persuade the native population to support the United States. Once in Puerto Rico, General Miles ordered the creation of a volunteer group known as the Porto Rican Scouts. The PRS, a cavalry unit of seventy men, was attached to Gen. Theodore Schwan's brigade. Miles also ordered the creation of the Porto Rican Guards to keep the public order and named a Puerto Rican as the unit's commanding officer.[9] Puerto Ricans volunteered as skirmishers, provided intelligence, and organized small foot and mounted raiding parties across the island that scourged the Spaniards and their allies by burning their plantations and stores and seizing their property.[10] These actions hindered the Spanish defense and accelerated Miles's advance.

Miles's gamble paid off, as Puerto Ricans sided with the invading force. In early August, the gobernador general of Puerto Rico, Manuel Macías y Casado, complained to the Spanish minister of war: "The majority of this country does not wish to call itself Spaniards, preferring American domination. This the enemy knows and is proven to him by greetings and adhesions in towns that are being occupied."[11]

Puerto Rico in Lieu of Indemnities

Miles's carefulness in not aggravating the population responded to U.S. designs for the island. On May 26, Capt. Alfred T. Mahan, Secretary of War Alger, Navy Secretary John D. Long, and General Miles held a war council.[12] The United States had considered invading Puerto Rico before Cuba to force the Spaniards to support the war in Cuba from their own home shores. The Navy, however, discarded this plan because it did not need Puerto Rico in order to win the war in Cuba. Furthermore, the Navy was concerned about dividing the fleet between Cuba and Puerto Rico, which could lead to an unfortunate sea fight that could alter the balance of maritime power in Spain's favor. Thus the United States decided to mount two expeditions in the Caribbean, but not simultaneously. Santiago de Cuba would be the first target, and Fajardo in Puerto Rico would follow. Once Santiago had fallen, and with it Adm. Pascual Cervera y Topete's fleet, there would be no need to attack Havana.[13]

On May 1, 1898, Adm. George Dewey's command destroyed the Spanish fleet in the Philippines. On July 3 the U.S. Flying

Squadron stopped Cervera y Topete's fleet when it attempted to escape the U.S. blockade, and on July 13, the 35,000 troops who made up the Spanish garrison in Santiago de Cuba and its department surrendered. At that moment, the war was practically over. Even Mahan conceded that there was nothing else for the Spaniards to do but to surrender.[14] There was no need to invade Puerto Rico to win the war. The United States had achieved such military superiority over Spain that Adm. William T. Sampson opposed Miles's request for armored vessels to escort his transports to Puerto Rico.[15] Still Miles received the order to proceed to Puerto Rico on July 18 and invade seven days later. The motive for such action was to occupy the island before the end of hostilities prevented the United States from doing so. Quickly after the destruction of the Spanish fleet in the Pacific, Assistant Secretary of the Navy Theodore Roosevelt wrote a personal letter to Senator Henry Cabot Lodge urging him not to make peace until "we get Porto Rico." Lodge assured Roosevelt that the administration was "fully committed to the larger policy we both desire."[16] President McKinley's administration had decided to annex Puerto Rico "in lieu of indemnities," and the physical presence of the U.S. military on the island would undoubtedly strengthen the U.S. position. That Puerto Rico came to be a U.S. colonial possession did not stem from historical accident but rather from a calculated design. The United States did not become an empire by default.[17]

On July 18 the Spanish had asked the French government to approach the United States and request a cease-fire as a preliminary to peace negotiations. The French ambassador to the United States, Jules Cambon, communicated the Spanish request to the White House on July 26. McKinley rejected the offer, for it did not say anything about Puerto Rico or the Philippines. On July 30, through the office of the French ambassador, McKinley delivered armistice terms to Spain, demanding that it relinquish control of Cuba and cede Puerto Rico, other islands in the Caribbean, and the Ladrones in the Pacific. Spain replied on August 1, asking if any other territorial indemnification could be substituted for Puerto Rico, and Washington responded negatively.

Defeated in the Philippines and in Cuba and unable to win in Puerto Rico, the Spaniards agreed to U.S. terms, and an armistice went into effect on August 12, 1898.[18]

From Spanish Colony to U.S. Colony

By the Treaty of Paris of December 10, 1898, which officially ended the war, the United States gained full control over Puerto Rico, Guam, Wake Island, and the Philippines and limited control by the Teller Amendment over Cuba. Spain officially relinquished control over Puerto Rico, and on October 18 the change of sovereignty was completed with the evacuation of the last Spanish troops and the raising of the American flag in all public buildings. That day witnessed the inauguration of a military government that lasted until May 1900.

The way in which the Puerto Rican campaign had been conducted and the high regard that Puerto Rican politicians had for the United States and its republican institutions allowed for a widespread sense of goodwill among the general population.[19] There was a belief that the island would be given independence or become an American state. The latter option seems to have had the most support among both the elite and the masses. The annexationist movement dates back to 1898 when the former autonomist leadership formed two parties, the Federal and the Republican, both with statehood as their goal.[20] As discussed by Rafael Bernabe, both Republican and Federal leaders in Puerto Rico saw the United States as a political entity, a republic providing space for many nations and peoples to coexist in equality while enjoying the benefits of constitutional democracy.[21] Former autonomistas who had defined "Puerto Rico as a regional entity within the larger Spanish polity" had little trouble applying the same view to the American metropolis.[22] Roughly 90 percent of the population in Puerto Rico favored annexation to the United States during the first years after the war.[23] Nonetheless, neither independence nor federated statehood was granted. Instead the United States installed a military government.

As is evident from the diplomatic correspondence during the war, the United States intended to keep Puerto Rico as a permanent possession. The local political elites and the popular sectors overwhelmingly favored becoming a U.S. state. This situation begs the question: Why did Puerto Rico become a colony as opposed to an incorporated territory on its way to federated statehood? The type of territorial and political expansion of the United States helps to understand the reluctance to incorporate Puerto Rico as a territory. As the United States expanded westward, the indigenous inhabitants of the continent were eliminated, displaced, or forcefully relocated. Settlers of mostly European background re-peopled the new territories, and Congress moved toward statehood once the socioeconomic and political structures of such territories were firmly in the hands of Euro-Americans.[24] Although the leaders of the annexationist movement knew this history, they believed that as a "civilized" and "Christian" people fit for self-government, the Puerto Ricans would be smoothly incorporated into the United States.[25] What escaped the annexationist leaders was that in the United States, Catholicism was not considered the religion of the "civilized," nor were Catholics viewed as having the aptitude for democratic self-government.[26] Worse yet, the Puerto Ricans were considered to be the result of miscegenation—an unholy mix of Indian, black, and Spaniard. In 1898, when the dictums of social Darwinism, pseudoscientific racism, the white man's burden, and manifest destiny combined to guide U.S. policies, the fact that the United States came to control Puerto Rico upset the plans of the annexationist movement on the island.[27]

Rationalizing Colonialism

The most popular narratives in support of intervention in the Cuban war of independence were based on gender and racial narratives. The yellow press in the United States portrayed Cuba and Puerto Rico as damsels in distress abused by Spain and in need of rescue by a virile Uncle Sam. Post-1898 imagery of the inhabitants of Cuba, Puerto Rico, and the Philippines presented them as apes or as pickaninnies in need of Uncle Sam's guiding hand.[28] These gendered and racial narratives were dominant at the time and served to rationalize colonialism in popular terms.[29]

Military service was an almost universal rite of passage into manhood.[30] Forbidding nonwhite males to serve in the military and questioning their martial prowess helped to perpetuate the myth that nonwhites were not fully men and hence were unworthy of full citizenship and unfit for self-determination and government.

African American soldiers who participated in the war of 1898 were portrayed as inferior to their white counterparts, prone to panic and cowardice, and only able to perform acceptably when firmly and often brutally led by white officers.[31] It is not coincidental that the U.S. military began to restrict the role of blacks in the military after the war and the subsequent Filipino insurrection against U.S. rule ended.[32] Precluding blacks from combat positions and denying them officers' commissions were justified on the grounds of the inability of darker races to achieve full manhood and self-government.

The gendered and racialized discourses used in support of the war in 1898 traveled with the U.S. troops. As military service became definitive proof of manhood and a prerequisite for full citizenship and self-rule, calling into question the military competency of Cuban and Filipino rebels became an expeditious rationalization for empire. Cuban rebels, instrumental in securing a U.S. victory, were portrayed as lacking even more in martial prowess and manliness than U.S. black troops.[33] The implications are clear. The African American soldier performed slightly better and was somewhat manlier than his Cuban counterpart because the blacks were led by white officers. In these skewed narratives, African Americans and Cubans evidenced their innate inability for martial prowess.

The infantilizing gendered and racialized discourses came from the highest sectors of the military establishment as well. Capt. Alfred T. Mahan, whose work influenced U.S. military strategy and foreign policy for decades, regarded the people in the new possessions as alien subjects impossible to assimilate and still in "race childhood."[34] Puerto Ricans came ashore with the invading U.S. Army, parties of Puerto Rican scouts aided the invasion, and hundreds of Puerto Ricans rose up against the Spanish establishment on their own while fighting alongside the Cuban rebels.

However, the new metropolis was quick to elevate the supposedly nonmartial and docile nature of the Puerto Ricans into an enduring myth, even as it mobilized them.[35] Illustrative of this contempt, the War Department and the first American military governor of the island reported that there were no capable local men to form part of a civilian government in Puerto Rico, and a military government ensued until 1900.[36]

The rationale used to keep Puerto Rico as a colony, as well as the Philippines, was that the majority of its inhabitants were not capable of self-government mostly due to their racial composition and centuries of Spanish obscurantism, which made them an easy prey for European powers.[37] The ethno-racial assignments of the new colonial subjects under the American imperial umbrella were built on the premise of their men's compromised manhood as evidenced by their supposedly inadequate or nonexistent martial spirit.

Mahan believed that the racial composition of the new territories posed a threat to the social fabric of the United States.[38] In his opinion, the purpose of acquiring colonies should be limited to strategic naval bases. For this reason, Mahan opposed annexing the Philippines. He was solely interested in obtaining the military bases needed to reach the Asian and Latin American markets and protecting the sea lines and the racial integrity of the United States. Regarding the new colonies, Mahan argued that the United States should follow the "beneficial and parent-like approach of the British instead of the inhumanly oppressive Spanish model" because "alien subjects were still in race-childhood."[39] In short, Mahan proposed to use "uplifting benevolence" to pay for the acquisition of the bases needed to ensure the prominence of the Anglo-Saxon race. In the process, he established a dictum in U.S. extracontinental expansion.

The McKinley and successive administrations, as well as much of the American public, operated under the presumption that colonies were necessary from a military and economic perspective but that their inclusion as states would threaten the racial integrity of the United States.[40] Consequently, in 1898 U.S. imperialism became colonial in nature. The old imperial republicanism that had driven the westward expansion died when the United States acquired territories with populations that could not be removed or assimilated according to opinion makers.[41] That Puerto Rico was simultaneously wanted and unwanted had an impact on everyone's plans for the island. Puerto Rican elites, who had their own racial and gender baggage, understood U.S. discourses and would apply them to their understanding of American rule.

The Foraker Act and de facto Autonomismo

Neither independence nor the path to federal statehood for Puerto Rico were political options for the McKinley administration. This situation led to the passing of the Foraker Act of April 12, 1900. According to historian María Estades Font, that political factions and the population supported the Americans and a military native corps and a native insular police led by American officers guaranteed U.S. sovereignty, facilitated the transition from a military to a civilian government in Puerto Rico.[42] Secretary of War Elihu Root, who initially opposed ending military rule, chose Puerto Rico to try out the new colonial policy of no incorporation based on the aforementioned conditions, and as recommended by Mahan, he emphasized following the British imperial model.[43] The United States decided to create a tutelary colonial state in Puerto Rico.

Named for its sponsor, Ohio senator Joseph B. Foraker, the act established a civilian government for Puerto Rico. The colonial administration was headed by a governor and an executive council appointed by McKinley. Six of the eleven members of the council were continental Americans. The people of Puerto Rico, as defined in Article 7 of the act, would elect thirty-five members for the island's Chamber of Delegates and a nonvoting representative to Congress. The Foraker Act also established a political body to be known as the "Puerto Rican people." According to this article, those Spanish subjects who resided in Puerto Rico by April 11, 1899, and their offspring, would be recognized as citizens of Puerto Rico unless they opted for keeping their allegiance to Spain. By virtue of named citizenship, this political body, the Puerto Ricans, was under the protection of the United States. The act also declared Puerto Ricans to be American nationals.[44]

The Foraker Law disillusioned the leadership of the Republican and Federal Parties. When general elections took place on November 6, 1900, to elect the Puerto Rican representative to Congress and members of the Chamber of Delegates, the Federals abstained from participating.[45] The Republicans, on the other hand, immediately took part in the colonial government.[46] Some Federals ran in the elections of 1902, breaking the monopoly of the Republicans. In the elections of 1904 and 1906, the Federals, former members of the Federación Libre del Trabajadores (FLT), and some dissenters from the Republican Party joined together in the creation of Partido Unión de Puerto Rico and gained control over the insular House of Representatives.[47]

As argued by Rafael Bernabe, the early colonial policies of the U.S. government paved the way for de facto autonomisimo. Even when annexationists controlled all the positions opened to Puerto Ricans, they could do no more than to engage in the administration of the colonial regime.[48] Initially local political leaders challenged the United States and shifted their goals. However, they did so within the parameters established by the United States. Ironically, by serving in the colonial administration, Puerto Rican leaders, many of whom were ardent anticolonialists, showed acceptance of the regime, which further legitimized American control over the island.

Mass Political Organization

There were other reasons for accepting, or at least not opposing, the American presence on the island. Puerto Rico may not have moved politically in the direction that the native political leadership desired, but there had been real changes for the masses. One of these was the creation of the Partido Obrero Socialista in June 1899, led by Santiago Iglesias Pantín. For the first time, workers on the island enjoyed organized representation. This development was followed by the creation of labor organizations such as the Federación Libre de Trabajadores. Moreover, universal male suffrage was established in 1904, and the voting population more than doubled in a single generation.[49]

Access to political representation increased under U.S. rule, and urban and rural workers found themselves enfranchised. Legalization of labor organizing "opened the door to the possibility for a collective empowerment and degree of worker organization not experienced under the Spanish."[50] Such headway would have not been possible if the McKinley administration, its successors, and the U.S. courts did not believe in upholding the principles of freedom of the press, assembly, speech, and worship in the territories. The United States was engaging in colonialism, but it was liberal colonialism.[51] As argued by Ángel Quintero Rivera, the criollo leadership of Unión lost appeal due to the metropolis's influence among the working class. The working classes used the liberal aspects of the metropolis, such as suffrage and free association, to oppose the "conservative and *senõrial*" independence project of Unión and the unflappable pro-Americanism of the Republicans.[52] Whether intended or not, the United States was creating political spaces that weakened the economic and political power of the old elites.

Americanizing the New Colony

As discussed above, Puerto Rico, like the other territories acquired during the war, was not to be incorporated into the United States, but that did not mean that the population and the territory itself should not be molded into something more "American." In this regard on February 16, 1899, President McKinley accepted the "burden of the Philippines, to safeguard the happiness of their inhabitants," and later included the other territories, as he proclaimed a campaign of "benevolent assimilation."[53] The United States would rule the new territories, and in exchange it would civilize and modernize the natives. From socioeconomic structures to individuals, the U.S. colonial administration attempted to reshape the new territories in the image of the continental United States.[54] The new project of nation-building would seek to Americanize but not to include the natives as part of the American nation. U.S. colonial policies of assimilation seemed aimed at creating satellite nations orbiting the U.S. mainland.

In 1898, most Puerto Ricans were Catholic, spoke Spanish, and had deep cultural differences with mainstream Americans, who were perceived as being English-speaking, Anglo-Saxon, and

Protestant. They were well on their way to developing strong national identities mostly due to the exclusionary policies followed by the Spanish colonial authorities after the Lares revolt of 1868. It has been noted that the development of strong national identities occurs in opposition to a more discernible Other.[55] In the aftermath of the war of 1898, the U.S. soldiers on the island and the subsequent colonial administrators presented the Puerto Ricans with a different Other. However, the Americans were soon gone and replaced by local troops. The new metropolis did not send English-speaking settlers to displace the natives as it had been the case during the westward expansion. The new colonial bureaucracy was indeed small and dependent on local elites.[56] The U.S. officials did not pose a socioeconomic challenge to the local elites as the peninsulares once did to the criollos.

There were cultural differences between the new metropolis and the natives. The United States tried to overcome them with material superiority, which allowed the new metropolis to project cultural superiority.[57] U.S. economic resources enabled it to embark on infrastructure projects, to launch health and relief campaigns, and to create a public education system where the Puerto Rican youth could be Americanized. Moreover, political enfranchisement became a reality for previously marginalized groups, and the criollo elite actively participated in the political institutions. More important, perhaps, is that the military remobilization of the Puerto Ricans began during the first months of the American occupation. All this served to create a sense of inclusion as opposed to Spanish policies of exclusion and displacement.

Assimilation via Education

The popularization of education on the island by the creation of a comprehensive public education system was one of the most important policies followed.[58] The public education system is perhaps one of the most effective tools to promote the culture, ideals, and beliefs of the hegemonic group. English was the language of instruction, and courses on U.S. history and American mainstream cultural values were the cornerstone of the system. In that regard, the administration had the help of criollo elites

1. "Porto Ricans" in the American Colonial Army in El Morro Castle's parade field. This and other images were used to portray "America's colonial success," 1899. Postcard from author's collection.

who clamored for the establishment of such system. It would not take long before the island's elites began to send their youth to study on the mainland.[59]

The prompt enlargement and restructuring of public education by the colonial administration was intended to Americanize the population. For over two decades, the Department of Education in Puerto Rico remained firmly under U.S. control. The department's memos and guidelines openly called for policing those native teachers who strayed from the approved curriculum to include Puerto Rican culture in their lessons, as well as those who criticized the colonial regime.[60] However, recent scholarship has shown that even though English was used as an Americanization tool in the schools, that effort "was not coupled with censorship or institutionalized persecution of Spanish or other cultural forms."[61] The public school system was nonetheless a space for the cultural assimilation of the empire's new subjects. Solsiree del Moral has recently argued that in the case of Puerto Rico, the school system was intended to create second-class Americans or "tropical Yankees" through "the teaching of English and the celebration of U.S. history and patriotism." However, the metropolis's plans were challenged by Puerto Rican educators who shared "ideas and practices with others in the neighboring Caribbean and Latin American countries." Chief among these ideas is using schools and history lessons as tools for nation-building. As del Moral points out, the matter is further complicated by the fact that the new state imagined by both the Americans and the native educators was a colonial one.[62] That is not to say that the public school only served U.S. interests. By popularizing education, the colonial administration weakened the position of the local elites and created opportunities for socioeconomic mobility among groups with no previous chance for such a thing.[63]

Military Service and Americanization

The military was instrumental in promoting the Americanization of the Puerto Ricans. The militarization of the island under U.S. rule has been studied from a diplomatic and strategic point of view; however, the role that military institutions played in altering national identities and the influence of these soldiers in the political development of the island have been mostly ignored.[64] The island was under direct military rule between October 18, 1898, and May 1900. Even after a civilian government replaced the military regime, Puerto Rico continued under the control of the Bureau of Insular Affairs.[65] The BIA was an organ of the U.S. War Department created in the aftermath of the war of 1898 to administrate the overseas colonies. Puerto Rico was under direct control of the War Department from 1909 until President Franklin Delano Roosevelt placed it under the Department of the Interior in 1934.

Military Interactions with the Population

Military involvement had both a direct and an indirect approach, and both roles generated ties with the Puerto Rican peasantry and further Americanization. Direct involvement refers to the remobilization of the Puerto Ricans and their inclusion in the armed forces. Indirect involvement concerns any interaction of a nonmilitary nature between the U.S. Army and civilians, especially during catastrophes. The military government soon found itself fulfilling that function after August 8, 1899, when Hurricane San Ciriaco destroyed crops and dwellings and killed roughly 3,400 Puerto Ricans.[66] The population received military rations from the troops garrisoning the island as well as medical care. The role of the U.S. military went beyond immediate relief. As estimated by military authorities, the Army had to assist a vast portion of the population for several months.[67]

It was during the relief effort after San Ciriaco that a junior medical officer discovered the cause of chronic anemia, the worst ailment afflicting the Puerto Rican peasantry in the early twentieth century. While in charge of the medical detachment in Ponce, Dr. Bailey K. Ashford realized that the poor physical condition of the Puerto Rican jíbaro was caused not by the climate but by hookworms (*Ancylostoma duodenale*). The remedy was simple enough: purging the parasites by administering the patients a concoction of Thymol, a phenol found in the oil of thyme diluted in alcohol. The medical establishment in the island had long argued that the chronic anemia or "laziness" affecting the peasants, which was responsible for one-third of all deaths in the island, was due to the climate, nutrition, bad hygiene, malaria, or a combination of these factors, and as such it was endemic in the mountains and coastal plains where the jíbaro lived. Ashford recounts that when asked how their relatives had died, most peasants would respond, and physicians would confirm: "De la anemia—la muerte natural, of anemia—natural death." His wife, who came from prominent criollo families, explained to him "that is the anemia of the country. They all die of it eventually."[68]

Ashford could hardly believe that an entire "agricultural class" was dying of anemia. As his tests showed, it was anemia indeed, as the white corpuscles in blood known as eosinophils, which should not exceed 4 percent, were running up to 40 percent in the blood of the peasants he sampled. He was dumbfounded by the upper classes' lack of interest in treating such a preventable and curable disease. After years of trying to persuade the medical establishment to adopt the easy cure for pandemic anemia, Ashford was finally able to secure the creation of the Porto Rico Anemia Commission with a budget of $5,000 in 1904. After initially setting up the anemia camp in Bayamón, Ashley decided to move to Utuado, almost at the center of the island but with roads connecting to the northwest, so those more in need of treatment could reach him. That first campaign treated 5,490 patients. For the year 1905–6 the Anemia Commission moved its base to Aibonito, another mountain town but near the southeast. By the end of the second year, the Commission had treated 170,000 patients, and the death rate had been reduced to 0.12 percent for those treated. Deaths from anemia fell from 11,875 in 1900–1901 to 1,758 in 1907–8. The campaign lasted seven years. Between 1904 and 1911, more than 310,000 people were successfully treated for the anemia.[69]

Ashford also discovered that if the cause of the anemia was parasitical, it was severely aggravated by the peasants' malnutrition. He recommended that socioeconomic problems such as extremely low income, which he believed accounted for the malnutrition and ignorance plaguing the jíbaro, should be addressed to finally eradicate once and for all preventable diseases crippling the Puerto Rican peasantry. Only that way, he believed, would the Jíbaro awaken from his long sleep and small world and become an integral part of Puerto Rican society. He wrote: "Yet this is the man of whom we have to make a citizen, a man with a vote and a say in the affairs of the island. He has been through the awakening of Rip Van Winkle, and he has awakened into a world that leaves him gasping, stunned. He is neither a degenerate nor a fool."[70] Adopting a paternalistic stance, the military establishment in the island, from infantry to medical officers, took the jíbaro as a ward to be protected and reshaped.[71]

A special relationship between the U.S. military and the peasantry developed during the early days of the American occupation as a result of the relief efforts and sanitary campaigns. As discussed by historian Estades Font, the motives behind such practices were not exclusively humanitarian. She explains that controlling tropical diseases was economically and militarily vital for American expansion. The labor force of the new territories, the occupation troops, and the civilian population of the mainland needed to be protected.[72] Most of the relief, sanitary, and humanitarian campaigns carried out by the military and civilian colonial authorities in Puerto Rico targeted formerly disenfranchised groups: the peasantry and urban workers. In this respect, these efforts served a broader strategic agenda: securing their loyalty and promoting pro-American feelings. This type of military involvement could only be perceived as a positive gesture. In many respects, the services provided by the military and its interactions with the population facilitated the development of a special relationship and thus eased the acceptance of American rule.

Remobilization of the Puerto Ricans

Military involvement in the island was not limited to providing aid or functioning as a de facto government. As early as 1899 Puerto Ricans were serving in U.S. army units.[73] This phenomenon was the result of several factors. Once the war was over, U.S. politicians began to feel the pressure from their constituencies to bring the troops home. Consequently, they started to pressure the McKinley administration. By August 23, 1898, General Miles was proposing to return as many as a third of the invading troops to the mainland. Shortly after, the War Department decided to send fresh regular and volunteer troops to conduct the occupation.[74] However, after the transfer of sovereignty, continental politicians demanded the return of these fresh troops, too, especially the volunteer state militias.

The manpower situation was further complicated by the Filipino insurrection, which aggravated the shortage of regular U.S. troops. With state officials clamoring for the return of their respective states' militias and a well-organized insurrection against the American occupation forces in the Philippines, there was little support for continuing to occupy Puerto Rico, especially when the United States faced no organized political resistance or strong opposition from the general population. The island, however, which had been secured from Spain mostly for its military value, had to be policed and defended. It was within this framework that Puerto Ricans began to serve formally in the U.S. military.

U.S. politicians and strategists used gender and racial narratives to explain why Puerto Rico would be neither a state nor an independent republic. It was quite easy for local elites to believe that the illiterate rural masses were the "problem."[75] Furthermore, they were not averse to the belief that military service created better and manlier men, and neither were they oblivious to the link between it and self-government. Puerto Rico's pre-1898 military and political history moved the island's socioeconomic elites to try and secure positions within the U.S. military soon after the war had concluded. In the decades previous to the American invasion, the local elites had witnessed how the Spanish authorities demobilized the Puerto Rican peasantry and effectively limited the political power of those born on the island. In general, the island's political leadership believed that demobilization had weakened their position when dealing with the Spanish metropolis while making the Puerto Ricans complacent. For these reasons, local elites had sought participation in the U.S. military since the early days of the American invasion.[76]

Precisely because of their understanding of the links between martial prowess, manhood, and self-rule, Puerto Ricans from different sectors of society demanded access to the military. Cayetano Coll y Toste, a civilian secretary to Brig. Gen. George W. Davis, the military governor of Puerto Rico, claimed that he encouraged Davis to form a battalion of native volunteers to replace the U.S. troops on the island while touring Spanish military installations.[77] In fact, the process of organizing a native military had been initiated under Davis's predecessor, Maj. Gen. Guy V. Henry. Additionally, the first proponent of Puerto Rican military service in the U.S. military was a most unlikely figure, Eugenio María de Hostos.[78]

On January 20, 1899, Hostos, as one of the Puerto Rican commissioners traveling to Washington to discuss the future of the island, urged President McKinley to reduce the occupation forces and to create a native militia of at least three hundred men.[79] The same petition included the replacement of the military government with a civilian one while Congress decided, with the consent of the Puerto Ricans, the future of the island. Regarding education, Hostos proposed that "the military schooling of the people of Puerto Rico be considered as one of means we need for the education of our people." Military instruction, he argued, "is a tool for the physical strengthening and discipline of the life and character of the Puerto Rican people."[80] He also proposed the establishment of seven institutes in which military training would be used to promote discipline of the body and soul and to teach strong work ethics and concepts of rights and obligations. Hostos believed that the right type of military training promoted civic virtues. He envisioned "civilian schools to be military schools and the military training in our schools to be civic learning for life."[81] For Hostos, military service could speed up the Americanization process, which he understood as the political modernization of the inhabitants of the island and as a way to lead to self-determination, democracy, and modern republicanism.[82]

Hostos thought that Americanization "would prepare Puerto Rico to effectively assert its independence." Those thoughts were not contradictory. Hostos believed in self-determination but feared that centuries of oppression had weakened the Puerto Ricans to the point to where they might not even constitute a people. According to Hostos, to exercise self-determination, the Puerto Rican needed to adopt the ideals guiding the creation of the United States, which he considered to be "the most complete civilization in existence."[83] For Hostos, military education and service might very well serve to speed the Americanization—understood as political modernization—of the Puerto Ricans and their eventual self-determination. Other prominent politicians adopted or shared Hostos's philosophy.[84] The popular masses were viewed by the local elites as ignorant, weak, complacent, and docile and thus collaborated in the establishment of a tutelary state.[85]

Early U.S. Puerto Rican Units

With no initial opposition from the elites, with the blessing of the military governors, and with the real need of manpower elsewhere, and counting on the eagerness of the local elites to volunteer the Puerto Ricans into military service, the remobilization of the islanders under American rule proceeded swiftly. On March 2, 1899, Congress, through the Army Appropriation Bill, authorized the creation of a native corps in Puerto Rico. On March 24, Maj. Gen. Guy V. Henry, commanding officer of the Porto Rico Military Department, ordered the recruitment of natives to form a battalion. In early May, the four hundred men needed for the Battalion of Porto Rican Volunteers had been recruited, equipped, and trained. On May 20, 1899, Gen. George W. Davis, who had replaced Henry, published General Order No. 65 activating the battalion.[86]

The battalion of volunteers was primarily regarded as colonial troops and only expected to defend the island.[87] The military authorities added a cavalry battalion and changed the name to the Porto Rico Regiment United States Volunteers in 1900.[88] The change in name is significant if only for the fact that the words "United States Volunteers" drove home the point that Puerto Ricans were now U.S. nationals as established by the Foraker Act. Over the following year, the Puerto Rican volunteers replaced the continental troops garrisoning outposts throughout the island.[89] In 1905 all soldiers on the island except their commanders were natives of Puerto Rico.

2. Porto Rico Provisional Regiment of Infantry parades before the Teatro Tapia in San Juan, ca. 1903. Puerto Rican National Guard Museum.

The native corps became a regiment of the U.S. Army on July 1, 1908, by an act of Congress.[90] That same year Unión consolidated its political power. Unión represented a challenge to the U.S. colonial administration, since it demanded more autonomy or even independence, and as electoral results showed, the ardently pro-American Republicans were losing their appeal. In 1909 Unión, which dominated the Chamber of Delegates, defied the colonial administration by refusing to pass the governor's budget. President William Howard Taft (1909–13) moved swiftly to curtail the means of political opposition and obtained from Congress an amendment to the Foraker Act enabling the governor to use the budget from the previous year if the Chamber of Delegates did not approve his proposal. This amendment also authorized the president to place the island under the War Department's Bureau of Insular Affairs. Estades Font has emphasized that it was in the interests of the United States and its colonial administrators to weaken Unión, which was heavily dominated by coffee growers who had gradually lost socioeconomic influence since 1898 and were aggravated by the perpetuation of the colonial status.[91] President Taft's decision to put the island under direct control of the War Department when local politicians demanded more autonomy and a path toward self-determination is a perfect example of militarization as an integral component of colonial domination.

Why was the United States so decisive and harsh in dealing with the Puerto Rican Chamber of Delegates? Had it not been elected by a vast majority of Puerto Ricans and presumably held their allegiance? Furthermore, the U.S. soldiers on the island and the police, with the exception of most senior officers, were Puerto Ricans in U.S. uniforms. Was there not a possibility that these soldiers and policemen in charge of the security apparatus might turn against the administration if its policies became too unpalatable? In 1909 the native regiment and the insular police were trained and commanded by U.S. officers. This situation surely strengthened Taft's determination to deal harshly with the Chamber of Delegates. As governor of the Philippines, President Taft had opposed creating a Filipino regiment led by Filipino officers but supported creating it under the command of U.S. officers. He argued that under U.S. commanders, Filipino soldiers would be "entirely loyal" to the United States and would perform efficiently while Filipino commanders could lead the troops "into either ladronism or insurrectionism."[92] The colonial administration's policies to deal with Unión show that in fact Taft was confident of having the upper hand regarding the loyalty of the troops and the police as well as that of the majority of the population as well.

Americanization campaigns targeted mostly the disenfranchised groups. Likewise, the military remobilization of the Puerto Ricans exploited anti-Spanish sentiments. It is very telling that the first volunteers to serve in the native corps came from the town of Lares, where anti-Spanish and pro-independence sentiments had been strong for decades and the only place where the 1868 revolt against Spain had succeeded.[93] Moreover, the majority of those enlisting in the U.S. military were of humble origin.[94] Puerto Ricans from the upper classes joined the military and eventually became officers and noncommissioned officers (sergeants), but most of those in service came from more lowly backgrounds.[95] The U.S. military on the island was a tool for strengthening colonial rule while also acting as a vehicle for socioeconomic mobility and political enfranchisement in early twentieth-century Puerto Rico.

The military remobilization of the Puerto Rican served the metropolis very well during the first decades of American rule. The colonial administrators knew this only too well. In his report to Congress in 1900, Military Governor Davis stated: "The native troops . . . may be relied upon for performance of the principal military service for Porto Rico. They are a selected body of men, and exercise a most beneficial influence. The inhabitants of the island generally are proud of them, and the criminals hold them in wholesome fear."[96] So impressed was Davis that he recommended further reductions of continental troops, which at the time represented less than half, or 735 of the 1,635 U.S. troops on the island. He believed that with the added 475 officers and men of the insular police, a mere third of the police agents under Spain, the island's security needs could be easily met.[97]

American leaders liked showcasing their apparent colonial success by bringing the Puerto Rican troops to Washington. The band and first battalion of the native regiment participated in the inaugurations of President McKinley in 1901 and Theodore Roosevelt in 1905.[98] But the main role of these troops was to highlight the virtues of American rule before their compatriots. The native troops had a very visible role. They performed as firemen and had their own baseball team, which participated in the local tournament, while the regiment's band appeared at public events.

In a telegram dated March 11, 1901, Charles H. Allen, the first appointed civil governor of Puerto Rico, communicated to Secretary of War Elihu Root that it was advisable to make the regiment a permanent outfit. Allen believed that native troops, under the command of continental officers, would be adequate to garrison the island. Commenting on troop loyalty Allen wrote: "They have been tried in almost every emergency except that of meeting in arms people of their own country. Whether they would be found wanting at such an important moment, should it ever arise, I do not feel competent to say. But it can be said that in many discussions on the subject with the officers that they would be loyal to the sovereignty of the United States and implicitly obey the orders of their commanding officers. As an arm of safety their presence is therefore desirable."[99] The question of whether they would fight against their fellow countrymen would not have to be answered until 1950.

By wearing the U.S. Army uniform, Puerto Rican soldiers were to spread pro-American feelings among the population. The native soldier, Allen stated, had become "an object lesson to the communities in the neighborhoods of their posts . . . and from that standpoint, as from many others, has undoubtedly been a very potent educational influence. Each man of the battalion will be a committee in himself to spread among the natives, stories of American prestige. . . . The soldiers feel a pride in their service and there is an undoubted stimulant by it toward general loyalty.[100]

Several trends that would mark Puerto Rican participation in U.S. military institutions are identifiable in Allen's statements. First, a professional and loyal military integrated by natives of the island would guarantee stability for the metropolis. Second, service in the military was identified with progress and modernity. Third, the native soldiers, by becoming a model for the population, would be an instrument for the Americanization of the island further consolidating the command of the metropolis over its colonial subjects. When a real impasse emerged between the criollos leading Unión and the American colonial administrators in 1909, the metropolis flexed its muscles, for it was certain that it could count on the native military apparatus and the general public's support. These trends would become more obvious and would be further developed and challenged by the native leadership during the First World War. However, before the war, the military and paramilitary apparatus in the island was firmly in the hands of the metropolis.

Under U.S. rule, access to military institutions for the "hijos de este país" was reestablished while political participation, to a certain degree, was opened to the masses. Soon after the war ended, natives of the island began to replace U.S. continental soldiers. From the beginning the new insular soldiers did not become part of a home militia or National Guard but elements of the U.S. Army tightly controlled by the colonial administration. Additionally, the new metropolis gradually allowed for a higher degree of political participation, creating the space for mass electoral enfranchisement. These two apparently disconnected trends facilitated the transfer of sovereignty over the island from Spain to the United States, and they influenced the character of Puerto Rican national identities. The inclusion of Puerto Ricans in the armed forces of the new metropolis and mass political mobilization, especially of the rural sectors, gradually led to competing national identity narratives based on modernity, gender, and race discourses.

The United States also embarked on a comprehensive buildup of the public education system, which was intended to modernize the inhabitants of the island, while launching massive sanitary and relief campaigns. Hence, although cultural affinity might have been absent between Puerto Ricans and Americans in 1898, the metropolis's control of the education system allowed for the projection of American material superiority disguised as cultural supremacy. Furthermore, sanitary and relief campaigns allowed for positive interaction between the new metropolis and its colonial subjects. Whether these attempts were successful in "Americanizing" the Puerto Ricans is not the issue. What is important is that even the people living in the most remote corners of the island started to learn about the United States and the culture of its dominant groups.

The fact that the military institutions, the political arena, and the public school system were opened to previously disenfranchised groups began to profoundly alter the islanders' loyalties. Participation in American institutions provided unifying experiences, which allowed for the strengthening of national identities but with an American touch. Public schools offered a homogenized pro-American experience for hundreds of thousands of Puerto Ricans while the opening of the U.S. military to groups previously excluded from it and other sectors of Puerto Rico's society conferred these groups with a sense of inclusion. Access to education and military positions also offered an opportunity for mobility and the chance to challenge or even overthrown old socioeconomic hierarchies, a phenomenon that led to the creation of upwardly mobile classes and neo-elites who owed their well-being and thus their political allegiance to the new metropolis.

Puerto Rican politicians' participation in the military and civil government further legitimized the American presence on the island. The former autonomists became annexationists, and a vast sector of the population in Puerto Rico favored becoming a state during the first years after the war. Recognizing the pro-American sentiments of the population during the early stages of the occupation, the political leaders in Puerto Rico decided to exploit it by supporting participation in the political institutions set by the United States and emphasizing military service. Puerto Rican elites and the popular sector participated actively in the institutions of the new metropolis, further legitimizing U.S. sovereignty.

Early attempts to create a modern "Americanized" Puerto Rican via military service—which were supported by the elites, including champions of independence—were curtailed by the limited scope of the project. There was no dearth of interest or lack of enthusiasm among American officers and local elites to embark on this project, nor was the general population unenthusiastic. However, the small size of the U.S. military apparatus, which because of its mission did not require massive armies, limited the size of the military in Puerto Rico and its effect on the population. Nonetheless, the remobilization of the Puerto Ricans began during the first years of American rule as Puerto Ricans came to wear U.S. Army uniforms and replaced continental troops garrisoning the island. Furthermore, a special relation started to emerge between the military and Puerto Rico's population as military doctors and engineers combed the mountains and towns of the island, building sanitary facilities, roads, and schools and launching massive health and relief campaigns. The First World War would provide the grounds to retry the projects of Americanization and modernization via military service at levels previously unimaginable and with more players involved.

3

A New Day Has Dawned

World War I and Mobilization of the Peasant

> Downtrodden . . . as he has been, he is now in the limelight. The testing and refining process will be hard for him. But he and his brother will become the nucleus of a new Porto Rico. The anemic disease warped man will be a thing of the past. And the domain of the jíbaro will at last come into its proper place in the great Economic and Social scheme of this island.
> —*Porto Rico Progress*, July 12, 1918[1]

In 1908 the U.S. government strengthened its control over the military apparatus in Puerto Rico by making the native military corps a regular regiment of the U.S. Army by an act of Congress.[2] As a corollary to this measure, the Taft administration attempted to augment the political power of the colonial administration in Puerto Rico by giving full control over the island to the War Department's Bureau of Insular Affairs (BIA) and by curtailing the ability of the Puerto Rican Chamber of Delegates to challenge the presidential-appointed governor.[3] After taking these steps, the U.S. colonial administration enjoyed a few years of relative political calm. Under American rule, as it had been the case under Spanish control, a crisis tended to highlight the military importance of Puerto Rico, which in turn affected the island's political development. On the eve of World War I, the United States faced strong local political opposition in the form of demands for more self-government, self-determination, and labor organization.[4]

In 1917, the metropolis extended American citizenship to the natives of Puerto Rico. American citizenship preceded the first mass military mobilization of Puerto Rico's popular sectors under U.S. rule. Since the very early days, the U.S. colonial administrators had argued that military training and values would "Americanize" and "modernize" the Puerto Rican. During the war, Puerto Rican elites, political leaders, and the press, who had supported military instruction and service since the invasion in 1898, joined the chorus arguing that serving in the military would create a new man out of the Puerto Rican. Puerto Rican elites were interested in mobilizing the peasantry, commonly referred to as jíbaros. They viewed military service as a regenerative experience that would transform the jíbaro into a new, manlier, modern man integrated into the socioeconomic structures of the island as a productive agent.

Since the eighteenth century, the figure of the jíbaro and the role it should play in Puerto Rico's society had preoccupied the local elites. Historically, the insular peasantry has been ambiguously represented as both capable of the most sublime nobility and as the truest icon of Puerto Rican identity, but also as a drawback for the island's society, as "rustic" men incapable of political consciousness. Francisco Scarano has traced the development of characterizations of *jibaridád* and the coexistence of almost-contradictory meanings assigned to it. He explains that in "the eyes of the modernizing, rationalistic elites, the tactics of peasant survival seemed barbaric, conducive only to vagrancy, crime, and political paralysis." However, by the middle of the nineteenth century, representations of a multiethnic jíbaro served as a type of proto-nationalist icon for elites. Liberal criollos used the "jíbaro masquerade to identify themselves as ethnically different from other members of the elite while maintaining the basic outlines of a colonial relation."[5]

After the United States gained control of the island in 1898, intellectuals and political figures reimagined a jíbaro figure in opposition to American domination. The jíbaro figure, "now absolutely whitened," was converted into the repository of a higher form of "patriotic morality, the very essence of the Puerto Rican nation."[6] As Lilian Guerra argues, the figure of the jíbaro is key for understanding the development of national identities in early twentieth-century Puerto Rico. For the modernizing elites, the peasantry's state of illiteracy and failure to modernize was responsible for the island's colonial status and economic maladies. Local elites thus tried to construct the figure of the jíbaro (and hence that of the popular classes) as a less threatening and more civilized "Other."[7] Up until World War I, the regeneration of the popular sectors using the figure of the jíbaro was attempted mostly through discursive narratives as Guerra points out; through mass health campaigns, and by trying to reduce the illiteracy rate among them, as Solsiree del Moral has demonstrated.[8]

World War I presented the local elites with the opportunity to further their projects by mobilizing the peasantry. Political leaders, elected officials, and opinion makers sought to reform or regenerate the jíbaro through military training, hoping that the peasantry's transformation would translate into socioeconomic and political advancement. Hence elites demanded access to the U.S. military. Supporting the war effort, some thought, would prove the Puerto Ricans' loyalty to the United States and to the ideals of democracy and freedom. Others believed that participating in the war would prove Puerto Ricans' manhood and adulthood, which would put the United States in a very awkward position if it continued to deny them political equality and to ignore their capability of self-government and of self-determination. Whatever their reasoning, mass military service became a tool for different factions who sought to achieve their goals by modernizing the Puerto Rican jíbaro—and by extension Puerto Rico—through military training and service.

Both the local elites and the metropolis were engaging in reshaping the very essence of the Puerto Ricans' individual and collective identities. And during the war, the United States and the native elites found themselves in a battle for control over the nation-building project via military service. Moreover, the elites had their own projects of Americanization and modernization.

Was extending American citizenship to the Puerto Ricans and the subsequent mass mobilization of the peasantry and the urban working classes a transformative experience? Did a new Puerto Rican emerge from this experience? Was the military-trained jíbaro integrated into the modern socioeconomic structures of the island? Was American colonial rule in the island as strong as it had been before the war? Did the first mass mobilization of Puerto Ricans under American rule bring political transformations?

World War I and U.S. Citizenship

On June 28, 1914, the assassination of the Hapsburg heir, Archduke Franz Ferdinand, in Sarajevo by the Bosnian-Serb nationalist Gavrilo Princip activated several European alliances. By August 4, five European empires were at war and would soon drag many other nations into the conflict.[9] On April 6, 1917, after almost three years of carnage and with both belligerent alliances unable to win a decisive victory on the western front, the United States entered the conflict on the side of the Entente. On March 2, 1917, Congress had passed the Jones Act, also known as the Jones-Shafroth Act. This law granted American citizenship to the people of Puerto Rico and served as the island's de facto constitution until 1952.[10] Unlike its antecedent, the Jones Act allowed Puerto Ricans to elect their own territorial legislature and provided for universal male suffrage.[11] The fact that Puerto Ricans became U.S. citizens in 1917 has been linked to the need for soldiers.[12] However, citizenship was just one of the act's provisions. The passing of the Jones Act was the result of years of negotiations between Puerto Rican and U.S. leaders.

American citizenship for the indigenous people of Puerto Rico (known then as Porto Rican citizens) had been contemplated by U.S. leaders well before 1917. President Theodore Roosevelt proposed granting American citizenship collectively to Puerto Ricans, but did not find much support in Congress. As a result of the political crisis of 1909 in Puerto Rico, officials at the War Department studied the possibility of granting citizenship. They concluded that even though the status would be well received, collective citizenship was a premature step, since the majority of Puerto Ricans, they argued, were illiterate and unprepared for full political rights. As an alternative, the Office of the Secretary of War suggested facilitating the individual acquisition of U.S. citizenship by natives of the island who were educated and owned businesses or land.[13] Senator Elihu Root opposed collective U.S. citizenship on the grounds that Puerto Rico could not be admitted as a federated state and hence such a move would create two classes of citizens, a practice he believed to be inconsistent with U.S. democratic traditions.[14]

Despite opposition from prominent congressmen, projects to grant U.S. citizenship to the Puerto Ricans were presented before Congress in 1912 and 1913. President Taft (and later President Wilson) and most of Congress supported these projects. Taft's appointee, Governor George Colton (1909–13), also endorsed taking this step, which he thought would improve the United States' image in Latin America.[15] Colton's support for citizenship was not an aberration. His successor, Arthur Yager (1913–21), was even more vocal.[16] These projects, as well as the support for granting U.S. citizenship to the Puerto Ricans shown by Taft, Wilson, the BIA (reluctantly), Congress, and opinion-making groups on the mainland responded to both local and international considerations.

The emergence of a radical wing within the dominant political coalition, Unión, which under the leadership of José de Diego demanded independence under an American protectorate, and the creation of the Independence and Socialist Parties in 1912 and 1915, respectively, underline the sociopolitical unrest festering in Puerto Rico.[17] Furthermore, in 1913 Unión, though still working toward autonomy, had made independence its final solution to the status question after a period of self-government under American tutelage.[18] However, as early as 1915, convinced that the United States would never grant independence or statehood to Puerto Rico, Luis Muñoz Rivera, moderate leader of the Unionistas and Puerto Rican representative in Congress (resident commissioner) between 1910 and 1916, came to believe that a type of self-government or autonomy like Australia's or Canada's was the best option for the island.[19] That the dominant political party in the island had renounced inclusion into the Union highlighted the growing discontent with American rule in Puerto Rico.

On the eve of World War I, it certainly looked as if the United States' control over the island was becoming precarious. Many

Puerto Rican political leaders opposed the granting of U.S. citizenship without statehood or a general referendum on it. Muñoz Rivera, though originally one of its main architects, opposed passing the Jones Act if it included U.S. citizenship. He believed that such action would freeze the political development of the island while doing little to eliminate the colonial relationship. Nevertheless, on May 23, 1916, the U.S. House of Representatives approved the legislation and sent it to the Senate, but it did not reach the Senate floor before Congress's recess. In view of the failure of the Senate to consider this bill before recess, President Wilson decided to cancel the elections on the island scheduled for November 1916 so there could be a special election once the Jones Act was approved the following year.[20]

Some of the provisions of the Jones Act irked Muñoz Rivera. One of his main concerns was that the version sent to the House of Representatives included restricted suffrage based on literacy and taxation.[21] Also, while extra powers would pass to the Puerto Ricans, such as the right to have a two-house elected legislature, the bill included veto power for the governor, who remained a presidential appointee. Moreover, collective U.S. citizenship was imposed on the Puerto Ricans, who were not allowed to have a referendum. They had the right to reject U.S. citizenship, but doing so would turn them into foreigners in their own land. The Unionistas, who had abandoned statehood as a goal in 1913, saw collective U.S. citizenship as a drawback.[22] Muñoz Rivera probably understood that the irreversible nature of collective U.S. citizenship for the Puerto Ricans could have a defusing effect with regard to political tensions, which could hinder the chances of advancing his party's political goals.

The colonial administrators also understood the political value of granting collective U.S. citizenship to the people of Puerto Rico. Probably no one was more adamant than Governor Yager. His campaign to bring U.S. citizenship to all Puerto Ricans was closely followed in the United States. In 1914 the *American Review of Reviews* observed that Puerto Ricans should be granted citizenship and measures of self-government to reward their "continued improvement under American tutelage." Additionally, American citizenship, the journal stressed, would eliminate "the germ of nationhood" fostered by the "ill-conceived Porto Rico citizenship." The article added that complete self-government was not an option because the Puerto Ricans "are a Latin American people with the characteristics and traditions of their forebears still clinging about them." This journal also made clear the dominant attitude toward the island among opinion-making groups and the true reasons for the change of heart regarding granting U.S. citizenship to the Puerto Ricans: "The interest of our own country and Porto Rico demand this perpetual connection. It is for Congress therefore to make the people of this tropical isle reasonably satisfied with our rule; for the Stars and Stripes cannot permanently wave over a discontented and rebellious people."[23]

Quenching social and political unrest on the island and restoring a positive image of the United States in Latin America had moved U.S. leaders and opinion makers to favor U.S. citizenship for the Puerto Ricans as early as 1909.[24] The outbreak of World War I probably accelerated the passing of the Jones Act; however, Congress did not extend U.S. citizenship to 1.5 million Puerto Ricans just to have more manpower for a war in which they were not yet involved, especially when at the time "dark races," including Puerto Ricans, were neither trusted nor wanted as fighting troops.[25] When the United States took over Puerto Rico in 1898, one of the main discourses used to retain the new colony, as well as the Philippines, was that Puerto Ricans were not capable of self-government mostly due to their racial composition, which was supposedly exemplified by their lack of martial spirit.[26] As the Filipino insurrection ended, Congress moved to restrict the role of African Americans in the military.[27] The prejudices used to explain segregation and black "inferiority" were applied to the new territories. Racial prejudice led military planners to prefer excluding Puerto Ricans from the military, at least as fighting troops.[28]

Furthermore, the Selective Service Act of 1917 (Draft Law) declared that all American nationals who, "on June 5, 1917, had attained the age of 21 and had not attained the age of 31 are subject to registration." Only "aliens who have not declared their intention to become citizens of the United States and who have entered the United States for the first time since June 5, 1917" were not subject to registration.[29] Puerto Rican were not aliens and, in fact, due to the Foraker Act of 1900, they were "American nationals," which means that they were subject to registration under the Selective Service Act even without the passing of the Jones Act.

Congress did not grant citizenship to Puerto Ricans in order to deter a German attack on the island either. Attacking Puerto Rico, regardless of the citizenship of its inhabitants, would have meant both an attack on U.S. soil and a flagrant violation of the Monroe Doctrine and thus a major *casus bellis*. The United States did not need Puerto Ricans to become U.S. citizens to exercise its right to protect the island, which was an American possession recognized as such under international law. However, the strategic location of Puerto Rico at the heart of the archipelago of islands blocking access to the Panama Canal indeed influenced the passing of the Jones Act in 1917.[30] A friendly native population that could assist in the defense of the island and that would not side with an invading force was deemed imperative by the Navy and the War Department.[31] The need to prevent unrest in such an important possession accelerated granting citizenship to the Puerto Ricans. Clearly U.S. politicians recognized the calming effect that granting citizenship and somewhat broadening political rights would have on the island. Moreover, by granting them citizenship, Congress and President Wilson were affirming that the United States intended to hold the island in perpetuity, since there was no precedent for an American territory populated with American citizens to be allowed to separate from the Union.[32] Puerto Rico had to be held as an American possession for its geo-strategic value, and U.S. citizenship might very well do the trick.

Finally Wilson's approach to international mediation, his "new diplomacy" based on "self-determination," was incompatible with the outright colonial status of Puerto Rico. On December 7, 1915, Wilson declared before Congress that it was imperative to solve the Puerto Rican question by granting them a higher degree of self-government. More important, Wilson tied the passing of the Jones Act to national security and defense preparedness.

He argued that it was also a matter of credibility: the world was watching to see whether the United States was serious about self-determination and freedom.[33] In his October 26, 1916, closing campaign speeches, Wilson became the first statesman to commit his government to the pursuit of a League of Nations and to "articulate a comprehensive synthesis of Progressive Internationalism and the New Diplomacy," based on the principles of the equality of nations, self-determination, peaceful settlement of disputes, freedom of the seas, disarmament, and collective security while making a call for social justice for women, children, and workers.[34] Securing the loyalty of the island's population and international credibility moved Wilson to adamantly support U.S. citizenship and some measures of self-government for the Puerto Ricans in 1915.[35] Wilson's promises would be well received and tested in Puerto Rico.

The Jones Act was finally signed into law on March 2, 1917, and for the most part it was welcomed by the Puerto Ricans.[36] In total, 287 people claimed Spanish or another foreign citizenship or asked to retain their former status as citizens of Porto Rico instead of becoming U.S. citizens. Some 800 people took the opposite step and used a clause in the Jones Act allowing anyone of "alien" (non-Puerto Rican) parentage to claim citizenship.[37] Muñoz Rivera did not live to see the passing of the bill. He had returned ill to the island in September 1916 and died on November 15. At least his concerns about restrictive suffrage, which were shared by all political factions and in particular by the Socialists, were addressed in the Senate, and the act finally approved came to include male universal suffrage.[38]

The United States Joins the War

On April 6, 1917, triggered by Germany's resumption of unrestricted submarine warfare and the public outrage created by the Zimmerman telegram, the Unites States declared war on Germany.[39] Three days later, the Porto Rico Chamber of Delegates, in a message to President Wilson, offered the "absolute solidarity of the people of Puerto Rico to you and the great American Nation in the conflict with Germany."[40] Immediately after the declaration of war, Puerto Rican leaders volunteered their service and that of their fellow countrymen, expressed their desire to enlarge the Porto Rican Regiment to brigade, and requested the acceptance of Puerto Ricans as volunteers. The secretary of war, while praising their loyalty and patriotism, declined the offer.[41]

On May 18, Congress passed the Selective Service Act of 1917 calling for all males between the ages of eighteen and thirty-two to fill out registration cards.[42] The territories of Alaska, Hawaii, and Puerto Rico were not included in the original Selective Service Act. Amid the furor and the demonstrations of patriotism taking place across the United States, the Puerto Rican legislature asked Congress to extend the draft to the island.[43] The local newspapers labeled the legislature's request an act of patriotism. President Wilson promised to remedy the situation.[44] The date for the initial registration day in Puerto Rico was not a matter decided solely by Wilson and Congress. On June 6, Yager informed the chief of the BIA, Frank McIntyre, that his administration was working out the system of registration and that they could be ready "to have the date fixed during the latter part of July although it would be necessary to have 10 or 15 days for publicity work among the Jíbaros and illiterate men of the mountain"[45] The colonial administration was indeed eyeing the peasantry to form the bulk of the National Army in Puerto Rico. A presidential proclamation set registration in Puerto Rico for July 5.[46]

Puerto Ricans responded enthusiastically to the draft.[47] On that first day, 104,550 Puerto Ricans registered. Eventually 236,853 men inscribed for selective service and 17,855 were called to service. All of those called, except for 139, reported for duty. A few days after the first registration day, Governor Yager declared: "This [the number of registered men] is larger than the official estimate and I think it is a great compliment to the people of Porto Rico that they should have met this situation so patriotically."[48] The first training camp for Puerto Rican officers began in August. The 200 slots allowed for the officers' camp had been filled by the local elites and professional classes.[49] The speed with which the war effort advanced and the eagerness to show support led Yager to comment that the "patriotism of the island has been stirred and intensified by America's entrance into the Great War as shown by the eagerness with which the people responded to the recent draft." Yager was quick to find the root of these demonstrations of patriotism stating that Puerto Ricans were "as eager to get into the big war game as any other class of citizens under the Star and Stripes."⁵⁰ For Yager it was clear that citizenship, even if of a different class, had bought much goodwill and secured the loyalty of the Puerto Ricans at a critical historical junction.

Yager's narrative of patriotism did not go unchallenged. In a letter to Frank McIntyre, chief of the BIA, the governor expressed his fear that an independence leader might attempt "some propaganda in the matter of renouncing American citizenship for the purpose of avoiding the draft law." Even after the show of patriotism during registration day to which he made reference in previous letters, Yager suggested having the first draft after September 2, 1917, when the allotted time for renouncing U.S. citizenship would have expired. He was also concerned about having a representative of labor on one or more of the General Board of Exemptions under the selective draft because Santiago Iglesias Pantín "would be the one and he would do it selfishly."⁵¹ As his correspondence indicates, Yager and the metropolitan authorities were aware of the challenges to American sovereignty and policies on the island. However, the plans for mobilizing the Puerto Ricans continued inexorably, with the support of the local elites.

In late September 1917, in the Tapia Theater in San Juan, behind a banner reading "Go Ahead Porto Rico" and surrounded by members of the colonial government, the mayors of the island, and Antonio R. Barceló (the Unionistas president of the newly created Puerto Rican Senate), two women in white dresses escorted Governor Yager's daughter while she drafted the first ballot in the island." This overly symbolic ceremony marked the beginning of Puerto Rican mass participation in the U.S. armed forces. Most of the press, both in the United States and on the island, reported that the day had been marked by "rejoicing and celebration through the island."⁵²

In accordance with the Jones Act, elections had been held on the island on July 17, 1917. Again, Unión came up as the dominant political force, winning more than half the votes casted. More important, the Unionistas elected Félix Córdova Dávila as resident commissioner in Washington, a position held by Muñoz Rivera until his death. Unión also elected thirteen senators and twenty-four representatives to the new insular legislature, which gave them a majority in both houses.[53] José de Diego, leader of the separatist faction within Unión, became speaker of the insular house of representatives, and Antonio R. Barceló, Unión's president, became leader of the senate.

Since Yager supported more self-government for the island and liberal reforms but not statehood, an unwritten alliance developed between the governor and Unión during the war. The Republican Party, which preached 100 percent Americanism and desired nothing but federated statehood, found itself at odds with Yager, who seemed to favor some liberal reforms for the colony but not much else. The Socialists, however, suffered the harshest antagonism from the governor, and the attitude was reciprocated.[54] This is not to say that participating in the war was opposed by political groups alienated by Yager's courtship of the Unionistas. The situation only provided for far more complex approaches to the war effort, but nonetheless favorable ones. Mobilizing the Puerto Ricans came to be the means to different ends for the Republicans and Unionistas, as well as for the metropolis, which sometimes found itself at odds with Yager's own project. Yager fears proved unfounded. The weak opposition to military service stemming from pro-independence leaders was marked more by their silence than by outspoken opposition. Moreover, prominent separatist leaders of the stature of Nemesio Canales, José de Diego, and Luis Lloréns Torres supported joining the war effort.[55]

100 Percent Americanism and the Puerto Rican Division

President Wilson envisioned the creation of a National Army that would unify the multiethnic United States into one nation. Fearing that the 15 million immigrants who had reached the United States between 1900 and 1915 might not support the United States (especially the German American population), Wilson's administration launched a campaign promoting 100 percent Americanism. He believed that the war would end the hyphenations of ethnic and national groups in the United States. Wilson proclaimed: "Any man who carries a hyphen around with him carries a dagger that he is ready to plunge into the vitals of the republic." The blind patriotic mind-set promoted by the Wilson administration under the "100 percent Americanism" rubric is evident in the efforts of the Committee on Public Information to promote "unanimity of thought and action that would translate into victory on the battlefield and the realization of the melting pot ideal at home."[56] The Wilson administration believed that if the war was to bring an end to all hyphenations and the emergence of a single American nation, it would have to be fought on cultural grounds as well as on actual battlefields.[57] The War Department took Wilson's unifying rhetoric to heart.

As the war in Europe continued, military plans accelerated in the United States, and the War Department authorized the creation of the 94th Infantry Division to be composed of four Porto Rican regiments.[58] Although unconvinced of their value as first-line combat troops, the War Department believed that mobilizing the Puerto Ricans would prove useful. These soldiers could relieve white American soldiers from noncombat assignments, freeing them for combat duty while inspiring loyalty among the island population. The political and economic value of mobilizing as many Puerto Ricans as possible was well understood by the War Department. In December 1918 Frank McIntire, chief of the Bureau of Insular Affairs, wrote a memorandum to the chief of the War Plans Division informing him of the political, economic, and social benefits of mobilizing Puerto Rico's "large surplus population, that is, a population for who in the present there is no continuous employment." Dealing in strict utilitarian terms and after making clear that his views were not of a military nature, McIntire reported that the men who had gone through military training on the island "have been very much improved, physically and otherwise, and are better off for having had it and to that extent are of greater economic value."[59]

Not only did the colonial administration expect military training to improve the value of the trainees as workers, but while in service, their absence from the employment pool should alleviate the island's chronic unemployment. With regard to the impact these men would have in the island's sociopolitical structures, McIntyre argued that their training "will have given them a new point of view, their return to the civil life will establish a different and better element in the body politic."[60] It is clear that the BIA believed that the trainees, even if full Americanization proved impossible, would be at least more pro-American and more productive after receiving military training.

The Republicanos were quick to adopt the "100 percent Americanism" campaign launched by the Committee on Public Information. This was evident by their leaders' actions and words as recorded in the insular legislature. Through their newspaper, *El Águila de Puerto Rico*, the Republicanos more than echoed Creel's campaign of blind patriotism and Americanization.[61] Exhortations and instructions to "Prove that you are a 100% American" and slogans such as "Today is an honor to say: 'I am an American'" were accompanied by drawings of Puerto Rican families, boys dressed in military garments, an older father with his hat off, and a mother carrying a baby, with all solemnly watching the Puerto Rican troops marching under the American flag.[62] *El Águila*, like many local newspapers, routinely published long stories about recruitment, Puerto Ricans serving in continental units, "heroes" who had fallen in Europe, the training of the Puerto Rican troops, and the commissioning of officers on the island.[63] The narrative espoused by the Republicanos was of full cooperation with the war effort while underlining what they believed was the unbreakable ties between the United States and the island. They also defended the idea of modernizing the jíbaros through soldiering. The Republicanos were among the most ardent proponents of showing the Puerto Rican's Americanism, social and political maturity, and readiness to become a state of the Union by participating in the war.

The Unionistas, divided between separatistas and autonomistas, wanted the war effort and the mobilization of the Puerto

Rican to lead to independence or more self-government, respectively. Hence they approached mobilization as if they were raising a Puerto Rican army and not a contingent for the U.S. Army. Córdova Dávila attempted to secure that the units were truly composed, trained, and led by Puerto Ricans. In this regard he wrote to the secretary of war, Newton D. Baker (March 9, 1916– March 4, 1921), offering the creation of new regiments but also requesting that more Puerto Ricans be trained as officers and that those serving in the regular army be allowed to transfer to the island.[64] By mid-May 1918, the War Department approved the voluntary transfer of Puerto Ricans serving in the United States to Puerto Rico. Soon officers and noncommissioned officers serving in the regular army began to apply for transfers to the Porto Rican detachment.[65] Meanwhile Yager was trying to secure the creation of a Puerto Rican national guard despite the opposition of the War Department, which preferred that all resources be directed toward the creation of the Puerto Rican division to be part of the National Army.[66] Yager's attempts to secure the creation of a national guard followed the initiative of his predecessor, Governor Colton, in 1910.[67] Like Colton, Yager believed that the creation of the National Guard on the island would enhance the islanders' loyalty to the United States by instilling a sense of national pride and strengthen the political ties between the mainland and Puerto Rico.[68] In 1910, just as in 1917, the War Department did not heed the governor's plans.[69]

Transforming the Puerto Rican Jíbaro

Where to train the Puerto Rican soldiers was one of the first battles the Unionistas fought over control of the mobilization process. For the metropolis, the issue became a matter of economic value, racial prejudice, and part of the Americanization campaign. On November 19, 1917, the *Washington Post* announced that 8,000 white Puerto Ricans were to be sent to Camp Jackson in South Carolina to the 81st Division, while "4,000 [Puerto Rican] negroes" would be sent to Camp Upton Yaphank in New York as part of its colored division. Based on comments from War Department officials, the article stated:

> It is also felt that by training them in connection with our own citizens the Porto Rican soldiers will come to feel themselves as part of the Army of the United States. The psychological influence will be a considerable factor in making the Porto Rican American soldier in no way distinguishable from the men from New York, Michigan, or California. They will be led in English under native Porto Rican and American officers.[70]

These men were not only expected to look like any Americans but they also were supposed to come out of their training thinking and behaving like them. The War Department was indeed bent on fulfilling Wilson's idea of creating one nation through the military.

Though Yager believed that military training would create a new Puerto Rican, he opposed sending the recruits overseas for training. In a letter to the chief of the BIA, Frank McIntire, Yager urged him to train the troops in Puerto Rico. He stated that it would be humiliating to the soldiers and their officers to send them straight to the continental United States because: "Perhaps, 1/3 of these men who will be accepted for service have never worn shoes in their lives. They wear nothing but a cotton shirt and cotton trousers and have nothing else to wear unless it is furnished to them." He had faith in the redeeming qualities of scientific military training but feared that to the common U.S. observer they would look "like a bunch of ragamuffins and tatterdemalions out of which an observer who doesn't know the actual condition here would think it utterly impossible to make them soldiers." He insisted that if training in Puerto Rico was not possible, then, whatever the cost, the Puerto Rican recruits should be given "at least some preliminary training and organization, equipped, uniformed and fed for a while and on regular army rations."[71] It is evident from Yager's statement that the bulk of the Porto Rican soldiers were coming from the files of the malnourished peasantry.

Yager, with the aid of the Unionistas, also made the case for the unfairness of training abroad when the island could use the economic injection of building training facilities and hiring the required civilian staff and services to run the camps. McIntyre responded by informing Yager that it was too expensive to train on the island and that "wherever [Puerto Rican] troops are trained they will be a great economic advantage to Porto Rico due to large war pay, allotment to dependents, and insurance." Moreover, seeking to outmaneuver Córdova Dávila's request that the Puerto Ricans be allowed to fight in a truly Puerto Rican unit, McIntyre informed him that were Puerto Ricans to train on the island, "they would be sent abroad in small unit contingents to fill vacancies in units abroad and would lose their identity as Porto Rican troops." He also reminded Yager that training in the United States would "make them better men on returning to Porto Rico, physically and otherwise, this, even though they should not go abroad at all for service."[72] Besides pointing out the transformative experience the BIA believed military training to be, this statement is also indicative of the expected nature of a Puerto Rican contingent's participation in the war. They were not considered fit to join the fight in Europe, even after training in the United States alongside continental Americans.

Despite the BIA's opposition, Yager and the Unionistas' efforts, especially Córdova Davila's personal plea to President Wilson, paid off, and the War Department agreed to train the Puerto Ricans on the island. Córdova Dávila soon took credit for keeping the troops in Puerto Rico.[73] To house the trainees, a large military training facility was built in Puerto Rico. Located in Santurce, east of San Juan, and with an area of 537 acres, Camp Las Casas served to train more than 500 Puerto Ricans as officers of the U.S. Army and roughly 18,000 soldiers.[74]

It is very telling that the camp bore the name of fray Bartolomé de las Casas, the Dominican friar who in 1522 wrote *A Brief Account of the Destruction of the Indies* (*Brevísima relación de la destrucción de Las Indias*) detailing the Spaniards' atrocities committed against the indigenous population of the Caribbean. Las Casas's defense of the native peoples of the Americas earned him the title "Champion of the Indians." By choosing his name for the training camp, both the colonial administration and the criollo elites were satisfied. The former, subordinated to the Bureau of Insular Affairs, itself modeled on the Bureau of Indian Affairs, could very well see themselves as protectors of the Puerto Ricans, whom many regarded as Indians, at least institutionally.[75] The latter could go beyond that role and pin the friar's name to redeeming Hispanic and Catholic values, which Puerto Rican elites continued to hold as a symbol of their own whiteness and modernity.[76]

Elites Mobilize for War

Yager and Córdova Dávila were also allied in their efforts to secure the opening of spaces in the military for traditional and emerging criollo elites. In July 1915, the War Department's judge advocate had to send a memo stating that there should be no different legal status between Puerto Rican West Point graduates and their continental American counterparts. Citizenship, the judge argued, was not a requirement to serve as an officer of the U.S. Army. The appointment of Luis Raúl Esteves as a second lieutenant in the Porto Rico Regiment of Infantry quickly followed this decision.[77] The Porto Rico Regiment, however, with its excess personnel, waiting lists to join, and its colonial nature was not the best place to advance in rank. As soon as the United States entered the war, officers of the regiment started to resign their commissions so they could enter the regular army and advance in promotion.[78] The need of instructors for Las Casas also opened the door for sergeants of the Porto Rico Regiment to obtain commissions as officers.[79]

The mass mobilization of the Puerto Ricans, the manpower committed to the war effort in Europe, and the occupation of Haiti and the Dominican Republic made the United States and the colonial administration in Puerto Rico more dependent on the local elites. Mobilizing the Puerto Rican peasantry and carrying out other extra-insular services for the BIA became a means for the elite to assert their political power and to move forward their political goals.[80] Securing the training as officers of traditional Puerto Rican elites and emerging professional classes served to preserve a certain social hierarchy, since such training would place them in command of the thousands of peasants and workers mobilized for war. The local elites and the emerging professional classes were to have a role in the war as long as it was a leading one.

Yager did not shy from using colonial subjects to run his share of the American empire. He fought hard to ensure that they received the training to carry out their colonial duties. As early as May 1917, he had tried to arrange for an extra five presidential appointees from the island to attend the U.S. Naval Academy at Annapolis. The governor was not alone in these efforts. Puerto Rican representative to Congress Córdova Dávila also pressed this matter and wrote to President Wilson asking him to give five of his fifteen presidential Annapolis appointments to Puerto Ricans claiming that Hawaii and Alaska, territories smaller in population than Puerto Rico, had already that many.[81] By early 1919 new legislation was in place allowing for an extra five appointees to be nominated by the resident commissioner, and he made good use of his power.[82]

Again, as with any other opening of the U.S. military to Puerto Ricans, the press celebrated the event. On July 3, 1919, the newspaper *El Tiempo* published an editorial congratulating Córdova Dávila "for his efforts to secure this new evidence of confidence in the American citizens of Porto Rico." The article stated that the new legislation and Córdova Dávila's work indicated a "veritable union between the island and the Nation." Gauging the meaning of the event, *El Tiempo* reminded its readers that the only ones entitled to nominate candidates for Annapolis were the senators and representatives of the United States and the delegates from the incorporated territories. That Puerto Rico was "put on the same level as the states and territories in so far as the quota for the Naval academy" should show the "independentistas of the tropical republic" how the "Great Republic, of which we form a part, is each day giving us another proof of confidence in us, opening the doors of all institutions of the country to Porto Rican American citizens and putting them on the same place as citizens of the mainland."[83]

Obtaining capable personnel to help the BIA fulfill its colonial duties was one of Yager's priorities when he fought for more access to military institutions for the Puerto Ricans. Securing the loyalty of the local elites and the island's population while bettering the international image of the United States were added bonuses.

Yager's efforts to secure more spaces in the military for the Puerto Ricans were generally applauded. Only the issue of race gained him real criticism during this period. The United States military was still a segregated organization during the war. In this regard continental officers and Yager himself expressed pro-segregationist views to McIntyre. In one of his letters, Yager informed him that it had been necessary to "keep the blacks out because of prejudice amongst the soldiers of the [Puerto Rican] regiment themselves who did not want blacks in the regiment." However, Yager argued, "blacks are anxious to join the regiment and I'm told they make excellent soldiers under white officers and I'm confident a full regiment of them could be formed in the island."[84] In further correspondence Yager complained: "Many Porto Ricans seem to feel that the Governors and officials in the states consider all Porto Ricans as Negro troops: but that of course touches the sensibility of the white people here." The governor, referring to "our race problem, just as they have it in South Carolina," agreed to train black and white soldiers together if absolutely necessary but warned that "they must be separated."[85] Whether or not Yager wanted to segregate Puerto Ricans in the military by race was mostly irrelevant, since it was the policy of the U.S. Army to segregate troops racially. To that effect, the 375th Regiment was designated to train and field black Puerto Ricans.[86]

Regarding the decision to segregate the troops in the island, the newspaper *Justicia* commented: "Under the administration of Arthur Yager the line separating the men of color is finally established in Puerto Rico" followed by "the old racist fart from Kentucky accused of being the instigator."[87] The editorial continued by arguing that "the complete triumph [of the United States and the Allies] will also defeat all privileges." *El Diluvio*, one of the most vociferous critics of the Yager administration, took special interest in the 375th Porto Rican Colored Regiment and wrote a series of articles detailing their training and progress. An editorial asserted that those soldiers were not "the less intelligent, nor the less smart, neither the ones less disposed to learn and ready themselves to defend with honor the name of Puerto Rico." Instead, "the more apt, humble and the most attentive of the recruits are those of the 375." The editorial also mentioned that "the boys of the 375 will one day respond to the call of arms with the same unconditional bravery and tenacity shown by the colonial French troops and the brave Black soldiers of America."[88] José Celso Barbosa, as leader of the Republicans, took interest in the well-being of the Porto Rican Negro Regiment, the 375. He wrote to the regiment's commander, Col. Frank C. Wood, expressing his willingness to accept that the "national citizenry were divided in organizations and racially," but hoping that when the war ended the men's willingness to sacrifice in "defense of their nation" would help to erase such divisions."[89]

Puerto Rican participation in the armed forces was strongly encouraged, and there was consensus about wanting to see the United States emerge victorious, but that did not blind the press and political leaders to the fact that many of the freedoms espoused by Wilson were not enjoyed by Puerto Ricans. Moreover, local politicians continuously sought to link inequalities, prejudices, and injustices at home with the ideals espoused by Wilson when making the case to go to war.

The attitude of Puerto Rican leaders was similar to that of African American leaders, including W.E.B. Du Bois, who supported the war effort by encouraging black participation. Black leaders, who had argued that disdain of dark races was the real cause of the war, identified the United States and the Allies as the lesser of two evils and thus as their best chance for advancement. They adopted a policy of "first your country, then your rights" and of "close ranks" with "our fellow white citizens."[90] In Puerto Rico, the narratives were similar. However, the issue of race, as determined by skin color, was not the main concern of Puerto Rican leaders. Since the island had an undecided political status, there were several approaches to what came after closing ranks "with our co-citizens from the North." Nonetheless, just as African American leaders, so Puerto Rican leaders hoped to advance their respective agendas after showing the willingness and readiness of their people to come in the defense of the

United States and the ideals of freedom and democracy in times of need. They expected that participating in a war sold as a crusade against totalitarianism, colonialism, and militarism would bring decolonization and equality at home.

The New Jíbaro and the New Americanism

Another difference between Puerto Rican and African American leaders, even if both wanted to use military training to erase racial biases and prejudice, was that the former wanted to remake the very essence of the Puerto Rican through military training. As the recruits arrived at Las Casas for training, an editorial in the *Porto Rico Progress*, a publication adamantly pro-American, observed: "So a new day has dawned for Porto Rico's jíbaro." The training acquired in the military, the editorial argued, would prepare the jíbaro to join the drive toward a modern Puerto Rico: "Downtrodden . . . as he [the jíbaro] has been, he is now in the limelight. The testing and refining process will be hard for him. But he and his brother will become the nucleus of a new Porto Rico. The anemic disease warped man will be a thing of the past. And the domain of the jíbaro will at last come into its proper place in the great Economic and Social scheme of this island."[91]

The same journal and other newspapers reported that the majority of those joining the U.S. Army were jíbaros who wore shoes for the first time in Camp Las Casas after induction.[92] *El Buscapié* affirmed: "After the war, these soldiers will be our greatest leaders, teachers, and champions of freedom and democracy." Commenting on the attitude of the public when seeing the Porto Rican soldiers, the editorial continued: "Nobody can watch them without feeling a revolution in their blood and in the spirit which moves them to support in any possible way our soldiers, be it with a simple smile or with exhortations of courage and steadfastness."[93]

Addressing the poor physical state of the inductees, Francisco del Valle Atiles wrote for *El Buscapié* (a publication that constantly celebrated U.S. expansion in the Caribbean and Latin America and the role of Puerto Rico as the center of the imperialist venture) that military training would correct the "organic poverty" shown by the physical examination of the recruits. He was quick to add: "While the Puerto Rican may be lacking in physical condition due to malnutrition and disease, he overcompensates in spirit," a trait he identified with Hispanic gallantry. Moreover, in a Puerto Rican version of *Arielismo*, this editorial argued that the Puerto Rican "requires the material and industrial might of the continental American," identified as the Anglo-Saxon, to correct such deficiencies.[94] After assimilating such Anglo-Saxon characteristics, the jíbaro inductee would create a space for the "two great cultures of the American hemisphere—the Hispanic and Anglo-Saxon—to coexist."[95]

According to these narratives, military training would fuse material and moral progress, political and cultural identity into one being, the jíbaro. This interpretation of the potential role of military training for modernizing Puerto Rico's peasantry was found in almost all the local newspapers and was voiced by all political parties, especially the Republican. The autonomist wing within the Unión, which held political control during the war years, benefited more than any other political faction from the ambivalent narratives used to promote the war effort.

Soon after the armistice, the *Porto Rico Progress* reported derisively that the Unionistas claimed that the "Puerto Rican soldier has created a New Americanism," one that allowed for "these two great cultures" to coexist.[96] The New Americanism espoused mainly by the autonomistas and certain separatistas from Unión challenged both the Republicans, who would accept nothing but the complete assimilation of the Puerto Ricans, and the assimilation project of the metropolis. The Unionistas' approach to the constructed identity of the new Puerto Rican (as exemplified by the new jíbaro) and the New American was appealing indeed. Editorials in pro-American outlets such as *El Águila* and the *Porto Rico Progress* essentially made the case of the Unionistas, mostly due to their ambivalent national discourse and patriotism.

Eager to cooperate with the war effort and the defense of the "nation," the Red Cross, women's clubs, and in many cases the townspeople made sure that the departing recruits received care packages. A newspaper commented that "all soldiers arrive with a bill book with the inscription 'Adelante Soldado Portorriqueño.' And many of them received, besides the normative ration of cigars, cigarettes, and some cash, items that appealed to their national spirit, such as cloth with the inscription "Recuerde el Carolina" (a ship carrying Puerto Rican workers to the United States sunk by a German submarine) and the words of "La Borinqueña," considered at the time a national hymn that would become the national anthem in 1952.[97] It is obvious that the feelings toward the nation and the understanding of the nation itself were, to say the least, complex. A jíbaro told a reporter that his wife and children were crying when he left for training, but that he said to them, "It was for the Patria and the Patria would protect them if I fought to protect her."[98] It is clear that this jíbaro-soldier expected his sacrifice not to be in vain. In his understanding, he was not fighting for a foreign power; he was fighting for his motherland, and in case he made the ultimate sacrifice, the motherland would take care of his offspring. Luckily, he would not have to make such a sacrifice.

Armistice and Demobilization

By October 31, 1918, three of the four regiments authorized for the Porto Rican division had been trained and manned with 10,600 officers and soldiers. On November 11, an armistice between the Allies and the Germans went into effect, ending hostilities in Europe.[99] Amid fireworks, dancing, the colors of the United States and of the Allied nations, out of the gates of Las Casas came marching the 12,000 soldiers and trainers of the Porto Rican contingent of the National Army. The celebration climaxed with a military review of the Porto Rican Division in the Plaza 2 de Marzo in Condado, commemorative of the Jones Act of 1917. Knowing that demobilization would come rather sooner than later, the *Porto Rico Progress* announced that the men from Las Casas "no matter what their future may be, cannot help being better men for the few months of training they have had."[100]

On December 18, 1918, demobilization orders arrived, and in January 1919 the Puerto Rican division had been completely demobilized. The soldiers training in the island did not see combat. A soldier lamented after receiving his discharge papers and examining the document and the blank space reserved for "battles, engagements, and skirmishes": "If there were only three or four names in that line, how proud I'd be."[101] Other outlets published similar stories. Choosing to highlight the men's desires to see combat had political value. Local leaders who sought to advance their goals through war participation thought that had the Puerto Rican Division reached the European theater and bled alongside the Allied soldiers, their political standing would have been strengthened. The Puerto Rican soldiers, the local narratives claimed, had been willing to prove themselves in the battlefield.

The old Porto Rican Regiment saw its role extended during the war. Brought to full strength in 1914, the regiment had been sent to defend the Panama Canal in 1917.[102] It is significant that these troops were sent outside the island to take over defense of the Isthmian Canal. The Canal was vital for American projection of power and national security, hence the importance of receiving such an assignment. However, even though the regiment was combat-ready in 1914 and the United States had an acute shortage of trained military personnel, let alone combat-ready infantry regiments, military authorities did not even consider sending the Porto Rican Regiment to France. Instead, it replaced white troops in the Canal Zone. The role of the Puerto Rican regiment ceased to be solely of a domestic nature, but it continued to be subordinated and colonial in nature. The local press, however, interpret sending the regiment overseas as a sign of confidence in the Puerto Ricans. Reflecting their new political identity, upon their return to Puerto Rico, the men of the "Porto Rican Regiment" found their unit's name changed to the "65th Infantry, U.S. Army" through the National Defense Act of 1920.[103] Significantly, the term "Porto Rican" was dropped, as the regiment was included in the renumbering of federal units.

Demobilization came swiftly, but that was not to be the end of the "Porto Rican contingent." The three regiments from Las Casas were reorganized in 1922 as part of the Army Reserve Corps. In 1919, Secretary of War Baker authorized Yager to organize an infantry regiment and a cavalry battalion, officially creating the Porto Rico National Guard. In 1923 this corps was reorganized into the 295 Infantry Regiment, PRNG. Responding both to the prestige that came from wearing a military uniform and to economic hardships, neither the National Guard nor the regular army outfits on the island lacked volunteers to fill their ranks, and there were waiting lists to join these units.[104]

As the victory celebrations subdued, Puerto Rican politicians tried to use any political leverage they believed they had earned because of their support of the war effort. Still convinced that the soldiers who trained on the island would become the nucleus of a new Puerto Rico, some moved to secure that any benefits granted to World War I veterans in the United States were also extended to the Puerto Rican veterans. Roughly a month after the armistice, *Diluvio*, which had been very critical of Yager's administration throughout the war period, began a campaign promoting the inclusion of Puerto Rican soldiers as beneficiaries of the Secretary of Interior's proposed benefit for veterans, which sought to provide soldiers with the opportunity to buy farmlands with low interest loans. *Diluvio*'s editor, Norberto Escabí, argued that in Puerto Rico there were over 200,000 *cuerdas* of public lands—and hundreds of thousands more in private absentee idle hands that could very well be put to good use by the more than 15,000 soldiers who were peasants.[105] The editorial warned that the majority of the Puerto Rican soldiers had developed new worldviews, habits, and ideas through the hard training and labor of the military camps, and consequently the old standards of living would not satisfy them now.[106] The editorial was appealing to the colonial authorities' perennial fear of sociopolitical unrest. *Diluvio* also called for putting a stop to the Puerto Rican labor exodus. It argued that the training of the soldiers and the farmland legislation should help to create the necessary conditions to make the labor exodus unnecessary.[107]

Some steps were taken to prepare the soldiers for their return to civilian life. As part of the demobilization process, the soldiers attended a series of talks and seminars. C. Hendrickson, director of agriculture on the Food Commission, Félix Reina and F. G. Rodil, a functionary and the director of education, spoke to the men of the 374 and 375 about reentering civilian life. By means of these talks, the trio stated, they wish to prepare the soldiers to continue to work on food conservation and food crop development. They also covered pest control, production of food substitutes, and development of new agricultural industries. Hendrickson and Reina commented that it was for the soldiers to exploit what they were to learn and to create a new "relation of Porto Rican soldiers with the agricultural life," while Rodil discussed the opportunity of "making Porto Rico a self-supporting country."[108] The soldiers indeed received a tall order. The publications advocating for the extension of rights to Puerto Rican veterans and covering their demobilization training were the Socialist-leaning *Diluvio* and the staunchly pro-American *Porto Rico Progress*. Unionistas and Republicanos were too busy positioning themselves in order to further their respective political goals.

The Postwar Political Landscape

The Unionistas demanded a solution to the status issue and that Puerto Rico be allowed to send a delegate to the Peace Assembly in France to demand independence for the island. Republicans and colonial administrators soon labeled the Unionistas as selfish and irresponsible in view of the earthquake and tidal wave that punished the island in November 1918 and the subsequent cholera epidemic that crippled the west coast.[109] The next month Representative Cayetano Coll y Cuchí, who after de Diego's death in 1918 became the most prominent separatist among the Unionistas, passed a memorial and resolution in the insular legislature urging President Wilson to support self-determination for the Puerto Ricans. Coll y Cuchí's resolution stressed that failing to act positively would undermine the moral grounds of the American representatives in the peace negotiations and thus jeopardize their mission. Puerto Rico, he argued, "has demonstrated its fitness and capacity for self-government, that is being at present and always has been denied the island."[110]

Coll y Cuchí reminded the president that Porto Ricans "let out a cry of joy when the American Congress extended its laws to the island territory and called its sons to arms in order that they might play part in the great task of giving liberty to the world.

And our soldiers gathered in the camps and our riches flowed into the vaults of the government without the slightest doubt delaying the decided impulse of our spirit. Thus was seen the rare spectacle of a people who was itself not free hastening to give the blood of its sons to defend other nations." The Porto Rican soldiers, he continued, "left their homes to fight for democracy, resting in the belief that when the war was over, victory won, and peace established, Porto Rico would be given the same freedom for which it fought." He linked Wilson's international rhetoric to Puerto Rico's issues. The resolution continued: "Our culture and civilization and the pride of our glorious race oblige us to decline to accept as legitimate a government that does not spring from our own will."[111]

The easy passing of the nonbinding resolution emboldened the Unionistas, who tried to pass another one the following week. This time they sought approval for a resolution, calling on the president and Congress to allow the organization of a Republican form of government on the island. Manuel Rossy, Republican leader of the house, still espousing 100 percent Americanism, denounced the bill: "I am an American citizen and I stand for American sovereignty. That is my Americanism." He argued that Unionistas had poorly worded the resolution to disguise their true goal, independence. Speaker of the House Miguel Guerra had tried to persuade legislators to pass it unanimously by appealing to the need for a more liberal and democratic government. Defending democratic and nationalist aspirations, he declared that the day for Puerto Rico to voice its desire for self-government had indeed arrived. Frustrated by the intransigence of the Republicanos, Ponce's representative, Manuel Lastra, challenged Rossy to claim full responsibility before the people of Puerto Rico for the defeat of a plan for a more liberal government. Rossy riposted: "You [the Unionistas] stand for the Republic of Porto Rico, and we stand for statehood in the Union. We travel different roads and we seek different ends. We will not be one at this late hour to content ourselves with a loosely worded proposition that leaves in doubt the kind of sovereignty we want."[112] Guerra replied to Rossy's comments making a distinction between the old Americanism, which Rossy represented, and the new spirit of Americanism. Guerra explained that while holding in high esteem the old Americanism, and while being loyal to the teachings of American statesmen, the younger generation and their new Americanism believed in the future of Puerto Rican nationality.

Officially Unión did not demand independence. However, their leaders spoke openly about it and spared no effort in fighting against statehood. Undeterred by the failure of the resolution, Coll y Cuchí challenged the metropolis, declaring to the press that "year after year we have demanded independence or statehood . . . without achieving any" and "the Jones Act, let's be honest, does not satisfy the aspirations of the portorrican people." Coll y Cuchí linked Puerto Rico's need for "independence nationhood" to Wilson's "self-determination" rhetoric. He added that Córdova Dávila's proposal in the U.S. House of Representatives to create a referendum to decide the political status was not a surprise and that "we [the Unionistas] had always believed that after the war ended, there would be the opportunity to move the island toward that goal [independence]." The reporter himself was quick to link the goal of the separatistas in Unión to a long line of revolutionaries and champions of independence.[113] There was much opposition to any referendum on the status question, especially while Unión retained political power. During the war *Buscapié* had derided the idea of having a plebiscite to define the status, arguing that the hundreds of thousands of Puerto Ricans who registered for the military draft had already decided that issue.[114]

For a while it seemed as if the Unionistas would be able to realize their goals with considerable support from the general public. Unión dominated the 1920s election, but its success hid the deep-rooted divisions splitting its members into almost irreconcilable bands: those who wanted independence (initially led by José de Diego and succeeded by Coll y Cuchí, Barceló, and Córdova Dávila among others) and those who wanted to secure autonomy and who still spoke of pro-Americanism, led by Juan B. Huyke and Martín Travieso. In 1920 Barceló traveled to the United States with the purpose of gauging how much had changed in Washington with the election of the Republican candidate,

Warren H. Harding, as president. He proudly declared: "Let me go to Washington to demand independence." But once in New York he showed the ambivalence and division of his own party by declaring that the Unionistas' immediate goal was to obtain the right to elect their own governor and that they were happy and proud of having U.S. citizenship. Moreover, he declared that Puerto Rico would accept either independence or statehood as final solutions to the status question.[115]

In his inaugural speech in July 29, 1921, Harding's appointee as governor of Puerto Rico, E. Montgomery Reily, let political leaders know that he would not tolerate foreigners inciting political unrest or demanding independence. Reily stated that as long as the Stars and Stripes flew over the United States, it would continue to fly over Puerto Rico. He also warned the Socialists by declaring that he would not allow labor leaders to incite unrest among workers. Montgomery Reily's inaugural speech was well received by the Republicans. It made the Socialists weary and left the Unionistas feeling betrayed. On August 3 the leadership of Unión met in assembly. At the end of the meeting, a crowd accused Córdova Dávila of collaborating with the new governor and knowing beforehand what Reily would say in his inaugural speech. As the crowd chanted, "Viva la independencia," Córdova Dávila yelled back, "Viva Puerto Rico Americano."[116]

In January 1922 Congressman Philip Campbell, Republican from Kansas, and Senator William King, Democrat from Utah, introduced the Campbell bill. This bill for the first time mentioned openly the creation in Puerto Rico of a Estado Libre Asociado, which unlike the one created in 1952 included an American commissioner in Puerto Rico and a governor to be chosen by the elected Puerto Rican legislature, not by the people.[117] With the leaders of Unión in disarray as a consequence of internal divisions and the latest political developments, the party temporarily adopted the Estado Libre Asociado as its goal.

The Puerto Rican soldier and the heavy burdens the local elites put on him, as well as the promises made to los hijos de este país, quickly disappeared from the politicians' minds as they ushered the island into an era of political alliances. Incessant fighting for political survival and dominance left no room or interest for much else.

The combination of political developments, in the form of American citizenship for the Puerto Ricans and an elective legislature in 1917, and the military mass mobilization of the island's peasantry and urban workers, further complicated the relationship between the metropolis and the colony. The War Department, through the BIA, would have preferred to continue treating the island as a giant reservation. U.S. citizenship, however, invested the Puerto Ricans with more legal rights and recourses, making unpopular policies easier to challenge by the different political groups on the island as well as by individual citizens, educators, and business and agrarian associations.[118] The immediate goals of the War Department and the Wilson administration were achieved (securing the loyalty of the Puerto Ricans by granting them American citizenship and silencing critiques of imperialism). But this victory would prove a double-edged knife in the long run.

Mass participation of Puerto Ricans in the U.S. military, the newly created Puerto Rico National Guard, and the willing support of the newly elected Puerto Rican legislature for the war effort temporarily cemented American control over the island and over the islanders' loyalty to the United States. The unwillingness or inability of most Puerto Ricans to resist becoming U.S. citizens and their determination to participate in the war reflected the impact that the institutions of the American metropolis had had on the Puerto Ricans. That same institutional influence would lead the Puerto Ricans to expect more political and socioeconomic opportunities, if not equality. Oblivious to the transformation occurring in Puerto Rico, the United States was slow to respond to these challenges, and no major political changes would take place after 1917 until yet another world war highlighted the strategic importance of the island.

The mass mobilization of the Puerto Rican peasantry and urban workers and the initial enthusiasm shown by the inductees hid the fact that control over the military apparatus in the island was no longer the exclusive prerogative of the U.S. colonial administrators. The traditional and emerging local elites, as well as the professional classes, had to be called upon to train and lead the massive army of peasants soldiering in the island. Out of sheer necessity, the United States broadly opened the officers' corps to los hijos de este país, providing in the process the tools for the local elites and emerging professional classes to attain and consolidate political power. By the war's end, local leaders had succeeded in wresting exclusive control over the nation-building project via military service from the U.S. authorities. This situation, even if not immediately apparent in the postwar years, would eventually put the local elites in a better political position than they had been before World War I.

The passing of the Jones Act and extending U.S. citizenship to the Puerto Ricans, accompanied with the death of Luis Muñoz Rivera, temporarily weakened the Unionistas. The coming of the war brought the temporary resurgence of the Republicans who were the first to tie the war effort and the 100 percent Americanism campaign to their own political goal, statehood. By the war's end, however, by turning President Wilson's promise of ending the hyphenations in the American nation into a call for a New Americanism that promoted creating a new Puerto Rican out of Hispanic gallantry and Anglo-Saxon industrialism, the autonomistas within Unión had found an image they could use to sell their third way, the Libre Asociación, to the general population. This was in essence a return to Hostos and Matienzo Cintrón's idea of Americanizing the Puerto Rican, which meant creating a modern political individual without losing the essence of Puertorriqueñismo, only this time economic modernization superseded political modernization. The autonomistas had found a new philosophy and an agent to incarnate it. There could be a space for the Anglo-Saxon and Hispanic cultures to coexist. The jíbaro would be that new man and Puerto Rico that new space. The autonomistas of the 1920s were not able to fully exploit or develop their new popular philosophy, but the seed had been planted for the generation coming of age during the war, and they would retake this narrative decades later.

Over 18,000 Puerto Ricans served in the U.S. armed forces

during World War I. After the armistice, these soldiers were quickly demobilized and returned to the hills and coastal valleys. Neither the U.S. government nor the colonial administration created vocational or capacitating projects. The promises of a new jíbaro, integrated into the economy as its driving force and as the "new teachers of freedom and democracy," remained mostly unfulfilled. Discontent with the war's aftermath helps to explain the attitude of former soldiers and officers who after becoming teachers argued that patriots were created neither in the battlefield nor in the military but in the schools.[119]

The creation of the Puerto Rico National Guard in 1919 and the transformation of the provisional regiment into a regular U.S. Army regiment (*el 65*) absorbed many of the soldiers and restarted the military in Puerto Rico as a professional career. Many of the future career officers (and certainly the vast majority of the troops) identified themselves simply as jíbaros from Cabo Rojo, Cayey, Lares, here and there . . . and became an important emerging socioeconomic and political group. These soldiers and officers did not interfere directly in politics, as they followed the strict subordination to civilian authority practiced by the U.S. Army. Local politicians, however, tried to employ the soft enticements of the military (prestige, manliness, heroism) and its tangible aspect (socioeconomic improvement) to boost different political projects, from simply redefining the parameters of the colony to full decolonization. But this would have to wait.

The United States had secured the islanders' loyalty in part by extending citizenship to them, but the fact that the island remained mostly dormant after World War I, even after the promises of integrating the jíbaros as the axis of progress did not materialize, was a function of the temporary economic boom brought by the war. The Great Depression would bring unrest to the circum-Caribbean basin in the 1930s and mark the end of economic and political stability in the American informal empire, especially Puerto Rico. Yet another war would force the United States to mobilize the Puerto Ricans. The challenges to the metropolis would be stronger and more direct. Overreliance on the local elites to mobilize and control the peasantry and urban working classes would continue to undermine the United States' control over the military apparatus and the political structures in the island. A new challenge in the form of nationalist clandestine paramilitary units would be more than a military challenge and recognition of the political value of the military in the island's society.

In his later years, Gen. Luis Raúl Esteves commented that he believed that Camp Las Casas served as the "first blood transfusion received by our tired people. Not only did it [military training] awaken our jíbaro, but it taught him how to live a better life." Esteves had doubted that the "malnourished *jibaritos*" he encountered at Las Casas would ever be ready to serve as combat troops, and he longed serving with his continental unit, the 23rd Infantry. However, his opinion changed: "I witnessed our boys' physical transformation becoming aware of their disciplined spirit and military pride inherited from our ancestors; I changed my mind and felt proud of serving with *Boricua* troops."[120]

Esteves's assessment may have been lost to the dominant political leaders in the early 1920s, but the emerging leadership, among them Luis Muñoz Marín and Pedro Albizu Campos, were not to forget what they witnessed or experienced during the Great War. The jíbaro, who had been presented at best as a romantic figure and at worst as a reason for the island's backwardness had proven that his alleged shortcomings were a function of the structural social inequalities inherent to the island and not a characteristic of his persona. As mature leaders, both Albizu Campos and Muñoz Marín would try again to re-create the Puerto Ricans' national identities and the island's socioeconomic structures by virtue of military training. Their different paths would eventually lead to an armed struggle between *los hijos de este país*.

4

War against the Yankees!

Prelude to the Battle over Modern Puerto Rico

> Nationalism has organized and mobilized the vital strength of Puerto Rico to counter the enemy. The nation has passed from passive resistance to counterattack. The entire nation has condemned these killings and it is firm in its resolution that they will not be repeated. . . . It is the plan to exterminate the Puerto Ricans. But Nationalism has destroyed all Yankee inventions. The enemy has now left only the traditional arms of assassination. The country will vindicate the killings of its heroes, Pagán, Quiñones, Rodríguez-Vega, and Santiago. The Yankee Chief of police, Colonel Francis Riggs, has declared to the nation that there will be war. The Nationalists recognize his frankness and pick up the glove. There will be war. War against the Yankees!
> —Pedro Albizu Campos, November 2, 1935[1]

The 1930s in Puerto Rico were marked by economic distress and political instability. The economic misfortunes of the island were not simply a matter of the metropolis's economic problems extending to its colonies. Puerto Rico's problems had started before the Great Depression. As the Depression castigated the U.S. mainland, it aggravated preexisting conditions on the island. Puerto Rico's dire economic picture—an unemployed or overworked, underpaid, malnourished rural population and a rapidly failing urban sector—stirred widespread discontent. As hunger became the norm, the economic situation led to political violence. A virulent Nacionalista anti-American campaign and the colonial authorities' belligerent and often criminal persecution of the Nacionalistas characterized this decade. The Nacionalistas, however, were not passive victims; they fought back to the point that the island came to be called "America's Ireland" or the "Ireland of the Caribbean."[2] In fact, before U.S entrance into World War II, the metropolis and its colonial administrators used the militarized Puerto Rico Insular Police to fight a brief war against the Nacionalistas' political wing and their paramilitary units. The fear of social unrest during the early 1930s, followed by a reign of political violence, forced the federal government to take a closer look at the island's economic and political situation.

As economic distress afflicting the island turned into political discontent, emerging political leaders Pedro Albizu Campos and Luis Muñoz Marín used such discontent to further their own projects. The history of the rise of Albizu Campos and the Nacionalistas is well known. Albizu Campos was born in Ponce on September 12, 1891. His maternal grandmother had been a slave. His mother, an Afro-Puerto Rican domestic worker, died in his childhood. His father, Alejandro Albizu Romero, came from a wealthy family of Spanish immigrants. Albizu Campos received a scholarship to study at the University of Vermont after graduating with honors from the Ponce High School in 1912, a school mostly reserved for Puerto Rico's southern white elite. After two years in Vermont he transferred to Harvard University and graduated in 1917. He then volunteered to serve in the U.S. Army during World War I. After completing the officers' training camp at Las Casas, he earned the rank of first lieutenant in 1918. He was honorably discharged in April 1919 from the 375th Regiment, an outfit created on the island for black Puerto Ricans. Albizu Campos resumed his studies in Harvard after the war, eventually graduating with a law degree in 1923. During his later years at Harvard he became an admirer of the Sinn Fein Irish separatist movement. He returned to Puerto Rico after marrying Laura Meneses, a Radcliffe-educated Peruvian, and joined the Unionistas as a staunchly pro-independence champion. However, when he was not selected by the Unionista leadership as a candidate to the legislature in 1924, he joined the Nationalist Party, created by Unionista dissenters.[3] Eventually Albizu Campos came to believe any means, including a violent campaign, should be employed to free the island of the

American grip (which he identified as the cause of all of Puerto Rico's troubles). He thus waged war against the colonial authorities, hoping that the Puerto Rican masses would rise up and expel the Americans.

Luis Muñoz Marín, the bohemian "bard of politics" and patrician heir of Luis Muñoz Rivera, would spend the 1930s vacillating between socialist ideals (especially the socioeconomic restructuration of the island) and his belief in attaining independence via peaceful means. He was a self-proclaimed Nacionalista and advocate of independence, and he rejected violence, preferring political means and preserving good relations with the United States to achieve that goal. Although in the mid-1930s his fortunes indicated otherwise, shortly before U.S. entry into World War II Muñoz Marín would emerge as the dominant political leader.

Both Albizu Campos and Muñoz Marín benefited and suffered immensely from the same conditions plaguing the island. What transpired during these years of political violence was also a battle for control of Puerto Rican identities. Albizu Campos had no chance of militarily overthrowing the colonial government. However, though tactically insignificant from a military point of view, the Nacionalistas' daring attacks against the metropolis's agents fulfilled their intended role; these attacks gained local, national, and international attention to Albizu Campos's cause. His movement, however, had little possibility of success if it could not turn Puerto Ricans against Americans. Using Hispanic and Catholic iconography for his party and paramilitary units, and emphasizing Spanish traditions and conservatism, were but a call to the Puerto Ricans to see themselves as completely different from continental Americans. Albizu Campos was appealing to what he believed was Puerto Rico's true national identity. Eventually the Nacionalistas would challenge not only the American presence but also the legitimacy of the Insular Police and the U.S. Army and National Guard units on the island as truly Puerto Rican or as national institutions representative of the Puerto Ricans. In this regard, the Nacionalistas paramilitary units played an important role in winning the support of popular sectors.

Liberales Flirt with Independence

Before Muñoz Marín emerged as the leading politician in the late 1930s, he had to fight his way to center stage. For the elections of 1924 the Unionista leader, Antonio R. Barceló, made a political alliance with the staunchly pro-American Republicanos to form the Alianza, which faced the Coalición made up of Santiago Iglesias Pantín's Socialistas and dissenting Republicanos who had created the Partido Constitucional Histórico (originally known as Republicano Puro). Barceló's move secured the prevalence of Unionistas and Republicanos over the emerging Socialistas in 1924.[4] Before the general elections of 1928, however, the Alianza lost a significant number of Republicanos, who joined the rank and file of the Coalición. Although the Alianza again dominated the elections, the Coalición, especially its Socialista wing, was weakening the Alianza's grip on Puerto Rican politics.[5] Soon after the elections, the Unionistas from the Alianza, unhappy with having to divide government positions equally with their minority Republicano partners, splintered into two groups, and Barceló moved to dissolve Alianza. On January 1932 what was left of Alianza joined the Republicanos Puros led by Manuel F. Rossy, forming the Partido Unión Republicana. With this stroke Barceló's Unionistas lost the right to continue calling their party Unión. After failed legal attempts to regain their name and party insignias, the Unionist leaders rebranded themselves as Partido Liberal Puertorriqueño (PLP).[6]

Shortly before the election of 1932, the reunited Republicanos and some Autonomistas from the former Alianza entered into a pact with the Socialistas in what came to be known as the Coalición Republicana Socialista. It certainly seemed as if the political career of Barceló was coming to an end. The dire situation faced by the Liberales drove Barceló to act boldly, and he soon moved to embrace the ideal of independence. Many within the Liberales were in fact Autonomistas but by taking up eventual independence as part of their platform, the PLP gave the impression of unanimous thought with respect to the island's political future. During the campaign, a firebrand Independentista Muñoz

Marín emerged as an inspiring young leader. His articles in *La Democracia*, his father's newspaper, gave him a platform from which to attack the colonial administration and political opponents. Running for the Liberal Party, he was elected as "Senator at large" (*por acumulación*). Although the Liberales obtained more votes than any other party, the Republican and Socialist coalition dominated the elections and split the most important positions in government (that of resident commissioner in Washington, president of the senate, and speaker of the house) among them.[7] The staunchly pro-American and annexionist Republicanos and Socialistas were returned to power. Or so it seemed.

Although the Liberales did not dominate the elections, their performance was quite impressive. The electoral power gained by the Liberales derived from two sources. First, the popularity of their leading figures, the hardened veteran Barceló and the charismatic Muñoz Marín, made the PLP a recognizable organization. Second, Muñoz Marín's anti-monopoly and pro-labor rhetoric was appealing to the masses due to the extreme economic conditions plaguing the island. It did not take long for Muñoz Marín to identify the economy as the principal issue for most Puerto Ricans.

Under American control, land concentration and the proletarianization of the peasantry had advanced hand in hand in Puerto Rico. The monopolization of lands by absentee-owned sugar corporations meant that most of the island's arable land was dedicated to growing and exporting that crop, which in turn made the Puerto Ricans more dependent on imports for food. Land concentration, high population density, and dependence on exports exacerbated economic hardships in Puerto Rico. This process gradually led to the pauperization of the Puerto Rican peasant, especially the cane workers and their families.[8] The economic situation in Puerto Rico deteriorated tremendously in the late 1920s. In 1928, Hurricane San Felipe crippled the coffee industry, which saw its production reduced from 32 million pounds to just 5 million the next year and the loss of its remaining European markets.[9] In 1930 the Brookings Institution, an independent public policy think tank, presented the 700-page study, *Porto Rico and Its Problems*.[10] The study described the economic situation of the island as "deplorable" with rural families' annual income averaging between $250 and $275. Urban families earned a little more, but in these areas the cost of living was higher and there were fewer opportunities to have home orchards to supplement dietary requirements. In addition, the Organic Acts used to govern Puerto Rico (Foraker and Jones) required that imports be carried exclusively by the U.S. merchant marine, the most expensive in the world, which made foodstuffs on the island 8–14 percent more expensive than in New York. The cost of food on the island was aggravated by the fact that daily wages in Puerto Rico were less than one dollar while in New York they were four to ten dollars.[11] In fact, manufactured goods were so expensive that "in 1930 only one person in four had ever worn shoes."[12] On September 26, 1932, another hurricane, San Ciprián, caused 225 deaths and left more than 3,000 wounded and more than 100,000 Puerto Ricans homeless. San Ciprián also ruined the small producers' minor fruit crops on the northern coast.[13] When the Great Depression made its way to the colony, Puerto Rico was in no shape to withstand its assault.[14]

While most politicians continued to engage exclusively with matters of political arrangements and patronage, such as the political status of the island and positions in the colonial bureaucracy, Muñoz Marín was preoccupied with the economic and social maladies affecting the peasantry and urban working classes. He challenged the Brookings Institution's conclusions, which blamed overpopulation as the main cause for Puerto Rico's socioeconomic distress, instead holding capitalism and the sugar corporations accountable for the situation.[15] The Liberales benefited from Muñoz Marín's early and deep understanding of the popular sectors' dire situation. Meanwhile, on the mainland, Franklin Delano Roosevelt was elected president, bringing a very liberal agenda to the White House. The coalition of Republicanos and Socialistas would soon find their politics out of tune with the reformist drive of FDR's administration. The Socialistas and Republicanos may have dominated the elections on the island, but it would be

Muñoz Marín who would be seen constantly in Washington and as having the Roosevelt administration's ear.[16]

Nacionalistas Abandon the Electoral Process

The Liberales were not the only political faction benefiting from economic hardships. The Nacionalistas, who had reorganized their party in 1930 and elected Pedro Albizu Campos as their president, also participated in the elections of 1932.[17] They hoped to elect Albizu Campos to the senate, which seemed a reasonable proposition, since his frequent public speeches were usually attended by a multitude of people. The Nacionalistas, however, were weak to the point of requiring the unrequested, albeit welcome, assistance of the Republicanos to obtain the 30,000 signatures needed to inscribe their party.[18] The Nacionalistas obtained only 1.4 percent of the votes in the general elections of 1932 and failed to elect Albizu Campos as senator at large (who with 11,882 votes doubled his party's tally). This bitter experience eventually drove Albizu Campos to withdraw from the electoral process. Obtaining independence through any means necessary became the mission of the Nacionalistas. The 1932 elections were instrumental in radicalizing Albizu Campos and his followers.[19] Soon after the elections Albizu Campus challenged the legitimacy of American sovereignty over the island, basing his claims on the legal relationship between Spain and Puerto Rico before the 1898 invasion as established by the Autonomous Charter of 1897.[20] If American sovereignty was illegal, then the United States had no right to exert any authority over Puerto Rico, nor was it the Puerto Ricans' duty to obey or cooperate with what then constituted an occupation force. Political tension would soon lead to a shooting war between the colonial authorities and the Nacionalistas.

On July 1, 1933, Roosevelt replaced the competent governor James Beverly with the inadequate Robert H. Gore.[21] During Gore's short term there were no fewer than eighty-five workers' strikes and labor conflicts, and a bomb was found in the governor's summer residence in Jájome. The Coalición, which had won the elections of 1932, threw its support behind the governor, who sought to quench labor protests using the Insular Police.

The Liberales and most of the press openly challenged and ridiculed the governor. The Coalición's support of the governor, who defended antilabor initiatives, started to create a schism between workers and the Socialist Party. Within this context, Albizu Campos gained support among workers. His harsh attacks against the insular government, absentee corporations, and the Federación Libre de Trabajadores (which he accused of betraying the workers) gained him the attention of the sugar cane workers. In 1934, a general strike of sugar cane workers in Puerto Rico allied this labor sector (for the very first time) with the Nacionalistas and effectively ended the era of political stability on the island.[22] The workers requested the assistance of Albizu Campos, who negotiated on their behalf. However, shortly after the strike was resolved, he lost their support. Fixated on obtaining the island's independence, the Nacionalistas had not developed a labor ideology that could win them the loyalty of the working classes permanently.[23]

The Imperial Stick and Carrot

Aware of Gore's inability to govern the island and the endless cycle of strikes, Roosevelt feared that Puerto Rico was on the brink of anarchy. Persuaded by Muñoz Marín's personal plea to remove Gore, Roosevelt chose retired general Blanton Winship to replace him.[24] Winship assumed this role on February 5, 1934. Before his departure, Gore was pressured by Senator Millard Tydings to name his close friend, Elisha Francis Riggs, as chief of the Insular Police.[25] Riggs had served in the War Department's Military Intelligence Division and had retired as a colonel.[26] Under Winship, the militarization of the Insular Police acquired special relevance, especially after 1935. The police were issued submachine guns and riot control gear, and their training was intensified under Winship's personal supervision.[27] FBI agents and officers and sergeants (noncommissioned officers) from the 65th Infantry (whose intelligence section, S-2, redacted weekly reports on "subversive activity") conducted the training at Fort Buchanan.[28] One of the darkest chapters in Puerto Rican history was about to be written.

Labor conflicts and the Nationalist challenge notwithstanding, there was little evidence to indicate that political violence on the island would increase sharply. Roosevelt's administration had taken some steps to relieve the political pressure in Puerto Rico. Besides removing the publicly ridiculed Gore, Roosevelt changed the administrative arrangement on the island. In March 1934 the president signed Executive Order 6.726, which transferred supervision of Puerto Rican affairs from the War Department to the Department of the Interior headed by Indian rights' advocate Harold Ickes.[29] Within the Department of the Interior the newly created Division of Territories and Island Possessions (DTIP) took over the role of the Bureau of Insular Affairs (BIA). The DTIP was itself entrusted to Ernest Gruening, a longtime friend of Muñoz Marín.[30] War Department officials opposed the transfer, which they blamed on special interests, while defending the department's record as Puerto Rico's fair champion. An official from the War Department declared: "This transfer has long been agitated by special interests bent upon commercial and political exploitation of Porto Rico. The sinister machine of the sugar lobby against Porto Rico has long been strongly resisted by the secretary of war and the BIA."[31] The transfer, however, went into effect on May 22, 1935. Removing the last vestige of military rule over the island was a symbolic gesture that appeased politicians but had little value for the vast majority of Puerto Ricans, who were more concerned with feeding, clothing, and housing their families. This is not to say that Roosevelt's administration was oblivious to the economic hardships troubling the island and fueling political unrest.

In 1933, to combat the effects of the Great Depression, the Federal Emergency Relief Administration came to exist by virtue of the Federal Emergency Relief Act. Initially the program was extended to Puerto Rico in what came to be known as the Puerto Rico Emergency Relief Administration (PRERA). Though its director immediately set to work, his efforts were hindered by Gore and the Coalicionistas, who sought to control the institution.[32] On May 28, 1935, an executive order created another agency to tackle the deep-rooted economic problems on the island.[33] The Puerto Rico Reconstruction Administration (PRRA) was directed by a prominent Puerto Rican, Carlos Chardón. Its mission was ambitious, and its focus on reducing unemployment and poverty provided the chance to remove causes of unrest. The socioeconomic reconstruction plan for Puerto Rico was designed by Carlos Chardón, Rafael Menéndez Ramos, and Rafael Fernández García, but it had much influence from Muñoz Marín and some even referred to it as Plan Muñoz.[34] Yet the PRRA's offices were not fully staffed until the end of the year. Meanwhile, political unrest continued to escalate.

America's Ireland

On July 4, 1935, the Nacionalistas detonated bombs in the PRRA's office in San Juan and several other government buildings. A few weeks later a bomb went off at the U.S. Court Building in Puerta de Tierra, followed by the bombing of a police station. The bombings continued throughout the summer, but so far there had been no casualties.[35] Meanwhile, Albizu Campos carried on with his islandwide tour. On October 24, the Insular Police detained Nacionalistas armed with revolvers near the University of Puerto Rico in Río Piedras. The UPR students were protesting against Albizu Campos, who supposedly had called the students "effeminate" and "prostitutes" for failing to be at the vanguard of the fight for the island's independence.[36] On their way to the police station, a gunfight left four Nacionalistas and a policeman dead and forty wounded. There had been outbursts of political violence in the previous years, but nothing came close to the outright war that had just started between the Nacionalistas and the Insular Police.[37] Reacting to the incidents, Chief Riggs declared to the press:

> We regret the events in which five citizens lost their lives. But the police has strict orders to enforce the Law prohibiting the carrying of arms. It would be anarchy if we allowed armed people to walk freely on our streets, a constant threat to peace and tranquility. I'm not disposed to tolerate this state of disorder. Every citizen has the right to express and defend his political principles, but within the order and serenity which should characterize the actions of every citizen. No one has the right—unless properly authorized—to carry an illegal weapon and to establish a state of

mayhem in the community. I will let it be known that if anyone persists in committing these crimes, there will be war, war without end, not against politicians, but against criminals. Whoever resists arrest by an agent of the public order is a criminal and a savage.[38]

Roughly a week later, Albizu Campos answered Riggs's comments.

> The country will vindicate the killings of its heroes, Pagán, Quiñones, Rodríguez-Vega, and Santiago. The Yankee Chief of police, Colonel Francis Riggs, has declared to the nation that there will be war. The Nationalists recognize his frankness and pick up the glove. There will be war. War against the Yankees![39]

Albizu Campos wasted no time in mobilizing his troops. During the nationalists' funeral on December 8, the Nationalist Party declared the formation of the Ejército Libertador and warned that for every dead nationalist, an American would be killed.[40] Albizu Campos declared that the whole party was now a liberating army and reminded his followers of the "sacred oath" they had taken to defend the fatherland.[41] The next month, the Nationalist Party ordered the general drafting into the military of all nationalists eighteen years old and over as an immediate necessity for "national security." Albizu Campos issued a party resolution "to declare military service compulsory for all members of the party" who would join the nationalist paramilitary force, Cadetes de la República, trained by Albizu Campos and José Enamorado Cuesta since 1932.[42]

The situation appeared to escape the control of the Insular Police, threatening to become a military problem. The creation of paramilitary units gave the impression that Albizu Campos had decided to defy U.S. sovereignty by force, which brought the federal authorities to the island to conduct an investigation of the Nacionalistas and their activities.[43] The Cadetes de la República and the Ejército Libertador, however, were not much of a military challenge. In fact, it seems that the role they would eventually play in Puerto Rican politics stemmed from Albizu Campos's recognition of the political and symbolic value of the military on the island's society.[44] It is apparent that Albizu Campos understood the symbolic and political power of military service and the impact it had on the self-perception of Puerto Ricans. After all, he was himself a World War I veteran.[45]

In an interview published on the weekly *Los Quijotes* on June 11, 1927, Albizu Campos defended volunteering for military service and stated:

> I have always believed that our participation in the European War could had been a great benefit for the people of Puerto Rico. The military organization of a people is necessary for its defense, and that is only attainable through the painful sacrifices imposed by a war. If 30,000 or 40,000 Puerto Ricans had returned from France lamed, one-eyed, or mutilated in any other way, today there would be an organized resistance that would make the American Empire respect us. The European war offered us that splendid opportunity to organize our collective value. For Puerto Rico the armistice was premature, hence recruitment contributed to the demoralization of the people.[46]

Since few Puerto Ricans saw combat during World War I, and no Puerto Rican unit reached Europe, there were few men, if any, with combat experience who could join the Nationalists in an open war against the colony's police and military. As historian Marín Román has noted, Albizu Campos himself never went beyond the initial training for an officer to lead a platoon or command a company. He was trained as an infantry officer, which means that he was instructed in open warfare tactics, and that was a kind of war he could not hope to win against the Insular Police or the National Guard. In sum, his training did not prepare him to organize, train, and lead an army. The Ejército Libertador was too small, undertrained, and poorly equipped to present a serious challenge.[47] Albizu Campos was aware of these facts, but he also understood the symbolic value of the military. In order to fully exploit the symbolic power of the Nacionalistas' paramilitary units, the Ejército Libertador had to be as conspicuous as possible. He decided to call publicly for the creation of the Ejército, to have the Cadetes wear uniforms, to organize them as a regular army, and to have them conduct military exercises and parades in broad daylight and in public spaces.[48] The paramilitary nationalist units sought to appeal to the Puerto Ricans' sense of honor, duty, and manhood and to Puerto Rican identity, which the Nacionalistas identified with the island's Hispanic legacy including the Spanish language and traditional Catholicism.

Albizu Campos was not mistaken in his assessment of the role that the military played in the Americanization process. The 65th played an essential role that extended beyond the remaking of the men who joined the regiment. The 65th provided facilities and training for the Boys Scouts of America in Puerto Rico. The organization counted more than 1,500 Boys Scouts just in San Juan. On some occasions, Nacionalistas had disrupted Boys Scout meetings by throwing rocks at them. They intended to replace the Boys Scouts with the "Cuerpo de Exploradores Puertorriqueños." The 65th also participated in cultural activities such as carnivals while the regimental band provided entertainment in the towns' plazas and on radio shows. Albizu Campos recognized the impact that the 65th Infantry was having on the population and condemned those cultural events as "distraction from the terrorism that prevails through the nation."[49]

Military Intelligence and Subversive Activity

When the FBI set a bureau in San Juan in November 1939, it depended on other services for its intelligence.[50] These included the office of the U.S. Marshalls, the Office of Naval Intelligence, the Commissioner of Immigration, Customs, the Insular Police, and the intelligence section of the Porto Rican Regiment (known as the 65th since 1920), headed by a senior officer known as the "S-2." All of these organizations collected intelligence on "subversive activity" in Puerto Rico. There was little coordination or collaboration among these entities. Foreign agents and citizens, the labor movement, and political parties and their leaders were the main concerns of military intelligence in Puerto Rico.[51] The Insular Police collected its intelligence from its own men, witnesses, and informants. The 65th's S-2 was a continental senior officer while its operatives were Puerto Rican officers and enlisted men from all its units. The S-2 combined its intelligence with that collected from the other agencies to generate weekly and monthly reports. Between 1899 and 1933, the commanding officer of the U.S. Army Forces Intelligence Section in Puerto Rico had also served as chief of the Insular Police. Francis Riggs (1933–36) and his successor, Enrique Orbeta (1936–42), had retired from the military when they served as chiefs of the Insular Police.[52]

As Marín Román argues, the documents of the s-2, even when they failed to understand the idiosyncrasies of the Puerto Ricans, remained highly informative and useful. The s-2 officer had to be critical in his analysis of intelligence and formulation of hypothesis while avoiding unsubstantiated assumptions.[53] While the individuals gathering intelligence and writing these reports may have had biases, we have to assume that they tried to present a picture as accurately as possible. This is not to say that we should take the reports at face value. Like any other historical document, they must be questioned and scrutinized.

According to a U.S. Army report on subversive activity in late January 1936, "units [of the Nationalist Party had] begun to drill in violation of Sections 7–8 Chapter 1 of the Federal Penal Code of 1910."[54] The nationalist units, sometimes armed with machetes, chose to have their own military exercises (drills) across from the Puerto Rico National Guard (PRNG) armories, which apparently unsettled the commanders of such units.[55] That the Nacionalistas attempted to provoke and intimidate the PRNG was apparent. These incidents were also a clear attempt to contest the legitimacy of the Puerto Rico National Guard as a true national corps. Moreover, while the Nacionalistas' drills sent the unequivocal message that they were preparing militarily, which was probably intended to daunt the guardsmen, the fact that they did not carry weapons precluded the Insular Police from stopping their drills, and so they were free to continue harassing the PRNG units.

The Nacionalistas' War Plans

Meanwhile, Albizu Campos was gaining a strong foothold at the University of Puerto Rico. A Puerto Rican captain in the 65th Infantry reported that he had gained the trust of a nationalist student "who informed him that he is a captain in a Nationalist company, part of a battalion of 175 members in Río Piedras," and that they "are raffling a submachine gun amongst them to raise funds to buy more weapons."[56] The report shows two weaknesses inherent to the Nacionalistas. First, evidently it was not such a hard task to infiltrate the organization and to get their members to openly discuss their plans. Second, the fact that they had to raffle weapons to obtain funds in order to secure more weapons indicated the financial weakness of the movement but not of their members. This second point is important because the Nacionalistas had seen their movement grow during times of economic hardship. While pride and a sense of having a mission may for a while content the unemployed and malnourished to the point of even expressing fanatical support for a cause, in the long run, the leaders of such movements have to provide for the well-being of their followers or see their ranks dwindle. The Nacionalistas were not ready to fulfill that role, and it would cost them dearly. While they could attract young middle- and upper-class Puerto Ricans, they did not have the same appeal among the popular sectors.[57]

According to Army intelligence, the Nacionalistas, who boasted of having 10,000 members in the Ejército Libertador, had plans to take over the island.

> The [nationalist] leaders are planning a coup to take place in the no distant future, during which all police stations and National Guard armories, except San Juan and Cayey where the 65th is too strong, will be attacked simultaneously, to gain arms, ammo, and complete control of the island. The Nationalists have made a black list of persons to be killed.[58]

The plan was indeed sensible. The National Guard, a reserve component made of multiple units scattered throughout the island, left its installations with a skeleton crew when they were not conducting exercises. Moreover, even when the PRNG conducted monthly exercises, they did not train in unison, which meant that at any given time there were dozens of targets that could be quickly overrun. Once weaponry was secured from the

PRNG armories, the planned assaults on police stations would have a better chance to succeed. Taking on the 65th, which, as a U.S. Army regular unit, was well trained, armed, and manned to operational levels, was the Nacionalistas' biggest challenge, and apparently they had no plans to do so.

Riggs's Assassination

While uniformed cadets openly challenged the colonial authorities and the PRNG, other Nationalist elements were targeting the Insular Police and Puerto Rican and Continental government officials. Going after individual policemen became a favorite tactic employed by the Nacionalistas. This trend continued until October 1935 when the Nacionalistas set their sights on political leaders from the other parties and valuable targets from the colonial administration.[59] On February 23, 1936, Nationalists Hiram Rosado and Elías Beauchamp killed the chief of the Insular Police, Colonel Riggs, and were in turn executed while in police custody. After Riggs's murder, Ruby Black, a journalist and biographer of Eleanor Roosevelt and a personal friend of Muñoz Marín, wrote to his wife, Muna Lee, that the act had been a stupid crime because Riggs supported independence for Puerto Rico.[60] Riggs's death would have a deep impact on the independence movement.

The Intelligence Section of the 65th reported that roughly 8,000 people attended the funeral of the Nacionalistas held the very next day in Santurce. Albizu Campos, who had sworn to avenge the death of the four nationalists killed by the Insular Police the previous year near the University of Puerto Rico, addressed the crowd gathered at the cemetery late in the afternoon. He declared that the death of the young nationalists had not been in vain because "for every nationalist killed we gain 100 adherents." The intelligence section agreed in principle with Albizu Campos. The report stated that it was "evident that the public sentiment is running high against the Insular Police for the shooting of the nationalists after they had been arrested."[61] Emboldened by the growing support shown to the Nacionalistas, Albizu Campos publicly celebrated the assassination:

> Colonel Riggs, a tyrant, has fallen. Colonel Riggs ordered the murder of our comrades in Río Piedras last October.... On the occasion of their funeral a solemn promise was made. Beauchamp and Rosado have made good their promise. They are dead, but they have done their duty.[62]

He went further and implicated the governor and his superiors with the murders. "General Winship is following higher authorities attempting to kill any nationalist sentiment which may be developing in the people."[63] Local leaders were not exempt from Albizu Campos's threats.[64] He accused the whole directive of the Liberal Party (the other party seeking independence), the local press, and the functionaries of the PRRA of complicity with Winship and Riggs. Ironically, the Liberales, just like the local press, had been extremely sympathetic and accommodating toward Albizu Campos and very supportive of the Nationalists. The Liberal leadership went as far as condemning the political targeting of Nationalist leaders. The Liberals, especially Muñoz Marín, were in fact the only effective opposition to Winship. Muñoz Marín's Independentistas had been so effective in challenging Winship and his predecessor, and in uniting different factions, that military intelligence considered him a bigger threat to the colonial administration than Albizu Campos.[65] Albizu Campos apparently considered that the existence of a party seeking independence by peaceful means, and of an agency bent on alleviating the economic situation on the island (PRRA), would rob him of potential adherents and momentum.

The 65th intelligence section warned that "Colonel Riggs was very popular but indignation against his assassination has been overshadowed by strong popular indignation against the police for what is considered the murder of the young assassins by them."[66] The report concluded by pointing out the weaknesses of the Nacionalistas but warning "that if this party movement is unchecked there will be other assassinations attempted." Furthermore, the intelligence section saw "no danger of general uprising but these young men and their organized companies encouraged and abetted by [Albizu] Campos may attempt such coup against police and National Guard armories."⁶⁷ The officers of the 65th, a mostly Puerto Rican unit tracing its lineage to 1899, evidently believed they would enjoy the support of the population and emerge victorious from a faceoff with the Nacionalistas. The report highlighted police brutality as one of the main causes behind the Puerto Rican public's support of the nationalists. The warning fell on deaf ears, and the violence would continue to escalate.

The United States and its colonial authorities responded to the Nationalist challenge by misusing the legal system to prosecute the Nationalist leaders and by threatening the island with independence. The FBI joined the surveillance of the Nacionalistas. U.S. Marshalls and Insular Police carried out raids in March and found military equipment, weapons, and a bomb in the Nationalists' possession. On March 5, 1936, Albizu Campos and other seven Nationalist leaders were arrested and charged with sedition and conspiracy to overthrow the U.S. government.⁶⁸ The next month, a federal grand jury submitted accusations against Albizu Campos and other leaders of the party.⁶⁹ Local newspapers and politicians, as well as the American Civil Liberties Union were against trying the Nationalist leader for sedition instead of murder or conspiracy to commit murder. Albizu Campos's defense argued that it was preposterous to try him for sedition when Congress was in the process of preparing an independence bill for the island.⁷⁰ The federal government, however, had had enough of the Nacionalistas and sought to strengthen its authority on the island by trying and convicting Albizu Campos in a federal court. The s-2 reported that the Nationalists claimed that they could muster 15,000 men and were confident that the federal government would not find a jury brave enough to declare the Junta Nacionalista guilty. If they did, the Nacionalistas would execute all the members of the jury within a week. During the trials, soldiers from the 65th's intelligence section dressed as civilians to support the police. Fearing that a nationalist commando might liberate the Nacionalistas under trial, Marshall Donald A. Daughan tried twice to put the Junta Nacionalista in the Army's custody, but the Army refused him.⁷¹ A predominantly Puerto Rican jury did not convict the defendants. Albizu Campos's standing among Puerto Ricans had reached its zenith. On July 31, a second trial, with a jury composed of ten continentals and two Puerto Ricans, concluded with a guilty verdict.[72] Albizu Campos and Luis Velazquez were sentenced to seven years in the Atlanta federal penitentiary.

A Punitive Bill of Independence

A month after the Riggs assassination, Senator Millard Tydings, a Democrat from Maryland, introduced a bill to grant independence to Puerto Rico. The bill had been drafted by the Department of the Interior, and Secretary Ickes picked Senator Tydings to introduce it.[73] Tydings presided over the Senate branch of the Committee of Territories and Insular Affairs and, as a close friend of Colonel Riggs, was enraged by his assassination. If Riggs's death was not enough to move Tydings to introduce the punitive independence bill, his racial beliefs undoubtedly drove him to propose such a measure. As the coauthor of the Tydings-McDuffie bill of 1934 to grant independence to the Philippines, he had declared that the Filipinos were a "burden for the federal budget and a menace to the racial composition of the United States."[74] According to the bill introduced by Tydings, Puerto Rico would obtain its independence in four years at the end of which full economic tariffs would be established between the two countries. Moreover, if Puerto Rico voted for independence, all federal aid would cease immediately, and the transitional government would assume responsibility for the defense of the island. As the island's economic relief and reconstruction had come to rely on the federal monies channeled through the PRRA, the passing of such a bill meant economic ruin for Puerto Rico.

President Roosevelt, Secretary of the Interior Ickes, and Secretary of the Division of Territories Gruening gave lip service to the Tydings bill. In fact, they did not consider granting independence to the island as a real option. The president secretly gave his support to the Tydings bill because the harsh measures that were included in it guaranteed that it would be rejected, not only by most Puerto Rican politicians but by the masses, resulting in a de facto popular vote to preserve the colony intact. This strategy was designed to enhance the image of the United States in Latin America and to shield Roosevelt's administration from accusations of imperialism. In that regard, Secretary Ickes declared to the *New York Times* that the administration would give sympathetic considerations to any "political demand which is responsibly backed by a majority of the people of Puerto Rico."[75] In other words, the responsibility for moving toward independence was put, falsely, on the Puerto Ricans. Knowing that the bill would not pass in Congress, and that if for some reason it did, it would be rejected by the Puerto Ricans, Ickes reasoned that introducing the bill in Congress would have a quieting effect among separatist elements in Puerto Rico.

Gruening, who had been a close friend of Muñoz Marín, felt even more aggravated by Muñoz Marín's reluctance to condemn Riggs's assassination than by the act itself. In fact he believed Muñoz Marín had stabbed him in the back by refusing to publicly condemn Riggs's assassination. Muñoz Marín, on the other hand, thought that Gruening was in essence asking him to blame all Puerto Ricans for the assassination while keeping quiet on the matter of Rosado and Beauchamp's execution while in police custody. When Muñoz Marín finally condemned the assassination of Riggs and Beauchamp and Rosado's execution, Gruening had already decided to wage war on Muñoz Marín and the Liberales. Gruening, a former opponent of Winship, quickly turned into the governor's ally. He hit where it hurt Muñoz Marín the most, with a purge of Liberal elements from the PRRA.[76] According to a continental PRRA employee, the purge created a sense of fear and killed the agency's dynamism. Furthermore, with Muñoz Marín out of political favor, the PRRA became ineffective. After all, to Puerto Ricans, even to his detractors, "Muñoz was the PRRA."[77]

The Tydings bill had the desired outcome of arresting the independence spirit among many Liberal leaders.[78] Muñoz Marín thought that the intention was to "obtain from the people of Puerto Rico under duress a mandate for a continuation of the colonial system." The bill divided the Liberal Party by causing a schism between Muñoz Marín and Barceló. Muñoz Marín believed that participating in the elections of November 1936 would be fatal for the Liberales, who would lose the elections because they would be identified with an independence that meant economic ruin. He reasoned that abstaining from the elections of 1936 would give the Liberales time to regroup and to secure economic guarantees that would make independence viable and thus more attractive to Puerto Ricans. His plan was to participate in the elections of 1940 from a position of strength.[79] Barceló, however, did not share Muñoz Marín's convictions and led the party during the campaign for the November elections. Although he did not run for office, Muñoz Marín campaigned strenuously for the Liberales. Barceló, showing how disconnected he was from the socioeconomic maladies afflicting the island's population, declared that he would welcome independence "even if we starve to death."[80] Such declarations did little to persuade the already starving peasantry and urban workers to vote for the Liberales.

Soon after the defeat of the Liberales in the general elections of 1936, Barceló issued an ultimatum to Muñoz Marín, urging him either to follow the party's policies or to form his own party.[81] After failed attempts at reconciliation, on March 31, 1937, Muñoz Marín and his followers were expelled from the party. He and close to 40 percent of the former Liberales founded the Popular Democratic Party (Partido Popular Democrático, PPD) on July 22, 1938. An object of derision after its creation, the PPD would become an important force in Puerto Rican history. Before Muñoz Marín and the Populares emerged as the dominant force in Puerto Rican politics, relations between the island and the United States would deteriorate even further.

The Ponce Massacre

Incarcerating Albizu Campos did little to silence the Nationalists. In fact, political violence increased after his capture. On October 25, 1936, a group of nationalists wounded the Socialist leader Iglesias Pantín during a rally in Mayagüez. In November, a nationalist mob attacked a political meeting held by the Liberales because the latter were using the Puerto Rican flag. Such acts, and the introduction of the Tydings bill, had started to dissipate popular sympathy for the Nacionalistas, and many Nationalists leaders began to leave the party disgusted with the violent campaign.[82] These events, however, paled in comparison with the colonial administration response to the nationalist challenge.

On March 21, 1937, the Insular Police opened fire on a group of unarmed Nacionalistas parading in the southern town of Ponce. Originally the Nacionalistas had been denied permission to hold the parade. The mayor of Ponce, José Tormos Diego, later approved the event as a "civic parade" with the Nacionalistas' promise that the event would not have a military character. The new chief of the Insular Police, Col. Enrique Orbeta, rushed to Ponce under Winship's orders and urged the mayor to revoke the permit. Orbeta and Tormos notified the Nacionalistas and warned them not to proceed with the march. Roughly eighty cadets in black shirts followed by the Daughters of the Republic and the Nationalist Nurses prepared to march. Police Capt. Guillermo Soldevilla, leading a contingent of more than 150 policemen armed with rifles, carbines, and submachine guns, ordered the Nacionalistas to stop as they initiated the march. A single shot was heard followed by a police barrage. When the shooting was over, seventeen Nacionalistas and spectators had been killed and roughly one hundred lay wounded. Two policemen also died from bullet wounds.[83] The slaughter of the unarmed Nacionalistas, which came to be known as the Ponce Massacre, led to widespread discontent if not open hostility toward the police and Governor Winship. The massacre did little to weaken the Nacionalistas. In fact, it won them more sympathizers. *El Mundo* reported that more than 15,000 people attended the funeral in Ponce and roughly 5,000 in Mayagüez.[84] The American Civil Liberties Union concluded that the event had been a massacre.[85]

Local newspapers published full-page photos of the massacre on a daily basis. *El Imparcial* offered a $25 prize to the person making the best analysis of the shooting and providing "the best evidence of the first shot." The 65th intelligence section complained that *El Imparcial* "will not publish any theories blaming the nationalists."[86] Such theories may have been hard to find. Even members of the National Guard were openly critical of the Insular Police. Asked by a reporter, Lt. Col. Miguel A. Muñoz

(PRNG) criticized police tactics such as encircling the crowd and failing to provide an avenue of escape to the Nationalists. In what eventually emerged as the most accepted explanation, he stated that the wounded and dead policemen (the prosecution's evidence that the Nacionalistas initiated the shooting) had probably been hit by friendly fire. Colonel Muñoz was not an anti-metropolis pundit. In fact, he had served the colonial administration in several positions including that of assistant attorney general. There was no evidence at all to put into question the loyalty of this former commander of the American Legion in Puerto Rico and vice commander of the National American Legion. Nonetheless, the 65th intelligence officers stated that his analysis of the Ponce Massacre was "unbecoming of an officer of the guard" and believed that "he [would] be forced to resign" by Winship.[87] Winship was so determined to eliminate the Nacionalista threat that he would not tolerate the mildest dissent or opposition.

Under Winship, the decapitation of the Nationalist leadership and the silencing of the opposition continued unabated.[88] On April 16, the anniversary of the birth of Puerto Rican politician and poet José de Diego, who tirelessly fought for independence, the atmosphere was undeniably tense. For the last few years the Nacionalistas had been holding a mass and a rally near de Diego's tomb. Winship was so determined to deny the Nacionalistas any opportunity to celebrate de Diego's birthday that he put regular army units and the National Guard on alert. Across the island, the Insular Police impeded groups larger than two persons from entering the cemeteries to present flowers to the "Puerto Rican patriots."[89]

The Nacionalistas, however, promptly wasted any sympathy obtained after the Ponce Massacre by perpetrating a series of attacks on judges and even the governor. On July 25, 1938, Winship sponsored the celebration of the fortieth anniversary of the U.S. military invasion of Puerto Rico. This yearly celebration was usually held in San Juan or Guánica, the place of the original U.S. landings. In what could only be seen as a show of force and calculated provocation, Winship decided to hold the celebration in Ponce, roughly a year after the massacre of the unarmed nationalists. More than 50,000 people congregated to watch the parade and to listen to Winship's speech. A battalion of the 65th Infantry was marching past Winship and the parade's guests of honor when at least five Nacionalista shooters opened fire. Ángel Esteban Antongiorgi fired more than ten shots directly at Winship, who remained undisturbed as the rest of his entourage ducked for cover.[90] A detective shot and killed Antongiorgi. The commander of the 296th Regiment of the Puerto Rico National Guard, Col. Luis A. Irizarry, a well-known and respected Puerto Rican officer, died in the shooting which also left thirty-two wounded. Once order was reestablished, Winship delivered his speech as planned. Colonel Irizarry's death provoked a wave of public outrage against the Nacionalistas. On September 28, several Nacionalistas were convicted in connection with the attempt against Winship, further debilitating the party's leadership.[91] The fallout of the shooting was even more troublesome. Any chances of persuading Roosevelt to remove Winship, a priority for Secretary Ickes and whom Muñoz Marín had continued to attack from *La Democracia*, dissipated after the attack.[92]

Police brutality had gained the Nacionalistas much support on the island. However, they apparently did not understand that the islanders' sympathy was also a repudiation of violence. The events of July 1938 eroded the support they had amassed. The press, insular, and continental politicians were quick to point out that the blood spilled that day was Puerto Rican blood, and that fact undermined the Nacionalistas. Even the remaining official leadership of the Nacionalista Party sought to distance itself from the incident. Rafael Medina Ramírez, speaker of the Nacionalista Party on the island, condemned "anarchical" acts even if planned with "good faith" and "conducted patriotically and heroically" because they only provided an excuse to the colonial administration to implement the "most barbaric of official terrorisms."[93] The Nacionalista leaders' statements evidenced the breaking of communications between the political arm of the party and its armed wing and a growing schism between Albizu Campos and moderate elements in the Nationalist Party. As the party's leadership crumbled, the ranks of the Nacionalistas petered out. Even more disheartening for the Nacionalista leaders was that whenever opportunities arose to obtain a job, even if it meant working for the colonial administration or for the U.S. armed forces, party members quickly applied for such jobs.[94]

Shortly after the failed attempt to assassinate Winship, political violence subsided. Winship's persecution of the Nacionalistas, which succeeded in incarcerating the most militant wing of the party, had much to do with decreasing violence. Many remaining militants went underground to avoid arrest. Scores of Nacionalista leaders disenchanted with Albizu Campos's radical tactics switched allegiance, mostly joining the Populares or the Independentistas. However, the main reason for the abating violence was the Nacionalistas' failure to mobilize a considerable segment of the population, especially the urban and rural working classes, to continue engaging the colonial authorities.

A Weakened Independence Movement

The Nacionalistas' failure to win the support of a sizable portion of the population was also a rejection of their iconography and emphasis on Spanish traditions. After all, most Puerto Ricans had been born under U.S. sovereignty, and those lucky enough to have been educated had been exposed to a curriculum based on the New England public school model. In other words, the nostalgic discovery of the "Hispanic" past was an alien concept to the Puerto Rican popular sectors of the 1930s, except for the elites who still traced their lineage to the peninsula. Moreover, for all means and purposes, the Nacionalista "rediscovery" of the island's Hispanic past was incongruent with the drive toward progress and a modern Puerto Rico. Both progress and modernization, and hints at industrialization, were at the core of the PRRA's effort to improve Puerto Rico's socioeconomic condition. Many Continental and Puerto Rican politicians had accepted the PRRA's plan as a solution for the island's maladies. The Nacionalistas could not compete with the metropolis's material superiority and its implied promise of a better future. Hence the combination of violent acts, the lack of an alternative path forward, the disconnection with the popular sectors' socioeconomic realities, and the emphasis on Spanish tradition were as responsible for the Nacionalistas' demise as was political persecution.

As the island descended into a shooting war between the police and the Nacionalistas, the police ranks swelled. The National Guard also expanded during this period, although the expansion had little to do with the Nacionalista challenge. Nonetheless, it is very telling that whenever volunteers were requested for the National Guard or the 65th Infantry, the Puerto Ricans, even Nacionalistas, quickly moved to fill those positions.[95] While the Insular Police stained their record and lost much credence in their battle against the Nacionalistas, the National Guard and the regular U.S. Army on the island stayed out of the fray, at least in the public's eye. The U.S. military in Puerto Rico had always functioned as a possible avenue of socioeconomic advancement, which appealed to a large segment of the island's population. Its prestige remained unblemished by this period's violence. That the Puerto Rican military units were not involved in the brutal repression of their fellow countrymen would ease the conscience of tens of thousands of Puerto Ricans who would soon join the armed forces of the metropolis. Albizu Campos had challenged the Insular Police and the legitimacy of the armed forces on the island as true national corps and had lost the duel.

Albizu Campos was not the only one losing in this battle. The independence movement was seriously weakened by the Nacionalistas' radicalism. Locally the separatist leadership was balkanized, and popular support for independence seriously waned due to the endless cycle of violence. Outside the island such violence worked as a self-fulfilling stereotype. If there ever was any doubt in the minds of Continental politicians that Puerto Rico would descend into chaos if it became independent, there was the proof. The independence movement would never fully recuperate from this blow. To add to the island's calamities, the split of the Liberal Party and Muñoz Marín's fall from Washington's grace hindered the progress of the socioeconomic reconstruction effort led by the PRRA. In a sense, those who could afford to lose the least lost more than anybody else.[96]

The Resurrection of Luis Muñoz Marín

Ruby Black sent Muñoz Marín a letter on July 3, 1936, that helps to explain the latter's attitude toward independence, which he thought could only be attained through peaceful means and without creating an adversarial relationship with the United States. Black wrote that peaceful negotiations were the only way toward independence because of the military and industrial might of the United States; because the American national pride required it; and because the U.S. government would never recognize as legitimate any independence movement that did not adhere to the rule of law that turned to violence or even pacific insurgency.[97]

Further, Muñoz Marín understood that the islanders' indignation was a rejection of all types of political violence. He had condemned Riggs's assassination and the subsequent execution of Beauchamp and Rosado by the Insular Police in 1936, as well as the Ponce Massacre of 1937. This stand gained him the antipathy of Tydings and Winship and of many other metropolitan administrators. It also cost him his friendship with Ernest Gruening. Muñoz Marin's political career almost ended after 1936 as a consequence of Riggs's assassination and the Tydings bill. Unfettered, Muñoz Marín immediately condemned Irizarry's assassination, but he also denounced what he considered to be the root of the incident. He declared:

> We emphatically condemned and repudiate violence, as well as when it comes from the government as when it comes from individuals. Our opposition to violence—as an evil itself, and as a danger to our people's future democracy and freedom—is so strong and unequivocal that we condemn it even in cases when the most extreme provocation may seem to justify it.[98]

Muñoz Marín was slowly emerging as a better option to the seemingly endless cycle of violence between the Nacionalistas and the Insular Police. He skillfully denounced the Winship administration for provoking the incident while also condemning the nationalists. His attempts to appear fair and balanced endeared him with the Puerto Ricans, and while his actions may have irked colonial administrators and continental politicians, he presented the metropolis with a more palatable alternative to political violence. Furthermore, although at the time he did not hold any official position, Muñoz Marín had been associated by the public with both the PRERA and PRRA. Thus Muñoz Marín presented himself as fair-minded leader apparently in touch with the socioeconomic problems of the island while campaigning to end the colonial relation. He would eventually rise to power with a popular mandate to tackle the first issue and with the personal conviction of advancing the latter. These two concerns eventually would become the pillars of his new party's platform.

Whereas Muñoz Marín had initially amassed political power riding on his father's brand-name and thanks to his position as a Washington insider, his comeback to the political center stage was to be fueled by hundreds of thousands of votes coming from the Puerto Rican rural and urban workers. Very early Muñoz Marín and the Populares focused their campaign on appealing to the peasantry and in securing the support of the organized labor sector.[99] The young professional classes on the island would desert traditional parties and join his new party to try and lead the island out of its economic malaise, but it would be popular support that gave Muñoz Marín and the Populares the political strength to demand from Washington the needed economic reforms and the decolonization of the island.

The high point of Muñoz Marín's political trajectory lay ahead. In great measure his rapid ascendance was facilitated by the outbreak of war in Europe on September 1, 1939. But that he emerged as the most prominent leader in Puerto Rico during the war years was also the result of the political chaos prevailing on the island before the outbreak of the war. The shooting war between the Nacionalistas and the Insular Police was detrimental to Roosevelt's Good Neighbor policy and forced Congress and the president to take a more pronounced interest in the political and socioeconomic conditions of the island. It was necessary to complement the Good Neighbor policy with a domestic corollary for Puerto Rico, which was after all a Caribbean and Latin American nation. This newfound interest in Puerto Rican politics and socioeconomic matters helped to bring Muñoz Marín to the insular political scene with strength that he did not enjoy before and that he probably would have not held if Roosevelt had not found it suitable to improve the relations between the United States and Puerto Rico.

During World War II, Muñoz Marín would use the military-diplomatic value of the island to advance the decolonization project while extracting every possible economic concession with the intention of fixing socioeconomic problems and readying Puerto Rico and the Puerto Ricans for eventual independence. The Puerto Ricans, and especially the jíbaros, were about to be mobilized both politically and militarily on a scale and fashion never seen before. During the war years, the island would undauntedly start its movement toward industrialization as a way to a modern Puerto Rico and toward decolonization. The peasants and urban workers turned soldiers would spearhead the effort.

5

Education, Industrialization, and Decolonization

The Battlefields of World War II

> After two years, the War Department has given Puerto Rican Americans the same opportunities as any other American, to enter the United States Army and fight for the nation as well as to obtain such benefits as could certainly be of advantage to the underpaid, inadequately educated Puerto Rican, who has little opportunity to improve himself. Puerto Ricans, it is stated, will now be able to enter the army and have their lots improved learning trades that will not enable them to help win victory, but will afford them a means to a better livelihood after the war, thus benefiting themselves and raising the standards of their communities and of Puerto Rico.
> —Editorial, *Puerto Rico World Journal*[1]

With the end of the Second World War in sight, U.S. congressmen discussing a bill to make the office of the governor of Puerto Rico subject to election could not help but wonder what impact this measure would have on helping to modernize and democratize the island. Puerto Rican and continental Americans residing on the island testified before Congress that through their willingness to support and participate in the war effort, the Puerto Ricans, especially the tens of thousands who joined the U.S. military, had shown they could be trusted to carry out both tasks.[2] Congressmen were notably worried about the possibility that the returning soldiers might cause unrest on the island if reemployment opportunities were not readily available. Those testifying on the matter were quick to stress the need to create economic opportunities, but they also pointed out that political development was necessary and ultimately linked to the returning Puerto Rican soldiers and the peaceful decolonization of the island.³ Echoing the island's press, Elmer Ellsworth, a continental American and insular senator, stated: "The GI Bill will help them [the Puerto Rican veterans] in the creation of a better Puerto Rico."⁴ That better Puerto Rico, however, had to offer more than economic opportunities. A congressman asked: "Will the [1944 governor] bill alleviate tensions in Puerto Rico and ease the comeback of Puerto Rican soldiers?" Jesús T. Piñero, a leader of the Popular Democratic Party, promptly answered: "That is the urgency of the bill, so the boys feel that some steps have been taken in the right direction."⁵

World War II was a catalyst for socioeconomic and political change in Puerto Rico. With the exception of Franklin Delano Roosevelt's decision to transfer the island from the War Department to the Interior Department on March 1934, no major changes to Puerto Rico's political relationship with the metropolis had occurred since 1917, when Congress imposed U.S. citizenship on the Puerto Ricans and created an elective insular legislature through the Jones Act.⁶ War yet again highlighted the strategic importance of the island and provided for faster negotiation between the metropolis and the colony. The years preceding the U.S. entrance into World War II were marked by economic distress and political instability in Puerto Rico. In fact, a shooting war between the Nacionalistas and the militarized Puerto Rican police briefly threatened to become a full military affair. By 1939, however, the colonial administration had gained the upper hand over the Nacionalistas. Puerto Rico did not become the dreaded "Ireland of the Caribbean."⁷ Still, the political violence that reigned in Puerto Rico in the 1930s forced the federal government to take a closer look at the island's socioeconomic and political situation. The winds of war, even before the juggernaut of the German and Japanese militaries became apparent and the United States slowly started to ready itself for war, made continental politicians more open to finding solutions to the island's plight and to avoiding a repetition of the 1930s. Thus war brought the promise of political and economic advancement by rekindling Puerto Rico's strategic value. Once more the Puerto

Ricans were called to arms and responded with overwhelming enthusiasm. Different projects of decolonization and modernization, which included the revitalization of the economy and the Puerto Ricans' regeneration through military service, rested on the roles these soldiers were about to play.

Politicians and opinion makers sought to advance projects through military collaboration and participation. The United States first tried to secure stability and the loyalty of the Puerto Ricans by bringing measures of relief via federal projects and then by allowing their mass entry into the military. The idea of Americanization and modernization through military service and public education made a strong comeback as war engulfed Europe. Concurrently, the United States became more inclined to grant a higher degree of self-government to Puerto Rico, since it would serve to support FDR's narrative of a war fought for freedom while also serving to quench political unrest on the island.

Federal plans, however, had to compete with those of local politicians. Aware of Puerto Rico's military and diplomatic relevance, Luis Muñoz Marín, leading the Popular Democratic Party, followed a strategy that supported the war effort, linked the Allies' narratives of a war fought for the preservation of democracy and freedom to the Populares' own programs, and made the socioeconomic restructuring of the island a priority while using the participation of Puerto Rican soldiers in the war and the island's strategic position as leverage to extract political concessions. Historian Jorge Rodríguez Beruff has recently discussed how U.S. military strategy dominated White House policy-making toward the island even before the outbreak of World War II in Europe. Moreover, he has shown that Muñoz Marín supported FDR's domestic and foreign policies and equated them to the Populares' reformist agenda.[8] Further, as the war was coming to an end, Muñoz Marín and the Populares tried to secure veterans' benefits so these men and women could attempt to change the dire socioeconomic condition of the island. Muñoz Marín's strategy was threefold: supporting the war effort and avoiding the status issue to regain Washington's trust; using the participation of Puerto Rican soldiers in the war and the island's strategic position to barter political concessions; and using the soldiers' benefits and training to advance the socioeconomic restructuration of the island.

Betting on the returning soldiers to lead the march to a modern industrial Puerto Rico and as a key to further the decolonization project was but the logical extension of the role played by the military during the war. Historian José L. Bolívar Fresneda has demonstrated that during the period 1939–48 instead of state or national capitalism—as most of the historiography on the period argues—a military economy dominated the island and served as a transitional phase between agrarian and industrial Puerto Rico. He has shown that military expenditures on the island (in particular funds assigned to the construction of military installations) and repatriated rum excise taxes saved Muñoz Marín and the Populares during the critical years of 1942–44 and were responsible for the creation of the infrastructure needed to industrialize Puerto Rico in the postwar years. It also created a pool of more than 50,000 men who trained and worked on modern construction and building industries for the first time. They would prove essential during the industrialization phase.[9]

The military economy created the right conditions for social change, economic development, and political progress.[10] But the key to postwar development was the mass military mobilization of Puerto Ricans, and it would prove essential to the Populares' reconstruction and decolonization plans. The role of the soldiers went beyond offering economic relief and the promise of future development. When Muñoz Marín called the Puerto Ricans to arms, he did not appeal to their sense of duty as "Americans' or "U.S. citizens," as was the case during World War I.[11] Instead he appealed to the virility of the Puerto Rican men who would join with others, including the United States, to defend their rights and freedoms. As Rodríguez Beruff has argued, Muñoz Marín saw war as emancipatory. In similar fashion to how Pedro Albizu Campos and countless champions of independence had perceived war, he saw the people of Puerto Rico as valiant and combat as an opportunity to face hardships that would strengthen their virility.[12] Thus the Puerto Rican peasants and agrarian workers turned soldier were expected to bring more than economic respite or technical knowledge. These soldiers were also supposed to erase a colonial inferiority complex by showing that they could bear the same burden as any other man.

This chapter analyzes two very different projects. On the one hand, the metropolis sought to show Puerto Ricans that they were regarded as American as any continental, which would generate loyalty to the metropolis and simultaneously enhance the United States' image as emerging leader of the free world. On the other hand, the dominant political leader during this period tried to use military participation to advance the decolonization of the island by obtaining concessions from the metropolis and by turning the experience of these soldiers into a lesson on self-confidence and manhood, and in more practical terms by using their veterans' benefits and skills learned in the military to reconstruct the island and its socioeconomic structures. These political projects were not impervious to the needs of the masses being mobilized to carry them out. Actually, both the metropolis's and the Populares' projects were influenced, if not outright changed, by the sudden enfranchisement of tens of thousands of peasants and urban workers. This enfranchisement was in part possible due to military mobilization. Thus the military mobilization of the Puerto Rican had a political, socioeconomic, and very popular character.

The First Populares Campaign

War in Europe seemed imminent by 1938, while Japan continued its inexorable march in China. The American public, however, was not prepared to support involvement in a European war, nor were the armed forces ready to participate. If the Good Neighbor policy had put Puerto Rico's problems in the sight of FDR's administration in the early 1930s, the impending war and the reluctance of the American public to consider participating in it moved the island to the center stage of U.S. preparedness and defense efforts.[13] FDR's administration decided to base its military strategy on the concept of hemispheric defense.[14] The United States would stay out of the war and concentrate on strengthening the defenses of the Western Hemisphere to stop any assault on the Americas far from the mainland. Puerto Rico was to play a vital role in this strategy. For decades, the island had been crucial to the defense of the Panama Canal. This time, however, its importance went beyond protecting the canal. This design was an extension of Alfred T. Mahan's strategy for the defense of the American empire. The U.S. Navy planned to stop naval aggression far from the mainland in what it called the Caribbean Sea Frontier. The waters surrounding Culebra, a Puerto Rican municipality lying off the east coast, would be the stage for such a battle.[15] Puerto Rico effectively became the center of the hemispheric defense strategy and the first American line of defense against German or Japanese aggression.

The importance of Puerto Rico in the defensive plans of the United States is best expressed in a presidential letter to Congress dated September 28, 1943:

> When the present war became imminent, however, it was obvious that the chain of islands stretching in a great arc from Florida to the shoulder of South America, enclosing the Caribbean Sea, formed a vast natural shield for the Panama Canal, suited in distance and conformation to the use of the military plane. And of the island shield Puerto Rico is the center. Its possession or control by any foreign power—or even the remote threat of such possession—would be repugnant to the most elementary principle of national defense.[16]

The fortification of the island became a priority, and by 1939 the construction of multiple army, naval, and air bases was well on its way.[17] The Roosevelt administration, however, was concerned about the possibility of American troops finding themselves without the support of the island's population, which in case of an invasion might mean that these bases would become nothing more than isolated outposts. Consequently, the administration sought to improve relations between Puerto Rico and the United States, which had deteriorated to an unprecedented low due to the events of 1936, the Ponce Massacre of March 21, 1937, and the continuation of the shooting war between the Insular Police and the Nacionalistas.[18] The first positive step taken by FDR was the removal of the unpopular Governor Blanton Winship. Roosevelt replaced him with Adm. William D. Leahy, the highest-ranking U.S. naval officer, who took charge of that office on September 11, 1939. Leahy was entrusted with supervising plans for military expansion in Puerto Rico and the Caribbean and with advancing military coordination with South American countries.[19] Of equal relevance was his mission to promote social and political stability in Puerto Rico, which the administration considered essential to its defense plans. Urged by Muñoz Marín, Leahy worked to prevent fraud in the general elections of 1940, the first in which the Populares would participate.[20]

The Popular Party was weak after its creation in 1938. Most analysts and political rivals dismissed Muñoz Marín's intention of participating in the elections as a Quixotic if not an outright act of foolishness. However, by 1940 the political picture in Puerto Rico seemed to favor the rise of the Populares. Albizu Campos was still a federal prisoner in Atlanta, and movement had been seriously weakened. The Nacionalistas remained dormant in 1939 and 1940.[21] Meanwhile, the dominant traditional parties faced a series of setbacks. Barceló, the Liberal leader, and Iglesias Pantín, the Socialist leader, died in 1938 and 1939, respectively.[22] After Barceló's death, the new president of the Liberales decided to make statehood the political goal of the party, and most Autonomistas and Independentistas abandoned the PLP to join the Populares. Unión Republicana's leader, Martínez Nadal, was absent from most of the campaign as he fought against cancer, finally succumbing in 1941. To make matters worse for the annexationists, García Méndez left the party and formed the Partido Unión Republicana Progresista months before the election. Unión Republicana honored the pact with the Socialistas and continued the Coalición while Unión Republicana Progresista and the Partido Laborista Puro, which splintered from the Socialistas, joined what was left of the Liberales to create Unificación Puertorriqueña Tripartita.[23] This incessant splintering and confusing net of tactical alliances further weakened the traditional parties. The nature of their alliances also showed that their priority was political survival, not addressing the socioeconomic problems of the island.

While campaigning for the 1940 general elections, Muñoz Marín spoke of alleviating the socioeconomic problems of the island. The insignia of the PPD, a *pava* (the traditional hat of the Puerto Rican jíbaro) and the slogan "*Pan, Tierra, Libertad*" (bread, land, freedom) proclaimed the priorities of the Populares. Claiming that the rural masses distrusted him because of his association with independence, Muñoz Marín announced in a meeting in San Juan that "el status no está en issue."[24] Resolving the political status of the island was not to be his party's immediate goal. This position was resented by the Popular Party's *independentista* wing. The outbreak of World War II in Europe a year before the elections helped Muñoz Marín convince the most pro-independence elements in his party that it was not the right time to fight for independence. Muñoz Marín was thus able to keep the masses' support and avoid a schism in his new party. At any rate, due to his connections with White House insiders, he knew as early as 1938 that Washington was not to grant independence to the island until the world crises had passed. The outbreak of war in Europe in 1939 and the strategic relevance of Puerto Rico made it impossible for a political party to share colonial power without expressing its loyalty to the United States' goals, and independence became even more unlikely.[25]

Muñoz Marín wasted no time in linking his campaign to the war effort and to FDR's domestic programs. Not only would the status question be put on hold for the duration of the conflict, but the Populares committed themselves to supporting the hemispheric defense plans and the war effort. Recognizing the change in Roosevelt's attitude toward Puerto Rico, as well as the cause for such change, the renewed military importance of the island, Muñoz Marín would use the latter to promote social and economic development, which he thought essential in advancing the decolonization of the island.[26] The mass political mobilization of the jíbaros and urban working masses had started, but not as imagined by Albizu Campos, who remained in jail. Tactical decisions, however, tend to alter broader strategic views and goals.

Muñoz Marín may have temporarily adopted the jíbaros' point of view with regard to independence in order to win the political battle, but what he had learned from them during the 1936 and 1940 campaigns had started to erode his own *independentismo*.[27]

With the votes of hundreds of thousands of peasants, jíbaros, and urban workers, Muñoz Marín and the Populares surprised the coalition of Socialistas and Republicanos, as well as the Unión Tripartita of Liberales, Progresistas, and Laboristas Puros by obtaining a pyrrhic victory.[28] FDR publicly congratulated Muñoz Marín, who became president of the Puerto Rican senate, and offered his full support for his project of "social justice and economic rehabilitation."[29] This was a significant change. Years after serving as governor of Puerto Rico, Rexford Tugwell wrote that Muñoz Marín's support for the Nationalists in the 1930s had "succeeded in alienating both Secretary Ickes and President Roosevelt" and that FDR distrusted Muñoz Marín, whom he considered a Nationalist. Distrust of Muñoz Marín was also the product of the imperialist side of Roosevelt, "the navy man," who could not support autonomy wholeheartedly because "he just never thought that Puerto Ricans were the equals of Continental Americans."[30] As Rodríguez Beruff has argued, Muñoz Marín's reconciliation with Washington occurred because of his expressions of support for FDR's domestic and foreign policies, his adherence to social peace and stability in Puerto Rico, his avoidance of the status issue during the war years, and his support for military preparedness.[31] But overall, Muñoz Marín's victory and the Populares' ability to build upon it left FDR with few other options. Once in power, Muñoz Marín and the Populares sought to control the socioeconomic reconstruction effort on the island while carefully moving forward the process of political decolonization.

A New Deal for Puerto Rico

In many respects, Muñoz Marín benefited from FDR's concerns regarding the island. World War II was responsible for bringing the New Deal to Puerto Rico. Roosevelt took a significant step by naming Rexford G. Tugwell as governor of the island in August 1941. Governor Leahy had secured clean elections in

1940 and started Roosevelt's plans to make Puerto Rico an island fortress with a friendly population, but Tugwell would lead the island during the war.[32]

Tugwell was more a scholar than a politician and had become one of the foremost champions of the New Deal as well as one of its leading ideologues. His appointment as governor could only mean that FDR's administration was serious about improving social and economic conditions on the island. The president told Tugwell that his first duty as a representative of the United States in Puerto Rico was to "shape civil affairs . . . so military bases, which might soon have to stand the shock of attack, were not isolated in a generally hostile environment."[33] Moreover, Roosevelt and Secretary of the Interior Harold Ickes had made it clear that sending such a prominent New Dealer like Tugwell to Puerto Rico would help to undermine the charges of imperialism coming from Latin America since the early 1930s.

Tugwell and Muñoz Marín, though many times at odds, were natural allies. They both believed that a restructuring of the island's economy and society was badly needed. However, Muñoz Marín was still contemplating eventual independence for the island while Tugwell did not believe such status to be practical. In this regard Tugwell thought that liberalization of the political status, granting more autonomy and powers to the island, or even moving toward statehood were the best options for both the Puerto Ricans and the metropolis. In order to push his goal forward, Tugwell used the strategic importance of the island to convince the president and Congress that political change was needed. In a letter to FDR dated March 10, 1942, Tugwell expressed concerns about the loyalty of the population in case of an attack. In this letter Tugwell made clear that both the British and Dutch had lost their possessions in the Pacific to the Japanese because these countries never won the loyalty of the native populations, who saw them as foreign rulers. The United States had to prevent that from happening in Puerto Rico. To guarantee the loyalty of Puerto Ricans in case of an attack, Tugwell recommended that the president ought to support "a new status for Puerto Rico now." Moreover, he wrote that such a gesture would disassociate the United States from "the colonial empires" and could serve to avoid "the risk of a Malaya or Java here [in Puerto Rico]."³⁴

Elected Governor's Bills

The Caribbean Advisory Committee (CAC), a local version of the Caribbean Commission established between Great Britain and the United States in 1942 to study possible collaboration in the Caribbean, recommended to FDR in March 1942 that he should support an amendment to the Organic Act of Puerto Rico, which had remained unchanged in all major respects since 1917. The suggested amendment would make the office of governor an elected one. This measure, the CAC believed, "would in fact have the effect of converting Puerto Rico into a state, except for income tax purposes and for voting representation in Congress." Moreover the letter expressed that such a move would show that the "United States has no ambition to be a colonial power" and that this measure was submitted more "for its general than for its local effect."³⁵ These events followed a unanimous request made on February 10 by the Puerto Rican legislature (Muñoz Marín's initiative) to Congress and the president to allow Puerto Ricans to find a solution to end the colonial regime on the island. The letter did not make reference to the issue of the elective governor, which Muñoz Marín did not fully support as it could block the path to eventual independence.³⁶

FDR did in fact move to support the creation of an elective governor for Puerto Rico. On March 9, 1943, he asked Congress to consider "as soon as possible an amendment of the Organic Law of Puerto Rico to permit the people of the island to elect their own Governor and redefine the functions and power of the Federal government and the government of Puerto Rico." The previous day, Roosevelt had ordered Secretary Ickes to establish a commission of four Puerto Ricans and four Americans to make a study and report on the amendments required to provide for such measures.³⁷ Tugwell and Muñoz Marín were members of this committee, which met in Washington from July 19 through August 7. On September 28, in a special message to Congress on the status of progress in Puerto Rico, Roosevelt urged once more that Congress adopt the recommendations of the committee as a matter of "right and justice for Puerto Ricans."[38] FDR saw "no reason why their [the Puerto Rican's] Governor and other officials should continue to be appointed from without."[39]

In a letter to New Mexico senator Dennis Chavez, chairman of a subcommittee of the Committee on Territories and Insular Affairs, Muñoz Marín expressed his support, although not enthusiastically, for the Governor Bill and added that it was essential to incorporate the necessary provisions so that Congress could not alter the Organic Act unilaterally.[40] To support his demands Muñoz Marín referenced the military participation of Puerto Ricans in the world conflict as well as the ideological icons used by Allied propaganda, particularly democracy, national self-determination, and the principle of the consent of the governed.[41] On February 15, 1944, the bill, with the proposed amendments, was approved by the Senate. It would not reach the House of Representatives until August, when war in Europe appeared, incorrectly, to be nearing its end.

With the bill sent to the House, leaders from the PPD launched yet another campaign to secure the passing of the Governor Bill with the proposed amendments. Jesús T. Piñero declared before the House that doing so was essential for the peaceful decolonization of the island by showing the returning Puerto Rican veterans that "some steps have been taken in the right direction."[42] Elmer Ellsworth, a native of Massachusetts but longtime resident and senator in Puerto Rico (PPD), accused Congress of excessive paternalism and urged the representatives to approve the bill. Ellsworth declared that Puerto Rico should be an example for "all the islands being liberated in the Pacific that they too would be free." Moreover, Ellsworth was quick to point out that approving the bill "will clear the atmosphere throughout all Latin America of accusations of Uncle Sam's merciless exploitation of Puerto Rico."[43] Such strategic considerations as well as the impact that the Governor Bill could have regarding U.S. foreign relations did not escape federal officials. Abe Fortas, undersecretary of the interior, declared during the House hearings that approving "this substantially increased measure of home rule" would be seen as an indication of goodwill being "most beneficial in reaffirming the leadership of the United States in world affairs." Fortas emphasized that "not only will it have that effect upon the people of Latin America but also throughout the world."[44]

The bill died, however, over the issue of denying Congress the right to change the Organic Act without the concurrence of the people of Puerto Rico or their elected representatives. The House would not approve it without eliminating this provision, and Muñoz Marín, disillusioned with the limited nature of the bill, asked Secretary Ickes to let it die. The proposal to allow Puerto Rico to elect its governor failed because of protests from Puerto Rico and indifference from Roosevelt, who did not make an effort to push the bill after his letter to Congress of September 1943.[45] Presidential support was absent when the House convened in August 1944 to discuss the bill approved by the Senate in February. The president's support might have persuaded Congress to grant Muñoz Marín's requests. The war situation, however, had changed by August 1944 on all major fronts. War in Europe appeared to be nearing its end, and Japan did not pose a threat to the Caribbean, the Panama Canal, or the U.S. West Coast any longer. As the military importance of the island declined in comparison with other war theaters, promoting a change of its political status ceased to be a pressing matter for the administration. It was no longer imperative to pass the bill.[46]

Independence Bill of 1943

Muñoz Marín also had to contend with the separatist wing within his own party. The Independentista faction within the PPD urged Senator Millard Tydings to present yet another independence bill, which he did on April 2, 1943. Hearings were held in the Senate the following month.[47] During these hearings, however, the assistant secretary of war, John J. McCloy, made it clear that the military was against the independence of the island because Puerto Rico was "irreplaceable for Caribbean defense" and that its independence "was not in the best interest of the military."[48] Senator Robert A. Taft, a member of the Committee on Territories and Insular Affairs, declared that Puerto Rico was still necessary to secure the military control of the Caribbean.[49] For all purposes, the fate of the 1943 independence bill was sealed with the testimony of McCloy.

The Tydings bill not only lacked support among American officials but also among Puerto Ricans. A letter from Muñoz Marín addressed to Senator Tydings, dated April 29, 1943, reminded Tydings of the resolution approved unanimously by the Puerto Rican legislature on February 10 requesting a referendum to end the colonial regime as soon as the conditions allowed it, and of President Roosevelt's decision to create a committee to work on reforms to the Organic Act. Muñoz Marín stated that he could not support the bill, since doing so might break the delicate equilibrium that had led to the resolution from the Puerto Rican legislature requesting a referendum on the political status.[50] Moreover, the military had made unequivocally clear that it would oppose independence for the island during wartime. Muñoz Marín was well aware of the military's and the administration's position. Not only had his friend and Washington insider Ruby Black informed him as early as 1938 that there would no independence until the international crises were resolved, but war in Europe in 1939 and the strategic relevance of Puerto Rico made it impossible for a political party to share colonial power without a clear signal of loyalty toward the United States.[51] Muñoz Marín's understanding of the geopolitical situation had influenced his decision to campaign under the slogan "El status no está en juego." A vote for the PPD was not a vote for independence.

The Independentistas in the PPD wanted the party to support Tydings's bill openly, but Muñoz Marín believed that this option was the equivalent of political suicide. He was aware that not only the president but most congressmen and the military were opposed to independence during war. At any rate, explaining support for an independence bill to his constituency would have been extremely difficult if not impossible when even the Nacionalistas were remaining dormant and at least paid lip service to supporting the war effort.[52] Muñoz Marín's position with respect to independence was evolving due to local and global realities, and he came to believe that independence had no future under the current situation. As early as 1936, he noted that whenever he spoke to the jíbaros about independence, their response was one of fear and uncertainty. Most of them, he said, were afraid of independence and would not vote for it.[53] Muñoz Marín then ran the first PPD campaign based on social and economic reform and avoiding the status issue. He kept independence as his goal, but he had to secure enough economic guarantees from the United States for the survival of the new republic in order to persuade the jíbaros to vote for independence.

Additionally, the new Tydings bill was only a slightly improved version of the one rejected by most Puerto Rican politicians in 1936. Although the bill provided for a period of twenty years before full trade tariffs were implemented between Puerto Rico and the United States, federal aid to the island was to be cut almost immediately. Moreover, the armed forces let it be known that they would not support any independence bill that would not guarantee the retention of all military installations and their right to appropriate lands for expansion of those bases as needed. In other words, independence under the Tidings bill would mean that the U.S. military, especially the Navy, would control much of the island and that Puerto Rico would not enjoy the benefits of any federal aid or special trade arrangements. This was not independence but a de facto transfer of its sovereignty from Congress to the military, which would not have the responsibilities that Congress had but would enjoy all of its rights and then some more. Lacking support from the military, the State Department, or even from Committee members, and with the backing of only the staunchest Independentistas in Puerto Rico, the bill did not survive for long.

The Military Economy

The new Tydings bill did not offer the economic guarantees or the full sovereignty that Muñoz Marín deemed necessary for independence to be viable.[54] During his first campaign he had asked the popular sectors to let him borrow their vote and to remove him from office, along with the rest of the Populares, if they strayed from their campaign promises of socioeconomic justice or betrayed them by moving toward independence.⁵⁵ To that end and before the famous Operation Bootstrap (*Manos a la Obra*) was launched in 1948, Tugwell and Muñoz Marín embarked in several public-sponsored ventures seeking to promote the industrialization of the island and the creation of industrial jobs and small business.⁵⁶

Muñoz Marín had embraced the New Deal in the 1930s, and it would be no different during the war. He was aware of the massive economic aid brought to the island by the Puerto Rican Reconstruction Administration and the Work Projects Administration. Before the military mobilization of the Puerto Ricans became relevant for island's economy and society, a labor mobilization through federal programs and war preparedness took place. In 1939, FDR requested $1.48 billion for the WPA (at the national level), $10 million for the PRRA, and $68 million for military expenses in Puerto Rico. The WPA spent $43.6 million in Puerto Rico in just four years. The WPA employed 36,552 workers in 1942. These workers earned between $19 and $33 a month, which compared very favorably with the wages for workers in the sugar ($33), tobacco ($18), and needle industries ($19).⁵⁷ By March 1942, naval installations' construction workers started to earn $2.25 per day, which was at least 40 percent more than sugar workers received. Since sugar cane workers only worked for seven months, construction workers' wages were in fact more than double that of sugar workers.⁵⁸

During the war the island grew ever more dependent on federal funding. In 1942, without federal intervention the economy would have collapsed. In that year, the WPA employed 36,552 workers to provide service and build military installations, and federal expenses on the island more than tripled prewar expenses (which were still marked by war preparedness), going from $33.3 million in 1939 to $110.1 million in 1942.⁵⁹ In December 1942, however, the White House announced that the WPA would end in the following year (August in Puerto Rico). This was detrimental to Puerto Rico's economy, which did not have any military industries.⁶⁰ In economic terms 1943 would prove to be the worst year for Puerto Rico. Military expenditures on the island and revenue from repatriated rum excise taxes, which totaled more than $1 billion between 1938 and 1948 kept the island's economy from collapsing during the war.⁶¹ Meanwhile, the state factories created by the Puerto Rican colonial state under Muñoz Marín and Tugwell represented an investment of merely $10.7 million and created 992 jobs.⁶² As argued by Bolívar Fresneda, economic development was secondary to military strategy, but military investment had long-lasting effects on the Puerto Rican economy. The military economy that dominated the 1939–48 period also served as a transitional phase between the agrarian and the industrial phases. During this period the infrastructure needed for the eventual industrialization of the island (modern roads, airports, and docks) was built to turn Puerto Rico into the centerpiece of U.S. hemispheric defense strategy. Beyond infrastructure, the war provided the opportunity for roughly 50,000 workers to train and learn the skills necessary to work in the modern construction industry and would prove essential for the postwar industrialization of the island. More important, the war created the conditions necessary to generate social change by making the PPD agrarian and social reforms viable.⁶³

Seen under this light, Munoz Marín's change of heart with regard to the political status should not be surprising. He had embraced the New Deal because it offered a way out in economic terms in the 1930s. By 1943–44 if not earlier, historians Ayala and Bernabe argue, he "became convinced that independence as he envisaged it was impossible," economically unviable. Hence he abandoned his former harsh critique of capitalism and started to trust "beneficial effects of free trade and absentee capitalism." He came to see the United States as a kind of "harmless empire that had stumbled into Puerto Rico in 1898 and mismanaged it since then." More important, he had always had an attachment to the United States and always harbored the idea of political and economic independence closely aided by the United States. When he realized that "the former could not be attained without the metropolis's support, he redefined his objectives accordingly. Imperial constraints and domestic pressures pushed him in the same sociopolitical direction" The war economy served to reinforce Muñoz Marín's beliefs.⁶⁴

3. First Lieutenant Cipriani, communications officer of the 65th Infantry, accompanied by Sergeant Navares, supervises the work of Technical Sergeant Santiago and Private Rivera in Caguas, Puerto Rico, November 1941. Center of Military History/Army Signal Corps.

The Puerto Rican Induction Program

To alleviate unemployment, Muñoz Marín promoted the military mobilization of the Puerto Ricans, especially the peasantry and urban workers. This gave him another card with which to advance political decolonization in his dealings with Washington. If he and Tugwell disagreed on the path to political decolonization, they certainly agreed on the importance of military preparedness and mobilization to improving conditions on the island. The economic impact of the military preparedness was hard to miss.

In November 1939, as the United States accelerated readiness procedures in response to the war in Europe, the War Department decided to augment the army units in Puerto Rico, which at the time consisted of the 65th U.S. Army Infantry Regiment and the 295th and 296th regiments of the Puerto Rico National Guard.[65] After announcements were made to that effect, the press reported a wave of volunteers congregating outside the induction centers on the island.[66] The boards on the island gave priority to men who had volunteered to be called. The unemployed, regardless of age were admitted first.[67] Mobilization on the island moved speedily and Army units expanded exponentially. The selective service on the island, with 122 local boards, led and staffed mostly by Puerto Ricans, registered roughly 535,000 men between the ages of 18 to 64. Of those who registered 224,559 were examined and 47,000 accepted. The rejection rate was 91 percent.[68]

During this first period Puerto Ricans were accepted under the same standards (with the exception of English literacy) as their continental counterparts.[69] To process the Puerto Rican recruits, an army reception and induction center was established in Fort Buchanan, a basic training station at Camp O'Reilly (Gurabo), and an advanced training center at Camp Tortuguero (Vega Baja).[70] The 65th was quickly brought to war strength, attached to the U.S. Army Second Army Corps, and sent to Panama in January 1943. The regiments 295 and 296 of the PRNG were called into active service in 1940 and gradually took over the 65th's responsibilities, first on the island and later on throughout the Caribbean Basin.[71]

Continental and local politicians were not the only ones invested in the mass mobilization of Puerto Ricans. Convinced that "Puerto

Rican men inducted under U.S. standards were drastically inferior to continental troops," the U.S. Army's Puerto Rican Department unilaterally set higher standards for natives to be admitted in the service in July 1942, including twice the schooling of that of continental Americans.[72] The War Department had authorized the commanding general of the Puerto Rican Department to require an eighth-grade education from natives of the island in order to be considered for service. The Puerto Rican Department was also authorized to "weed out the most undesirable men" thought to be "inferior physically, mentally, and in other ways" to continentals. More satisfied with the men selected after the new requirements were instituted, the War Department decided to use these men to replace continental troops in the Caribbean area. The Puerto Rican monthly quota was raised as the reports on the new inductees' performance showed improvement, and more than 16,000 men were inducted using the new standards.[73] Such policy, however, was taken as demeaning by local leaders. In October 1943, the Mayagüez Lions Club initiated the complaint that culminated with the War Department reestablishing same parameters for Puerto Rican and Continental recruits.[74] In March 1944, under pressure from civic groups and local politicians, the War Department ordered the local selective service unit on the island to reinstate the fourth-grade education requirement for admittance into the army and to set the monthly inductee quota at 1,500 men. Between March 1944 and April 1, 1945, roughly 18,380 men were inducted into the Army. The War Department, however, decided that these new troops would be used as "fillers for Puerto Rican units and as service troops in overseas theaters."[75] Thus the War Department still found a way to deny equal opportunity to those born on the island.

It was the general attitude that Puerto Ricans, as colored troops, were not suited for combat duty. The Bureau of the Budget's report on the inductee program on the island declared that "Puerto Ricans obviously are not as valuable as Continentals for Army service because of lower educational and physical standards, racial and historical traditions and background, aptitude, etc."[76] Not only did the War Department believe that their race poorly

4. Just like many other civic groups, the Club Damas de Puerto Rico supported the war effort in Puerto Rico. Puerto Rico National Guard Museum.

suited nonwhites for combat duty, but that it also made them intellectually inferior to white soldiers. Although the same regulations with regard to schooling were applied to Puerto Rican recruits, and then doubled, continental officials still believed that Puerto Ricans were deficient in intellect, which they blamed on the recruits' race. Furthermore, the report reiterated the myth of Puerto Rican docility used by local elites before 1898 to explain the inability of Puerto Rico to obtain independence, and ignored the island's military tradition. A Bureau of the Budget report stated that the use of native officers in the Puerto Rican units was "a major reason for the retention of many men whose effectiveness and/or efficiency is questionable in comparison with Continental troops."[77] The conclusions of this report with regard to the protective role played by Puerto Rican officers, however, goes against many of the troops' preferences for serving under continental officers who they saw as less demanding than their Puerto Rican counterparts. According to these soldiers, Puerto Rican officers always seemed to have something to prove, the proverbial chip on the shoulder, and were more demanding than continental officers.[78]

The War Department's low opinion of the Puerto Ricans was set before recruitment began. In the Puerto Rican Induction Report prepared by the Bureau of the Budget in 1945, it is stated that the Puerto Rican inductee "admittedly, was not generally suited for front line duty" but would be valuable for other duties and "thousands of potential actual combat U.S. Continental personnel would thereby be released from secondary services." A War Department adamant in showing that all "available sources of non-father (pre–Pearl Harbor) manpower were being exhausted before fathers were called" thus proceeded to mobilize thousands of Puerto Ricans, which it did not trust nor did it intend to send into battle. According to the Bureau of the Budget, the Puerto Rican Induction Program admittedly had another purpose "not directly related to the actual prosecution of the war." The War Department, through induction, sought to "provide employment for many idle Puerto Ricans classified as 1-A."[79] FDR, members of Congress, and the military had continuously expressed their fear of local unrest. Excluding able and unemployed Puerto Ricans from the military could have been taken as an outright insult, especially considering that unemployment on the island went from 99,100 in July 1941 to 237,000 in September 1942 because of the strain imposed on the island by German U-boats, rationing, the prioritization of military needs, and the failure to establish war industries in Puerto Rico.[80]

That Puerto Rican soldiers were excluded from the battlefield was not the result of any refusal on their part. Soldiers, local leaders, the press, and the general public on the island demanded the opportunity to see action.[81] Local leaders interested into getting as many Puerto Ricans as possible into the military were aware of the economic and political value as well as the regenerative effect of military training. However, Puerto Rican leaders did not want military participation to be a handout. It was important for Puerto Rican leaders to debunk the myth of the Puerto Rican soldiers' inferiority (and thus of the Puerto Ricans in general), and so they pushed the matter of sending the troops into action, just as they had done during World War I. The War Department may have wanted to save face by including Puerto Ricans in the military but restricting them to service duties, an opinion shared by continental politicians, but local leaders and soldiers demanded a chance to prove their worth in the battlefield. For once, there was the symbolic regaining of manhood. This could be attained by first being able to support their families and second by sharing the burden of "national defense" by fighting and, if necessary, dying in war. Furthermore, many local leaders, including Muñoz Marín, thought that active participation in the war would convince Puerto Ricans that they could stand on their own, individually and collectively, and that they could in fact run the island by themselves. Being allowed to fight was perceived as a means to end what some perceived as psychological and sociological perceptions and complexes of inferiority. As local leaders encouraged the population to support and join the military, economic opportunity and personal improvement joined national duty as part of the rationale used to exhort the Puerto Rican peasantry and working urban classes to join the military.[82] Economic hardships and the call for national defense, with everything that it entails, combined to drive the Puerto Rican masses into recruiting stations. The War Department casually reported: "The number of volunteers appears to be comparatively much higher than in the Continental United States. Some months, it is stated, volunteers supplied the complete quota."[83]

Economic distress was not missed by military officials when asked to comment on Puerto Rico's exceptionally high volunteer rate. Citing the senior commander of the U.S. Army Puerto Rican Department, Maj. Gen. James Lawton Collins, an editorial in the *Christian Science Monitor* observed:

> Since Puerto Rico's economic problems are so acute, a grocery store clerk in a small coastal town would probably never have earned more than a few hundred dollars a year before becoming a soldier. His Army pay plus the Government's allowance to his wife and family will be actually a raise in income.[84]

Lawton Collins's comments rang especially true to the peasantry and the jíbaros.[85] An old saying in the 65th declared, "Poverty takes me to war. If I had any money, I would not go."[86] That seemed to be the case for many Puerto Ricans who joined the military before and during World War II. Victor Vargas, who joined the 65th Infantry in 1940 at age sixteen, stated: "I joined because of the economic situation. I used to go downtown on a donkey to sell vegetables and tubers, but there wasn't any money. When the war came, I took that opportunity and started to earn $21 per month."[87] Francisco Salinas, who enlisted in 1939, declared:

> For many Puerto Ricans there is no better institution than the Army. The Army gives the Boricuas housing, clothes, order, recreation, school, a pension, three hot meals [last tres calientes], and a decent pay. Where is the Boricua going to find all that?[88]

The veterans who most frequently cited economic reasons for joining the army also stated that once in the army they were very happy and took pride in wearing the uniform. Their pride came from the respect and admiration they received from the rest of the community and a feeling of being needed.[89] Lawton Collins, commander of the Puerto Rican Department, identified other reasons besides economic improvement for Puerto Rican participation in the war effort: "It would be hard to find any community where civilians have cooperated more wholeheartedly and unselfishly with the army than in Puerto Rico. We have several gifts of lands from individual Puerto Ricans for army projects here."[90] The overwhelming support for the war effort and the numbers of Puerto Ricans joining the military even started to worry the Nacionalistas, who understood the symbolic value of military service with regard to national identities.[91]

Bolívar Fresneda has calculated that the average annual salary for the Puerto Rican soldier was roughly $902, which almost doubled that of the sugar cane cutters ($506). Based on a conservative estimate of 47,000 Puerto Rican soldiers serving by 1944, that translates into $23.6 million to $118.4 million if the soldiers sent between 15 and 70 percent of their salaries to their families. He concludes that it is possible that soldiers' remittances surpassed government revenues even in 1944, when the latter reached its high for the period 1941–47.[92] The mobilization of tens of thousands of Puerto Ricans went beyond personal economic improvement. Entire families and communities were affected by it. According to the Bureau of the Budget, federal payments in the form of dependents benefits and "readjustment payments" (a type of unemployment benefit after being discharged) to soldiers were bringing $28,074,000 annually into the economy by 1944.[93] The BoB estimated that after the war at least 30,000 veterans would seek unemployment benefits under the Servicemen Readjustment Act of 1944. Entitled by this act to a weekly unemployment pay of $20 for 52 weeks ($1,040 annually), these soldiers' readjustment pay meant a monthly boost to the local economy of $600,000 or $31,200,000 annually in wages.[94] The readjustment weekly benefit was substantially more than the $12 weekly pay a veteran could earn working as a waiter in Fort Brooks Officers Club, itself a higher pay than what most Puerto Ricans earned at the moment.[95] Many veterans in fact made use of this provision. Miguel A. Muñoz, director of the Veterans Administration on the island, informed Muñoz Marín that by June 30,

1948, roughly 49,000 veterans had received unemployment readjustment pay for a total of $40,755,971.[96] However, those numbers show that although almost twice the number of the expected veterans received unemployment payments, the total payments remained close to the Bureau's 1945 estimate. This indicates that veterans were not sitting idle to receive a paycheck, as the BoB had feared, but were seeking employment or retraining under the provisions of the Readjustment Act. The economic impact of mobilization would continue to be felt after the war ended. Federal expenses in Puerto Rico for the period 1939–46 show that veterans' benefits in 1946 rose to $22 million from $700,000 the previous year. Veterans' benefits thus represent the third largest source of federal expenses only behind rum repatriated excessive taxes ($26.6 million) and military agencies' expenditures ($84 million). For the whole period, veterans' benefits are fourth behind unemployment benefits.[97]

Regarding the Puerto Rican units being created, the report concluded that "few, if any, foresaw the cost of creating this comparatively small segment of the Army." The Puerto Rican soldiers averaged 2.6 dependents, which meant an annual dependent payment of $560 per man. Moreover, Puerto Ricans were entitled to overseas payment while serving on the island (an overseas possession), which translated into their pay being equal to those troops deployed around the world and between 10 and 20 percent higher than soldiers stationed in the continental United States.[98] Those were policies instituted not by local officials but by the War Department based on Puerto Rico's political status and geographical location. Furthermore, annexationists on the island preferred the island to be treated as a state, even if that meant a decrease of the War Department's moneys assigned to the island.[99]

The BoB took special aim at dependents benefits. It blamed the local selective service boards, "whose member are predominately, if not entirely Puerto Ricans," of failing to verify dependents claims and of fomenting the steady increase of inductees applying for dependents benefits. The BoB report stated that it was "almost unbelievable that 97 out of every 110 men inducted (more of 60 percent being single) were supporting an average of

2.6 persons when joining the Army."[100] The report did not take into account that by 1933, families in Puerto Rico already averaged five members.[101] Ironically, the BoB, which used the cultural and social conditions of the Puerto Ricans to argue against their usefulness as fighting troops, overlooked the extended Puerto Rican families, many of which were led and supported by the oldest son, whom among his patriarchal duties counted being the first to go to war. The BoB ignored that, especially in rural areas, many Puerto Rican couples lived as concubines, which meant that many of those labeled as "single" likely had a partner and children from their unrecognized unions. Moreover, as it is evident from the BoB report itself, local members of the selective service board were strictly following this institution's and the War Department's guidelines, as well as the laws passed by Congress. The BoB also complained that the local government was bent on helping recruits to secure documentation for purposes of dependents benefits. However, this was no different than in any of the states on the mainland to the point that many of the initiatives devised by the local government in Puerto Rico to aid the veterans and recruits in securing benefits were verbatim copies of continental states' legislation.[102]

The Bureau of the Budget's report denied that the induction program in Puerto Rico functioned as a "glorified WPA" or a "WPA in 'uniform.'" Proportionally, the report indicated, Puerto Rico received a larger monthly dependent benefit than any other state of the Union. The report accused local officials of treating mobilization as a workers program and of "expending large sums of money haphazardly" while "groundwork is being laid [by the Puerto Rican senate] for continuing postwar expenditures in whatever form of pensions may be finally adopted."[103] The Populares were in fact counting on the Puerto Rican soldiers to bolster the socioeconomic reconstruction effort in the postwar years.

Reintegration of Veterans into Civil Society

The Americans who fought in World War II enjoyed some tangible benefits not experienced by their World War I predecessors. The Populares would make sure that no benefit (i.e., vocational

5. "Learning lathe work in off-duty hours are GI's of Antilles Department," ca. 1944–45. During World War II, the military effort in Puerto Rico included educational programs with formal classes, study groups, and vocational training. Center of Military History/Army Signal Corps.

rehabilitation, unemployment benefits, reemployment, discharge compensation, life insurance, medical assistance, mortgage loans) remained unclaimed by Puerto Rican veterans. The PPD leaders also fought to extend the same benefits to World War I veterans. Altogether, the world war veterans residing in Puerto Rico in 1947 totaled 70,426 men and 210 Women Army Corps veterans.[104] Even though a fifth of World War II veterans were no longer residing in Puerto Rico in 1947, roughly 10 percent of the male-eligible population consisted of veterans. The sheer number of veterans eligible to participate in the several federal readjustment programs facilitated the Populares effort to change the nature of the island's socioeconomic structures and eventually to embark on the industrialization of the island with native know-how.

Arguably, the most important of those benefits was the Servicemen's Readjustment Act of 1944, better known as the GI Bill, which allowed almost eight million World War II veterans in the United States to go to college—a feat that has been credited with the dramatic expansion of the middle class on the mainland.[105] The GI Bill had a similar effect on the island. Understanding that many Puerto Rican soldiers would not be able to use the benefits of the Servicemen's Readjustment Act, for too many had little formal schooling, Muñoz Marín and the Populares designed training and vocational state programs for the returning soldiers so they could make use of these benefits. The returning soldier was not to go back to the fields; high schools, vocational schools, and the University of Puerto Rico were waiting for him.

The Department of Education and the Veterans Administration worked closely to retrain and in most cases to help the veterans finish high school. In 1946–47 the Department of Education had readied itself for the returning soldiers and trained 1,167 academic teams that employed 3,677 people to cater to 36,584 veterans. Besides primary and secondary teachings, the DoE conducted more than 650 workshops, and 8,418 veterans received diplomas that first year. The DoE was spending more than $3 million annually to run these programs. During the academic year of 1947–48, the local government helped 40,000 veterans to obtain the necessary credentials or certifications necessary to receive an education under the Servicemen's Readjustment Act. That year the DoE again counted 36,584 veterans finishing high school, 1,798 in vocational (industrial) schools, and 936 pursuing vocational agricultural studies. According to a report from Pedro Gil, director of the Veterans Division of the Department of Education, 48,075 veterans were receiving some kind of secondary education. More than 2,000 were receiving vocational industrial training, and roughly 1,200 were enrolled in vocational agricultural studies. The report boasted that 50,000 veterans were receiving some kind of instruction.[106]

The enrollment in the University of Puerto Rico increased 24 percent from 5,869 students in 1941–42 to 7,300 for 1944–45, and it would continue to expand mostly in part to accommodate a growing veteran population that now had the means to go to college. The veteran population for the academic year 1947–48 rose to 2,074 students. The next year 2,307 attended the UPR.[107] As the UPR grew in terms of enrollment, it was also restructured to emphasize the teaching of social sciences with the intention of producing a harvest of economists, public administrators, social workers, and all types of professions associated with public service. Moreover, as explained by Henry Wells, strengthening the social sciences core did not diminish interest in applied sciences, which in turn supplied the new commercial and industrial enterprises' demand for accountants, statisticians, engineers, scientists, managers, and all types of technicians.[108]

On August 1947, the University of Puerto Rico inaugurated an industrial arts school with 1,200 students, mostly veterans. The school, which when finished would have room for 7,000 students, covered twenty-two acres and had twenty-five classrooms, one administrative building, fourteen buildings for practical workshops, four classroom buildings, a bakery, and a cafeteria. This school offered more than fifty courses designed to train carpenters, electricians, auto mechanics, sheetmetal workers, and cast iron workers, as well as auto, aviation, and general mechanics, plumbers, experts on refrigeration, and welders. Five more of these schools were eventually built in Ponce, Mayagüez, Arecibo, Humacao, and Guayama. The director of the Veterans Administration on the island understood the priority of these schools and stated that although they were not exclusively for veterans, former servicemen would receive preference for admission.[109] The importance of these thousands of soldiers who received technical training went beyond that of providing technicians. They subsidized the schooling of thousands more because their tuition, books, and other expenses were paid in full by the federal government, which allowed the UPR to expand in other areas while keeping tuition rates low and offering scholarships. Hence it is not surprising that the UPR administration went out of its way to make sure that "not a single veteran who wished to enroll in the University of Puerto Rico and who met the admission requirements was denied the opportunity to attend either Río Piedras or Mayagüez because of lack of space."[110] These citizen soldiers, through vocational and college education, were to become the technicians and technocrats of a new political framework, the "commonwealth" and of its main project, the modernization of Puerto Rico's economy via industrialization.

But before Muñoz Marín moved decidedly toward the commonwealth formula, he had already engaged the military in promoting the island's industrialization and in providing essential services commonly reserved for state agencies or the private sector. The National Guard (and the State Guard) were occupied with providing entertainment during towns' *fiestas patronales* and helping public schools with extracurricular activities ranging from athletics and field days to conducting seminars on industrialization for civilians and veterans.[111] Moreover, through their own radio show, the National Guard provided entertainment while engaging with communities hosting guard units. The PRNG also appointed godmothers and honorary officers in these communities seeking to create a sense of belonging.[112] The military was in fact busy with community and state building projects as it continued to take on civilian roles to fill the vacuum of nonexistent civilian structures. This added another dimension to the role of the military on the island beyond providing economic relief by direct and indirect employment and beyond its character and nation-building role as proposed by local and continental leaders. In many areas the military on the island had taken a leadership role in the effort to reconstruct Puerto Rico. Unsurprisingly, many of the officers of the National Guard also worked for the relief and reconstruction agencies on the island. Furthermore, many of the enlisted men and officers had trained or were training to fill the needs of the coming insular industrial revolution. National Guard officers led many of the federal and state agencies involved in the island's reconstruction.[113]

Autonomismo at the War's End

With the help of Tugwell, Muñoz Marín and the Populares had been able to plant the seeds of socioeconomic change during the war and afterward. However, political advancement had been limited by an intractable Congress and by the most militant independence wing within the PPD, which tended to align with Tydings. The PPD won the elections of November 1944 in a landslide, even after bitter accusations between Muñoz Marín and the Independentistas in the PPD were made public.[114] The Independentistas had wanted the total rejection of the governor bill and a compromise to celebrate a referendum to vote for independence a month after the general elections of 1944. Once again Muñoz Marín ran the PPD's campaign on social and economic reform, allegiance to the war effort, and assurances that a vote for the Populares was not a vote for independence. The platform of the PPD, however, made clear the intention of the Populares to submit to the direct decision of the Puerto Ricans, "not later than the moment when the world peace is structured, the question of the final political status desired by the people of Puerto Rico."[115] Muñoz Marín, who followed the war closely, probably thought, as many did, that the war would be over before Christmas that year. Thus the PPD platform of 1944 was a repetition of that of 1940 with an emphasis on ending the colonial regime, as soon as the fighting was over, via a referendum in which all the political sectors had a chance to promote their status preference.

On January 10, 1945, Tydings presented yet another independence bill, identical to the one introduced in 1943. During the public hearings held March 5–8, the position of the differ-

6. Dozens of veterans gather in support of Insular House Project 536, which exempted veterans in public vocational schools from taking examinations to receive their certification as electricians, ca. 1947–48. Signs read, "Industrialization needs us" and "Puerto Rico needs electricians." El Mundo Collection, University of Puerto Rico, Rio Piedras.

ent groups with interests in Puerto Rico remained the same as in 1943. Capt. G. B. Parks, representing the Office of the Chief of Naval Operations, officially declared that "from the viewpoint of national security Puerto Rico is of great strategic value as a site for a naval operating base," and that after the war the facilities on the island were to be used to locate the "Task Force in charge of defending the Caribbean to deny the approach of any threat from east or south." For that reason, the Navy was "opposed to any bill for Puerto Rico independence that does not provide for the retention of the naval and military reservations, and does not also provide for the right of expansion and the selection of new sites at any time in the future."[116] The armed forces' position clearly indicated that the military leaders planned to continue using Puerto Rico to project U.S. power over the Caribbean Basin after the war ended and that they wanted a free hand with regard to expanding their footprint in Puerto Rico.

The death of President Roosevelt in April 1945 brought an inexperienced and uninformed Harry S. Truman to the presidency of the United States. This event could have not been more relevant.[117] Truman was willing to support self-government for the island, a position that FDR had abandoned. He also made clear to Tugwell that he was against independence for Puerto Rico. In an attempt to secure a fair referendum, Tugwell tried to convince Truman that "if there is a plebiscite, neither of us should say so in a way to influence Puerto Rican's choice," and Truman agreed that he thought the Puerto Ricans "should have the right to make even a disastrous choice."[118] Unbeknownst to Truman, he was, in fact, reversing his predecessor's policy. However, without outright support from the president, there was little chance of convincing Congress to grant independence to the island.

As had been the case in 1943, Muñoz Marín could not support the independence bill of 1945. He wanted economic guarantees and a chance for the Puerto Ricans to vote on status options. Moreover, these options should be guaranteed by Congress. Muñoz Marín was still operating under the assumption that once the war was over, the sacrifices made by Puerto Rico and its loyalty to the Allies' cause would be rewarded with a referendum sponsored by Congress to find a formula to decolonize the island.[119] The Department of the Interior had come to believe that Puerto Rico should not sever its ties with the United States but that home rule was a must. Ironically, the position held by Muñoz Marín, who was already recognized by the U.S. government as the most influential and popular leader in Puerto Rico, strengthened the Interior's opinion.[120]

On October 16, 1945, in a special message to Congress on Puerto Rico, Truman declared that it was the policy of his administration to promote the political, social, and economic development of people who have not yet attained full self-government, "and eventually to make it possible for them to determine their own form of government." Truman went further and emphasized that it was time to "ascertain from the people of Puerto Rico their wishes as to the ultimate status which they prefer within such limits as may be determined by the Congress," with the end of granting Puerto Ricans the kind of government which they desire. Truman probably did not intend to curtail the right of Puerto Ricans to choose their status, but he was concerned that they might vote for a formula that Congress was not ready to support. Such occurrence would undoubtedly have diplomatic repercussions for the United States at a moment when it was trying to assert itself as the leader of the free world. Therefore, Truman suggested that Congress consider four possibilities: "(1) the right of the Puerto Ricans to elect their own Governor with a wider measure of local self-government; (2) Statehood for Puerto Rico; (3) complete independence; and (4) a Dominion form of government [similar to the political arrangement between Canada and the United Kingdom]."[121] Congress, which was not interested at all in a referendum, did not even hold public hearings for the new Tydings-Piñero bill.[122]

Cornered by the Independentistas in the PPD, by another American president who did not support the independence of Puerto Rico, by a Congress that would not give Puerto Rico an independence that the island could survive, compelled by the loyalty he felt to his constituency, which had elected him on the premise that a vote for the PPD was not a vote for independence, and aware of the island's growing dependency on federal funds, including veterans' benefits, Muñoz Marín began to turn decidedly toward autonomismo. In 1946 he expelled the Independentistas from the PPD, who responded by forming the Partido Independentista Puertorriqueño, or PIP. The third Tydings bill and its sequel, the Tydings-Piñero bill, had an unexpected effect. It almost destroyed the PPD, and in the end it forced its leadership to define the party's status preference. Muñoz Marín had come to the conclusion that the United States would not offer enough guarantees to make independence viable, nor could he persuade the people to vote for it. This experience finally moved Muñoz Marín to seek autonomismo or a higher degree of self-government, a formula that he knew Truman would support.

The reluctance of Congress to consider a referendum drove Muñoz Marín to endorse yet another governor bill in 1947. This time he expressed his enthusiasm for the bill in a long cablegram to Congress.[123] The PPD immediately mobilized in favor of the bill. Piñero, whom Truman had appointed as governor of Puerto Rico (the first Puerto Rican to serve in this position), and Antonio Fernós Isern, the new Puerto Rican resident commissioner in Washington and a member of the congressional committee studying the bill, hurried to express their support and to educate the members of the committee on the benefits of approving the bill.

Showing the new, although limited, decolonization spirit of the White House, the new secretary of the interior, J. A. Krug, declared that Article 76 of the UN charter made the approval of the governor bill necessary.[124] Krug convinced the committee that approving it would send a message to "the nations of the world, and particularly of South America," that the United States adhered to the principles of democracy and self-government and had no colonial empire." He also called on Congress to commit itself to sponsoring a referendum to decide the political status of Puerto Rico in the near future. In his deposition Piñero followed the anticolonial line and emphasized the global prestige that this bill would bring to the United States. During the hearings, he promoted a Congress-sponsored referendum and hinted at the possibility of a third status.[125]

James A. Beverly, a former governor of the island, informed Congress that more than 99 percent of Puerto Ricans were intensely loyal to the United States (and that their war service was evidence of such loyalty) and that approving the bill would not affect national defense. Moreover, he advocated the idea of a holding a referendum as soon as possible.[126]

During the hearings before the House, a single letter from the Independentistas and the personal testimony of Ruth M. Reynolds, secretary of the American League for Puerto Rico's Independence, expressed opposition to the bill. Reynolds argued that Puerto Rico should be granted independence and that American sovereignty over the island was illegal.[127] In fact, of the eighty letters and cablegrams included in the records of Congress, only the one sent by the PIP opposed the bill. The rest, signed by mayors, senators, independent organizations, and common people, supported it.[128]

Representative Fred L. Crawford, who during the hearings expressed his preference for Puerto Rican statehood, made clear on the record that he was completely against independence.

> I do not propose to give Puerto Rico its independence. Statehood is a different proposition, change of political status is a different proposition, but the United States will either defend Latin America, including Puerto Rico and Santo Domingo and Haiti and South America, or we [the United States] will come under the domination of some power in Europe.[129]

Adhering to the rationale used to take over Cuba and Puerto Rico during the Spanish-American War of 1898, Crawford emphasized that although he trusted Puerto Ricans, he believed that some European power might attempt to gain a foothold there from which it could operate against the United States, and therefore independence for the island would be a blow against national defense.[130] Unlike the independence bills' hearings of 1936 and 1943, in which Senator Tydings made clear that Congress would never grant statehood to Puerto Rico, in 1947 Congress's attitude toward Puerto Rico had shifted considerably to the point that statehood was actually being considered by members of Congress and the military.[131] Undoubtedly, the first consequence of the cold war was to revive or, more accurately, to increase the military importance of Puerto Rico, which made independence unthinkable for Congress. The United States, however, had also emerged from World War II as the self-proclaimed leader of the free world, a position quickly challenged by the Soviet Union. The decolonization of Puerto Rico thus assumed more relevance than ever before, especially with the intense propaganda that characterized the cold war. The diplomatic value of decolonizing the island rivaled its military worth, a point that politicians on both sides were quick to realize.

The governor bill of 1947 was approved by Congress after the Interior Department and the political leaders of the island went out of their way to establish that its passage would not curtail the powers of Congress over Puerto Rico.[132] This time Muñoz Marín did not try to obtain guarantees that Congress would not make further changes to the Organic Act except with the consent of the people of Puerto Rico.[133] He had bigger plans for the island and had been busy gaining support of the Interior and powerful congressmen to find a formula to decolonize Puerto Rico with a future referendum. On August 5, 1947, President Truman signed the governor bill, which became Public Law 382, providing for the election of the governor of Puerto Rico. The significance in passing the governor bill was that the Interior and powerful congressmen established without doubt the military and strategic significance of Puerto Rico, but more important, they recognized the diplomatic gains that decolonizing the island offered the United States. In a visit to Puerto Rico on February 21, 1948, Truman reiterated his commitment to local self-government and labeled the nomination of an island-born governor, that of Jesús T. Piñero, and the elected-governor bill as significant steps toward the increasing measure of self-government in Puerto Rico. More relevant, perhaps, was the fact that Truman pointed out that the relationship between Puerto Rico and the United States was mutually beneficial and that it was an example to the world of how well the "democratic approach to the problem of national existence in the modern world" worked. Moreover, Truman stated that

Puerto Rico represented "what the American people are trying to encourage in the world at large."¹³⁴ The president recognized the value of Puerto Rico in global politics, a point that Puerto Rican politicians did not miss. In 1948 Muñoz Marín became the first elected governor of Puerto Rico.¹³⁵ From this office, with firm command of the political apparatus and with overwhelming popular support, Muñoz Marín would launch a new offensive to decolonize the socioeconomic and political structures in Puerto Rico. The Puerto Rican veterans and the military units still active on the island in many ways would spearhead the new campaign.

When men of the 65th Infantry Regiment returned home on November 9, 1945, they were received as heroes by an enthusiastic multitude crowding the streets of San Juan and waving both Puerto Rican and American flags.¹³⁶ The victory parades did not stop until the spring of 1946 as Puerto Rican units continue to return from overseas deployment.¹³⁷ In several speeches Muñoz Marín made clear the reasons for sending Puerto Ricans to join the fight overseas. The common Puerto Rican, Muñoz Marín argued, was forging democracy abroad and at home. He did not hesitate to identify who those heroes were: soldiers, citizens, and jíbaros. "Soldier Ocasio, citizen Ocasio, jíbaro Ocasio, soldiers and citizens and jíbaros in all the hills in Puerto Rico, in all fronts and camps throughout the world, you are Puerto Rico's hope."¹³⁸ That the returning Puerto Rican "heroes," the island's hope, wore U.S. Army uniforms and that they were received by crowds waving the island's unofficial flag and the Stars and Stripes evidenced the intricate nature of national identities on the island.

During the war, the metropolis and the local politicians' projects had in common their emphasis on creating a modern Puerto Rico and Puerto Rican. Modernization had meant political Americanization as understood by some local politicians as early as 1898 and as late as the 1920s. For the metropolis, however, Americanization was still intrinsic to modernization, but it also entailed cultural assimilation, not just political. Thus the initial projects of both the metropolis and the local elites had presupposed some type of modernization via Americanization with the meaning and extent of the latter varying accordingly. These projects were not completely rejected by the masses but reimagined as they went through the metropolitan institutions, usually cheered by a cacophony of modernizing discourses echoed and distorted by the Puerto Rican elites.

Cultural and political assimilation had been at the core of modernization projects for four decades. During World War II, however, the emphasis was on economic modernization, first suggested during World War I.[139] The socioeconomic reconstruction programs in Puerto Rico have been studied by overemphasizing either a pure economic or political focus. They center on relief agencies such as the PRERA, PRRA, and WPA and economic strategies like the Plan Chardón, Rex G. Tugwell's and Muñoz Marín's promotion of local industry during World War II, and the subsequent and world famous Operation Bootstrap leading to the final industrialization of the island. Such narratives have left out the role of tens of thousands of Puerto Ricans serving in the U.S. military during World War II. Initially they represented an economic boom—in the form of new wages and unemployment relief—just by serving in the armed forces. Furthermore, as military mobilization advanced, their salaries and benefits came to eclipse the funds available to both the PRERA and PRRA. However, through their service they provided more than temporary economic relief as previously discussed.

Unlike World War I veterans, before World War II ended the Puerto Rican soldier could count on a generous package of benefits designed to ease the soldier's reentry into civilian life. A march toward a "modern" Puerto Rico had started, and these soldiers would be leading such a movement. That Luis Muñoz Marín came to depend on the votes of the peasantry and rural working classes to attain political power and on their military mobilization to advance the socioeconomic restructuring of the island would eventually force him to change his personal political goals, first tactically and later definitively. Fittingly, militarization and enfranchisement of the Puerto Rican masses during World War II coincided with a growing dependence on the island on the federal government's political, legal, and financial intervention.[140]

Old metropolitan ideas regarding the impact of military training on Puerto Rico's social and economic structures resurfaced during the war.[141] This was not a new theory. Immediately after the 1898 invasion and during World War I, military service had been considered as a builder of character and national identity and as a way to remake the Puerto Ricans in the continental image. But even in World War I, the metropolis's nation-building project, which heavily relied on modernizing the Puerto Rican via military service, had started to escape the hands of its administrators. History repeated itself during World War II as the plans of the metropolis—including type, size, and length of mobilization—had to contend with an empowered Puerto Rican senate led by a popular and skillful politician such as Muñoz Marín. Moreover, Muñoz Marín worked incessantly to make the Puerto Rican soldier an integral part of the socioeconomic restructuring of the island. By the end of the war, control of the nation building project via military service was firmly in the Populares' hands. Thus while the U.S. military had envisioned service as a way to build a new Puerto Rican and thus a new Puerto Rico, as early as 1898 and most certainly during World War I, this project really came to bear fruit when it was appropriated by Puerto Ricans. Nonetheless, the military in Puerto Rico, be it the National Guard or the regular Army units, remained part of the U.S. military and depended entirely on federal funds to function. This could only allow for a third path as the Populares continue to employ the military for nation and state building.

The first mobilization of the Puerto Ricans during World War II was more political in nature than military, and it happened in 1940 with the Populares' first electoral victory. The second mobilization of the Puerto Ricans was military. It involved an economy dominated by military expenditures and rum tax excises (itself related to the war effort), which allowed the PPD to embark on its reforms. Tens of thousands of Puerto Ricans became soldiers. This effort had a strong economic impact in terms of federal monies transferred to Puerto Rico and unemployment relief. The third mobilization was social in nature as the Puerto Rican soldiers moved from the fields to classrooms and put to good use the skills learned while in the military and the benefits to which they were entitled. World War II ended with the island moving toward socioeconomic restructuration very rapidly and with LMM accepting the third way. Initially a tactical decision born out of the need of securing the vote of the peasantry and urban workers which did not see independence as a solution to their everyday problems, the idea that the "Status no está en issue" became a kind of end in itself as political decolonization took a backseat and socioeconomic decolonization became imperative. At this historical junction, the popular sectors' needs and will coincided with one of the greatest social reconfigurations in U.S. and Puerto Rican history. After World War II, the island moved rapidly to achieve the socioeconomic change envisioned by Muñoz Marín and Tugwell. Shying from independence, Muñoz Marín had started to adopt the third way of autonomism, a place between independence and statehood. The Korean conflict would become a propaganda war to support such a third way, which entailed a new Puerto Rican for a new Puerto Rico. The fourth mobilization of the Puerto Ricans would happen during the Korean War. It would be sociopolitical and cultural in nature as military mobilization became essential for the creation of the Estado Libre Asociado. The figure of the jíbaro-turned-soldier presented as a hybrid that allowed for a political identity and a cultural one to coexist would become one of the archetypal figures representing that new Puerto Rican and a living example of the commonwealth ideology.

6

Fighting for the "Nation"?
War at Home and Abroad

> For fifty-four years, we, the Puerto Ricans, have lived under the political tutelage of our co-citizens of the North. We have assimilated their entrepreneurial spirit and industrial skills and fed our soul and thoughts with the most sacred of men's attributes: their admiration and respect for freedom, justice, and equality . . . without adulterating our Hispanic heritage, nor have we soiled it with artificial trends of Sajonic assimilation, and without relegating our Hispanic culture, sentiments, and traditions, which we conserve pure, like the most precious legacy of our gallant and noble ancestors.
> —Juan César Cordero, August 13, 1952[1]

During the Second World War and its immediate aftermath, military mobilization served both as a political bargaining chip and as a tool with which to advance Puerto Rico's socioeconomic restructuring. Luis Muñoz Marín and the Populares also relied on the popular sectors' sheer electoral power to demand and embark on a reform of such a grandiose scale. The combination of economic imperatives—the effect of the Great Depression and the New Deal on the island and military expenditures and rum tax excises during the war—made Puerto Rico even more dependent on U.S. capital and federal transfers. The military in Puerto Rico became an essential instrument for political and socioeconomic modernization as the island shifted closer to the United States. Not only was Puerto Rico increasingly more dependent on federal transfers to effectively run reconstruction and relief agencies (not to mention the military), but as shown by the tens of thousands of peasants and urban workers who became soldiers, there was a growing acceptance of U.S. values and institutions (which were mostly led by Puerto Ricans) throughout the island. This phenomenon curtailed the ability of Muñoz Marín to move toward independence, and soon after becoming Puerto Rico's first elected governor in 1948, he began to work on a third option between federated statehood and independence.² That third option would eventually be known as the commonwealth formula, or Estado Libre Asociado. The outbreak of the Korean War in 1950 would not only provide the opportunity to mobilize tens of thousands of Puerto Ricans and to make them part of the socioeconomic reconstruction of the island (as their World War II counterparts had been). It would also provide a space where the Puerto Rican soldier would incarnate the ideals of the commonwealth formula. However, the symbolism of such participation with regard to national identities and the PPD's project of decolonization, and thus the acceptance of the commonwealth formula, was of the utmost importance. That the Estado Libre Asociado came into existence in 1952 is well known. The part played by the Puerto Rican soldiers fighting in Korea to advance this formula, however, has been almost completely ignored.³

From Point Four to Public Law 600

In his inaugural address of January 20, 1949, President Harry Truman made public to the world that the United States, as leader of the free world, was bent on combating the "false philosophy" of communism, not just by strengthening its military alliances with "peace-loving" countries but by its determination to "work for a world in which all nations and all peoples are free to govern themselves as they see fit, and to achieve a decent and satisfying life." He emphasized that the United States sought no territory, that "we have imposed our will on none," and that "the old imperialism—exploitation for foreign profit—has no place in our plans." Moreover, the United States was to embark on a new plan to make its technology and expertise, as well as its capital, available to the underdeveloped world. This policy, known as Point Four, was a global version of the Good Neighbor policy. Truman believed that to defeat communism, the United States had to convince the world that it did not intend to create a world empire, nor did it want to possess colonies. Accordingly, decolonizing Puerto Rico became a priority for his administration.

On March 13, 1950, the new Puerto Rican resident commissioner in Washington and PPD ideologue Antonio Fernós Isern, inspired by Truman's Point Four, introduced a bill in the House (H.R. 7674) to provide for the organization of a constitutional government in Puerto Rico. Senator Joseph C. O'Mahoney, then chair of the Committee on Interior and Insular Affairs, introduced the bill in the Senate (S. 3336) that same day. In a statement before a joint Senate and House committee, Muñoz Marín declared that approving these bills would be of great value to the United States, "which is constantly accused by the Latin American countries and the Communists of running a colonial system."[4] Unlike his remarks regarding previous bills, Muñoz Marín's statements were not adversarial. In fact, he had offered to make Puerto Rico into a world showcase of Truman's Point Four.[5] The gesture was reciprocated. The atmosphere during these hearings was congenial, at least between the Populares and the members of Congress.

Most congressmen agreed with Muñoz Marín's views, and one even pointed out the positive effect that a recent visit to Haiti by elected Puerto Rican officials had on their Haitian counterparts. Moreover, members of Congress noted that passing this bill could only "elevate our position before the United Nations," especially since the United States was a signatory to the United Nations charter and therefore had to adhere to the calling for self-government included in it. Others emphasized that its adoption would advance the "defense of democracy in the eyes of the world, and especially with our fellow Americans south of Rio Grande." Although the Independentistas tried to call into question the legitimacy of the legislation and of Muñoz Marín's government, Congress gave its blessing to the Senate version of the bill. On July 30, 1950, Truman signed the Congress Act of July 3 (S. 3336) into Public Law 600, giving the Puerto Ricans the right to create their own constitution and to establish a relationship with the United States in the nature of a compact. P.L.

600 authorized the people of Puerto Rico to organize a republican form of government pursuant to a constitution of their own choosing. That act, adopted by Congress, would become effective only when accepted by the people of Puerto Rico in a referendum. As these hearings were coming to an end, congressmen exhorted Inés Mendoza, Muñoz Marin's second wife, to address the audience. She declared: "This growing solidarity will be paid back to the United States someday." Her words could not have been more prophetic. Soon los hijos de este país would be fighting in the hills of Korea alongside the United Nations and against each other in the hills and towns of Puerto Rico.[6]

A referendum was set for June 4, 1951, in which the Puerto Ricans would cast a vote to accept or reject the provisions of P.L. 600. Muñoz Marín and the Populares enjoyed broad support. Having overwhelmed all the other political parties and alliances during the general elections of 1948, they were firmly in control of the political apparatus in Puerto Rico.[7] Acceptance of P.L. 600 in the coming referendum was hardly in doubt. This is not to say that there was no opposition. The staunchly pro-American Estadistas opposed—at least in principle—what they regarded as a perpetuation of the colonial status and an obstacle to achieve federated statehood. Nonetheless, even though they had come in second in the 1948 elections, the PPD had obtained more than four times the Estadistas' votes. The only chance the Estadistas had was to persuade the voters to reject P.L. 600 and to have a Congress-sponsored plebiscite including statehood and independence as options. The Independentistas were in a similar predicament. They had obtained even fewer votes than the Estadistas, and their efforts to stop passing of P.L. 600 in Congress were fruitless. They chose to campaign against the acceptance of P.L. 600 by exhorting their members to abstain from voting in the referendum or vote against it. However, even when combining their mass appeal with the rest of the parties opposing the PPD, they were still unable to match the Populares' strength. In fact, Independentistas, Estadistas, and Socialistas had continued their exodus to the PPD after 1948. Furthermore, the Socialist Party supported P.L. 600, which made its passing almost inevitable.

War among All Puerto Ricans: The Nationalist Insurrection

The traditional parties were just too weak to stop the PPD by peaceful means. The Nacionalistas, however, had long ago shunned the electoral process. A violent confrontation pitting the Nacionalistas' Ejército Libertador against the Puerto Rico National Guard and police was about to shock the island.[8] Albizu Campos, who had been convicted of sedition and conspiracy to overthrow the U.S. government in 1937, returned to Puerto Rico from New York City on December 15, 1947, four years after being released from federal prison on probation.[9] He immediately started a campaign to derail the PPD's projects and ordered the mobilization of the Ejército Libertador once more. Only a day after his return, Albizu Campos held a press conference and warned the United States that after depleting all peaceful means to obtain independence, the "Nationalist Party would resort to the use of force to attain its goals." His threats also targeted Muñoz Marín. Albizu Campos declared that "Muñoz must be stopped and we will stop him." Muñoz Marín publicly warned him to abstain from violence. Albizu Campos responded by questioning Muñoz Marín's Puertorriqueñidad while demanding that the Puerto Ricans abstain from voting in the 1948 general elections. He also condemned the teaching of English in Puerto Rico, declared that "every person serving in the Selective Service Boards should be shot," and commanded the Nacionalistas to start arming themselves with "revolvers, rifles, guns, shotguns, knives, and daggers to defend the cause of the Revolution." Despite Muñoz Marín's warnings, Albizu Campos's campaign continued unabated. On September 23, 1950, the anniversary of the Lares revolt of 1868, he addressed the crowd gathered in Lares's Plaza Pública. He spoke against P.L. 600 and harshly condemned the participation of Puerto Rican soldiers in the Korean War. He ended his speech by calling on Puerto Ricans to defy the United States and its colonial pawns in the same way that "the men of Lares defied despotism, with revolution!"[10]

That the Nacionalistas were planning a coup or insurrection was hardly a secret. Emboldened by the apparent inaction of the insular government, Albizu Campos continued his call to arms against the United States and its representatives on the island: Muñoz Marín, the Populares, and anyone who served the United States. In his speeches Albizu Campos defied the hated gag law (*Ley de la mordaza*) of 1948. Jesús T. Piñero, as appointed governor of the island, signed Law 53 (the gag law's insular nomenclature) on June 10, 1948. Muñoz Marín was still the president of the senate and Puerto Rico's most powerful politician when the bill was passed. The gag law declared it a felony to urge people to violently overthrow the island's government. Publishing any material encouraging people to engage in such activities and creating any kind of organization to carry out these acts became felonies. The law, which was derogated in 1957, closely resembled the U.S. Alien Registration Act (also known as the Smith Act) passed by Congress on June 29, 1940. This act made it illegal for anyone in the United States to advocate, abet, or teach the desirability of overthrowing the government.[11] A month earlier, the insular police had established the Internal Security Unit, which worked closely with the local FBI unit to keep the Nacionalistas, Communists, and Independentistas under surveillance. While Communists and other leftist groups were the primary target of the Smith Act, the insular version was instrumental in the suppression of Nacionalistas and other Independentista groups in Puerto Rico. The insular government, despite appearances, was not inactive with regard to the Nationalist threat.

On October 27, 1950, the police detained one of the cars of Albizu Campos's motorcade and found explosives, weapons, and ammunition in its trunk.[12] Throughout the island the Nacionalistas rushed to hide their weapons, and the chaos led to a gunfight with the police. After this second event, the police started a series of raids against known Nacionalistas. Albizu Campos immediately ordered the Ejército Libertador to launch a general attack against the police, political leaders, and elected officials at midday on October 30. The insurrection actually begun on October 28, as the Nacionalistas helped some 112 inmates escape from the island penitentiary. Long considered a diversion, the mass escape was in fact designed to secure additional manpower and weapons for the insurrection. The leader of the inmates who escaped that day, Pedro Benejam Álvarez, who was in jail for stealing military weapons and ammunition from Camp

O'Reilly, had promised to hand over the stolen weapons to the Nacionalistas in exchange for his freedom.[13] Plans had to be accelerated because of the events of October 27, and the Nacionalistas helped Benejam Álvarez and others to escape. The mass escape served in fact as a diversion as it kept the police occupied, but it also alerted them of the impending battle.

As ordered by Albizu Campos, the Nacionalistas launched their attack on October 30 on what is known as the Jayuya Uprising. The revolt became a series of gunfights between Nacionalistas and police in the cities of Ponce, Arecibo, Mayagüez, Naranjito, and San Juan, including the attempted assassination of Muñoz Marín in , La Fortaleza.[14] Albizu Campos designated the town of Utuado as the rendezvous point for all Nacionalistas to converge, believing its geographical location and topography would allow the Ejército Libertador to resist for at least a month. In that time they expected to gain enough international attention and support as to force the UN General Assembly to intercede in their favor. The local Nacionalistas attempted to take the town, but after a gun battle with the police, they had to take refuge in a few houses. Aided by the National Guard, the insular police quickly overwhelmed the Nacionalistas in Utuado.[15]

The Nacionalistas were able to take and briefly hold the central mountain town of Jayuya. They burned the police station, the U.S. post office, and the equipment and records found in the Selective Service offices. Just like the other Nacionalista cells, they were supposed to make their way to Utuado. But a lack of vehicles, disorganization, and the prompt mobilization of the National Guard prevented them from doing so. During that first day Blanca Canales, one of the few women involved in the insurrection, proclaimed the Republic of Puerto Rico. But in fact the Nacionalistas in Jayuya were trapped, and the revolt was quickly coming to an end. The Air National Guard bombed and strafed the town as an infantry company surrounded it. Those Nacionalistas who were able to escape the encirclement fled to the hills. With the National Guard in close pursuit, and alerted that their leader had surrendered in San Juan, the remaining Nacionalistas came down the mountains to surrender on November 2, 1950.[16]

7. Puerto Rico National Guardsman and Insular Police officer. The National Guard was activated during the Nationalist uprisings in 1950. Library of Congress.

The battle in Puerto Rico was over. By no means had it been bloodless. Eighteen Nacionalistas had been killed and eleven wounded. Seven policemen and a guardsman were killed, and twenty-one police officers and eleven soldiers were wounded. A fireman and two civilians also died during the gunfights.[17] After his arrest, still defiant and jubilant, Albizu Campos declared that the "nation was undergoing a glorious transfiguration." Muñoz Marín instead talked of the "tragic and useless death of 31 Puerto Ricans." He was quick to link the revolt to the "island's Communists" who had joined Albizu Campos and his diehard followers. He warned the Nacionalistas that "a government founded on votes cannot be destroyed."[18] Muñoz Marín linked the revolt to what was perceived as the biggest enemies of western democracies: fascism and communism.

The revolt also had an extra-insular chapter. On November 1, 1950, Nacionalistas Oscar Collazo and Griselio Torresola attempted to assassinate President Truman in front of the Blair House in Washington. Torresola was killed in the attempt, and Collazo was seriously wounded and captured. One White House guard was shot and killed by the assailants, and two other guards were wounded. During a press conference the next day, shrugging off the attacks and lamenting the unnecessary loss of life, President Truman reaffirmed his commitment to support the right of Puerto Ricans to write their own constitution.[19]

Governor Muñoz Marín passed his first test with flying colors as he quickly suppressed the revolt and succeeded in discrediting the Nacionalistas, especially after the assassination attempt. Furthermore, the local and continental media presented the insurrections as a local affair. Even though martial law was declared—which entitled the White House and the Army troops on the island and in the Caribbean region to have a more prominent role in containing the insurrection—Muñoz Marín and the colonial administration made sure that only the insular police and the Puerto Rico National Guard participated in the affair. The commander of the U.S. Army units in Puerto Rico and the Antilles, Brig. Gen. Edwin L. Sibert, turned his units' ammunition over to the National Guard during the insurrection, but did not provide aid in any other way.[20]

The insurrection was in fact a Puerto Rican affair. All of those involved and all the dead and wounded were Puerto Ricans commanded by Puerto Ricans. But besides the nationality of the participants, the revolt was a Puerto Rican affair in the sense that it was the Nacionalistas' desperate attempt to stop P.L. 600. They had hoped to bring the international community to their side but succeeded in doing the opposite. The revolt was suppressed quickly and with almost the same number of casualties on both sides.²¹ The outcome of the revolt served to prove the viability of a Puerto Rican autonomous state and that the island would not descend into chaos if left in the hands of the Puerto Ricans.

The timing of the revolt, as discussed by Eileen Suarez Findlay, also benefited the Populares. In the preceding months, the local press had been highlighting the plight of Puerto Rican migrant workers in Michigan. The scandal that ensued regarding breach of contracts and poor working conditions threatened the PPD's plans for socioeconomic restructuring, which in great part depended on labor migration. Known as the Michigan affair, this issue became a thorn in the PPD's side. However, as the Nationalist revolt in late October became the dominant topic in Puerto Rico, the farmworkers' ordeal disappeared from the island's press.²² Furthermore, the insurrection made opposing P.L. 600 by peaceful means even more difficult.²³ On November 3, Muñoz Marín made a personal radio call for all women to register for the coming referendum and the next day for all males.²⁴ Far from blocking P.L. 600 or at least casting a shadow on the process as the Nacionalistas wished, a record 779,695, including 157,393 new voters, registered themselves to vote in the coming referendum.²⁵ The Nacionalistas' military wing had been defeated, their leaders imprisoned, and their ideology soundly rejected.²⁶

The Korean War

While the fighting on the island subsided, Puerto Rican soldiers were engaged in battlefields half a world away. On June 25, 1950, war had broken out in Korea. The North Korean People's Army (NKPA) quickly overran most of the Korean peninsula, forcing South Korean and U.S. forces into a small perimeter in Pusan.²⁷

The United States was unprepared to deal with the crisis, as it had quickly demobilized its vast military after World War II and was suffering an acute shortage of manpower. Maj. Gen. Edmond L. Almond, the commander of X Corps during the Korean War, believed that when war broke out, the U.S. Eighth Army, the only force the United States had available to thrust into combat, was just 40 percent effective.[28] The Eighth Army was not prepared physically or psychologically for battle in the summer of 1950.[29]

Structural racism had kept Puerto Rican units from seeing combat during the world wars.[30] Maj. Gen. Luis Raúl Esteves, a Puerto Rican West Pointer and adjutant general of Puerto Rico's National Guard, declared in 1951: "I was greatly discouraged [during World War II] when the blindness of the Federal Military Authorities in Puerto Rico denied us that opportunity [to fight]." General Esteves thought that the Puerto Rican regiment in the U.S. Army, the 65th Infantry, was never trusted in combat because the federal authorities believed that "although the Puerto Ricans were valiant individuals, they could not be trusted in their collective abilities and valor."[31] Racial prejudice was part of mainstream tenets which, backed by pseudo-science and popular writings, stated that the inferiority of colored races justified segregation at home and imperialism abroad—in essence, a dogma for domination and imperialism based on a racial hierarchy of power. On July 26, 1948, President Truman signed Executive Order 9981, "calling on the armed forces to provide equal treatment and opportunity for black servicemen."[32] In compliance with the executive order, the Army reluctantly started to integrate its forces. Yet as late as 1950, Puerto Ricans still did not receive any assignments that promised action. As a result, they were not sent either to basic school or to the Army Command and Staff General Staff College, which trained company and field grade officers in the fundamentals of higher command.[33]

The outbreak of the Korean War brought a striking change to the mission of the Puerto Rican soldier in the U.S. military. The gravity of the moment was the most important consideration. There were two reasons why the U.S. Army did not assign the 65th Infantry to supporting roles during the Korean War as it had during the two world wars. The first was the army's lack of manpower.[34] The second was the regiment's (and the Puerto Rican National Guard's) performance during a training exercise, Operation Portrex.[35] However, had there not been such an acute shortage of military personnel, Puerto Rican units might have had to fulfill the same supporting roles they had carried out in the previous wars.

Participating in the War as a Decolonization Strategy

In Puerto Rico, the National Guard was activated and the 65th Infantry mobilized and secretly sent to Korea. Recent works on Puerto Rico's participation in the war and the role of the 65th have approached the issue from the perspective of traditional military history or have focused on the injustices suffered by the men of the regiment.[36] For our discussion, highlighting the political, social, cultural, and symbolical value of fighting in the Korean War is of the utmost relevance. As part of the decolonization project, participating in the war was significant as it helped to shape and consolidate the commonwealth formula in both abstract and practical terms.

Unlike previous wars, Puerto Ricans were entering this conflict very early, and they were going in as first-line combat troops. Their role could very well undermine the basis for imperial racial hierarchies of power—the supposed inferiority of darker races—and prove to the Puerto Ricans themselves that they were not inferior to continental Americans (specifically to white Americans) or anybody else—as commentators in the local press argued.[37] Obtaining political equality and decolonization via military service was neither a new strategy nor the prerogative of the Puerto Ricans. As in the previous wars, service, equality, and decolonization were tied to manhood and modernity. The same familial language and metaphors used by PPD officials to make the reformed colony more palatable to Puerto Ricans and the notion that "Puerto Rico as a nation was growing up into manhood, and deserved to be treated as such" were extended to Puerto Rican participation in the war.[38] In fact, throughout the war the Puerto Rican soldiers came to epitomize that new and transformed modern man and the new Puerto Rico.

For political leaders in Puerto Rico, the outbreak of the Korean War gave them an opportunity to prove that their people were ready for self-determination, that they had learned the ways of democracy and freedom, and that they would fight in defense of what was popularly promoted as America's values. In a sense, military service could prove that Puerto Ricans were politically mature according to the parameters of the western world. Consequently, most political leaders in Puerto Rico actively supported the participation of tens of thousands of Puerto Ricans in the conflict. That local leaders believed that participating in the war might accelerate the decolonization process or advance their political goals was rooted in the island's history. The development of the political status of the island and the role of Puerto Rico's participation in the U.S. military had followed parallel paths. Moreover, P.L. 600, signed into law on July 30, called for Puerto Ricans to write their own constitution through a constitutional convention, and that document was to define both the status of the island and its relationship with the United States. Every political party had reasons to believe that supporting the war effort would promote their particular goals. Consequently, all political factions except the Nacionalistas supported the war effort.

Both the Estadistas and the Socialistas supported participation in the war, believing that the full incorporation of Puerto Rico into the Union would end the colonial regime. The leadership of these parties saw in the Korean War the opportunity to prove, not only to Americans but to Puerto Ricans themselves, that Puerto Rico was ready to join the United States on equal terms. The rationale was that Puerto Ricans had learned the American ways and were willing to do their share for the Union, even if that meant dying in defense of the nation. On the other hand, the Independentistas supported the war because its leaders hoped to prove that if Puerto Rico became independent, it would not turn anti-American or Communist. Just like their ideological antagonists, the leaders of the independence movement also sought to demonstrate that Puerto Rico was politically responsible and mature.[39] The Nacionalistas orchestrated the only opposition to military participation. But after the failed insurrection and attempt to assassinate President Truman, Muñoz Marín succeeded in discrediting their movement.[40] The only voice opposing Puerto Rico's cooperation with the U.S. military was silenced in the early days of the war.

If anything, the Populares were more invested in supporting Puerto Rican participation in the war than any other party. The military mobilization of tens of thousands of Puerto Ricans and military expenditures during World War II had provided economic relief and the means and infrastructure to launch the most comprehensive socioeconomic restructuring in the island's history with U.S. capital but with local manpower and know-how. World War II and military mobilization had in fact allowed the Populares to keep their promises of social justice. Mobilizing the Puerto Ricans again carried the implicit promise that another generation of veterans could receive all the opportunities and benefits to which the World War II veterans were entitled and use those benefits to join in the socioeconomic restructuring of the island. For the Populares, however, who had moved to support a third way (the commonwealth), participating in the war also provided a battleground to test the viability of the new political status and promote its main discourse with regard to political and cultural identities. Korea would be the arena where Puerto Ricans would show that Anglo-Saxon and Hispanic cultures (identified by the press and politicians as the two great cultures of the hemisphere) could coexist not just in one place but in one body.[41] Hence throughout the war the PPD would vigorously call the Puerto Ricans to arms and use every opportunity to link the war effort with their own decolonization project, the socioeconomic restructuring of the island, and the making of a new Puerto Rican for a modern Puerto Rico.

Support for the war effort and the call to send Puerto Ricans to Korea started soon after the outbreak of hostilities. In early August 1950, Fernós Isern, serving as Puerto Rico's resident commissioner, declared in Washington that the island was ready to field an army of 75,000 men to join the UN forces.[42] Fernós Isern believed that if Washington asked for this volunteer force, the quota would be easily filled. Although Fernós Isern probably considered the economic situation in Puerto Rico when he calculated such a high number of volunteers, he did not mention it in his declarations. Instead, he stressed the patriotism of Puerto Ricans, asserting they would not fail to come to the defense of democracy and the nation.[43]

Ordered to prepare the Puerto Rican 65th Infantry Regiment for duty in Korea, the commanding officer, Col. William W. Harris, asked permission to recruit about 2,000 volunteers to bring the regiment to 10 percent above war strength. The Pentagon agreed, and Harris proceeded to solicit recruits over the radio and through the local press. At first Harris doubted he could collect all the men he needed, but he soon was surprised to find the streets and sidewalks leading to the recruiting and induction center at Fort Buchanan jammed with men waiting to get in. In his memoirs Harris stated, "We could have recruited fifty thousand if we needed that many. We literally turned them away in droves after we reached our quota."[44] The island's deteriorating economic situation helps to explain the enthusiasm described by Harris. The island's economy had improved greatly during World War II due to mobilization and the war economy. However, as the war ended and federal military expenditures on the construction of installations completely ceased in 1948, unemployment rose dramatically while the island experimented inflation and a decrease of the Real Per Capita Net Income.[45] Moreover, the previous war experience (World Wars I and II) had not been a traumatic event for the soldiers who served in Puerto Rican units, due to the War Department's policy of using them in supporting roles far from active battlefields. And thanks to the Veterans Readjustment Act of 1944 (the GI Bill), World War II veterans in Puerto Rico had found a path toward education and middle-class status. The combination of these factors made military service very attractive for Puerto Ricans, even during wartime.

Any doubts Puerto Ricans may have had about joining the U.S. military were eased by the stance of the island's political parties. The fact that Governor Muñoz Marín publicly exhorted Puerto Rican youth to respond to the call of the 65th and to defend other peoples' right to democracy because it was "our privilege . . .

Fighting for the "Nation"?

as our people has developed one of the best democracies in the world" surely helped fill the ranks.[46]

The Puerto Rican press echoed the call to arms linking participation in the U.S. military with decolonizing the island. Even as late as 1950, the press ran editorials in which the autonomous period of 1897–98 stood as the minimum standard to which Puerto Rico should aspire. Moreover, the press called for a greater degree of autonomy, which was to be accomplished by allowing Puerto Ricans to draft their own constitution. A journalist wrote: "Under the Autonomic Charter of 1897 we enjoyed a relative sovereign life, until it was brusquely replaced by an intractable military regime as a consequence of the war of 1898." These calls for more autonomy appeared beside articles lauding the 65th Infantry (nicknamed the Borinqueneers in an English transliteration of *Borinqueños*) and citing the regiment as a possible catalyst in forging a new national identity. Moreover, these editorials ran alongside commentaries praising Muñoz Marín and Fernós Isern for their commitment to earn the right for the Puerto Ricans to write their own constitution.[47]

The rationale behind these articles was that the Borinqueneers' commitment to Korea as first-line troops "will help Puerto Ricans to come out of their complexes of insularism, and erase the marks of inferiority, which are the byproduct of hundreds of years of colonial type regimes."[48] This statement adds another factor to explaining why support for military service, especially combat duty, was so widespread. The modernizing local elites agreed that fighting alongside U.S. and United Nation soldiers could help to prove, not only to Continental Americans but also to Puerto Ricans themselves, that they were the equals of their co-citizens from the mainland. Both the press and the political leadership thought it necessary to convince the people of Puerto Rico that they were ready to decide their own future.

On October 12, 1950, the press announced that the 65th was fighting in Korea. The mood that day came to resemble a holiday more than anything else. The island's newspapers were full of stories, pictures of the 65th, and the ceremonies held previous to their departure. The private sector joined the chorus with paid advertisements wishing the 65th a prompt return, and exhorting Puerto Rican soldiers to uphold the ideals of democracy and freedom. In both leading newspapers, *El Mundo* and *El Imparcial*, the tone was the same. The latter proclaimed, "As it was yet another symbol of the United Nations, under the American flag flies the flag of the 65th Infantry Regiment, this flag flies today in Korea." The colors of the 65th came to represent not only the regiment, but Puerto Rico as a whole.[49]

In a farewell speech published two months later in the press, Muñoz Marín told the departing soldiers that their fight was one for freedom and democracy. He stressed that they were fighting not for a clichéd democracy but for a democracy that entailed a fight against "scarcity of economic means; scarcity of knowledge; scarcity of wisdom."[50] Muñoz Marín had lost no time in linking participation in the war to the Populares' platform, which prioritized economic freedom and social justice over political sovereignty. The island's media also reminded Puerto Ricans what they were fighting for. "This regiment (the 65th) goes again overseas in defense of our Nation's freedom," asserted *El Imparcial*.[51] Another editorial in *Periódico el Mundo* stated, "It should bring great satisfaction to Puerto Rico that the military authorities in the United States found the 65th competent and qualified to actively take part in this vital endeavor that encompass so much for the Christian world."[52] Even before the 65th was mobilized, the press ran patriotic news and editorials that sought to comfort fathers and mothers "before the imminent probability that their sons will soon find themselves obliged to carry on their patriotic duties by participating in the conflict."[53] Defense of the nation, democracy, and freedom mixed with patriotism and local pride in the narrative, put forward by the island's press. The call for decolonization and the creation of the new Puerto Rican glued these narratives.

As political leaders and the press issued a call for fighting in defense of the nation, Puerto Ricans responded en masse. On several occasions the military authorities in Puerto Rico had to announce that they did not need more volunteers. Even when the war had turned into a bloody stalemate and long lists of casualties appeared almost every week in the Puerto Rican press, the recruiting stations never lacked volunteers, at least not until 1953.⁵⁴ Eventually more than 61,000 Puerto Ricans served in the U.S. armed forces during the Korean War: 43,434 fought in the Korea, most of them with the 65th Infantry, and some 91 percent of the soldiers were volunteers.⁵⁵ Puerto Rico's poor economic situation after World War II compelled Puerto Ricans to join and stay in the U.S. military as previously discussed. But as the Korean War became a bloody stalemate, other reasons also influenced the decision to volunteer for service. The narratives put forward by Muñoz Marín and most of the political elites and the press created a hero cult around the Puerto Rican soldiers fighting in Korea. Periodically large groups of veterans returned to the island after being replaced by new recruits and were treated to official receptions and parades. Soldiers killed in action (KIA) received full military burials in Puerto Rico, some of which the governor attended. The wounded (WIA) were welcomed as heroes by the governor and elected officials, and their hometowns organized parades in their honor. Those facts may explain why Puerto Rico sustained a high enlistment ratio, notwithstanding a high casualty rate among its troops. Those men were praised as heroes because they served, were maimed, or died defending the nation.

Puerto Rican leaders, the press, and the common folk continued to show their support for the war effort and especially for the 65th's soldiers throughout the conflict. On May 21, 1951, scarcely two weeks before the people of Puerto Rico voted to accept the provisions of P.L. 600, roughly three hundred veterans of the 65th arrived in San Juan. This group was the first contingent of Puerto Ricans to finish their tour of duty under the U.S. Army's rotation system. They received an extremely warm welcome from both the leaders and the people of Puerto Rico. The governor declared the day a national holiday and hosted a ceremony to honor the returning "heroes and their families."⁵⁶ Avenues and plazas were named in honor of the regiment, while monuments went up to commemorate the dead. The coat of arms of the 65th was painted on all the public buses in the capital and on the sides of train engines and freight and passenger carts. Groups of parents collected and sent tons of packages containing Puerto Rican food, music, letters, and gifts to their soldiers. Newspapers sent free copies to Korea for distribution to the soldiers. Muñoz Marín had his speeches taped and sent to the Puerto Rican soldiers in Korea.

Some of the farewell messages from soldiers of the 65th embarking for Korea support Fernós Isern's presumption that Puerto Ricans would respond patriotically to the call to arms. "We will fight for our motherland until victory is achieved," wrote one departing soldier. "I will fight for the motherland until we secure victory and thus enjoy eternal peace and democracy," vowed another Borinqueneer.[57] Though at first glance these statements may read as the usual discourse of soldiers yet to see battle, it would be wise to consider the deep implications of such comments. First they referred to Puerto Rico when talking about the motherland (usually *patria* or *madre patria*) but to the United States when referring to the nation. Their statements show that they accepted the defense of the American nation as their duty as Puerto Ricans. Second, fighting in the war as part of the U.S. military and the UN command was perceived as a way to secure democracy and freedom at home, which went along with the Populares' new political formula.

That the leading newspapers handpicked the statements that more closely resembled the developing ideology behind the commonwealth formula is a possibility, but it is likely that Muñoz Marín and the Populares and the views of the thousands of peasants and workers turned soldiers had finally aligned. After all, in his previous three campaigns Muñoz Marín had campaigned on social justice and not independence as his party's priority. Furthermore, the fact that these two newspapers, which more often than not were at odds with Muñoz Marín, chose to present these narratives (which clearly benefited the Populares' plans) shows the growing support for the commonwealth project throughout the island.

Puerto Ricans responded to a call to defend the United States, reaffirming that they considered themselves part of it. But the call to arms also emphasized the attributes of Puerto Rico and its *Ante-American* heritage even if in the elite's and the Populares' discourse it was limited to the notion of Hispanic legacy. By responding to this call, Puerto Ricans demonstrated their complex identities, which allow them to be Puerto Ricans and Americans simultaneously and interchangeably and to negotiate and synthesize cultural and political identities. This in fact became the essence of the national identity sponsored by the Commonwealth architects in its early days. The Anglo-Saxon/Hispanic binary would eventually be replaced by the racial triad (Spaniard, Taino, and African) as the Puerto Ricans' colonial identity matrix as the reformed colonial state continued to engage in the sponsoring and sanctioning of identities.[58] But during the crucial years of 1950–52, the Puerto Rican soldiers who went to fight in Korea, especially with the 65th Infantry, became national icons and the incarnation and champions of the commonwealth's philosophical matrix. These soldiers became an energizing element in the fight for decolonization as the Populares envisioned it.

Linking the Korean War and the active participation of the Puerto Rican soldier to their project of political decolonization helped the PPD to ensure the acceptance of P.L. 600. Muñoz Marín equated the battles being fought in Korea to those being fought at home. On May 28, 1951, he held a ceremony honoring the guardsmen, policemen, and firemen who fought the nationalist insurrection. Addressing those about to be awarded medals for their service during the insurrection, Muñoz Marín declared that just as their brothers in Korea were doing, they had put "their lives between the assailants of freedom and peace and the people of Puerto Rico." The Nacionalistas, he argued, believed that they had the right to "impose their views on the people by violent means" and could not respect the will of the people as expressed through the electoral process.[59] The Nacionalistas had hoped to derail the referendum and the Populares' project. Ironically, the revolt provided the Populares with the opportunity to link their project to local and global decolonization and democracy.

On June 4, 1951, the people of Puerto Rico voted by a large majority to accept the provisions of P.L. 600.[60] Following the referendum, the Puerto Ricans elected delegates to a constitutional convention on August 27. The constitutional convention, led by

Fernós Isern, convened in San Juan on September 17, 1951, and concluded its deliberations on February 6, 1952. The constitution it adopted was submitted to the people of Puerto Rico in a referendum on March 3, 1952, and was passed by an overwhelming majority.[61] On April 22, 1952, in a special message, Truman recommended that Congress granted early approval of the constitution drafted by the convention and argued that such action would be evidence of the United States' adherence to "the principle of self-determination and its devotion to the ideals of freedom and democracy."[62] The constitution was approved by Congress on H.J. Res. 430, and signed into law by the president on July 3, 1952. Upon signing the constitution, Truman reiterated the importance of the event for the free world.[63]

After the acceptance by the constitutional convention of the conditions of approval and the issuance of a proclamation by Governor Muñoz Marín, the Constitution of the Commonwealth of Puerto Rico became effective on July 25, 1952, exactly fifty-four years after the American invasion. The date could not have been more symbolic, for the constitution was supposed to erase all traces of colonialism, including the anniversary of the island becoming an American colony. Many continental politicians thought that the establishment of the Commonwealth showed that the United States was not only "disposed to increase the well-being of Puerto Rican fellow citizens but was willing to allow them to define for themselves the relationship they would establish with the federal union."[64] Truman remarked that the "American people should take special pride in the fact that the constitution was the product of the people of Puerto Rico."[65] These comments are representative of how important it was for the United States to prove its adherence to the principles of self-determination. Soon afterwards Muñoz Marín asked President Truman to stop submitting annual reports on Puerto Rico to the United Nations, a decision which led the international organization to remove the island from the list of non-self-governing territories on November 27, 1953.[66] To both the Puerto Rican and the U.S. government, the island had ceased to be a colony, and the UN had certified the end of the United States as a colonial power.

According to its preface, the new constitution was intended to promote the "coexistence in Puerto Rico of the two great cultures [Anglo-Saxon and Hispanic] of the American Hemisphere."[67] Many Puerto Rican soldiers fighting in Korea thought they were doing just that. A copy of the constitution was sent to Korea before ratification along with Puerto Rican flags. One soldier commented, "We know and understand the things we are fighting for, but it is better to have a document of our own, stated in the words of our people." Another soldier added, "Now we have two Constitutions to defend."[68] It is significant that two corporals made these comments in 1952, which means that they were not part of the 65th Infantry's old guard but volunteers who joined the army after the war broke out. They enlisted to defend the nation to which they felt they belonged, but they were also proud of having a document expressing the will of the Puerto Rican people. Moreover, the 65th, which had been a regular U.S. Army unit since its early days, had become an instrument for nation and state building as the Populares envisioned it, just as the Puerto Rico National Guard had been since at least the 1930s. There was no question that Puerto Rican U.S. military units were loyal to the United States, but they were also fiercely loyal to the island's civilian government and its political and socioeconomic projects.

On August 13, 1952, exploding Chinese artillery rounds and the strains of the Puerto Rican national anthem, "La Borinqueña," set the mood as a group of Puerto Rican soldiers proudly raised their homeland's flag beside the Stars and Stripes on a mountainous battlefield in South Korea. The soldiers commemorated the creation of the Estado Libre Asociado after half a century of direct U.S. colonial rule. Col. Juan César Cordero, the first Puerto Rican commander of the 65th Infantry, felt that all Puerto Ricans in the U.S. military, especially those in his regiment, had contributed more than their fair share to the creation of the commonwealth. Addressing the troops in Spanish, Cordero stated: "Today more than ever, we the Puerto Ricans have motives to feel highly proud of our citizenship. Today we ceased to be group citizens taken by the hand and led by the rest of our co-citizens from the North." Cordero told his men that it was important

8. Chaplain Harvey F. Kochner of St. Louis blesses a Puerto Rican flag in Korea held by Lt. Col. Carlos Betances Ramírez (Cabo Rojo PR) and M. Sgt. Ángel J. Rivera (Coamo PR), August 31, 1952. Hilda Alicia Hernandez de Rivera (Humacao PR) sent the flag to the regiment. Center of Military History/Army Signal Corp.

9. In the fall of 1952 Puerto Rican flags would be carried by leading elements of the 65th Infantry during attacks. The flag and appeals to national pride and unity helped the Puerto Rican soldiers overcome shortcomings such as inadequate training, a language barrier, and deficient leadership. Flag of the Commonwealth of Puerto Rico presented to the 65th Infantry Regiment, 3rd U.S. Infantry Division, in Korea. *Left to right*: Maj. Silvestre Ortiz, adjutant, 65th; Maj. Edward D. Denges, 65th; Lt. Col. Clayton C. Craig, executive officer, 65th; Maj. Gen. Rovert L. Dulaney, commanding officer, 3rd Division; Col. Juan Cesar Cordero Dávila, commanding officer, 65th Infantry; Brig. Gen. Charles L. Dasher, 3rd Division; and Col. George Vivario, commanding officer, Belgium Battalion. Photo taken by Cpl. Chester Kryzack, U.S. Army Signal Corps.

10. Puerto Rican soldiers serving with the 65th Infantry in Korea hold the Puerto Rican flag, fall 1952. Photo taken by Marcelino Cruz Rodríguez, used by permission of Carlos Cruz and Mirta Cruz-Home; reproduction by Noemi Fuigueroa-Soulet.

that they continue to be American citizens, but he also emphasized that "we too have a constitution that emanates exclusively from our own will." He added, lest anybody forget, how they had obtained their constitution:

> Patiently but armed with faith in the great democratic attitudes of our great nation, we hoped for the day in which, not only we were allowed to enjoy our individual freedom and our rights as individuals citizens, but also to determine our own destiny.[69]

Not only had the Puerto Rican soldier waited but he had fought for such status and became instrumental in the battle for political and socioeconomic decolonization. Cordero expressed the complex paradigm of Puerto Rican national identities on August 13 in Korea:

> For fifty-four years we, the Puerto Ricans, have lived under the political tutelage of our co-citizens of the North. We have assimilated their entrepreneur spirit and industrial skills; and fed our soul and thoughts with the most sacred of men's attributes: their admiration and respect for freedom, justice, and equality.

Puerto Ricans, in Cordero's opinion, had assimilated and embraced what the United States represented, but without ceasing to be Puerto Ricans or "without adulterating our Hispanic heritage, nor have we soiled it with artificial trends of Sajonic assimilation: and without relegating our Hispanic culture, sentiments and traditions, which we conserve pure, like the most precious legacy of our gallant and noble ancestors."[70]

Nevertheless, Puerto Ricans had assimilated trends from American culture. It would have been impossible not to do so after half a century of U.S. rule and after going through the institutions set by the metropolis to Americanize its new subjects. But the Puerto Ricans did not renounce their *Ante-American* heritage but fused it with that of the newcomers. In the process, new national identities slowly but surely emerged, finally becoming hegemonic during the Korean War and the Puerto Rican soldier was instrumental in this process. The cultural and the political, the insular and the continental, the Puerto Rican (in all its manifestations) and the American could, according to the soldiers' and politicians' discourse, coexist and strengthen each other. The words of two Puerto Rican POWs may express this better. Released after two years of imprisonment in a Chinese camp, Corporal Fernando Arroyo told a correspondent of the *Pacific Stars & Stripes*, "They (the Chinese) often tell me about big trouble and revolution in Puerto Rico because American [*sic*] exploits masses. I tell them I am American and they are liars." Master Sergeant Enrique R. Fernández, Arroyo's prison mate, added: "We may come from Puerto Rico and speak a different language but the communists could not take away from us one thing, we are Americans."[71]

As discussed earlier, the historical juncture of 1898 gave way to the development of very complex national identities in Puerto Rico. This process was furthered by the U.S. presence and active campaigns to Americanize the natives on the island and by the active support given by Puerto Rico's political leadership to cooperate militarily with the metropolis. This, many thought, would bring about the decolonization of the island, either by becoming a state of the union or an independent republic. Paradoxically, military participation eventually made it easier for Puerto Ricans to embrace an identity that allowed them to negotiate between being Americans and Puerto Ricans or to be both simultaneously and hence, to embrace *autonomismo* in the form of the Commonwealth. Since the very early days of U.S. domination over the island, politicians and the press sought to hasten the decolonization process by using colonial instruments, and in this case, the metropolis' military. In the 1950s, however, a midpoint was chosen when it became apparent that after half a century under U.S. rule had not moved Puerto Ricans toward either full assimilation or full rejection of American culture, values, and institutions.

If the project of nation building through military service had passed from metropolitan to local elites' control during World War II, during the Korean War such project became popularized. As peasants and urban workers continued to join the armies of the metropolis and to support the Populares' project of social justice and the economic restructuring of the island, their views with respect to political and cultural identity became hegemonic.

Unable to convince his constituency of the viability of independence, incapable of winning elections without the support of the masses, faced with Washington's adamant opposition to independence, and aware of the significance of military service (and federal aid and support) for the reconstruction of the socioeconomic structures in the island, Muñoz Marín and the Populares revived and championed a political status which they thought offered the space for political, economic, cultural and social development.

In a very real sense, when the Puerto Rican soldier became the embodiment of the commonwealth formula, the political leaders involved in its design were responding to the peasants and urban worker's complex identities as reflected and empowered by their military service. Among other things, their national identities compelled them to defend the "American Nation" to show their *Puertorriqueñidad*. As such, the new status, at least for the time being, offered a space where most Puerto Ricans could feel comfortable. Throughout the war, the Populares and the press made it a point to highlight that, as it had been the case for World War II veterans, the majority of the Puerto Rican soldiers who fought in Korea came from the mountains, sugar cane plantations and the urban working classes. This is not surprising as those sectors constituted the bulk of the PPD's base. That the figure of the jíbaro-soldier was used to support the creation of the reformed colonial state supports Lilian Guerra's thesis of a jíbaro image firmly ingrained in Puerto Rican society as part of a nationalism that paradoxically does not "necessarily entail independence."[72] This is especially true for those jíbaros -turned soldiers during the Korean War. Military service made them the perfect embodiment of a noble, romantic past and a modern future as proposed by the ELA creators.

And just as the World War II veterans had done, the returning jíbaro-Soldier would renounce subsistence agriculture or life as a sugar cane-cutter. Many would become the technocrats and technicians of the Puerto Rican "industrial miracle" and would become the nucleus of broadening middle class.[73] But they did not renounce their identity. In fact many of those jíbaro/soldiers, who went on to study and became professionals, or started small and medium business, and/or remained in the National Guard or the active military, subsidized their plots of land with the income from their new professions. Ironically, the jíbaro, a heavily romanticized figure to be sure and the quintessential icon of the *Populares*, and of modern nationalist and independent movements in the island, survived as such in great part due to his military service.

Those Puerto Rican soldiers, who celebrated the creation of the Commonwealth by raising the Puerto Rican flag and by playing the national anthem in a forgotten hill in Korea, made another symbolic contribution to the emerging nation. The Puerto Rican *danza*, "La Borinqueña," composed in 1867 as a criollo version of the European waltz and quickly banned by the Spanish authorities, had been for a long time the unofficial anthem of the island. In 1922, the director of the 65th regimental band adapted "La Borinqueña" to be used as the regiment's march. In July 24, 1952, that version became the official anthem of the Estado Libre Asociado de Puerto Rico. Unbeknownst to these soldiers, their regiment, el *sesenta y cinco* had safeguarded that expression of Puertoricaness.

Conclusion

Usually when metropolitan powers engage in transforming the socioeconomic and political structures of colonies or territories, they call these projects "nation building" when in fact they are engaging primarily in "state building." The focus is on creating, altering, or reimagining the public and private infrastructures that should allow for a territory or country to operate per the rules set by the hegemonic world power or coalition, which are considered modern and therefore desirable. Among the structures that make a country or territory "modern" are sanitary health facilities, a monetary system tied to western banks, public education, political and judicial institutions that resemble those of the dominant power, a local constabulary, and a professional military. These institutions serve to change the self-perception (if not the loyalties) of individuals and groups in such territories, and since it is the metropolis's desire to do so, they are indeed engaging in nation building via state or institution building. Hence they create a state more in tune with the metropolis, ultimately affecting the sociocultural identities of the colonial subjects and their national identities.

Spanish and American imperialists tried to implement different projects in Puerto Rico (and elsewhere) in which exerting control over the identities of the colonial subjects was paramount. These projects, as Julian Go has argued, "were rarely if ever realized in full." Moreover, they were alternately aided, challenged, and altered by the local elites and popular sectors.[1] Metropolitan powers are not fully hegemonic in deciding what the colonial subjects are to become. Local realities and idiosyncrasies alter the metropolis's designs. Institutions must be adapted to such things as climate, geography, and cultural differences. Moreover, as elite colonial groups become engaged in nation building (an inevitable process, since the metropolis needs them to secure the loyalty of the colonies' popular sectors), imperialists are forced to negotiate with pre-metropolis or emerging colonial elites with regard to the socioeconomic and political structures of the colony.[2] Laura Briggs has argued that "internal power relations of gender, race, class, age, and so on can be worked out through the structure of colonialism (what structures are untouched by it) without being in any meaningful sense determined by them."[3] Even within colonial structures there is space to negotiate internal power relations. And these colonial institutions can also be turned around to resist the metropolis. Power relations are influenced by the metropolitan structures, but the colonial subjects have a say in altering the nature of these institutions, too.

To some extent, the degree of the colonial elites' engagement with the metropolitan structures may determine how liberal or at least how responsive metropolitan policies are to the colonial subjects' needs. The degree of participation in state and nation building is in itself influenced by the needs of the metropolis. And during periods of crisis, metropolitan-colonial negotiations tend to accelerate. The need to rely on local elites to command public support gradually leads to the criollization of the institutions and projects designed by the metropolis to control or assimilate their subjects. When this happens, there is a chance that the nation building project falls into the hands of the local elites. Depending on the nature of the local coalitions, there is also the possibility of these projects, and the institutions devised to carry them out, becoming popularized and that a very pluralistic polity supported by flexible and open national identities becomes hegemonic.

The more that Spain was able to exclude those born in Puerto Rico from the colonial administration and the military, the more repressive it became. The Spanish colonial administration had tried since the early nineteenth century to restrain the power of colonial elites by reducing the presence of those born on the island in the colonial militias. However, it was not until the once vast Spanish Empire was reduced to Cuba, Puerto Rico, the Philippines, and some smaller possessions that the Spaniards were able to concentrate on closing all avenues to enfranchisement, especially the military, to black men. After the failed 1868 insurrection of Lares and the final exclusion of the Puerto Ricans from the military, the liberal criollo political leadership moved toward autonomismo while the exiled leadership joined revolutionary juntas in the United States and continued to advocate for independence. By the dawn of Spanish control over the island, the Iberian metropolis had also tried to keep the island by passing the Carta Autónomica de 1897, but this gesture came too late and only placated the criollo political elite as it did not change quotidian dynamics for most Puerto Ricans. Though the Spaniards were able to quench political and military insurrection until they finally lost the island to the United States, they had alienated themselves from the general population, fueling the emergence of distinct Puerto Rican national identities. Hence when the U.S. troops landed in Puerto Rico in 1898, the Spaniards could not rely on the loyalty of the islanders. Four hundred years of history and dominance, however, are hard to erase. The natives of Puerto Rico probably started to develop distinct national identities during the last third of the nineteenth century, and while a majority felt no loyalty to Spain, they still retained a high degree of cultural affinity with the metropolis.

Under U.S. rule, access to military institutions for the hijos de este país was reestablished while political participation, to a certain degree, was opened to the popular sectors. Soon after the United States took over the island, Puerto Ricans started to replace U.S. continental soldiers. From the beginning the new insular soldiers became elements of the U.S. Army tightly controlled by the colonial administration. Additionally, the new metropolis gradually allowed for a higher degree of political participation, eventually creating the space for mass electoral enfranchisement. These two trends facilitated the transfer of sovereignty over the island from Spain to the United States, and they transformed the character of Puerto Rican nationalities. The inclusion of Puerto Ricans in the armed forces and mass political mobilization, especially of the rural sectors, gradually led to competing national identities.

The United States embarked on a comprehensive buildup of the public education system (which was intended to Americanize and modernize the inhabitants) and launched massive sanitary and relief campaigns. Although cultural affinity may have been absent between Puerto Ricans and Americans in 1898, the metropolis's control of education allowed for the projection of American material superiority disguised as cultural preeminence. Furthermore, simultaneous sanitary and relief campaigns allowed for positive interaction between the new metropolis and its colonial subjects. A special relation started to emerge between the military, in particular the Army and Puerto Rico's population as military doctors and engineers combed the mountains and towns of the island, building sanitary facilities, roads, and schools and launching massive health and relief campaigns.

The opening of military institutions, the political arena, and public schools to previously disenfranchised groups began to profoundly alter the islanders' national identities. Public schools offered a homogenized pro-metropolis experience for hundreds of thousands of Puerto Ricans while the opening of the U.S. military conferred them with a sense of inclusion. Access to education and military positions also offered an opportunity to overthrow old socioeconomic hierarchies, a phenomenon that led to the creation of upwardly mobile classes and neo-elites who owed their well-being and their political allegiance to the United States.

Early American attempts to create a new Puerto Rico via military service were curtailed by the narrow scope of the project. The small size of the U.S. military apparatus at the beginning of the twentieth century limited the size of the military in Puerto Rico and its effect on the population. Still, the remobilization of the Puerto Ricans began during the first years of U.S. rule as Puerto Ricans came to wear U.S. Army uniforms and to replace continental troops. It was not, however, until the First World War, when more than 18,000 Puerto Ricans served in the U.S. armed forces, that the United States had to rely heavily on the local elites to mobilize and lead thousands of Puerto Ricans. The chance could have not come at a better time for Puerto Rican politicians, who had started to aggressively challenge colonial policies. The First World War provided the grounds to retry the projects of Americanization and modernization via military service at levels previously unimaginable and with more players involved.

The coming of the war temporarily brought to power the staunchly pro-American Republicanos, who were the first to embrace President Wilson's 100 percent Americanism discourse and to tie it to their own political goal of federated statehood. By the war's end, however, by turning President Wilson's promise of ending the hyphenations in the American nation into a call for a "New Americanism" that promoted creating a new Puerto Rican by fusing Hispanic gallantry and Anglo-Saxon industrialism, the autonomistas within Unión had found an image they could use to promote a third way, the Libre Asociación, to the general population. In essence this was a return to Eugenio María de Hostos and Rosendo Matienzo Cintrón's early idea of Americanizing the Puerto Rican, which for them meant creating a modern political individual without losing the essence of Puertorriqueñismo.[4] But this time economic modernization superseded political modernization. The autonomistas had found a new philosophy and an agent to incarnate it. There could be a space for the Anglo-Saxon and Hispanic cultures to coexist. The jíbaro, the Puerto Rican peasant, would be that new man and Puerto Rico that new space.

After the armistice, however, the jíbaro soldiers were quickly demobilized and returned to the hills and coastal valleys. Neither the metropolis nor the colonial administration created vocational or educational projects to facilitate these soldiers' readjustment into civilian society. The promises of a new jíbaro, integrated into the economy as its driving force and as the "new teachers of freedom and democracy" remained unfulfilled. The autonomistas of the 1920s were not able to exploit or develop their new popular philosophy, but the seed had been planted for the next generation, and they would retake this narrative decades later.

The imposition of U.S. citizenship prior to U.S. entry into the war, the mass participation of Puerto Ricans in the U.S. military, the newly created Puerto Rico National Guard, and the willing support of the newly elected Puerto Rican legislature for the war effort temporarily cemented U.S. control over the island and over the islanders' loyalty to the metropolis. As some supporters argued during the war, the unwillingness or inability of the vast majority of the Puerto Ricans to resist becoming American citizens and their determination to participate in the war reflected the impact that the institutions of the new metropolis had had on the Puerto Ricans. That same institutional influence would lead the Puerto Ricans to expect—if not equality—at least more political and socioeconomic opportunities.

The mass mobilization of the Puerto Rican peasantry and urban workers and the initial enthusiasm shown by the inductees hid the fact that control over the military apparatus on the island was no longer the exclusive prerogative of the American colonial administrators. The traditional and emerging local elites, as well as the professional classes, had to be called upon to train and lead the massive army of peasants soldiering in the island. Out of sheer necessity, the metropolis broadly opened the officers' corps to los hijos de este país, providing the tools for the white elites and emerging professional classes to attain and consolidate political power.

Local leaders who supported the war effort had succeeded in wresting exclusive control over the nation-building project via military service from the United States. The criollization of both the military and nation building had begun. This situation, even if not immediately apparent in the postwar years, would eventually put the local elites in a better political position than they had been before World War I. Oblivious to the transformation occurring in Puerto Rico, the metropolis was slow to respond to these challenges, and no major political changes would take place until World War II rekindled the strategic importance of the island.

Before 1941, Puerto Rico had experienced natural disasters, the Great Depression, and the end of political stability. The emergence of the Nationalist Party as a radical force under the leadership of Pedro Albizu Campos is one of the most striking characteristics of this period. Albizu Campos, in Benedict Anderson's jargon, was one of many colonial subjects who discovered the "limit of their inward ascension" during his educational pilgrimage to the metropolis. According to Anderson, awareness of their exclusion from power circles would become the basis for the colonial subjects to see themselves as "nationals" separate from the metropolis.[5] Initially staunchly pro-American, Albizu Campos would eventually lead a virulent anti-U.S. campaign in an attempt to create the Republic of Puerto Rico. The Nationalists of the 1930s resorted to underlining the differences between continental Americans and Puerto Ricans while emphasizing Hispanic traditions. Recognizing the relevance of military traditions on the island and the impact that they had on the population, the Nacionalistas created their own paramilitary units.

The Nacionalistas' failure to win the support of a sizable portion of the population was also a rejection of their iconography and their emphasis on Spanish traditions. At the time, most Puerto Ricans had been born under U.S. sovereignty, and those lucky enough to have been educated had been exposed to a curriculum based on the New England public school model. The Nationalistas' nostalgic discovery of the "Hispanic" past was an alien concept to the masses of the 1930s but not to the elites, who still traced their lineage to Spain. Moreover, the Nacionalista "rediscovery" of the island's Hispanic past was incongruent with the drive for progress. Modernization and hints at industrialization were at the core of federal efforts to improve Puerto Rico's socioeconomic condition. The Nacionalistas could not compete with U.S. material superiority, which implied a vague promise of a better future. Hence the combination of violent acts, the lack of an alternative path forward, the disconnection with the masses, socioeconomic realities, and the emphasis on Spanish tradition were as responsible for the Nacionalistas' demise in the 1930s as was the brutal political persecution to which colonial authorities subjected them.

Old ideas regarding the impact of military training on Puerto Rico's social and economic structures resurfaced during World War II.[6] This was not a new theory. Immediately after the 1898 invasion and during World War I, military service had been considered a builder of character and national identity and as a way to remake the Puerto Ricans in the continental's image. But even in World War I, the U.S. nation building project, which heavily relied on modernizing the Puerto Rican via military service, had started to escape the hands of the metropolitan administrators. During World War II, the plans of the metropolis, including type, size, and length of mobilization, had to contend with an empowered Puerto Rican senate led by Muñoz Marín. Moreover, Muñoz Marín worked incessantly to make the Puerto Rican soldier an integral part of the socioeconomic restructuring of the island.

By the war's end, control of the nation- and state-building project via military service was firmly in the Populares' hands. The U.S. military had envisioned service as a way to build a new Puerto Rican and a Puerto Rico, as early as 1898 and most certainly during World War I. This project, however, came to bear fruit when it was appropriated by Puerto Ricans. The military relevance of the island, the immense size of the U.S. military and the Puerto Rican contingent (with over 65,000 islanders serving in the armed forces), allowed for the Criollization of the military and of the agencies in charge of reconstructing the socioeconomic structures of the island. Very tellingly, Puerto Rican military officers came to preside over many of these agencies and openly supported Muñoz Marín and the reconstruction effort. Nonetheless, the military in Puerto Rico, be it the National Guard or the regular Army units (specifically the 65th Infantry), remained part of the U.S. military and depended on federal funds to function. Using the military for nation and state building reinforced the island's dependency on the federal government.

The first mobilization of the Puerto Ricans during World War II was more political than military in nature, and it happened in 1940 with the Populares first electoral victory. The second mobilization of the Puerto Ricans was, in fact, military as the island became an integral part of the U.S. war effort and Puerto Ricans were called to arms. Military expenditures during the war provided a boost to the economy, curbed unemployment, and created the infrastructure and the right socioeconomic conditions for reform.[7] The third mobilization was social in nature as the Puerto Rican soldiers moved from the fields to the classrooms and put to good use the skills learned while in the military and the benefits to which they were entitled through the GI bill of 1944. World War II ended with the island moving toward socioeconomic restructuring very rapidly and with Luis Muñoz Marín beginning to accept the third way, the commonwealth.

Initially a tactical decision born out of the need of securing the vote of the peasantry and urban workers who did not see independence as a solution to their everyday problems, the idea that the "Status no está en issue" became a kind of end in itself as political decolonization took a backseat and socioeconomic decolonization became imperative. Many have branded this change as a sellout or the co-optation of the people's will. But in fact Muñoz Marín was responding to the popular sectors' needs and will, which at this historical junction coincided with one of the greatest social reconfigurations in U.S. and Puerto Rican history. Even if the popular sectors had been supportive of independence, the political violence of the 1930s and the strategic role played by the island during World War II had moved the metropolis, in particular the armed forces, to adamantly oppose independence for the island.

Benedict Anderson has argued that a final wave of nationalism occurred during the post war era, especially in Asia and Africa, and that it was directly linked to those colonial subjects who made the educational peregrination to the metropolis and found out they belonged to another "family." These nationalist movements seeking political independence were led by "lonely bilingual intelligentsias unattached to sturdy local bourgeois," who read another language. This intelligentsia, however, was able to "bypass print in propagating the imagined communities" not only to illiterate masses but to "literate masses reading different languages."[8] It is tempting to fit Puerto Rico's postwar experience into Anderson's "final wave." After all, Muñoz Marín, the architect of the final commonwealth formula, for a time spoke a language different than that of the popular sectors, at least symbolically. Moreover, his campaigns were marked by the use of radio speeches to circumvent both the difficulties of traveling on the island and illiteracy. Instead of asserting this formula, I propose that a different wave of nationalism visited the island.

Criollization of the military and other metropolitan institutions paved the way for another phenomenon, which I call popularization. As criollization yields to popularization, the former metropolitan institutions, originally intended to change the colonial subjects into something more attuned with the metropolitan master, can turn into tools for resisting complete assimilation. This metamorphosis may occur when the metropolis finds itself in need of the colonial subjects' manpower, as in World War II, and the military and other metropolitan institutions have to open to the masses. In this instance the military can become a type of megaphone for the masses to express their voices, and there is a real chance of altering both the metropolis and the local elites' plans. The military and its project of nation and state building had fallen into the hands of the local elites during World War II, but the process of popularization had already begun as the native political leaders owed too much to these soldiers.

During World War II, the Populares used military service to begin their project of social justice and succeeded in gaining control over metropolitan institutions. Florencia Mallon has argued that the degree of military, paramilitary, and political mobilization of peasants and indigenous groups contributes to the depth of the liberal spirit of a country's polity. She believes that political groups not only sense a stake in nation state formation but also seek to participate in its design. Participation, she argues, is contested at the local level and filtered through regional politics until it moves to the national level, where negotiation continues and a contract is reached among contesting forces. Mallon calls this stage hegemony, a process that will continue endlessly as counterhegemonic forces keep challenging the hegemonic entity or polity.[9] Mallon emphasizes the construction of alternative national projects (popular, inclusive and liberal) through the political and military mobilization of peasants and other subaltern groups during periods of crisis. When subaltern groups are successfully integrated within the new hegemonic coalition, the popular sectors are incorporated into the country's polity and economy, and the state becomes a real negotiator between labor and capital while embarking on land reform. The combination of these factors attests to the liberal spirit of a hegemonic political alliance based on a national populist discourse. By World War II's end the political and military mobilization of popular sectors on the island started the drive toward a popular, inclusive, and liberal national project, and the project of political decolonization took on another meaning.

The next mobilization of Puerto Ricans took place during the Korean War, when the military became fully popularized. This mobilization had a sociopolitical character nature and was instrumental in the creation of the Estado Libre Asociado in 1952. Korea would become a propaganda war for sponsors of the third way, which entailed a new Puerto Rican for a new Puerto Rico. During this war, military service not only served as a path to political and socioeconomic enfranchisement for the Puerto Rican peasantry and urban workers. It also allowed for their national identities to become hegemonic and to translate into the political realm by virtue of the Estado Libre Asociado. That is not to say that everyone welcomed the ELA or the philosophy behind it. In fact, pro-annexation groups, echoing the Independentistas on the island, soon denounced it as a farce.[10] But the ELA's creation had a very popular, liberal, and pluralistic origin supported by an alternative concept of the Puerto Ricans' national identities.

The tens of thousands of Puerto Ricans turned soldiers during World War II and Korea had the opportunity to become part of an emerging or broadening middle class. The popular sectors' cultural discourses were characterized by neither a rejection nor an acceptance of the 100 percent Americanism espoused by some metropolitan agents and native politicians or the Hispanic revival of the nationalist movement. Instead, their discourse was a hybrid popular language that fused and accepted Americanism and Hispanismo as well as other cultural influences. The popular hybrid culture inched its way forward to eventually become the dominant cultural and political discourse. Had tens of thousands of Puerto Rican peasants and urban workers not been mobilized for war and then enfranchised, such popular discourse would have had a hard time becoming politically hegemonic.

This discourse was hard to accept by the nationalists. For the Nacionalistas, the "Nation" could not survive; in fact, it had no purpose at all if it did not have its own independent state. Becoming an independent state to secure the survival of the nation went from being the means to becoming the end. This vision did not attract vast sectors of Puerto Rico's society. Puerto Ricans obviously identified culturally with the island, although the influence of fifty years of U.S. institutions was noticeable in every aspect of Puerto Rican life. But politically Puerto Ricans were neither alien nor adversarial to U.S. precepts. In effect, even to this day Nacionalismo expresses itself in every possible cultural form but does not translate into political power. For Albizu Campos's Nacionalistas, the nation was a concept higher than the Puerto Ricans themselves, for they imagined the Puerto Rican nation as a sovereign political entity, as an independent republic. The Populares, on the other hand, switched the discourse by making the Puerto Ricans the nation. Thus political sovereignty in the form of an independent state came second to the welfare of the people. As long as the people were taken care of, the nation would survive. Muñoz Marín and Albizu Campos were part of the intelligentsia that Benedict Anderson identifies as the future leaders of national movements of decolonization. After his pilgrimage to the metropolis, Albizu Campos, was never able to speak against the language of the popular sectors, for he never understood that many Puerto Ricans had come to adopt traits of American culture as their own. Muñoz Marín, on the other hand, learned the language of the popular sectors.

The institutions and plans of the metropolis and local elites may have been changed by the popular sectors, but they were also changed in the process. After fifty years of U.S. dominance, Puerto Ricans identities were divided into a very Puerto Rican cultural side that mainstream mainly identified with Hispanic legacy, albeit with a heavy American influence, and a political identity attuned mostly with the precepts of Americanism. Puerto Rican society, where the political meets the cultural, provided the space for these two identities to merge. Nobody expressed the complexity of Puerto Rican identities better than the Puerto Rican soldiers who thought they ought to defend the American nation, to which they thought they belonged, because it was their duty as Puerto Ricans. In this regard, we find Puerto Ricans serving in the U.S. military during the Korean War, with the overwhelming support of the population, who were proud of their Puertoricaness and who saw no incongruence with proving their Puertorriqueñidad by defending the American nation and wearing a U.S. Army uniform. The colonial subjects going through these institutions, with the cheering of the local elites, found it hard not to be receptive to the metropolis's tenets. And thus these soldiers who cited "freedom," "democracy," "fighting for our nation," and "defending our nation in peril" had in fact adopted much of the metropolis's creed, even if criollized or popularized, and even with the inherent contradictions of a colonial subject fighting for his nation while wearing the uniform of the metropolis. By bleeding alongside the soldiers of the United Nations in Korea, the Puerto Rican soldiers became the local heroes of the emerging nation.

But as Mallon warns us, hegemony is always in contestation. Soon after the creation of the Commonwealth, the local elites tried to create a sanctioned national identity to fit the new state's official discourse. Arlene Dávila has argued that after Puerto Rico became a commonwealth, the PPD sought to counter the independence movement and thus secure the survival of the commonwealth by appropriating the Nationalist Party's icons and discourse. This, Dávila argues, led to the neutralization of independence as a political option.[11] However, Muñoz Marín abandoned independence as an immediate political goal after he became disenchanted with the cold reception that the masses in Puerto Rico gave to the idea of independence in 1936 and because he knew that at least during the World War II Washington would not support it in any way. Moreover, he did not appropriate the symbols of Puerto Rican nationalism. He identified them correctly and altered his political posture accordingly. And he did so only after spending another decade trying to secure independence for the island after realizing that important groups in the United States were starting to favor statehood for the island and recognizing that he would not command the loyalty of the Puerto Rican peasantry and urban workers if he moved toward independence. Most notably, Dávila has argued that the creation of the Racial Triad—the "brave and gallant" Spaniard, the "noble" Taino, and the "strong" black African—to encapsulate Puerto Rican culture and identities was the ELA's attempt to consolidate its position and defeat the Independentista movement, by dominating cultural identities on the island. The racial triad, however, was not an attempt to move the island away from independence or Puertorriqueñismo but an effort to hinder further Americanization. In essence, the new state-sponsored identity was intended to roll back half a century of American influence. Nonetheless, the popularization of the metropolis and the reformed colony's institutions meant that the local elites lost any control they could hope to have over the islanders' national identities. New national identities emerged in Puerto Rico, but they were and remain impossible to be controlled by the state.

AFTERTHOUGHT

In 1958 former Puerto Rican governor Rexford G. Tugwell predicted: "The [Commonwealth] Constitution might prove so satisfactory that it would arrest further progress toward union, at least temporarily, and would also make it impossible for Muñoz's successors to press farther toward independence."[12] The constitution indeed proved satisfactory to both American politicians and Puerto Ricans. The United States was able to shield itself against charges of colonialism and to proclaim itself as the true champion of the free world. In late 1952, the government of Puerto Rico asked President Truman to stop presenting annual reports on Puerto Rico before the United Nations, which led the international organization to remove the island from the list of non-self-governing territories on November 27, 1953.[13] For a while, Puerto Rico became a miracle, a window for the underdeveloped world to see what could be accomplished by aligning itself with the United States. For Puerto Ricans, the Estado Libre Asociado offered a higher degree of autonomy that few thought possible at the time, while retaining its relationship with the United States. It also brought a respite to a people that had been fighting for a change in their colonial status for more than fifty years. Both Puerto Ricans and Americans grew comfortable with the Commonwealth, perhaps too comfortable, and more than seven decades later the island still has the same political status.

NOTES

Introduction

1. Lilian Guerra argues that the figure of the jíbaro is key to understanding the development of national identities in early twentieth-century Puerto Rico. Local elites tried to construct the figure of the jíbaro (and hence that of the popular classes) as a less threatening "other." In general, the elites imagined the jíbaro as their racial equal (white due to European ancestry) but still subordinated to them. Guerra identifies this approach as an attempt to control popular classes that were "everywhere asserting their dissent" and their own identities. Guerra, *Popular Expression and National Identity*, 9, 83–85.

2. Michael C. Hawkins argues that imperial historicism was the "fundamental philosophy of American colonialism in the Philippines" and guided the metropolis's attempts at social and ethnological engineering. Further, no other period was as transformative and crucial for the Moros of the southern Philippine islands of Sulu and Mindanao's self-awareness and "ascent into homogenous modernity" as the fourteen years under American military rule. Hawkins claims that "American discourse and policy during military rule shaped the Moros' concept of themselves and the emergent postcolonial state in modernity." The Moros, however, "established the parameters of their own modern selves," as the new identity that emerged from that "collaborative colonial encounter" was negotiated, and the Moros both resisted and embraced American attempts at reimagining them. Hawkins, *Making Moros*, x–xi, 5–6.

3. The news clip stated that the "can of Korean dirt was handed over to the Red Cross, which will forward it to the Lions Club of Corozal. The frozen, snow-covered soil was taken from ground over which the Puerto Rican Regiment has battled and from an area where men have died. It will be placed in the cornerstone of the Corozal monument." INS, "Korean Earth to Puerto Rico."

4. In the 1970s Puerto Rican writers lamented the extinction of the jíbaro, beyond an "abstraction in which Puerto Ricans have invested the whole of their collective consciousness" due to "the realities of modernity." Guerra, *Popular Expression and National Identity*, 5–6.

5. "Sale el 65 hacia Corea," *Periódico el Mundo* (San Juan), October 12, 1950; "Opinión," *El Imparcial*, June 1950.

6. "Opinión," *Periódico el Mundo*, October 12, 1950.

7. Eileen Suárez Findlay analyses the familial narratives used by the Popular Democratic Party leadership to highlight the central role that migration played in the PPD's plans for the island. The familial language and metaphors used by PPD officials, she argues, made the reformed colony more palatable to Puerto Ricans. "Puerto Rico as a nation was growing up into manhood, and deserved to be treated as such" (Suárez Findlay, *We Are Left without a Father Here*, 48).

8. Burk, "Citizenship Status and Military Services," 503–5.

9. For a comprehensive study of the U.S. press representation of Cuba and Puerto Rico before and after 1898, see Johnson, *Latin America in Caricature*.

10. Bederman, *Manliness and Civilization*, Kindle ed.

11. Her analysis of the controversy and backlash after the black heavyweight boxer Jack Johnson defeated the white champion James J. Jeffries in 1910 clearly shows the domestic link between white supremacy and male power. The heavyweight title, an icon of masculinity and whiteness, had to be off limits to a black contender, for its mere contention by a nonwhite would put in doubt the claims of white virility that supported white males' commanding place in society. Bederman, *Manliness and Civilization*.

12. For example, in antebellum New York, African Americans were barred from serving in the state militia and then denied citizenship based on their failure to serve. Military service gradually became an almost universal rite of passage for white males to the point that during World War II, eight out of ten eligible men in the United States served in the military. Moskos, "From Citizens' Army to Social Laboratory," 85–86.

13. Hoganson, *Fighting for American Manhood*, 3, 8, 10.

14. Kaplan, "Black and Blue on San Juan Hill," 228–31.

15. In 1906 Congress even recommended barring African Americans from serving in the military. The black press denounced this action as a southern conspiracy to exclude African Americans from full citizenship. Dalfiume, *Desegregation of the U.S. Armed Forces*, 26–27.

16. Kaplan, "Black and Blue on San Juan Hill," 222–26.

17. See, for example, Mrinalini Sinha, *Colonial Masculinity*; Nye, *Masculinity and Male Codes of Honor*.

18. Ferrer, "Rustic Men," 667–69, 679. Ada Ferrer examines the court-martial of Quintín Bandera, a Cuban rebel officer who had served for more than thirty years for the cause of independence. He was the last of the famous nonwhite generals still alive in 1897.

19. "Clearly the boundaries of military leadership had to be made more impermeable than the boundaries of nationality; and the requisites for political power and leadership had to be stricter even than those for military power." Ferrer, *Insurgent Cuba*, 172.

20. Wagenheim and Jiménez de Wagenheim, *The Puerto Ricans*, 89.

21. Negroni, "Hostos y su pensamiento military," 275, 283–84.

22. The myth of the Puerto Ricans' docility originated with the local elites in the previous century. See Valle Atiles, *El campesino puertorriqueño, sus condiciones físicas, intelectuales y morales*, 151. Francisco Scarano has traced the development of characterizations of *jibaridád* and the coexistence of two almost contradictory meanings assigned to it. In "the eyes of the modernizing, rationalistic elites, the tactics of peasant survival seemed barbaric, conducive only to vagrancy, crime, and political paralysis." Scarano, "The Jíbaro Masquerade," 1400–1402. Part of the contradictory representations of the jíbaro by the island's elites included its docility, which "predisposed him to accepting his exploitation at the hands of others." See Guerra, *Popular Expression and National Identity*, 81, 109.

23. Briggs, *Reproducing Empire*, 198.

24. A small sample of recent scholarship that shows multileveled negotiation between the American empire and its colonial subjects include Hawkins, *Making Moros*; Levy, *Puerto Ricans in the Empire*; Moral, *Negotiating Empire*; and Go, "Chains of Empire."

25. Traditionally, Florencia Mallon argues, national democratic discourses have included promises of universal potential for autonomy, dignity, and equality for all peoples. In practice, however, entire groups have been barred from access to citizenship and liberty according to Eurocentric class, racial, and gender exclusionary criteria. Mallon associates this type of nationalism with the historical mission that the upper classes in a given country have reserved for themselves the creation of the nation and control of national identities. Subaltern groups, she contends, have nonetheless initiated projects for "collective identity based on a premise of citizenship available to all, and with individual membership beginning with the presumption of equality." Mallon, *Peasant and Nation*, 4, 6, 9–10. Also see Suárez Findlay, *Imposing Decency*, 9.

26. Suárez Findlay explores the role of marriage, sexual practices, and conceptions of morality, respectability, and honor with regard to the formation of national identities, class relations, and colonial state policies. Suárez Findlay, *Imposing Decency*, 2–4.

27. Go, "Chains of Empire," 335–37.

28. Anderson, *Imagined Communities*, 6–7.

29. Morris, *Puerto Rico: Culture, Politics, and Identity*, 12–17.

30. Lilian Guerra has argued that the image of the jíbaro is firmly ingrained in Puerto Rican society and part of a "nationalism that paradoxically did not necessarily entail independence." Guerra, *Popular Expression and National Identity*, 6.

31. *Criollo* is used throughout this work, unless citing works where *creole* is used, for the sake of accuracy. Puerto Rican elites appropriated the term *criollo* to signify those who had been born on the island and who were legally Spaniards in opposition to those Spaniards born on the peninsula, or *peninsulares*. The term had a pejorative origin that implied that those under this label had been contaminated by the ethnic and cultural diversity of the Americas. During the late Spanish empire, it was more widely used to refer to the relatively eco-

nomically successful, educated, and predominantly white native minority of Spanish lineage born in Puerto Rico. Astrid Cubano Iguina reminds us that neither some light racial mixing nor falling on economic hard times automatically excluded *criollos* from this class. Moreover, there was a political factor that defined the *criollos*. The *criollos* resented political marginalization and sought to establish their position vis-à-vis the "peninsular newcomers, whom they perceived as representatives of Spanish domination" and abuse. Cubano Iguina, *Criollos ante el 98*, 2–3.

32. Several scholars have noted that criollos and peninsulares had much in common and even relied on each other to hold on to power. Although both exploited the Puerto Rican masses, the *criollos* were successful in presenting the peninsulares, especially the merchant class, as the main cause for the masses' impoverishment. See, for example, Bergard, "Toward Puerto Rico's Grito de Lares," 636, 640–42. Astrid Cubano Iguina argues that "Spain was indispensable for the Criollos' survival as a dominant class" (*Criollos ante el 98*, 5–6).

33. The role played by the public education system in the Americanization of the island has been studied by several authors. See Negrón de Montilla, *La americanización de Puerto Rico y el sistema de instrucción pública*. Negrón de Montilla documents the attempts of the metropolis to reproduce in Puerto Rico an education system similar to that of New England in which English was the mandatory language and the teaching of U.S. history and American mainstream cultural values came to be the cornerstone of the system. More important, perhaps, is her detailed study of the department's memoranda and guidelines that openly called for policing those native teachers who strayed from the approved curriculum and included Puerto Rican culture in their lessons, as well as those who criticized the colonial regime. See Torres González, *Idioma, bilingüismo y nacionalidad*.

34. For example, see Hawkins, *Making Moros*.

35. As Solsiree del Moral has argued, in the case of Puerto Rico, the school system was intended to create colonial citizens through "the teaching of English and the celebration of U.S. history and patriotism." However, the metropolis's plans were challenged by Puerto Rican educators who shared "ideas and practices with others in the neighboring Caribbean and Latin American countries." Chief among these ideas is that of schools and history lessons as tools for nation-building. As del Moral points out, the matter is further complicated by the fact that the new state behind the revamping of the school system was colonial. See del Moral, *Negotiating Empire*, 7–9.

36. Allen to Root, May 1901, AGPR, Caja 224.

1. Birth of a Nation

1. All translations are mine unless otherwise indicated. I have tried to use the original Spanish version for titles, offices, and names throughout this narrative as long as it did not cause confusion to do so. Translations and abbreviations are offered and used throughout the text, but their use is limited.

2. By the time of el Grito de Lares few *criollos* served in the colonial administration, and the majority occupied subordinated roles that often offered no remuneration. Jiménez de Wagenheim, *El grito de Lares, sus causas y sus hombres*, 85.

3. Mallon, *Peasant and Nation*, 4, 6, 9–10.

4. López Alves, *State Formation and Democracy in Latin America*, 8–9, 32–33, 44–47.

5. By 1834 Puerto Rico had received some seven thousand Spaniards, many of them military men, from the crumbling empire. They soon monopolized the colonial bureaucracy. See Dietz, *Economic History of Puerto Rico*, 14–15; Jiménez de Wagenheim, *El grito de Lares*, 53; Cifre de Loubriel, *La inmigración a Puerto Rico durante el siglo XIX*, 49–53, 89, 99–101; and Cifre de Loubriel, *Catalogo de extranjeros residentes en Puerto Rico en el siglo XIX*, 35–37, 38–41, 50–56.

6. Dietz, *Economic History of Puerto Rico*, 23. The "Mexican situation" ended in 1810 with Mexico's separation from Spain.

7. Until the 1860s, the biggest challenge to Spanish rule in Cuba and Puerto Rico came in the form of slave resistance and rebellions. For example, a series of slave rebellions, plantation uprisings, and urban unrest of free people of color in Cuba from January through March 1812, known as the Aponte rebellion (dubbed a conspiracy by the colonial authorities), led to the execution of thirty-two and the imprisonment of some three hundred rebels. The Spanish authorities identified and executed a free black carpenter, José Antonio Aponte, as the leader of the rebellion. Although on a smaller scale, there were dozens of slave rebellions and conspiracies in Puerto Rico before slavery was finally abolished on March 22, 1873. See Childs, *The 1812 Aponte Rebellion*, and Baralt, *Esclavos rebeldes*.

8. The total population went from 80,246 in 1776 to 128,758 in 1797 to 583,308 in 1860 and 953,243 in 1899. The black slave population increased throughout the nineteenth century both in terms of numbers and as a percentage of the total population until 1846, when it began a radical reduction. The black slaves represented 11.4 percent of the population in 1846 but only 7.2 percent in 1860 and 5.1 percent in 1872. Dietz, *Economic History of Puerto Rico*, 31, 36; Jiménez de Wagenheim, *El grito de Lares, sus causus y sus hombres*, 53–56.

9. Dietz, *Economic History of Puerto Rico*, 17–19, 20, 27.

10. Dietz, *Economic History of Puerto Rico*, 72–73. Laird Bergard explains that a "nearly total separation divided the agrarian and commercial elites. Conflicts between producers and merchants often took on national characteristics, usually aligning creoles against Spaniards." Bergard, "Toward Puerto Rico's Grito de Lares," 636.

11. In Puerto Rico, the *hacendados* were owners of landed estates of some significant size devoted to agricultural endeavors.

12. Dietz, *Economic History of Puerto Rico*, 73.

13. Several scholars have noted that both criollos and peninsulares had much in common and even relied on each other to hold on to power. For the purpose of this study we do not need to delve into this debate. It will suffice to say

that political exclusion was real but that it affected a relatively small sector of the population that still saw in Spain a warrantor of their position in the island. Although both criollos and peninsulares exploited the Puerto Rican masses, the criollos were successful in presenting the peninsulares, especially the merchant class, as the main cause for the masses' impoverishment. See Bergard, "Toward Puerto Rico's Grito de Lares," 640–42. Astrid Cubano Iguina argues that "Spain was indispensable for the criollos' survival as a dominant class" (*Criollos ante el 98*, 5–6).

14. Jiménez de Wagenhein, *El grito de Lares, sus causus y sus hombres*, 119–21.

15. Wagenheim, *El grito de Lares, sus causus y sushombres*, 122–24.

16. Bergard, "Toward Puerto Rico's Grito de Lares," 640.

17. Juan de la Pezuela y Ceballos, gobernador y capitán general of Puerto Rico (1848–52), created the Reglamento Especial de Jornaleros. See Figueroa, *Sugar, Slavery, and Freedom in Nineteenth-Century Puerto Rico*, 142–48, 166–73. See also Dietz, *Economic History of Puerto Rico*, 43, 45–52, and Bergard, "Toward Puerto Rico's Grito de Lares," 640.

18. Bergard explains that the peninsulares' conspicuous wealth, reluctance to interact with the local population, failure to assimilate, constant travels to Europe, almost incestuous seclusion, and their replenishment with new arrivals made them an easy group to identify as both foreign and oppressive. Bergard, "Toward Puerto Rico's Grito de Lares," 638–40.

19. Bergard, "Toward Puerto Rico's Grito de Lares," 631, 637.

20. The Glorious Revolution culminated with Queen Isabella II being deposed. She was replaced by the Italian prince Amadeo de Savoy, who lasted two years as the head of a constitutional monarchy. He was followed by the First Spanish Republic, which lasted roughly two years (1873–74).

21. Since the exiles in New York had a "revolutionary" agenda, including the abolition of slavery, I use the term *revolutionaries* to refer to them. The leaders of the revolt in Puerto Rico, which included some slave owners who disagreed with the abolition of slavery, are referred to as *rebels*.

22. For the military aspect of the Lares revolt, see Negroni, *Historia militar de Puerto Rico*, 296–301. For an exhaustive study of the rebels who led the revolt and their motivations, see Jiménez de Wagenheim, *El grito de Lares*.

23. By order of the Dominican president, Buena Ventura Báez, Betances and his men were precluded from sailing to Puerto Rico. See Jiménez de Wagenheim, *El grito de Lares*, 192, and Negroni, *Historia militar*, 297.

24. See Gautier Dapena, *Trayectoria del pensamiento liberal puertorriqueño*, 103–5; Negroni, *Historia militar*, 298; Jiménez de Wagenheim, *El grito de lares*, 160–62.

25. Those threatened were the slaves and *jornaleros* working for landlords who were not part of the rebellion. The rebels apparently killed Agustín Venero, a freed black, for refusing to join them. See Jiménez de Wagenheim, *El grito de Lares*, 170–74, and Gautier Dapena, *Trayectoria del pensamiento liberal*, 108.

26. Francisco Ramírez was named president of the Republic of Puerto Rico, Clemente Millán as minister of justice, Federico Valencia as minister of the trea-

sury, Aurelio Méndez as minister of foreign affairs, and Bernabé Pol as secretary of state. See Jiménez de Wagenheim, *El grito de Lares*, 179–80; Negroni, *Historia militar*, 298–300; and Gautier Dapena, *Trayectoria del pensamiento liberal*, 107–8.

27. Jiménez de Wagenheim, *El grito de Lares*, 179.

28. See the original decrees in Gautier Dapena, *Trayectoria del pensamiento liberal*, 102–3. For an analysis of the decrees, see Jiménez de Wagenheim, *El grito de Lares*, 179–84. See also Negroni, *Historia militar*, 29, and García Ochoa, *La política española*, 150–52.

29. See Jiménez de Wagenheim, *El grito de Lares*, 179–80, 185–92; Gautier Dapena, *Trayectoria del pensamiento liberal*, 106; Negroni, *Historia militar*, 298–300.

30. See Jiménez de Wagenheim, *El grito de Lares*, 78, 82–85, 174, 182, and García Ochoa, *La política española*, 151.

31. For those who see the revolt as the birth of Puerto Rico's national identity, see Correjter, "The Day Puerto Rico Became a Nation," and Géigel Polanco, *El Grito de Lares: gesta de heroísmo y sacrificio*.

32. A more balanced history of the revolt is found in Cruz Monclova, *El Grito de Lares*. Economic and agrarian historians follow the second trend. See Bergard, *Coffee and the Growth of Agrarian Capitalism*, 41–45, 140, and Dietz, *Economic History of Puerto Rico*, 72–74. Bergard and Dietz agree that Lares was a manifestation of the attempt by members of the more powerful creole class to end the dominance of the hated Spanish merchants. Ricardo Camuñas-Madera also emphasizes the economic nature of the uprising. He argues that commercial relations between nonpeninsular (*criollo*s and foreigners) farmers and peninsular monopolists supported by the colonial regime in the island were dominated by the latter leading the hacendados from the coffee zone to opt for revolution to correct the unequal relationship. See Camuñas-Madera, *Desplazamiento y revolución en el Puerto Rico del siglo XIX*, 97–107. For a discussion of stated and unstated causes of the revolt and a synthesis of the economic, displacement, and discrimination theories, see Jiménez de Wagenheim, *El grito de Lares*, 82, 117.

33. Dietz, *Economic History of Puerto Rico*, 73.

34. Economic and agrarian historians follow the second trend. See Bergard, *Coffee and the Growth of Agrarian Capitalism*, 41–45, 140, and Dietz, *Economic History of Puerto Rico*, 72–74.

35. Dietz explains that as the strength of large landowners and small merchants increased, "Spanish domination and in particular, peninsular control over the largest commercial establishments and credit, it became an obstacle rather than an ally to the members of this class, as well as educated professionals, just as it had in the rest of the New World." See Dietz, *Economic History of Puerto Rico*, 73.

36. Bergard, "Toward Puerto Rico's Grito de Lares," 642.

37. Correjter befriended the nationalist leader Pedro Albizu Campos and became secretary general of the Nationalist Party in the 1930s. He was imprisoned in 1937, 1947, and 1950.

38. See Dávila, *Sponsored Identities*.

39. Jiménez de Wagenheim, *El grito de Lares*, 74.

40. See *Manifiesto de los patriotas borinqueños que dirigen el movimiento revolucionario*, in Gautier Dapena, *Trayectoria del pensamiento liberal*, 102–3.

41. The population grew from 138,758 in 1797 to 583,308 in 1860. Dietz, *Economic History of Puerto Rico*, 31.

42. During the first period identified by Cifre de Loubriel, military personnel and loyalists started to arrive after the defeat of the Spanish armies in the former empire and soon monopolized the island's bureaucracy. During the second period, there was a marked increase of peninsular immigration, but Lares and Yara soon made Puerto Rico less attractive to this group. The third period was characterized by a slow decrease in immigration, especially of peninsular origin. Although it could never overtake the *peninsulares*, foreign immigration held steady throughout the century. Immigration of peninsular origin and from Spanish insular possessions accounted for 88.2 percent of the century's immigration while foreigners accounted for 8.5 percent. It is noteworthy that foreign immigrants were mostly farmers, professionals, and artisans while peninsular immigrants were, for the most part, military personnel (including guardias civiles), merchants, and public employees. The vast majority of foreigners living in Puerto Rico resided in the south/southwest, the west, and the northwest tip of the island and the coffee region adjacent to these areas. See Cifre de Loubriel, *La inmigración a Puerto Rico durante el siglo XIX*, 49–53, 89, 99–101, and Estela Cifre de Loubriel, *Catalogo de extranjeros residentes en Puerto Rico*, 35–37, 38–41, 50–56.

43. Joseph C. Dorsey has questioned the longheld view that Puerto Rico had little involvement with the slave trade in the first half of the nineteenth century. His work shows that slave owners in Puerto Rico were actively engaged in the international Atlantic slave trade. The slave cargo landed first in the non-Hispanic Caribbean from which it made its way to both Cuba and Puerto Rico. The Spanish crown allowed for both African and American-born slaves from neighboring French, Danish, and Dutch Caribbean islands to be imported to Puerto Rico. Dorsey, *Slave Traffic in the Age of Abolition*.

44. Chinea, *Race and Labor in the Hispanic Caribbean*.

45. Chinea, *Race and Labor in the Hispanic Caribbean*, 150.

46. The African-born slave population in 1869 was tallied at 5,000 from a total of 39,000. See Jiménez de Wagenheim, *El grito de Lares*, 54. The white population grew faster than the nonwhite population after the 1840s. It is commonly accepted that the colonial authorities sought to promote white immigration while policing the nonwhite population. See Chinea, *Race and Labor in the Hispanic Caribbean*, 123–25. Kinsbrunner argues that a type of caste system continued to exist in Puerto Rico during the 1800s. As part of the system, the free men of color occupied a middle ground separating whites and slaves. He contends that by the end of the nineteenth century, Puerto Rican racial prejudice had evolved away from biological racism toward a "more culturally centered prejudice." Kinsbruner, *Not of Pure Blood*, 45.

47. See Jiménez de Wagenheim, *El grito de Lares*, 78, 82–85, 174, 182, and García Ochoa, *La política española*, 151.

48. Jiménez de Wagenheim, *El grito de Lares*, 55–56, 78. Almost 9 percent of the rebels captured in Lares were slaves, and African-born and Dutch-Caribbean émigrés were among the foreigners tried by the colonial authorities.

49. Ferrer, *Insurgent Cuba, Race Nation, and Revolution*, 7–8.

50. Cuban intellectuals such as José Marti denied the existence of race claiming that it was but a colonial tool "used locally to divide the anticolonial effort and globally used by men who invented 'text races' to justify expansion and empire." The anticolonial struggle in Cuba was also antiracist. National unity was possible due "joint political action by armed black, mulatto, and white men fighting in a war against the colonizer." Ferrer, *Insurgent Cuba: Race, Nation, and Revolution*, 3–4.

51. Sanz wrote, "Puerto Rico necesita reformar su instrucción pública españolizandola convenientemente y para ello se hace indispensable prescindir por completo de los profesores naturales de este país." He also argued for the "conveniencia de prescindir de ciertos puestos de empleados hijos de este país. Nunca pueden dar aquí buen resultado." He added, "En esta Provincia [Puerto Rico] sólo deben admitirse los empleados [born on the island] más subalternos, siempre que hayan dado pruebas inequívocas de un acendrado españolismo." See Leg. 5112. Expediente 15 *Memoria presentada por el Gobernador supr. Civil de Puerto Rico D. Laureano Sanz*, in Gautier Dapena, *Trayectoria del pensamiento liberal*, 46–47.

52. Writing for the *Boletín Histórico de Puerto Rico*, the Puerto Rican liberal leader Cayetano Coll y Toste lamented with ambivalence, bidding farewell to "our parents' and grandparents' flag. It was cruel with us; thoughtlessly, they often flagellated our faces with her, handled by unjust hands and desecrated by retrograde hands; and that notwithstanding, we loved her." Cubano Iguina argues that the fin de siècle criollos, in general, assumed Spanish nationality and identity consciously and identified Spain as a greater or "sublime" nation, a "Motherland" in which the "regional" patria (Puerto Rico) had a space. This regional patria was in turn "more intimate, and it is loved with passion." See Cubano Iguina, *Criollos ante el 98*, 7–8, 10–11, 17, 20–21, 29.

53. See Bergard, "Toward Puerto Rico's Grito de Lares," 640–42, and Cubano Iguina, *Criollos ante el 98*, 5–6.

54. Román Baldorioty de Castro and Luis Muñoz Rivera, leaders of the Autonomist Liberal Party (pro-autonomy) in Puerto Rico talked openly about the impossibility of obtaining independence through war. One of the reasons was the state of illiteracy and poverty of the peasantry, which they thought would not allow for an effective revolt or the survival of an independent republic. According to Jiménez de Wagenheim's findings, of the men taken prisoners after the revolt who were asked about their literacy, 40 percent responded negatively. Jiménez de Wagenheim, *El grito de Lares*, 79. Cubano Iguina describes the autonomistas as a movement of nativist inclination which, in search of political hegemony, sought to establish a distinction vis-à-vis the peninsular newcomers whom they perceived as representatives of metropolitan domination.

Cubano Iguina, *Criollos ante el 98*, 2–3, and Cubano Iguina, "Política radical y autonomismo en Puerto Rico," 155–57.

55. Negroni, *Historia militar*, 60.

56. Puerto Rico's capitanía general formed part of the Viceroyalty of the New Spain and of the Real Audiencia of Santo Domingo until the Real Audiencia de Puerto Rico was created in 1831.

57. See Negroni, *Historia militar*, 24–26, 66–67. The capitanías generales were located in strategic areas to protect the sea routes and the empire against indigenous peoples, foreign powers, and contraband. As part of the defensive perimeter designed by the Spaniards in the eighteenth century, Puerto Rico came to be known as the 6th Key (Llave de las Antillas y de las Indias). As such, the island received priority for military matters, especially the building of fortifications. There were another nineteen keys throughout the empire.

58. Negroni, *Historia militar*, 29.

59. Negroni, *Historia militar*, 218–20. Francisco Scarano has traced the development of characterizations of *jibaridád* and the coexistence of two almost contradictory meanings assigned to it. In "the eyes of the modernizing, rationalistic elites, the tactics of peasant survival seemed barbaric, conducive only to vagrancy, crime, and political paralysis." However, by the middle of the nineteenth century, representations of a multiethnic jíbaro served as a type of proto-nationalist icon for Puerto Rican elites. Puerto Rican liberal *criollos* used the "jíbaro masquerade to identify themselves as ethnically different from other members of the elite while maintaining the basic outlines of a colonial relation" ("The Jíbaro Masquerade," 1401–2). After the United States gained control of the island in 1898, intellectuals and political figures re-created a jíbaro figure in opposition to American domination. The jíbaro figure, "now absolutely whitened," was converted into the repository of a higher form of "patriotic morality, the very essence of the Puerto Rican nation" (1404).

60. See Dietz, *Economic History of Puerto Rico*, 18, 19, 31, and Negroni, *Historia militar*, 80–81.

61. The Real Cédula of October 7, 1540, signed by Felipe II of Spain, ordered all Spaniards (age twelve to sixty) living in the West Indies to join the militias. Before that cédula, the militias had organized themselves voluntarily in times of need.

62. Negroni, *Historia militar*, 62–63. The *milicia urbana* was to be composed of free white males between the ages of sixteen and sixty and was entrusted with public order and territorial defense.

63. Negroni, *Historia militar*, 66–67.

64. Negroni, *Historia militar*, 105.

65. Bayrón Toro, *Elecciones y partidos políticos de Puerto Rico*, 106, and Dietz, *Economic History of Puerto Rico*, 31.

66. In 1783 Governor Juan Dabán assigned the cavalry units of the *milicias disciplinadas* to deliver the mail, in fact creating the first postal service in the island, as a way to justify the expenses incurred in providing for this recently created body. Negroni, *Historia militar*, 66, 112.

67. Negroni, *Historia militar*, 131.
68. Negroni, *Historia militar*, 108.
69. Negroni, *Historia militar*, 117–20.
70. Since 1741 there had been artillery and infantry battalions in San Juan. Both *fijos* (permanent) and half the positions in it were opened to those born on the island. Negroni, *Historia militar*, 106–7.
71. Negroni, *Historia militar*, 128.
72. Negroni, *Historia militar*, 129. Negroni citing *Reglamento para la Guarnición de la Plaza de Puerto rico, castillos y fuertes de su juridisción, de febrero 12 del 1741*.
73. Negroni, *Historia militar*, 131.
74. Bayrón Toro, *Elecciones y partidos políticos*, 11–12.
75. Bayrón Toro, *Elecciones y partidos políticos*, 13.
76. Negroni, *Historia militar*, 118–19.
77. Negroni, *Historia militar*, 133.
78. Negroni, *Historia militar*, 133–34. Negroni citing the secretario de la gobernación de Puerto Rico, Don Pedro Tomás de Córdoba, who said, "No se ha podido desimpresionar a los puertorriqueños que la extinción [*sic*] de este cuerpo veterano no tuvo por causa la desconfianza que suponen; y es preciso conocer su carácter pundonoroso para graduar hasta qué extremo se creen lastimados por la extinción del regimiento." Tomás de Córdoba also pointed out that disbanding the Fijo closed the military as a career for most of the hijos de este país, who could not afford to send their sons to the peninsula.
79. Negroni, *Historia militar*, 119. The *Reglamento* set July 25 for the corps' annual inspection. That is also the date for the American invasion in 1898 and the creation of the Estado Libre Asociado in 1952.
80. Negroni, *Historia militar*, 120–21.
81. Negroni, *Historia militar*, 15, 120. The demobilization of the urbano, the largest paramilitary unit in the island, coincided with the implementation of the Reglamento Especial de Jornaleros of June 11, 1849, ordered by Gobernador y Capitán General of Puerto Rico Juan de la Pezuela y Ceballos. The reglamento was intended to provide cheap labor, especially for sugar plantations and other enterprises. This third attempt to coerce the lowest strata in Puerto Rico to work in the fields came during a period of low sugar prices, which made it imperative to lower production costs. See Dietz, *Economic History of Puerto Rico*, 44–45, and Ayala, *American Sugar Kingdom*, 159–65.
82. Bayrón Toro, *Elecciones y partidos políticos*, 23–26.
83. Bayrón Toro, *Elecciones y partidos políticos*, 30–35.
84. Bayrón Toro, *Elecciones y partidos políticos*, 36–38.
85. Bayrón Toro, *Elecciones y partidos políticos*, 35–41.
86. García Ochoa, *La política española*, 125–28, and Bayrón Toro, *Elecciones y partidos políticos*, 44–45.
87. The Spanish governor, José Núñez de Cáceres, announced the independence of Spanish Santo Domingo and the creation of the state of Spanish Haiti on November 30, 1821. Haiti's president, Jean-Pierre Boyer, decided to invade

Santo Domingo and to reunite the island under the Haitian flag. The twenty-two years of Haitian occupation led to deep resentment of Haitians among Dominicans. Fearing another Haitian invasion, the Dominican Republic returned under Spanish sovereignty on March 17, 1861, due to Dominican General Pedro Santana's negotiations with the Spanish ruling Liberal Union of General Leopoldo O'Donnell. Resistance to the reannexation soon materialized, and a war for independence began. On March 3, 1865, Isabel II of Spain approved a decree repealing the annexation of Santo Domingo. See Moya Pons, *The Dominican Republic*, 124.

88. Negroni, *Historia militar*, 291.

89. Bayrón Toro, *Elecciones y partidos políticos*, 47, 51–52. Of roughly 650,000 inhabitants, only 2,580 were allowed to vote, resulting in the election of seven conservative diputados and four liberals.

90. Negroni, *Historia militar*, 122.

91. The origin of the Guardia Civil goes back to Spain in 1844 when this body was created under shared command of the Ministry of War for Organization, Personnel, and Discipline and the Ministry of Government for Services and Mobilization. See Negroni, *Historia militar*, 125.

92. By 1898 the Guardia Civil included the offspring of peninsulares and had grown to about 800 men. These "new" criollos were of the most conservative stock. The peninsulares, being a group incapable of reproducing, since their offspring would be criollos or Americans, had to secure some positions for their children. Thus these positions were not completely closed to criollos but to liberals.

93. Negroni, *Historia militar*, 114–15.

94. Negroni, *Historia militar*, 139. Intended to provide officers for the island's garrison, this Academia de Caballeros Cadetes had room for thirty-two students, one for each company of the permanent garrison in 1784.

95. The examination for entrance into the Academia de Infantería included reading and writing, Castilian grammar, rhetoric, French, arithmetic, Spanish geography and history, notions of morality, and knowledge of the Spanish constitution. Negroni, *Historia militar*, 140.

96. The curriculum of the Academia de Infantería included algebra, geometry, trigonometry, military commands, tactics, psychology, logic and ethics, history, French, topographic drawing, gymnastics, cosmography, physics and chemistry, accounting, fencing, fortifications, the art of war, military law, ballistics and the use of small arms, and the principles of artillery. Negroni, *Historia militar*, 141.

97. Bayrón Toro, *Elecciones y partidos políticos*, 52–53.

98. Bayrón Toro, *Elecciones y partidos políticos*, 54–55.

99. These general elections conformed to the Spanish constitution of 1869, which allowed for fifteen diputados a cortes to be elected. The liberals obtained more than 90 percent of the votes (9,773 versus 1,004) and elected fourteen diputados. Bayrón Toro, *Elecciones y partidos políticos*, 58.

100. Bayrón Toro, *Elecciones y partidos políticos*, 58–59.

101. Bayrón Toro, *Elecciones y partidos políticos*, 65–66.

102. The Federal Republic's government fell in less than a year (January 3, 1874) with the pronouncement of Madrid's captain general, Manuel Pavía, calling for all parties with the exception of federalists and Carlistas to form a new government. The federalists had been weakened by the schism with the radicals.

103. Bayrón Toro, *Elecciones y partidos políticos*, 69–70.

104. Negroni, *Historia militar*, 123.

105. Negroni, *Historia militar*, 126.

106. It should be noted that the autonomists-liberals, boycotting the Ley Electoral Maura of 1892, which imposed a payment between ten and twenty-five pesos for electoral rights, did not participate in the general elections of 1893 and 1896. In the elections of 1891, the autonomistas elected two diputados a cortes, including Rafael María de Labra and Miguel Moya y Ojanguren, representatives from Sabana Grande and Ponce, respectively. Both districts are contiguous and located in the southwestern corner of the island. Bayrón Toro, *Elecciones y partidos políticos*, 70–103.

107. Bayrón Toro, *Elecciones y partidos políticos*, 91–92.

108. Bayrón Toro, *Elecciones y partidos políticos*, 95, with Bayrón Toro citing Cruz Monclova, *Obras Completas de Luis Muñoz Rivera*, 45. See Astrid Cubano Iguina, "Política radical y autonomismo en Puerto Rico," 155–57.

109. Bayrón Toro, *Elecciones y partidos políticos*, 105–6. The idea of the political pact comes from Muñoz Rivera and Rosendo Matienzo Cintrón, who were part of the autonomist commission entrusted with securing a political pact with a Spanish party. The other members of the commission were José Gomez Brioso and Federico Degetau, the latter opting for not participating in the final pact as he espoused federal ideals.

110. The conservatives (Incondicional Español) were not impervious to the rapid changes occurring on the peninsula and in the colonies. In 1897 a wing of the party was expelled and proceeded to form the Partido de Izquierda Progresista Incondicional (Leftist Progressive Unconditional Party), later to be known as Partido Oportunista (Opportunist Party). Bayrón Toro, *Elecciones y partidos políticos*, 106.

111. To read the document in its entirety, see Fernós López-Cepero, *Documentos Históricos-Constitucionales*, 19–37.

112. Bayrón Toro, *Elecciones y partidos políticos*, 106–7.

113. Fernós Lopez-Cepero, *Documentos Históricos-Constitucionales*, 29.

114. Of 121,573 votes, the *autonomistas* obtained 82,627 votes, the *ortodoxos* 15,068, the *incondicionales* 2,144, and the *oportunistas* 1,585. There seem to be more than 20,000 votes invalidated or not counted. Bayrón Toro, *Elecciones y partidos políticos*, 107.

115. Bayrón Toro, *Elecciones y partidos políticos*, 109.

116. The Cleveland and McKinley administrations were especially opposed to an independent Cuba. This posture was the result of a century-old policy that was ready to support Spanish sovereignty over the island. This rationale was based on the assumption that a Cuba controlled by a weak Spain would be

nearly as valuable to the United States as it was under American sovereignty. See Pérez, *The War of 1898*, 3–6, quoting Thomas Jefferson to James Monroe, June 23, 1823, in Washington, *The Works of Thomas Jefferson*; and John Quincy Adams to Hugh Nelson, April 28, 1823, in Ford, *The Writings of John Quincy Adams*; James Buchanan to Romulus Saunders, June 17, 1848.

117. Pérez, *The War of 1898*, 6.
118. LaFeber, *The New Empire*, 286, 292.
119. Pérez, *The War of 1898*, 94.
120. Prime Minister Cánovas del Castillo, emboldened by the death of the Cuban rebel general Antonio Maceo on December 6, 1896, offered very limited autonomy to both Cuba and Puerto Rico. The Cuban rebels immediately rejected the overture and eventually so did the autonomistas in Puerto Rico, who also decided not to participate in the elections. Cánovas del Castillo's offer convinced most of the autonomistas in Puerto Rico of the need to make a pact with Sagasta and the liberal fusionistas. See Rosario Natal, *Puerto Rico y la crisis de la Guerra Hispanoamericana*, 146–53.
121. There was plenty of support for intervening in Cuba. Since 1895 Republicans were calling for *Cuba Libre*, not least because the *Junta Cubana* in the United States kept the Americans interested in the war. Spanish criminal behavior was widely publicized, and perhaps exaggerated, by the yellow press, but reporters did nothing but write what the public wanted to hear. Furthermore, religious papers supported intervention on moral grounds, using the same axioms behind manifest destiny. By 1898 opinion polls agreed that something had to be done about Cuba. See Gould, *The Spanish-American War and President McKinley*, 18, 23–24, and LaFeber, *The New Empire*, 337.
122. The term *pacification* in the Teller Amendement allowed the McKinley administration to first establish a military occupation and ultimately to impose the Platt Amendment on the Cubans. The Platt Amendment defined American-Cuban relations for half a century.
123. See Negroni, *Historia militar*, and Nadal, *Guardia Nacional, sucesora de las milicias puertorriqueñas*.
124. In 1882, due to the inability of the peninsula to furnish enough troops, Puerto Ricans were again allowed to serve in the units garrisoning the island. Puerto Ricans came to be drafted into the Spanish military under the Ley de Reclutamiento y Reemplazo del Ejercito del 1878, effective in Puerto Rico in 1882. See Negroni, *Historia militar*, 136–37.

2. Puerto Rican a la Americana

1. Allen to Root, May 1901, AGPR, Caja 224.
2. On February 16, 1899, William McKinley accepted the "burden of the Philippines, to safeguard the happiness of their inhabitants," as he proclaimed a campaign of benevolent assimilation. See Gould, *The Spanish-American War and President McKinley*, 123. McKinley was adopting Capt. Alfred T. Mahan's views with regard to the territories acquired as a result of the war with Spain in

1898. See Mahan, "The Relations of the United States to Their New Dependencies," 247–49.

3. Ayala and Bernabe, *Puerto Rico in the American Century*, 74–86.

4. For a military account of the American campaign in Puerto Rico, see Trask, *The War with Spain in 1898*, 336–68, and Rivero, *Crónica de la Guerra Hispanoamericana en Puerto Rico*.

5. When it was discovered that Pvt. Louis J. de Haass of the Sixth Illinois Volunteers had defrauded a restaurant owner by paying with Confederate money, Miles recommended harsh punishment. After a court-martial, de Haas was sentenced to thirteen months of solitary confinement and hard labor. Trask, *War with Spain in 1898*, 365.

6. Trask, *War with Spain in 1898*, 366.

7. Trask, *War with Spain in 1898*, 351–53.

8. Trask, *War with Spain in 1898*, 355–56.

9. Negroni, *Historia Militar de Puerto Rico*, 367–69.

10. The *partidas sediciosas* (seditious parties) had the effect of forcing the *voluntarios*, who had been deployed far from their communities, to abandon their posts and return to their lands to protect them from these attacks. At first these parties were of a spontaneous and independent nature or sanctioned by the Americans and engaged in sabotage against Spanish lines and giving logistical support to the U.S. Army. There were also parties who sided with the Spanish army, but they were mostly voluntarios. Historian Fernando Picó has found some groups formed completely on Puerto Rican initiative. Both the pro-American and pro-Spanish parties had to procure their own supplies, which led to the ransacking of haciendas and appropriation of cattle. As the war ended, the parties continued the raids in what is known as the *tiznados* (black faces). These parties did in fact engage heavily in personal, economic, and political revenge, which was exemplified by the burning of credit and debt books as well as haciendas and plantations. See Trask, *War with Spain in 1898*, 356, 359–60, and Fernando Picó, *1898: La guerra después de la guerra*, 86–92.

11. Macías to Correa, August 5, 1898, in Trask, *War with Spain in 1898*, 360.

12. If someone could claim responsibility for the U.S. readiness to accomplish its project of extracontinental expansion, that would be Alfred Mahan. Congressmen, presidents, diplomats, and high-ranking military personnel were well acquainted with his work, and many even studied under him or befriended the prolific strategist. Among Mahan's friends were Theodore Roosevelt, Senator Henry Cabot Lodge, and John Hay, secretary of state under McKinley. In addition, in 1902 Mahan was elected president of the American Historical Association, the most coveted position for a historian. American leaders were divided between two expansionist theories, that of entrepreneur Andrew Carnegie, who applied Herbert Spencer's survival of the fittest theory to commerce and business, and that of Mahan. Carnegie disagreed with Mahan in that he saw an industrial competition, not a military one. For Mahan, however, the fittest often gained ascendancy through military power. What is more, the industrial

and commercial competition and expansion proposed by Carnegie would lead to rivalry for markets and raw materials, and thus sea power was needed. Mahan argued that in order to maintain economic power, the U.S. military should control vital sea lanes. This approach required securing territorial bases to guarantee its dominion of the regions important to its commerce. Moreover, military sea power was needed to ensure that the nation enjoyed peace and industry uninterrupted by wars. Furthermore, he was convinced that merely utilitarian arguments would never persuade or convert mankind to join the great mission of the west, the uplifting and remaking of lesser races. Thus military preparedness and civilizational discourse were fused in Mahan's view. See Mahan, *The Influence of Sea Power upon History*, 83–84; Mahan, *Naval Strategy*, 100–101; LaFeber, *The New Empire*, 97; and Anders Stephanson, *Manifest Destiny*, 88.

13. At least on paper, Mahan explained, the Spanish navy seemed almost the equal of its U.S. counterpart, to the point that even some American naval officers believed that after losing the *Maine* in Havana, the American edge over Spain had shifted in Spain's favor. Mahan, *Lessons of the War with Spain*, 30–34, and Gould, *Spanish-American War and President McKinley*, 74.

14. See Mahan, *Lessons of the War with Spain*, 30–34.

15. Trask, *War with Spain in 1898*, 348–50.

16. Influential industrialist Andrew Carnegie was of the same opinion. Wagenheim and Jiménez de Wagenheim, *The Puerto Ricans*, 89, citing *Selections from the Correspondence of Theodore Roosevelt and H. C. Lodge*, 299.

17. Since 1890 Mahan had been stressing the need to secure and preserve naval bases in the Caribbean to protect the American sea lines. According to Mahan, the goal in the Caribbean was to enforce the Monroe Doctrine and prevent a strong naval European power from gaining a hold on Cuba. Mahan understood the purchase of Louisiana and Florida as part of the Jeffersonian idea to remove European powers from the Americas, a philosophy that later extended to Cuba, Puerto Rico, Hawaii, and finally Panama. Following Mahan's doctrine, the main reason for the United States to intervene in the Cuban Revolution was to secure important bases in both Cuba and Puerto Rico. These islands undoubtedly enticed American entrepreneurs, but they were more important to defend the projected isthmian canal, which had been an American concern since the United States reached the shores of the Pacific. See Mahan, *Influence of Sea Power upon History*, 83–84, and Mahan, *Naval Strategy*, 349–50, 368.

18. The Cuban rebels, who had been excluded from American front lines, were also excluded from the armistice's deliberations and the signing of the Treaty of Paris, as were the Filipino rebels and the Puerto Rican delegates to the Spanish Cortes. Gen. Calixto García, the principal rebel leader in Cuba, and his troops were not allowed in Santiago. Even the Spanish general, Valeriano Weyler, had expected the Cuban *insurrectos* to conduct the last part of the campaign after the taking of San Juan Hill. See Pérez, *The War of 1898*, 94, quoting Valeriano Weyler, *Mi mando en Cuba*. In the case of Puerto Rico, Title VII, Article 43, of the Carta Autonómica of 1897, guaranteed the veto power of the

Puerto Rican parliament over decisions reached by the Spanish Cortes where more than a dozen Puerto Rican delegates sat with both voice and vote. Article 2 declared that the "present constitution shall not be amended except by a special law and upon petition of the insular parliament." Since the U.S. military disbanded the insular parliament, and there were no Puerto Rican delegates present to sign the Treaty of Paris on December 10, the passing of sovereignty over Puerto Rico to the United States was in violation of the legal relationship between Spain and Puerto Rico and thus illegal. This position would become the most compelling legal argument embraced by the independence movement some thirty years later.

19. Ángel Rivero Méndez was a Puerto Rican captain of artillery in the Spanish army and stationed in Puerto Rico, and he later served as interim governor and officially ceded the island to the U.S. authorities. He praised the way in which the invading force behaved. "Esta breve campaña del 1898, de 19 días de duración, es un modelo de guerra culta, moderna y humanitaria. La invasión del general Miles revistió todos los caracteres de un paseo triunfal, debido a su política de guerra sabia y humanitaria; se respetaron las costumbres y religión de los nativos; se mantuvo en toda su fuerza la autoridad civil, a pesar de la guerra; no se utilizó el abusivo sistema de requisar, sino que todo fue pagado, incluso el terreno donde se levantan las tiendas, a precio de oro." In Ángel Rivero, *Crónica de la Guerra Hispanoamericana en Puerto Rico*, quoted in Nadal, *Guardia Nacional: sucesora de las milicias puertorriqueñas*, 34–35.

20. Just as autonomistas had done in the 1880s, the 1898 annexationists defended the concept of a "regional patria" that could be independent within the American federation to justify their welcoming of the new metropolis. Edgardo Meléndez argues that annexationists sought to legitimize the control of the local dominant class over cultural matters and the economic and political structures with the support of the new metropolis. For an in-depth analysis of the autonomistas' transformation into annexationists and the economic, political, and social rationale behind the movement, see Meléndez, *Movimiento anexionista en Puerto Rico*, 9–33. Also see Cubano Iguina, *Criollos ante el 98*, 7–8, 10–11, 17, 20–21, 29.

21. See Bernabe, *Respuestas al colonialismo en la política puertorriqueña*, 13–15.

22. Ayala and Bernabe, *Puerto Rico in the American Century*, 75–76.

23. For a sample of the diverse support and pro-American feelings evident among the general population, see Carroll, *Report on the Island of Puerto Rico*.

24. López Baralt, *The Policy of the United States towards Its Territories*, and Duffy Burnett and Marshall, *Foreign in a Domestic Sense*.

25. Bernabe, *Respuestas al colonialismo*, 16–18. Also see Barreto, "Appurtenant and belonging . . . but not a part of."

26. Gribbin, "A Matter of Faith: North America's Religion and South America's Independence."

27. The term *manifest destiny* was first used in an article regarding the impending war with Mexico in the *Morning Star*, December 27, 1845. Manifest destiny's

religious character was summarized by the Reverend Josiah Strong. In 1895 the Evangelical Alliance published Strong's *Our Country, Its Possible Future, and Its Present Crisis*, which sold 176,000 copies. The basic characteristics of Strong's work were liberal theology, mission at home and abroad, social gospel, and the final competition of the races with God's blessings supporting the Anglo-Saxons who were supposed to command, Christianize, and civilize the world. Manifest destiny had several contributors in academia. After 1880 John Fiske, a historian and evolutionist, promoted the vision of history as a dualistic struggle of worldwide proportions between conquering civilization and retreating barbarism. This very popular author, also a philosopher, reconciled the traditional religious belief in creation with the then revolutionary new principle of biology, evolution. The consequence was a firm belief in the dominion of advanced races—of which the Anglo-Saxon was the most advanced—over lesser ones. John Burges, founder of political sciences at Columbia University and mentor of Theodore Roosevelt, was also instrumental in developing racial theories to explain the destiny of the United States. He believed that the civilized states, founded by various branches of the Teutonic races, had a "claim upon the uncivilized populations as well as a duty towards them, and that claim is that they shall become civilized." This version of survival of the fittest, called Aryanism or Teutonism, proposed that there was a common racial ancestor or master race as the root of all those people whose language belonged to the Indo-European family, and that in some races, especially the Teutons, the line was purer. See Stephanson, *Manifest Destiny*, 28, 43–42, 60, 79, 81, 83–84.

  On July 12, 1893, historian Frederick Jackson Turner in *The Significance of the Frontier in American History* announced the end of a formative era and the beginning of a new epoch. It was time for the Anglo-Saxon reunion under U.S. leadership. When Strong's sense of sacred mission, the expansive Anglo-Saxonism of Fiske, and the social Darwinism of Burges met the manifest destiny of Turner, it was time to look for new frontiers. These views were evident in Roosevelt's *The Winning of the West, 1885–94*, as well as in other authors' frontier novels. See Slotkin, *Gunfighter Nation*, 24, 34–35, and Stephanson, *Manifest Destiny*, 83. Also see LaFeber, *The New Empire*, 95, 98–99.

  28. Johnson, *Latin America in Caricature*.

  29. Kristin L. Hoganson has argued that in the United States, gender served as a "coalition building political method" that helped to consolidate contradictory arguments while unifying people from different walks of life in favor of war with Spain in 1898. Hoganson, *Fighting for American Manhood*, 3, 8.

  30. Moskos, "From Citizens' Army to Social Laboratory," 85–86.

  31. Kaplan, "Black and Blue on San Juan Hill," 228–31.

  32. Dalfiume, *Desegregation of the U.S. Armed Forces*, 26–27.

  33. Kaplan, "Black and Blue on San Juan Hill," 222–26.

  34. Mahan, "The Relations of the United States to Their New Dependencies," 247–49.

  35. See Valle Atiles, *El campesino puertorriqueño, sus condiciones físicas, intelectuales y morales*, 151, and Scarano, "The Jíbaro Masquerade," 1400–1402. Part

of the contradictory representations of the jíbaro by the island's elites included his docility, which "predisposed him to accepting his exploitation at the hands of others." See Guerra, *Popular Expression and National Identity*, 81, 109.

36. Picó, *La guerra después de la Guerra*, 66–68.

37. Mahan, "The Relations of the United States to Their New Dependencies," 247–49, and Johnson, *Latin America in Caricature*.

38. One of the most important points in Mahan's theory was that sea power, "as a national interest, commercial and military, rests not upon fleets only, but also upon local territorial bases in distant commercial regions." These territories, Mahan believed, had to be extensive and densely populated by people bound to the sovereign country by "those of interest which rest upon the beneficence of the ruler; of which beneficence power to protect is not the least factor."

39. Mahan, "The Relations of the United States to Their New Dependencies," 245–49.

40. Labor sectors and farmers in the United States opposed incorporating the new territories into the Union. Labor sectors believed that corporations would strengthen their hold over the means of production while the farmers feared that corporations would inundate the American markets with cheap tropical products, especially sugar. This last position especially worried beet producers. See Bernabe, *Respuestas al colonialismo*, 23–25.

41. In essence, that transformation was also the decision of the U.S. Supreme Court during the infamous insular cases that tested the relationship between the United States and the new territories. In the case of *Downes v. Bidwell*, 182 U.S. 244 (1901), Justice Edward D. White stated that following the doctrine of automatically incorporating newly acquired territories would curtail the ability of the United States to obtain territories needed to advance its foreign policy but undesired as part of the Union. The insular cases were brought before the U.S. Supreme Court mostly due to the passing of the Foraker Act, which made Puerto Rico a nonincorporated territory of the United States. During the deliberation, the Supreme Court basically considered whether "the Constitution follows the flag." The justices decided, in a 5–4 decision, that newly annexed territories were not part of the United States for purposes of the constitution in the matter of revenues and administrative matters. The court also noted that the constitutional guarantees of a citizen's rights to liberty and property were applicable to all. However, territories were only due the full protection of the constitution when Congress had incorporated them as an "integral part" of the nation. Justice White was a native of Louisiana, a Confederate officer, and a state senator. He was also the first Roman Catholic to serve on the Supreme Court (1894–1921). He was appointed by President Cleveland and made chief justice by President Taft. It seems as if his ruling had more to do with racial prejudice than with religious beliefs. Bernabe, *Respuestas al colonialismo*, 24–26.

42. Estades Font, *La presencia militar de Estados Unidos en Puerto Rico*, 107–10.

43. Bernabe, *Respuestas al colonialismo*, 113–114, citing Elihu Root, *The Military and Colonial Policy of the United States*, 161–71.

44. Fernós López-Cepero, *Documentos Históricos-Constitucionales*, 45, 55–72. As provided by the Foraker Act, public education was to be conducted in English, now an official language.

45. The Federals had participated in the municipal elections between October 26, 1898, and February 5, 1899. Led by Luis Muñoz Rivera, the Federals won in forty-four municipalities, and the Republicans secured the remaining twenty-two. Bayrón Toro, *Elecciones y partidos políticos de Puerto Rico*, 111–15.

46. The Republicans accused the Federals of being anti-Americans. Mobs of Republican supporters, known as Turbas Republicanas, organized as the Comite para la Defensa del Partico Republicano (Committee for the Defense of the Republican Party). These mobs harassed the Federals and the members of the Federación Libre del Trabajo (FLT), forcing Muñoz Rivera and Iglesias Pantín to flee the country. Bernabe argues against the belief that the Turbas Republicanas were engendered by the resentment against the old Spanish regime and the insular classes that benefited from it. As evidence, he cites the Turbas' violence against workers, especially the members of the FTL, and the dispossessed who had nothing to do with the old regime or the elites. Bernabe, *Respuestas al colonialismo*, 30–31.

47. Between 1908 and 1914 Unión would not lose a single district or the office of resident commissioner. In 1912, disenchanted with U.S. colonial policies, Unión discarded statehood as a solution. Independence, added as a possibility in 1913, would be renounced in 1922. The concept of the Libre Estado Asociado (Free Associated State), which had been the dominant one among members of Unión since the 1910s, became its only solution to the status question in 1922. See Bernabe, *Respuestas al colonialismo*, 48–51, and Bayrón Toro, *Elecciones y partidos políticos de Puerto Rico*, 111–42.

48. Bernabe, *Respuestas al colonialismo*, 27.

49. Those twenty-one or older who were literate or who paid taxes were allowed to vote. There were roughly 132,000 registered voters in 1898; 159,000 in 1902; 221,000 in 1910; and over 273,000 in 1914. See Bayrón Toro, *Elecciones y partidos políticos de Puerto Rico*, 120, 125, 128, 132, 136, 140, 144.

50. Guerra, *Popular Expression and National Identity*, 23–24.

51. Bernabe, *Respuestas al colonialismo*, 27–28; Ayala and Bernabe, *Puerto Rico in the American Century*, 76.

52. Quintero Rivera, *Conflictos de clase y política en Puerto Rico*, 70–82.

53. McKinley adopted Captain Mahan's views with regard to the territories acquired as a result of the war with Spain in 1898. See Gould, *Spanish-American War and President McKinley*, 123, and Mahan, "The Relations of the United States to Their New Dependencies," 247–49.

54. Go, "Chains of Empire," 343.

55. George M. Fredrickson explains that finding peoples of brown and bronze skin color in the Americas debunked the European belief that skin color was a chameleonic adaptation of the skin to a region's weather. It was instead a permanent characteristic. Although the new understanding of skin pigmentation became a pillar for racist beliefs and doctrines, it also influenced the emergence

of nationalist movement. For the first time there was a permanent Other. Anna Triandafyllidou proposes that the existence of a "significant Other" influences the development of the national identity of an inner community by presenting not only the inner community but the state with a model against which they can define themselves. See Fredrickson, *Racism: A Short History*, 39–40, and Triandafyllidou, "National Identity and the 'Other.'"

56. Ayala and Bernabe, *Puerto Rico in the American Century*, 76.

57. Religious differences, to a certain degree, were bridged by American Catholic clergy and Protestant missionaries. After the change of sovereignty, the Catholic Church lost half its clergy on the island, who decided to return to Spain rather than live under the American flag. Bishop Jaimes H. Blenk arrived on the island in 1899 and until 1906 worked to fill the vacuum left by the Spanish clergy. Soon after the invasion, the main Protestant churches in the United States launched missionary campaigns in Puerto Rico. Churches and private schools run by different Protestant denominations were soon built throughout the island. See Vega, "La situación de las Iglesias en Mayagüez en torno a 1898," 58–59, and Campbell, "Imperialismo sin un imperio colonial," 65–67.

58. Thirty-six schools had been opened by the end of the military government, raising the number from 551 to 587. Enrollment in public schools went from 25,644 on June 30, 1898, to 28,691 on April 30, 1900. However, only 19,752 students were actively attending in school in 1900 compared with 18,243 on June 30, 1898. The figures are more striking when considering that the school population was roughly 300,000. The Insular Commission on Public Instruction found that in most cases the schools lacked buildings and books and that absenteeism and unpreparedness among the teachers was the norm. Furthermore, regardless of attendance and performance, all students eventually graduated. "Civil Affairs in Porto Rico," *Reports of the War Department*, 1900, 121–29.

59. On October 30, 1898, less than two weeks after the transfer of sovereignty, an assembly of Puerto Rican educators and prominent figures decided that the American method of schooling should be adopted as soon as possible if Puerto Rico were to become a state of the Union. Furthermore, as historian Rosario Natal details, Puerto Rican newspapers were beginning to publish advertisements in English promoting U.S. universities. The assembly demanded coeducation, free and compulsory schooling, and the establishment of schools to prepare male and female teachers. The educators believed that only in that way could they reach their goal "that Puerto Rico becomes a state of the Union." Rosario Natal, *Puerto Rico y la crisis de la Guerra Hispanoamericana*, 254.

60. Negrón de Montilla, *La americanización de Puerto Rico y el sistema de instrucción pública*, and Torres González, *Idioma, bilingüismo y nacionalidad*.

61. Ayala and Bernabe, *Puerto Rico in the American Century*, 75–76.

62. Del Moral, *Negotiating Empire*, 7–9. Del Moral addresses issues of race, nation, gender, and empire by examining the history of schools and teachers in Puerto Rico and their relevance for understanding the process of colonial state-building.

63. Estades Font, *La presencia militar de Estados Unidos en Puerto Rico*, 88–89, and Bernabe, *Respuestas al colonialismo*, 14–21, 124–28.

64. Works dealing with military institutions in the island are García Muñiz, "El Caribe durante la Segunda Guerra Mundial"; Estades Font, *La presencia militar de Estados Unidos en Puerto Rico*; Morales Carrión, *Puerto Rico y la lucha por la hegemonía el Caribe*; and Negroni, *Historia militar de Puerto Rico*.

65. The Bureau of Insular Affairs (BIA) was established as a branch of the War Department by an act of Congress on July 1, 1902. The BIA's origins are found in the Division of Customs and Insular Affairs existing between 1898 and 1900 and the Division of Insular Affairs between 1900 and 1902. The BIA was almost a replica of the Bureau of Indian Affairs. The main difference was that instead of civilians, who were believe to be prone to corruption and to promoting their own economic interests, military officers, who were supposed to be impervious to corruption, would run the new colonial apparatus. Moreover, as most U.S. army officers had experience in the Indian wars, they were considered ideal candidates to deal with the population of the Philippines, Puerto Rico, the Panama Canal, and later the Dominican Republic. The BIA administered the customs and supervised the civil affairs of the Philippine islands between 1898 and 1939, Puerto Rico, 1898–1900, 1909–34, and Cuba, 1898–1902, 1906–9. It supervised the Dominican Customs Receivership from 1905 to 1939 and the Haitian Customs Receivership from 1920 to 1924. President William Howard Taft, who served as secretary of war between 1904 and 1908, put the island's affairs under the control of the War Department's Bureau of Insular Affairs as a response to the Puerto Rican chamber of delegates' reluctance to pass the governor's budget for 1909. Responsibility for Puerto Rico transferred to the Division of Territories and Island Possessions (later the Office of Territories and then the Office of Territorial Affairs) in the Department of the Interior by Executive Order 6.726, May 29, 1934. The transfer went into effect on March 2, 1935. The BIA was abolished by the Reorganization Plan No. II on July 1, 1939. The bureau was replaced by the Division of Territories and Island Possessions of the Department of the Interior, which operated between 1939 and 1950. See Records of the Bureau of Insular Affairs, http://www.archives.gov/research/guide-fed-records/groups/350.html, and Estades Font, *La presencia militar de Estados Unidos en Puerto Rico*, 120–23.

66. Relief efforts started before San Ciriaco. In December 1898 the military governor, Guy V. Henry, had requested from Muñoz Rivera a report detailing "any cases of poverty or destitution which cannot be relieved by the inhabitants of the place" with the intention "if possible, to help these people." Henry to Muñoz Rivera, December 12, 1898, AGPR, Caja, 135.

67. The military government estimated that relief efforts had to be provided for a full quarter of the island's population estimated roughly to be one million. See "Civil Affairs in Porto Rico," *Reports of the War Department*, 1900, 771. Also see "Informe sobre el Censo de Puerto Rico," *Departamento de Guerra*, 1899, 106; Ashford, *A Soldier in Science*, 40; and Wintermute, *Public Health and the U.S. Military*.

68. Ashford, *A Soldier in Science*, 3–5, 42–45.

69. In Ashford's account that number represented "1,600,000 visits over mountain trails and hot coast-lands to see the doctor." Ashford, *A Soldier in Science*, 56, 68–70, 82–83.

70. Ashford, *A Soldier in Science*, 77, 79–80, 92.

71. The military paternalistic approach to the new colonial subjects was not restricted to Puerto Rico. It was also applied to the Philippines. See Hawkins, *Making Moros*, x–xi, 5–6, and Go, "Chains of Empire," 334.

72. Estades Font, *La presencia militar de Estados Unidos en Puerto Rico*, 101, quoting President McKinley's second annual message of December 5, 1898.

73. See Negroni, *Historia Militar de Puerto Rico*, 367–69.

74. Trask, *War with Spain in 1898*, 366–67.

75. The illiteracy rate in 1899 was 80 percent. U.S. colonial officials and Puerto Rican elites questioned the capacity of illiterates to fully participate in government. Del Moral, *Negotiating Empire*, 9.

76. Muratti, *History of the 65th Infantry*, 2–3; Negroni, *Historia militar de Puerto Rico*; and Franqui-Rivera, "'A New Day Has Dawned for Porto Rico's Jíbaro.'"

77. Muratti, *History of the 65th Infantry*, 2–3; clipping, *Bexans Daily Growl*, November 5, 1950, LRR; and Negroni, *Historia militar de Puerto Rico*, 371.

78. Rafael Bernabe has discussed many of the political responses to American imperialism developed by Puerto Rican leaders by the turn of the nineteenth century. In a work that demystifies early independence and statehood defenders, Bernabe argues that many of the latter were in fact radical anticolonialists. Bernabe, *Respuestas al colonialismo*, 29–36.

79. Hostos, *Los rostros del camino*, 154–56.

80. "Deseo que la enseñanza militar del pueblo de Puerto Rico sea considerada como uno de los recursos que necesitamos para la educación de nuestro pueblo . . . la instrucción de los puertorriqueños en la enseñanza militar es un medio para su fortalecimiento físico y para la disciplina de la vida y del carácter." See Negroni, "Hostos y su pensamiento militar," 272–85, quoting Hostos, *Obras completas*, 5:91–92.

81. "Nuestras escuelas cívicas sean escuelas militares y que la enseñanza militar en las escuelas sea enseñanza cívica para la vida." See Negroni, "Hostos y su pensamiento militar," 283–84, quoting Hostos, *Obras completas*, 5:251.

82. In 1900, disillusioned with the policies of the McKinley administration, he stated that the president had betrayed the goal of Americanizing the island. Although Hostos preferred an independent Puerto Rico and ideally to be part of an Antillean Confederation, he considered that if the people of Puerto Rico so desired it, the island should become a state. "En vez de un plan de gobierno que habría americanizado a Borinquen en cuanto el Americanismo es un bien, y la habría preparado para ejercer eficazmente su independencia en la vida de relación con los demás pueblos de la tierra, McKinley y el sindicato político que no ven más allá de la continuación del partido republicano en el poder, no vieron otra cosa en Puerto Rico que el campo de explotación que creían dar

a la codicia de sus parciales o a la vana gloria del vulgo americano." "Carta al Director de *La Correspondencia de Puerto Rico*," October 1900, in Hostos, *Los rostros del camino*, 156–58.

83. Bernabe, *Respuestas al colonialismo*, 35–37, quoting Hostos, *Madre Isla: Campaña Política por Puerto Rico*, 8, 13, 15–17, 24–25, 82, 305.

84. Rosendo Matienzo Cintrón, one of the founders of the Republican Party in Puerto Rico and initially an annexationist, shared some of the ideas espoused by Hostos regarding Americanization. To Matienzo Cintrón, Americanization meant democratic modernization. Political freedom, democratic rights, secular education, separation of church and state, workers' and women's rights, and the utilization of research and science for the betterment of all aspects of human life were part of his understanding of democratic modernization. This radical position, as argued by Rafael Bernabe, would eventually lead him to organize the Partido de la Independencia in 1912. Like many others who admired the founding principles of the United States, Matienzo Cintrón grew disillusioned with the colonial apparatus established on the island by the McKinley administration via the Foraker Act of 1900. Like Hostos, Matienzo Cintrón denounced the "false Americanization" taking place. He believed that if Americanization was "democratic modernization," then by imposing a colonial regime on the Puerto Ricans, the U.S. government was engaging in false Americanization and thus betraying its founding principles. Bernabe, *Respuestas al colonialismo*, 30, 32–33, 34–35.

85. Del Moral, *Negotiating Empire*, 9; Go, "Chains of Empire," 335, 338.

86. The order set the unit's strength at four companies, A, B, C, and D, each with one hundred men. They were located in Mayagüez, Ponce, and San Juan. Muratti, *History of the 65th*, 2–3.

87. Muratti, *History of the 65th*, 2–3.

88. General Order No. 34 of February 12, 1900. The order allowed for the organization of companies E, F, G, and H as a cavalry battalion. These troops were stationed in Henry Barracks in the mountain town of Cayey. Norat-Martínez, ed., *Historia del Regimiento 65 de Infantería*, 11.

89. By February 23, 1901, U.S. troops remained on the island, but their role was limited to support duties. Hospital, signal, and artillery detachments and an infantry battalion were all that was left of the occupation forces as of December 15, 1900. See *Reports of the War Department. 1900*, 106; Norat-Martínez, *Historia del Regimiento 65 de Infantería*, 9–11.

90. The regiment's structural organization did not suffer any more changes until it began to expand in preparation for the First World War. Norat-Martínez, *Historia del Regimiento 65 de Infantería*, 12.

91. Estades Font, *La presencia militar de los estados Unidos en Puerto Rico*, 121–28.

92. Taft made his remarks in 1902 during the hearings on affairs in the Philippine islands before the Senate Committee on the Philippines. At that point the United States had 40,000 troops in the Philippines aided by thousands of Filipino volunteers. See Graff, ed., *American Imperialism and the Philippine Insurrection*, 121–23.

93. The residents of Lares who joined the battalion of volunteers on March 28, 1899, were Manuel González, Juan Feliciano, Maximiliano Grauláu, Primo Hernández, Antonio Montes, Vicente Rivera, and Ramón Santiago. José de Rodríguez and Agustín Carbonell, also from Lares, became the first Puerto Rican sergeant and corporal serving in the U.S. Battalion of Volunteers, and Fermín Rojas, another *lareño* who joined on March 30, was in charge, with José F. Santiago from San Juan, of creating the first mess hall. See Padrón, *El 65 en revista*, 22–23.

94. This is supported by the fact that the officers' corps was closed to natives until 1904. Since the pay of an enlisted man was much less than what a professional, merchant, or *hacendado* could make, not to mention that these classes expected to serve as officers, it is obvious that those joining were of humble means. In July 4, 1904, Jaime Nadal became the first Puerto Rican to be appointed as a second lieutenant in the regiment. Before Nadal, Puerto Ricans only served as noncommissioned officers and recruits. "Puerto Rican Provisional Regiment of Infantry," July 1901–October 1909, CIHPC, Caja 31. Public Law 160 of March 3, 1903, allowed the governor of Puerto Rico to nominate one midshipman to Annapolis. The resident commissioner could nominate five candidates under Public Law 8, 66th Cong., of July 11, 1919. See CIHPC, Caja 30.

95. Until World War I there were few Puerto Rican officers, and they mostly served in junior positions as field officers. These "native" officers belonged to the upper crust of the island's society, and many had received degrees from U.S. universities. Marín Román, *¡Llegó la gringada!* 220–26.

96. *Reports of the War Department, 1900*, 105.

97. According to 1st Lt. J. S. Battle (11th U.S. Infantry), the first inspector of the Insular Police, this corps was created to fill the vacuum left by the retreating Spanish forces. He reported that "the reign of terror was existing everywhere. Armed bands of assassins and incendiaries were in control of the largest part of the island, levying tribute from the merchants and planters." Since he found the American soldiers incapable of dealing with these bands due to their lack of knowledge of Spanish and the islands' topography, Maj. Gen. Guy V. Henry, military governor, ordered the creation of the Insular Police on February 7, 1899. Two clerks and the inspector were the only Americans in the initial force. *Reports of the War Department, 1900*, 105–6, 226–28.

98. Norat-Martínez, *Historia del Regimiento 65 de Infantería*, 11–13.

99. Allen to Root, May 1900, AGPR, Caja 224.

100. Allen to Root, May 1900, AGPR, Caja 224.

3. A New Day Has Dawned

1. "A New Day Has Dawned for the Porto Rican Jíbaro," CPUPRM, *Porto Rico Progress*, July 12, 1918. The *Porto Rico Progress* was published in English between December 8, 1910, and the early 1960s. Its tone was adamantly pro-American.

2. Norat-Martínez, *Historia del Regimiento 65 de Infantería*, 12.

3. Taft obtained from Congress an amendment to the Foraker Act of 1900 enabling the governor to use the previous year's budget if the elected Porto Rican chamber of delegates did not approve his budget proposal. Estades Font, *La presencia militar de los Estados Unidos en Puerto Rico*, 126–29.

4. Self-government and self-determination are not the same. The former refers to a higher degree of self-rule and the liberalization of the colonial regime, which some groups thought would lead to eventual independence. Self-determination meant allowing the Puerto Ricans to decide the political status of the island by themselves, be it inclusion in the Union as a federated state, independence, or any other political arrangement.

5. Scarano, "The Jíbaro Masquerade," 1400–1402.

6. Scarano, "The Jíbaro Masquerade," 1404, and Guerra, *Popular Expression and National Identity*, 9, 83–85.

7. Guerra, *Popular Expression and National Identity*, 81, 109.

8. Del Moral, *Negotiating Empire*, 7–9; Guerra, *Popular Expression and National Identity*, 9, 83–85; and Ashford, *A Soldier in Science*. The Republicans argued that when the illiteracy rate had been reduced to 29 percent, the island should be accepted as a state of the Union. Clark, *Puerto Rico and the United States*, 28.

9. Gilbert, *The First World War*, 14–17, 32–34, 473–80, 497–523.

10. "Ley Orgánica Jones," Artículos 5, 5a, 5b, 5c, in Fernós López-Cepero, *Documentos Históricos-Constitucionales*, 79–82.

11. The members of the legislature were required to know how to read and write in both English and Spanish. The senate would be composed of two senators for each of the seven electoral districts and five senators not attached to any district. The House would consist of thirty-nine representatives, one per district, and another four not linked to any district. The president retained the authority to appoint the governor, the education commissioner, and the island's supreme court judges. See "Ley Orgánica Jones," Artículos 5–5a 25–28 in Fernós López-Cepero, *Documentos Históricos-Constitucionales*, 93–96.

12. Those who believe that Puerto Ricans were made U.S. citizens included the last-appointed continental American governor of Puerto Rico, Rexford G. Tugwell. See Tugwell, *The Art of Politics*, 35–36.

13. This opinion was shared by Secretary Jacob McGavock Dickinson (March 1909–May 1911) and Secretary Henry L. Stimson (May 1911–March 1913), though Stimson shifted his position later. See Estades Font, *La presencia militar de los Estados Unidos en Puerto Rico*, 204–6, citing "Hearing upon the Bill Proposing to Amend the Present Organic Law of Porto Rico, January 31, 1910, to February 24, 1910."

14. Estades Font, *La presencia militar de los Estados Unidos en Puerto Rico*, 207, citing Root to Stimson, December 7, 1911.

15. President Taft appointed Colton as governor of Porto Rico in mid-September 1909. According to the *New York Times*, Colton who at the time was serving in the Philippines as a customs collector, had worked in a similar role in the Dominican Republic, spoke Spanish fluently, and had diplomatic ties with

many Latin American leaders. See *New York Times*, September 13, 1909; and Colton to Secretary of War, December 13, 1912, in Font, *La presencia militar de los Estados Unidos en Puerto Rico*, 208.

16. Yager served as governor of the island from 1913 to 1921. He was appointed by President Woodrow Wilson, a fellow Democrat and a former classmate from Johns Hopkins University. Yager had a PhD in political sciences and had headed Georgetown College in Kentucky. He served throughout Wilson's terms in office and was succeeded by President Warren G. Harding's appointee, Emmet Montgomery. See Albert Shaw, ed., "Puerto Rico under Dr. Yager: Citizenship in the New Bill."

17. In the general elections of November 3, 1914, Unión, which had controlled all districts in the island since 1906, lost the districts of Mayagüez, Aguadilla, and Ponce to the Republicans. However, it continued to be the dominating political force, receiving over half the total votes cast, winning fifty-one municipalities out of seventy-five, reelecting Luis Muñoz Rivera as resident commissioner in Washington, and securing nineteen of thirty-five seats in the chamber of delegates. Bayrón Toro, *Elecciones y partidos políticos de Puerto Rico*, 143–45.

18. The Socialist Party, led by Santiago Iglesias Pantín, and its union, Federación de Trabajadores de Puerto Rico, were associated with the American Federation of Labor presided by Samuel Gompers. The Socialists defended Americanization and permanent union with the United States. See Bayrón Toro, *Elecciones y partidos políticos de Puerto Rico*, 148–49. Between 1913 and 1922, Unión's dominant plan to change the political arrangement of the island consisted of three stages: securing autonomy, exercising such autonomy, and demanding independence. Historian Rafael Bernabe explains that this platform was more likely intended to restrain de Diego and his most radical wing than the party's actual goals. See Bernabe, *Respuestas al colonialismo*, 48–49.

19. Most of the discontent with the metropolis was voiced through *La Correspondencia*, which was first the newspaper of the radicals within Unión and later of the Partido de la Independencia (Independence Party). Wilson made it clear that the Unionist Party would have to abandon the goal of independence to get the administration's approval to amend the Foraker Act. Muñoz Rivera conceded, and autonomy became the goal of the Unionist Party. See Bernabe, *Respuestas al colonialismo*, 49–51.

20. Bayròn Toro, *Elecciones y partidos políticos de Puerto Rico*, 147–48.

21. Restricting suffrage on the basis of literacy and taxation was opposed by all political parties, as it would deny voting rights to 165,000 registered voters from a total of roughly 250,000. Pagán, *Historia de los Partidos Políticos Puertorriqueños*, 174–75.

22. The Unionistas believed that granting U.S. citizenship would kill the chances of independence by definitely incorporating Puerto Rico as a territory. That was the opinion of Speaker of the House José de Diego. See Pagán, *Historia de los Partidos Políticos Puertorriqueños*, 173–74.

23. This journal highlighted that in 1914, more than 200,000 children were attending public schools on the island. *American Review of Reviews*, 399–400.

24. Estades Font, *La presencia militar de Estados Unidos en Puerto Rico*, 126–27, 212–15.

25. See Butler, "African Americans in the Military," 7–9; Foner, *Blacks and the Military in American History*; Richard M. Dalfiume, *Desegregation of the U.S. Armed*, 26–27; and Morris J. McGregor, *Integration of the Armed Forces*.

26. Johnson, *Latin America in Caricature*.

27. To see the trajectory of the policy of excluding African Americans from combat positions, see Dalfiume, *Desegregation of the U.S. Armed Forces*, 26–27.

28. Ramírez, *To the Line of Fire! Mexican Texans and World War I*, and Franqui-Rivera, "'A New Day Has Dawned for Porto Rico's Jíbaro.'"

29. "Selective Service Act of May 18, 1917," https://archive.org/details/cu31924020164152.

30. Beisner, *From the Old Diplomacy to the New*, 132; Langley, *The Banana Wars*, 21, citing Herwig, *Politics of Frustration*, 101–9.

31. Mahan, *Lessons of the War*, 29, 245, 247–49.

32. The type of citizenship granted by the Jones Act is known as statutory citizenship, meaning that citizenship was granted by an act of Congress and not by the Constitution; hence it was not guaranteed by the Constitution.

33. Wilson also made reference to the Philippines in his speech. Pagán, *Historia de los Partidos Políticos Puertorriqueños*, 172.

34. Knock, *To End All Wars*, 97–98, 116–17.

35. In his first annual message to Congress on December 2, 1913, Wilson had expressed his positive opinion with regard to granting American citizenship to the people of Puerto Rico. Speech reprinted in Pagán, *Historia de los Partidos Políticos Puertorriqueños*, 171–72.

36. Republicans and Socialists celebrated the passing of the bill as a victory and stepping-stone toward equality. The Unionistas, under the new leadership of Antonio R. Barceló, welcomed the act but saw it just as a measure of self-government before the last stage of their political solution, independence, was attained. Although officially the Unionistas talked about self-determination, their leaders started to call for independence after the Jones Act passed. See Bolívar Pagán, *Historia de los Partidos Políticos Puertorriqueños*, 179–86.

37. Clark, *Puerto Rico and the United States*, 26–27.

38. U.S. citizenship and majority of age were the only requirement. See Pagán, *Historia de los Partidos Políticos Puertorriqueños*, 179.

39. Knock, *To End All Wars*, 116–17, and Gilbert, *First World War*.

40. Declaration reprinted in *El Águila de Puerto Rico*, April 10, 1917.

41. "Secretary of War, Memorandum," February 25, 1918, CIHPC, Caja 30.

42. "Document 10 A," CIHPC, Caja 18.

43. "A Bill to Amend the Organic Act of Puerto Rico, Election of Governor: Hearings on H.R. 3309," UMMC, May 19, 1947, 35–36.

44. "Document 10 A," CIHPC, Caja 18.

45. A native of Alabama, Frank McIntyre served on the Mexican border until the war with Spain of 1898. He was part of the invading force sent to Puerto Rico. From 1899 to 1902, McIntyre served in the Philippines. In 1905 he was sent to the Bureau of Insular Affairs, served as acting chief at least since 1910, and became the Bureau's chief proper in 1912, a position he occupied until 1929. That same year he became a brigadier general. McIntyre was a latecomer with regard to granting collective U.S. citizenship to Puerto Ricans.

46. "Document 10 A," CIHPC, Caja 18, and Muratti, *History of the 65th*, 8.

47. Muratti, *History of the 65th*, 8.

48. Yager to McIntyre, July 10, 1917, CIHPC, Caja 30.

49. Doctors, dentists, engineers, lawyers, professors, businessmen, industrialists, and landowners became the bulk of the Puerto Rican officers' corps. See Nadal, *Guardia Nacional, sucesora de las milicias puertorriqueñas*, 42. Yager was not easily impressed with the volunteers showing up. He wrote the chief of the BIA: "700 applicants for the officer's training camp, not the best quality. I'm sure that many more young men of a better class than this could have been secured." See Yager to McIntyre, July 20, 1917, CIHPC, Caja 30.

50. Memorandum, February 25, 1918, CIHPC, Caja 30.

51. Yager to McIntyre, July 20, 1917, CIHPC, Caja 30.

52. Newspaper clip, CIHPC, Caja 30; and Nadal, *Guardia Nacional, sucesora de las Milicias Puertorriqueñas*.

53. Unión obtained 90,155 votes while the Republicans tallied 60,319 and the Socialists 24,468. In 1916 Martín Travieso, *Unionista*, and Manuel V. Domenech, *Republicano*, had been named secretary of Puerto Rico and commissioner of the Interior, respectively. These were the highest-ranking Puerto Ricans in the executive council and for the first time Puerto Ricans had a majority in the council. Bayrón Toro, *Elecciones y partidos políticos de Puerto Rico*, 147. In the elections of 1917, the Republicans elected five senators and fourteen representatives while the Socialists elected one senator and one representative. Unión won fifty-two municipalities and recovered the Aguadilla district lost in 1914. See Bayrón Toro, *Elecciones y partidos políticos de Puerto Rico*, 149–52.

54. Bolívar Pagán, *Historia de los Partidos Políticos Puertorriqueños*, 189–90.

55. Paralitici, *No quiero mi cuerpo pa' tambor*, 25–29, 1998, 65–66.

56. As explained by Barbara L. Tischler in "One Hundred Percent Americanism," slogans, parades, speeches, posters, and news articles were among the means used by George Creel's Committee on Public Information seeking to create patriotic consensus in the ethnically diverse U.S. population. "While Creel did not use the term officially, the ideology of 100 percent Americanism permeated his writings and speeches."

57. Creel noted that other wars "went no further than the physical aspects, but German 'Kultur' raised issues that had to be fought out in the hearts and minds of the people as well as on the actual firing-line." Tischler, "One Hundred Percent Americanism," citing Creel, *How We Advertised America*, 3–5.

58. The 94th Division would consist of four regiments, 373, 374, 375, and 376. The first two were assigned to the Tactical Brigade 187 while the 375 Colored, and the projected 376 were to form part of Tactical Brigade 188. A Home Guard was also established to take over defense of the island in the unlikely case the Porto Rican division was sent overseas. Negroni, *Historia militar de Puerto Rico*, 422–23, 440–45.

59. "Memorandum from Chief of the War Plans Division," December 18, 1918, CIHPC, Caja 30.

60. The BIA estimated: "The National Army had for its Porto Rican contingent about 12,800 men organized into eight white and four colored provisional training battalions, provisional division of 3 provisional regiments." "Memorandum from Chief of the War Plans Division," December 18, 1918, CIHPC, Caja 30.

61. A semi-bilingual publication based in Ponce, *El Águila de Puerto Rico* was published between January 8, 1902, and July 3, 1931. It reappeared on January 1, 1934, but ceased to exist two months later. It always functioned as an organ of the Republican Party.

62. *El Águila*, October 6–9, 1918.

63. *El Águila* congratulated "our old friend don Pedro Albizu Campos, who in the recent graduation of cadets from the Officers Training Camp at Las Casas earned the rank of First Lieutenant in the Army reserve." *El Águila*, November 8, 1918, April 10–14, 1917, October 10, 1918, and December 6, 1918.

64. Córdova Dávila to Baker, January 10, 1918, CIHPC, Caja 30.

65. "Memorandum from Adjutant General of the Army," May 15, 1918, CIHPC, Caja 30.

66. Yager to McIntyre, July 10, 1917, CIHPC, Caja 30.

67. Brown to Colton, March 26, 1910, CIHPC, Caja 29.

68. Colton to McIntyre, September 24, 1910, CIHCP, Caja 29, Documento 8, and Pierson to Colton, April 9 1910, CIHPC, Caja 29.

69. McIntyre to Colton, September 16, 1910, CIHPR, Caja 29. Chief of Staff Leonard Wood's views were at odds with the War Department's. See Acting Secretary of War to Taft, July 23, 1910, CIHPC, Caja 29, and "Militia in the Island of Porto Rico: Memorandum," Baldwin to Taft, July 13, 1910, CIHPC, Caja 29.

70. *Washington Post*, November 19, 1917, CIHPC, Caja 30.

71. Yager to McIntire, November 9, 1917, CIHPC, Caja 30.

72. McIntire to Yager, November 24, 1917, CIHPC, Caja 30.

73. Córdova Dávila claimed that with the support of hundreds of cablegrams from businessmen and the mayors and legislators of the island, he persuaded Wilson to support training Puerto Rican troops on the island. Córdova Dávila also urged the War Department to buy Puerto Rican coffee for the military. Due to the inexpensive nature of Brazilian coffee and the high cost of the coffee produced in Puerto Rico, the War Department refused Córdova Dávila's proposal but agreed to buy local coffee for the Puerto Rican troops. *Porto Rico Progress*, March 8, 1918.

74. A total of 726 officers were trained and commissioned in Puerto Rico between August 27, 1917, and November 6, 1918. See "Report by Capt. Luis Raul Esteves, May 27, 1918," CIHPC, Caja 30, and Negroni, *Historia militar de Puerto Rico*, 440.

75. Rosa-Vélez, "The Puerto Ricans at Carlisle Indian School," Rosa-Vélez, "Acquiring the American Spirit," and Rosa-Vélez, "¿Qué pasó con los becados?"

76. Benedict Anderson has pointed out that the final replication of the former master's ways came in the obsession of the new states with legitimizing themselves through archaeological excavations that allowed scholars and administrators to connect them vertically to vanished civilizations and horizontally to European metropoles. Anderson, *Imagined Communities*, 120–27.

77. Crowd, "Memorandum to Chief of Staff," July 2, 1915, CIHPC.

78. Yager to McIntyre, July 10, 1917, CIHPC, Caja 30.

79. Yager to McIntyre, June 6, 1917, CIHPC, Caja 30.

80. Yager informed the BIA's chief that he was "looking for someone to aid the Governor of Saint Thomas to deal with Mr. Jackson and sugar laborers, but the war and Santo Domingo have taken many of Porto Rico's best men." Yager to McIntyre, June 6, 1917, CIHPC, Caja 30.

81. *La Democracia*, August 2,1918, CIHPC, Caja 30.

82. Miller to Córdova Dávila, August 7, 1919, CIHPC, Caja 30. Public Law 160–with 6700–6 of March 3, 1903, allowed the governor of Puerto Rico to nominate one midshipman to Annapolis while the resident commissioner could select five nominees. PL 8, 66th Congress 6700-With-27 of July 11, 1919. See Document 2 A, CIHPC, Caja 30. The colonial administrators also sought to secure equal treatment for their children born or residing on the island. See Miller to Hodges, circa 1918, CIHPC, Caja 30. Puerto Ricans were not the only colonial subjects attending the elite military institution. Emilio Aguinaldo Jr. was among the Filipino cadets sent to West Point. By 1924 eleven appointees from the Philippines and four Puerto Ricans had received commissions from the military institution. Osvaldo de la Rosa and Virgil Miller graduated from West Point in 1924. Luis Raul Esteves had graduated from West Point in 1915 and Francisco Cintrón in 1918; both remained in the Puerto Rico National Guard in the postwar years. See McIntire to Tower, June 16, 1924, CIHPC, Caja 30.

83. *El Tiempo*, July 3, 1919, CIHP, Caja 30.

84. Yager to McIntyre, June 6, 1917, CIHPC, Caja 30.

85. Yager to McIntyre, September 5, 1917, CIHPC, Caja 30.

86. *El Diluvio*, August 24, 1918.

87. "Acusan al viejo racista de Kentucky de ser el instigador. El triunfo definitivo derrotará también todos los privilegios," *Justicia*, San Juan, June 8, 1918, CIHPC, Caja 30, and *El Águila*, October 5, 1918.

88. *El Diluvio*, August 24, 1918.

89. *El Águila*, October 5, 1918.

90. Dalfiume, *Desegregation of the U.S. Armed Forces*, 11–14.

91. *Porto Rico Progress*, July 12, 1918.

92. According to these reports, quartermasters had trouble finding shoes for the majority of the men, who had never worn shoes and as a result "have feet almost as broad as they are long." Commenting on the need to stop drills often to allow the trainee to rest his feet, the editor continued, "Perhaps this is not a rigidly military proceeding, but the men so treated are going to fight to destroy militarism." *Porto Rico Progress*, July 5, 1918.

93. *El Buscapié*, January 14, 1918.

94. *Ariel* was published in 1900 by Uruguayan writer José Enrique Rodó and gave way to *Arielismo* as a literary and political movement. *Arielismo* offers an idealized picture of Latin American culture, which is marked by noble spirituality and gallantry as opposed to the United States, which represents materialism. Rodó took William Shakespeare's *The Tempest* to represent this cultural and spiritual divide between the United States and Latin America. The main characters in Rodó's versión are Ariel and Calibán. Ariel symbolizes Latin Americas' noble spirituality rooted in the Greco-Roman ideal of beauty and the Christian value of charity. On the other hand, Calibán (an anagram for Canibal) represents U.S. expansionism and utilitarianism. Latin America's spirituality, according to *Arielismo*, would help to create a better society by allowing the best men to flourish and lead the masses. The United States, however, engrossed in materialism and lacking Ariel's spirituality, is presented as utterly unable to escape mediocrity. Rodó, *Ariel*, http://www.pgdp.net.

95. *El Buscapié*, October 17, 1917. A few weeks later, this newspaper commented on the possible role of the island as a bridge between Latin America and North America: "Por nuestra condición de pueblo bilingüe, por ser este el punto de conjunción de dos civilizaciones y las dos razas predominantes en el hemisferio occidental; nuestra Universidad puede llegar a ser . . . la Universidad Panamericana." See *El Buscapié*, November 4, 1917.

96. *Porto Rico Progress*, December 13, 1918.

97. *Porto Rico Progress*, July 5, 1918. *El Carolina*, a ship carrying Puerto Rican workers to the United States, became Puerto Rico's USS *Maine* during the war after being sunk by a German submarine a few miles from the east coast. Several dozen Puerto Ricans drowned as a result of the attack.

98. Another commented about his wife and children: "They'll be all right. The Gobierno will take care of them." *Porto Rico Progress*, July 5, 1918.

99. The Treaty of Versailles of June 28, 1919, officially ended the First World War.

100. *Porto Rico Progress*, November 29, 1918.

101. *Porto Rico Progress*, December 27, 1918.

102. Within three days, the 654 vacancies of the Porto Rico Regiment were filled with volunteers. McIntyre to Yager, March 13, 1914, CIHPC, Caja 30, and Muratti, *Historia del Regimiento 65*, 9.

103. On July 1, 1908, under authority of an act of Congress approved on May 27, the Porto Rico United States Volunteers became officially part of the

regular army and was named the Porto Rico Regiment of Infantry U.S.A. See Muratti, *Historia del Regimiento 65*, 6.

104. Nadal, *Guardia Nacional, sucesora de las milicias puertorriqueñas*.

105. One *cuerda* equals 0.98 acres, so 200,000 *cuerdas* equal 194,244.38 acres.

106. "Pronto tendremos que afrontar el que la desmovilización del primer contingente de doce mil soldados portorriqueños, que acudieron presurosos al llamamiento de la nación, cuando peligró la libertad. La mayoría de esos labradores han aprendido a vivir una vida nueva. Todos, o su inmensa mayoría, han cambiado completamente sus puntos de vista. Lo que ayer les pareció natural; los standards [*sic*] de vida que aceptaron antes sin proferir un aqueja, con los nuevos hábitos e ideas adquiridas en la dura y provechosa labor del Campamento, no puede, no podrá satisfacerlos." *Diluvio*, November 16, 1918.

107. *El Águila*, November 23, 1918, and *Diluvio*, November 16, 1918.

108. *Porto Rico Progress*, December 27, 1918.

109. *Porto Rico Progress*, November 29, 1918.

110. *Porto Rico Progress*, December 6, 1918.

111. *Porto Rico Progress*, December 6, 1918.

112. *Porto Rico Progress*, December 13, 1918.

113. *El Mundo*, San Juan, February 18, 1919. The reporter asked Coll y Cuchí: "Do you believe that through Wilson's mediation the puertorriqueños will obtain the dream longed for by Hostos, Betances, and de Diego, that is, the independence of our motherland?"

114. This publication also defended the expansionist policies of the metropolis and declared that "when the war ended the U.S. would have absolute control of the Caribbean, and would continue its missionary colonization in the Caribbean." *El Buscapié*, November 4, 1917. This pro-metropolis publication, *El Buscapié*, as well as *El Águila* periodically wrote columns defending suffrage and full rights for women.

115. Pagán, *Historia de los Partidos Políticos Puertorriqueños*, 188–89, 201–2.

116. Montgomery Reily was despised by Socialists and Unionistas alike, and his arbitrary decisions even won him the antipathy of many Republicans. Iglesias Pantín came up with the rube nickname "Moncho Reyes" to deride the governor. Pagán, *Historia de los Partidos Políticos Puertorriqueños*, 205–6.

117. Pagán, *Historia de los Partidos Políticos Puertorriqueños*, 211–12.

118. For example, see Levy, *Puerto Ricans in the Empire*, and del Moral, *Negotiating Empire*.

119. Solsiree del Moral explains that when local newspapers reported that a majority of men who volunteered for service during World War I were rejected due to illiteracy, a crisis ensued. "If the majority of adult men were, in fact, illiterate and failed to meet that basic requirement of citizenship, teachers asked, how could they fulfill the duties of the newly granted U.S. citizenship?" Del Moral, *Negotiating Empire*, 3–5, 94–97.

120. Negroni, *Historia militar de Puerto Rico*, 442. Esteves stated that this experience moved him to fight for the creation of the National Guard in Puerto Rico.

4. War against the Yankees!

1. Pedro Albizu Campos, radio speech, printed in its entirety in *La Palabra*, November 2, 1935. The speech was in reaction to a gunfight near the University of Puerto Rico between the Insular Police and Nacionalistas the previous October 24, in which four Nacionalistas and a policeman lost their lives. See "Nationalist Party of Puerto Rico," FBI files, August 30, 1943, 50–51, http://www.pr-secretfiles.net. The chief of the Insular Police, E. Francis Riggs, had declared to the press: "If anyone persists in committing these crimes, I will let them know that there will be war, war without end, not against politicians, but against criminals. Whoever resists arrest by an agent of the public order is a criminal and a savage." *La Democracia*, October 26, 1935, 8.

2. In the *Baltimore Sun* edition of July 30, 1930, Luis Muñoz Marín had warned that the United States "does not wish to have a small Ireland on their hands by establishing a permanent satrapy in Puerto Rico." Muñoz Marín was particularly incensed by the apparent preference of the Brookings Institution report for getting rid of democratic institutions on the island, such as the legislature, for the sake of scientific efficiency in dealing with Puerto Rico's socioeconomic problems. Maldonado, *Luis Muñoz Marín*, 83–84. By 1937 Jay Franklin, Washington commentator for the Stern Papers, had labeled Puerto Rico the Ireland of the Caribbean. See Langley, *The United States and the Caribbean*, 72. On August 14, 1939, New York congressman Vito Marcantonio, while outlining his charges against Governor Blanton Winship's administration, which he described as "Five Years of Tyranny in Puerto Rico," used Stern's new nickname for the island to describe the political unrest during a speech on the floor of the House on August 5, 1939. Marcantonio had presented these charges to President Roosevelt and Secretary of the Interior Harold Ickes several months earlier. Ojeda Reyes, *Vitto Marcantonio y Puerto Rico*, 73–74.

3. His tactics were such that eventually he forced the founding leadership to leave the party. Cayetano Coll y Cuchi, cofounder of the Nationalist Party, declared that Albizu Campos's "intolerance and fanatism was going to alienate Puerto Rican people from the independence ideal." See "Nationalist Party of Puerto Rico," FBI files, 54–55; *El Águila*, November 8, 1918, April 10–14, 1917, October 10, 1918, December 6, 1918; Maldonado, *Luis Muñoz Marín*, 85–86, 87; Ferrao, *Pedro Albizu Campos y el nacionalismo puertorriqueño*, 43–48; and Marín Román, *El caldero quemaó*, 514–21.

4. Unión obtained 132,755 votes, the Republicans 30,286, the Socialists 56,103, and Constitucional Histórico 34,576. Altogether the Alianza received 163,041 votes versus 90,679 cast for the Coalición. The Alianza won seventy-one municipalities while the coalition secured four and elected two senators and three representatives. The Nationalist Party participated in the election, as well as the Federal Party and splinters of the principal parties, but did not win a significant number of votes anywhere. See Bayrón Toro, *Elecciones y partidos políticos de Puerto Rico*, 163–66.

5. Of 321,113 registered voters, 256,335 cast a vote in 1928. Alianza obtained 132,286 votes versus 123,415 for the Coalición. The Alianza elected Félix Córdova Dávila for the fourth time as resident commissioner in Washington and won forty-seven municipalities, elected eleven senators and twenty-first representatives, and won the senatorial districts of San Juan, Aguadilla, Mayagüez, and Guayama. The senatorial districts of Arecibo, Ponce, and Humacao were won by the Coalición (running under the name Socialistas–Coalicionistas), which also secured eight senators, eighteen representatives, and forty-seven municipalities. See Bayrón Toro, *Elecciones y partidos políticos de Puerto Rico*, 168.

6. Mathews, *La política puertorriqueña y el Nuevo Trato*, 26, 35, and Bayrón Toro, *Elecciones y partidos políticos de Puerto Rico*, 167–68, 173–76.

7. During the general election of 1932, registered voters increased to 452,783 (from 321,163) because for the first time women were allowed to vote on the island, made possible by Public Law 74 sponsored by Senator Manuel A. García Méndez. Of 383,722 votes cast, the PLP obtained 170,168, Unión Republicana 110,794, and the Socialistas 97,438. The Nacionalistas obtained 5,257, and Albizu Campos running for senator at large secured 11,882 votes. As a result, Santiago Iglesias Pantín became resident commissioner (a position he occupied between 1933 and 1939). The presidency of the senate and the house went to Rafael Martínez Nadal and Miguel A. García Méndez, respectively. See Bayrón Toro, *Elecciones y partidos políticos de Puerto Rico*, 168, 177, 181.

8. As explained by historian César Ayala, the proletarianization of the Puerto Rican peasantry was a function of land scarcity and high population density. This process accelerated after the passing of the Hollander bill of 1901 and by the implementation of U.S. tariffs on the island that were detrimental to the coffee industry in Puerto Rico, and forced small peasants and subsistence farmers to sell their lands. Ayala, *American Sugar Kingdom*, 159–61, 164–65.

9. Mathews, *La política puertorriqueña y el Nuevo Trato*, 17.

10. Important to include that *Porto Rico and Its Problems* was written after two years of research by seven scholars and professionals under the guidance of Victor S. Clark, formerly Puerto Rico's education commissioner. Excessive, inefficient government and partisan politics were to blame for Puerto Rico's maladies. But the main problem, according to the report, was overpopulation. See Maldonado, *Luis Muñoz Marín*, 82–84.

11. Dietz, *Economic History*, 127–29.

12. Ironically, Dr. Bailey K. Ashford's crusade to eradicate the hookworm-caused chronic anemia of the Puerto Rican peasant was undermined by the lack of shoes. By 1925 a study found that although the death rate related to hookworm had been dramatically reduced, the incidence of the disease had not. See Dietz, *Economic History*, 129, and Ashford, *A Soldier in Science*, 37–54.

13. Mathews, *La política puertorriqueña y el Nuevo Trato*, 28.

14. In 1935 the percentage of the male population with no economic activity on the island (ten years and older) reached an all-time high of 24.2 percent. The percentage of women engaged in economic activity, on the other

hand, had slowly increased, going from 15.8 percent in 1899 to 34.3 in 1935. Reportedly 150,000 heads of families were unemployed. Dietz, *Economic History*, 131, 153, table 2.14.

15. The report recommended making the sugar industry more competitive instead of limiting landownership, export quota, or raising workers' salaries. The report recommendations were in opposition to Muñoz Marín's understanding of the problems. For him, the root of the problem was capitalism and the sugar corporations, and so he was bent on enforcing the anti-monopoly federal law limiting corporation landownership to 500 acres. Maldonado, *Luis Muñoz Marín*, 82–84.

16. The Coalición found themselves as the Washington outsiders because their policies were unlike those of the New Dealers. Muñoz Marín had many contacts with the continental press, including Eleanor Roosevelt's biographer, Ruby Black, and Ernest Gruening. The latter was the first director of the Office of Islands and Territories, an office that took over the War Department's Bureau of Insular Affairs's responsibility over Puerto Rico in 1935. See Maldonado, *Luis Muñoz Marín*, 113–15.

17. Maldonado, *Luis Muñoz Marín*, 87.

18. The Nacionalistas had obtained 329 votes in 1928 and were thus required to reinscribe the party. The Republicanos sought to weaken the Liberales by splitting the pro-independence vote between the two. Mathews, *La política puertorriqueña y el Nuevo Trato*, 43.

19. Members of the Nacionalista Party, put off by Albizu Campos's radical extremism, left the party and founded the Partido Independentista on October 21, 1934. On September 23, 1934, the Partido Comunista Puertorriqueño was founded and later joined the International Communists. Bayrón Toro, *Elecciones y partidos políticos de Puerto Rico*, 183.

20. Albizu Campos based his arguments on the provisions of Title VII, article 43 of the Carta Autonómica of 1897, which guaranteed the veto power of the Puerto Rican parliament over decisions reached by the Cortes of the Kingdom where more than a dozen Puerto Rican delegates sat with both voice and vote. Article 2 declared that the "present constitution shall not be amended except by virtue of a special law and upon petition of the insular parliament." Since the military disbanded the insular parliament, and there were no Puerto Rican delegates present to sign the Treaty of Paris of December 10, the passing of sovereignty over Puerto Rico to the United States, the Nacionalistas argued, was a violation of the legal relationship between Spain and Puerto Rico and thus illegal. The discussion on this subject continued well into the 1940s and reached Congress. A Bill to Amend the Organic Act of Puerto Rico, Election of Governor: Hearings on H.R. 3309, UAMC, May 19, 1947, 15–16, 19. (Hereafter, H.R. 3309, UMAMC). To read the document in its entirety, see Fernós López-Cepero, *Documentos Históricos-Constitucionales*, 19–37.

21. Gore had contributed $10,000 to FDR's campaign and placed his three newspapers at FDR's disposal. He did not have any real experience that pre-

pared him to govern the island. He thought of Puerto Rico as Florida's insular junior partner, unaware that their economies were not complementary but in competition with each other. His lack of understanding of Puerto Rico's political arrangement led him to make a series of early mistakes while his disregard for the islanders' idiosyncrasies soon gained him many enemies. See Mathews, *La política puertorriqueña y el Nuevo Trato*, 68–109, and Díaz Soler, *Puerto Rico, sus luchas por alcanzar estabilidad económica*, 210–11.

22. In 1937 Esteban Bird calculated the yearly wages of cane cutters in Puerto Rico and their average family. He concluded that the cane cutter dedicated 94 percent of his income to food. At this rate the daily budget for food per family member was 12 cents. This was only 4 cents more than the daily food expense for feeding a hog in the United States. See Ayala, *American Sugar Kingdom*, 159–61, 164–65, 239, citing Esteban Bird, *The Sugar Industry in Relation to the Social Economic System of Puerto Rico*. In 1930, 400,000 or 25 percent of the population lived on lands dedicated to sugar cane production, which were 13.3 percent of the total land. That translated into sugar cane taking 50 percent of the arable land and 35 percent of the agrarian population. See Mathews, *La política puertorriqueña y el Nuevo Trato*, 150.

23. The Nacionalistas were "neither anticapitalists nor prosocialists." The party made no demands for reorganization of the economic structure beyond the transfer of ownership of the means of productions to Puerto Rican capitalists. See Dietz, *Economic History*, 161–62, and Díaz Soler, *Puerto Rico, sus luchas por alcanzar estabilidad económica*, 214–15.

24. Muñoz Marín had been the most vociferous opponent of Gore, even publishing an article in *La Democracia* entitled "Governor Gore, You Are a Damn Liar" on September 6, 1933. The article was in response to Gore's denial to Roosevelt that he had requested undated letters of resignation from all appointees to important government positions. Gore called the story a "Liberales fairy tale." Gore's removal was attributed to Muñoz Marin's efforts through the local press. In effect, a local journalist wrote: "He has overthrown his first governor!" and more than 50,000 people welcomed him in San Juan when he returned from Washington on January 21, 1934, coinciding with the news of Gore's replacement. Maldonado, *Luis Muñoz Marín*, 107–8, 115, and Mathews, *La política puertorriqueña y el Nuevo Trato*, 111–13.

25. Ferrao, *Pedro Albizu Campos y el nacionalismo*, 150–51.

26. Marín Román, *El caldero quemaó*, 505–6.

27. By 1937 special training for the Insular Police was given by the FBI chief in Puerto Rico, Edgar K. Thompson, and agent Myron E. Gurnes. Machine gun marksmanship, firing with tracer bullets, and firing from a cover position were among the subjects taught at Fort Buchanan by the FBI agents. See Ojeda Reyes, *Vito Marcantonio y Puerto Rico*, 76–78, and Maldonado, *Luis Muñoz Marín*, 120.

28. Marín Román, *El caldero quemaó*, 661–63, 666, and Ferrao, *Pedro Albizu Campos y el nacionalismo*, 152–56.

29. This is highly informative, and I will be the first one to put it in print. See http://www.archives.gov/research/guide-fed-records/groups/350.html, and Estades Font, *La presencia militar de Estados Unidos en Puerto Rico*, 120–23.

30. In the mid-1920s Gruening had published a series of articles penned by Muñoz Marín in the *Nation*. Muñoz Marín drove Gruening to Washington for his confirmation. See Maldonado, *Luis Muñoz Marín*, 131.

31. "This transfer has long been agitated by special interests bent upon commercial and political exploitation of Porto Rico. The sinister machine of the sugar lobby against Porto Rico has long been strongly resisted by the Secretary of War and the BIA. The great demons of the politicians for Porto Rican patronage have also been resisted. It was over their protests [the administrators of the BIA] that the Harding administration paid a political debt by appointing a Missouri politician [E. Montgomery Reily, who was actually from Texas] as governor of Porto Rico. It was over their protest that the present administration paid a political debt by appointing a Floridian [Robert H. Gore]." Clip from the *Washington Herald*, June 7, 1934, CIHPC, Caja 30. Senator Millard Tydings was behind the creation of a single bureau for all insular affairs within the Department of the Interior. Harold Ickes and Santiago Iglesias Pantín, the Puerto Rican representative in Congress, had recommended the change for years.

32. The Puerto Rico Emergency Relief Administration (PRERA) began its work on the island in 1933 with the main objective of reducing unemployment. Harry Hopkins named James R. Bourne as the agency's director. Although Bourne and his wife quickly set to work distributing aid, their projects were not on a big scale. Furthermore, since they hired many people associated with the Liberales, Coalition leaders accused them of using federal funding to strengthen the Liberales. See Mathews, *La política puertorriqueña y el Nuevo Trato*, 130–33, 150.

33. "It was to meet these conditions—to relieve unemployment—to remove as far as possible the causes of agricultural depression—to create new sources of wealth and income—to establish new standards of living—that there was created by Executive Order on May 28, 1935, the Puerto Rico Reconstruction Administration (PRRA) as the agency through which might be expended such Federal work relief and emergency funds as were available for Puerto Rico, towards the attainment of the above objectives." The objectives of the program were defined by the president in a letter dated August 1, 1935: "The Administration's program intends not merely immediate relief but permanent reconstruction for the island. To this end the projects in contemplation will see to insure every person on the island a position of reasonable independence and security. The economy of the island is, of course, agricultural and the solution of its problems must be in terms of agricultural rehabilitation. It will therefore be sought to secure for each citizen a place on the land which will give him a fair share in the fruits of his own labor and a position of independence and security. This will require the establishment of many persons on small farming units. It will also require that these small farmers be insured adequate processing and distributing facilities at reasonable cost. Diversifi-

cation of agricultural production will be sought by the program in order that the island may approach a self-sustaining status. Cheap and available electric power, good roads, reforestation, and adequate housing are also essential to the Administration's program. . . . I am anxious that the Government of the United States shall discharge fully its responsibilities to the Puerto Rican people." Immediately after the Executive Order was signed, by virtue of which the PRRA was created, the offices of the agency were established and in December 1935 the whole reconstruction administration program was already functioning. See Information Research Section, PRRA, "Facts about the Puerto Rico Reconstruction Administration," December 1938, http://newdeal.feri.org/texts/578.htm.

34. See Mathews, *La política puertorriqueña y el Nuevo Trato*, 167–96, and Maldonado, *Luis Muñoz Marín*, 131–36.

35. Maldonado, *Luis Muñoz Marín*, 137, and Ferrao, *Pedro Albizu Campos y el nacionalismo*, 157.

36. Mathews, *La política puertorriqueña y el Nuevo Trato*, 248–49.

37. On April 12, 1932, Albizu Campos and some eight hundred followers stormed the Puerto Rican legislature after being informed that the single star with five stripes flag designed by Puerto Rican exiles in New York in 1895 had been made the official flag of the island. In the scuffle trying to reach the legislative chambers, the rail of the stairs collapsed and a Nacionalista died. Santiago Iglesias blamed the police for being too lenient and attributed their leniency to the fact that the Nacionalistas were from the middle and upper classes. Had they been from the working class, Santiago Iglesias commented, "all their heads would have been cracked." Albizu Campos threatened the chief of Insular Police with death if a single Nacionalista died during the 1932 elections. See Negroni, *Historia militar de Puerto Rico*, 450–54; Mathews, *La política puertorriqueña y el Nuevo Trato*, 248–49; Bayrón Toro, *Elecciones y partidos políticos de Puerto Rico*, 182; and Maldonado, *Luis Muñoz Marín*, 89–90.

38. Riggs, *La Democracia*, October 26, 1935, 8.

39. Pedro Albizu Campos, radio speech, *La Palabra*, November 2, 1935.

40. *Report on Monthly Summary of Subversive Activities, December 1935–March 1936*, CIHPC, Caja 18.

41. Albizu demanded that party members took an "oath of honor" in which they swore to defend the Nacionalistas' ideals with their lives and belongings if necessary and to give unquestioning loyalty to "the leader." See Maldonado, *Luis Muñoz Marín*, 87, citing Ferrao, *Pedro Albizu Campos y el nacionalismo puertorriqueño*, 395.

42. *Report on Monthly Summary of Subversive Activities*, CIHPC, C. 18. Enamorado Cuesta was the general military instructor in the Nacionalista Party. He was a World War I veteran and served in the reserve with the rank of captain until 1929. He briefly served in the Republican Army in 1936 during the Spanish Civil War. See "Nationalist Party of Puerto Rico," FBI files, 50.

43. Ferrao, *Pedro Albizu Campos y el nacionalismo*, 160–61.

44. Luis A. Ferrao argues that the mobilization may have had a symbolic character designed to pressure the colonial government. Ferrao, *Pedro Albizu Campos y el nacionalismo*, 161.

45. In 1917 Albizu Campos interrupted his studies at Harvard to volunteer for service during the First World War. Ernest Gruening wrote that he was assigned to a black regiment that trained in the southern United States, which taught Albizu Campos "what it was to be a Negro, not only in the army, but in America. All his love for America turned to hate." Maldonado, *Luis Muñoz Marín*, 139, citing Gruening, *Many Battles: The Autobiography of Ernest Gruening*, 196–97. However, it seems that Albizu Campos never trained with African American units. Albizu Campos joined the Harvard Cadets Corps in 1916 (a precursor to the ROTC). After finishing the course he was recommended to receive a commission as first lieutenant. On May 15, 1917, he left Harvard to join the armed forces. It seems that from May to September he completed a military course offered by the French Military Mission in the United States. Late in September 1917, he offered his services to Frank McIntyre, chief of the Bureau of Insular Affairs during World War I, with the condition that he would serve with Puerto Rican troops. McIntyre recommended that he stay at Harvard. Albizu Campos entered federal active military service on July 10, 1918, as a private and was sent to officers training at Camp Las Casas in August. On November 5 he was commissioned as a first lieutenant of infantry and assigned to the Black–Puerto Rican 375th Regiment. In March 1919 he was discharged from the Army, and on April 2 he was commissioned as a first lieutenant in the Officers' Reserve Corps. Soon thereafter he resigned his commission and returned to Harvard. Marín Román, *El caldero quemaó*, 514–20.

46. Marín Román, *El caldero quemaó*, 519–20.

47. Marín Román, *El caldero quemaó*, 579–83, 727, and Ferrao, *Pedro Albizu Campos y el nacionalismo*, 161.

48. Albizu Campos emulated many of the policies and tactics of the Irish Sinn Fein, such as the oath to sacrifice life and property in order to achieve independence. He also copied from the Fascist and Nazi movements in Italy and Germany. The party's organ "published Benito Mussolini's 'Ten Commandments of Fascist Youths,' which included 'God and Fatherland' above all else; total surrender of the 'body and soul' to the Leader." The use of black shirts by the Cadetes and a black flag with a white cross were symbols of the conservative and right-wing nature of Albizu Campo's ideology. However, whether Albizu Campos or his followers were Fascists is debatable, especially because in the early and mid-1930s fascism was still taking form. See Maldonado, *Luis Muñoz Marín*, 118–19, and Ferrao, *Pedro Albizu Campos y el nacionalismo*, 165, 303–27.

49. Marín Román, *El caldero quemaó*, 666–67, 677–79.

50. https://www.fbi.gov/sanjuan/about-us/history-1.

51. Marín Román, *¡Llegó la gringada!* 498–99.

52. Marín Román, *El caldero quemaó*, 38–39, 505–6, 508–10, 661–63, 666; Marín Román, *¡Llegó la gringada!* 498–99, 505–6. From New York the reports

made their way with comments to the War Department's division of military intelligence in Washington. The reports written by the chief of the s-2 were sent to the G-2 section of the Second Corps Area (the 65th's parental unit) at Fort Jay, Governor's Island, New York.

53. Marín Román, *El caldero quemaó*, 510–12.

54. *Report on Monthly Summary of Subversive Activities*, CIHPC C.18.

55. "National Guard Major Samuel F. Howard reports that there are 2 Nationalist companies, one armed with machetes and another with no visible weapons, holding drills in front of armories disturbing the National Guard exercises." *Report on Monthly Summary of Subversive Activities*, CIHPC C.18.

56. *Report on Monthly Summary of Subversive Activities*, CIHPC C.18.

57. Santiago Iglesias accused the police of being lenient with the Nacionalistas and attributed their leniency to the Nationalists belonging to the middle and upper classes. After a nationalist riot in the insular legislature building, he stated that if they had been from the working class, "all their heads would have been cracked." See Maldonado, *Luis Muñoz Marín*, 89–80.

58. *Report on Monthly Summary of Subversive Activities*, CIHPC C.18. The 10,000 figure was taken from Albizu Campos's speeches. The FBI estimated that at the time the Nationalist strength was close to 2,000 members. See Nationalist Party of Puerto Rico, FBI files, 49.

59. In January a Nationalist wounded the chief police and another policeman in the mountain town of Utuado. On February 23, 1936, the same day the chief of the Insular Police, Riggs, was assassinated, the chief of police in Utuado was once again wounded by Nationalists. See Negroni, *Historia militar de Puerto Rico*, 450–54, and Mathews, *La política puertorriqueña y el Nuevo Trato*, 248–49.

60. Marín Román, *El caldero quemaó*, 604.

61. *Report on Monthly Summary of Subversive Activities*, CIHPC C.18.

62. *Report on Monthly Summary of Subversive Activities*, CIHPC C.18.

63. *Report on Monthly Summary of Subversive Activities*, CIHPC C.18.

64. A group of Nationalists wounded Iglesias Pantín during a public rally in Mayagüez on October 25, 1936. The next week a Nationalist mob attacked a political meeting held by the Liberales apparently because the latter were using the Puerto Rican flag. Domingo Saltari was eventually arrested for the Mayagüez incident and sentenced to ten years in prison. See Negroni, *Historia militar de Puerto Rico*, 450–54, and Mathews, *La política puertorriqueña y el Nuevo Trato*, 248–49.

65. As Marín Román argues, the U.S. military feared the "independentistas muñocistas more than it feared the nacionalistas albizuistas." They believed Muñoz Marín would be able to unify all the pro-independence forces in a single front. In the late 1930s and early 1940s, the Marine Corps conducted an exercise called "Small War Operations: The Puerto Rican Problem." As part of the exercise, the United States had granted independence to Puerto Rico. Conservatives had won the first elections and installed a pro-U.S. government. A young charismatic leader resembling Luis Muñoz Marín had gal-

vanized the Communists, Nationalists, and all the former liberal and radical Independentistas and with the support of the former 65th Infantry and one-third of the National Guard had declared a republic based in the southwest. The United States feared that the rebels would overthrow the pro-U.S. government and ally themselves with European Fascists. By the time the Puerto Rican president had requested military aid from the United States, it was too late and the rebels had taken San Juan. Marines would land in Aguadilla and Ponce to set up fields, dissolve the government troops still loyal (reform them as a constabulary), and get the president of Puerto Rico to put the island under the control of the U.S. military. From that point forward the officers in the exercise had to devise strategies to finish the campaign. Marín Román, *El caldero quemaó*, 654–58.

66. *Report on Monthly Summary of Subversive Activities*, CIHPC C.18, Ct. 4, Doc. 2 A. Colonel Riggs may have paid for the stubbornness of Winship. Riggs had tried to befriend Puerto Rican leaders including Albizu Campos. He was Catholic, spoke Spanish fluently, and was described by Gruening as being "sincerely interested in Puerto Rico's needs and aspirations." Muñoz Marín described him as a "humanitarian and liberal person." See Maldonado, *Luis Muñoz Marín*, 139, citing Gruening, *Many Battles*, 197, and Luis Muñoz Marín, *Memorias: Autobiografía Pública* 147.

67. *Report on Monthly Summary of Subversive Activities*, CIHPC C.18.

68. Mathews, *La política puertorriqueña y el Nuevo Trato*, 249–50.

69. The other defendants were Juan A. Corretjer, secretary of the Partido Nacionalista, Luis F. Velázquez, Clemente Soto Vélez, Erasmo Velázquez, Julio H. Velázquez, Rafael Ortiz Pacheco (who would later escape to the Dominican Republic), Juan Gallardo Santiago, and Pablo Rosado Ortiz. See Maldonado, *Luis Muñoz Marín*, 147–48.

70. On June 6, 1937, Albizu Campos was moved from Puerto Rico to Atlanta, and the following day Nacionalistas tried to assassinate federal judge Robert A. Cooper, who sentenced Albizu and the party's leadership to prison. See "Nationalist Party of Puerto Rico," FBI files, 42, and Maldonado, *Luis Muñoz Marín*, 148.

71. Marín Román, *El caldero quemaó*, 648–50.

72. The jury was selected to ensure a conviction. The statement of a member of that second jury, Elmer Ellsworth, an American residing on the island who would join the Populares and be elected as senator in 1940, denounced the unfairness of the trial. He stated: "I cannot refrain from saying that my associates on the jury seemed to be motivated by strong, if not violent, prejudice against the Nationalists and were prepared to convict them, regardless of the evidence. Ten of the jurors were American residents in Puerto Rico, and the two Puerto Ricans were closely associated with American business interests. It was evident from the composition of the jury that the Nationalists did not and could not get a fair trial." Ellsworth to Roosevelt, October 17, 1936, ACLU, vol. 2, 653.

73. Ayala and Bernabe, *Puerto Rico in the American Century*, 111.

74. Rosario Natal, *Luis Muñoz Marín y la independencia*, 80.

75. See Rosario Natal, *Luis Muñoz Marín y la independencia*, 78–79, quoting the *New York Times*, March 10, 1936, and *The Secret Diary of Harold Ickes*, 547–48.

76. Maldonado, *Luis Muñoz Marín*, 140–46.

77. Working for the PRRA Planning Division, Hanson and a team of planners prepared a report of the Tydings bill's effect on the island, which they described as "periods of chaos and dictatorship" after a U.S. withdrawal. Gruening ordered him to collect and burn all copies. Carlos Chardon and Rafael Fernández García resigned from the PRRA, and Rafael Menéndez Ramos left government altogether. José Padín, the education commissioner, who brought his first political defeat to Governor Gore (who had wanted him sacked for not being sufficiently pro-American and who as interim governor had calmed the students' protests against the Tydings bill) also resigned. Maldonado, *Luis Muñoz Marín*, 140–47, 150, citing Parker Hanson, *Transformation: The Story of Modern Puerto Rico*, 162, 168.

78. The Liberals were not the only political faction affected by the Tydings bill. The Republican leader Martínez Nadal was so offended by the terms of the bill that, if passed, he vowed to campaign for independence while the Socialists demanded that the statehood option ought to be included. The Republicanos finally agreed on demanding statehood but moving to independence if their demands were ignored by Congress. See Bayrón Toro, *Elecciones y partidos políticos de Puerto Rico*, 183–85; Pagán, *Historia de los Partidos Políticos Puertorriqueños*, 78, 82; and Maldonado, *Luis Muñoz Marín*, 144–45.

79. Rosario Natal, *Luis Muñoz Marín y la independencia*, 88–91.

80. See Pagán, *Historia de los Partidos Políticos Puertorriqueños*, 83–87; Mathews, *La política puertorriqueña y el Nuevo Trato*, 306–8; and Maldonado, *Luis Muñoz Marín*, 152–53.

81. Under the initiative of Socialist senator Bolívar Pagán, Puerto Rico ran its first elections with universal suffrage. The only requirements to cast a vote during this election were to be at least twenty-one years of age and legally registered. Voting was moved to closed colleges to guarantee secret ballots. Of 764,602 voters, 559,500 cast their votes. The Liberales obtained 252,467 votes, electing five senators, twelve representatives, and nineteen municipalities and controlling a single senatorial district. La Coalición obtained 296,988 votes: 152,739 and 144,249 votes were cast for Unión Republicana and the Socialistas, respectively. The Coalición was able to control six senatorial districts and elect fourteen senators, twenty-seven representatives, and fifty-eight municipalities. Bayrón Toro, *Elecciones y partidos políticos de Puerto Rico*, 185–86.

82. In 1934 the Junta Nacionalista de Mayagüez had argued for the dissolution of the Cadetes and in favor of a less bellicose approach. Ferrao, *Pedro Albizu Campos y el nacionalismo*, 190–94.

83. Moraza Ortiz, *La masacre de Ponce*, 81–83, and Negroni, *Historia militar de Puerto Rico*, 450–54.

84. Ojeda Reyes, *Vito Marcantonio y Puerto Rico*, 73.

85. Arthur Garfield Hays conducted the investigation that reached this conclusion. The ACLU believed that the police had panicked, resulting in a "police riot" and the subsequent massacre. The Insular Police insisted that the first shot had been fired from the Nacionalista Party's headquarters and later stated that a Nacionalista who was not part of the parade fired the first shot, killing a policeman. Ojeda Reyes, *Vito Marcantonio y Puerto Rico*, 74.

86. *El Imparcial*, April 1, 1937, in *Report to Chief National Guard Bureau*, April 27, 1937, CIHPC, Caja 19.

87. In 1936 Lt. Col. Miguel A. Muñoz was serving as executive officer of the 295th Regiment (PRNG). He served as a captain in Camp Las Casas during World War I, as commander of the Porto Rico American Legion, and as vice commander of the National American Legion. He graduated from Cornell's law school in 1913 and became the personal secretary of Governor Yager in 1914. During his legal career, he was assistant attorney general, judge of the district court of San Juan, acting prosecuting attorney of the supreme court of Puerto Rico, and president of the public service commission. "He was also a militant politician member of the Liberal Party and was removed from his last post by the Coalitionists in the senate." *El Imparcial*, April 1, 1937, in *Report to Chief National Guard Bureau*, April 27, 1937, CIHPC, Caja 19.

88. On January 10, 1938, Julio Pinto Gandía and other seven Nacionalista leaders were sentenced to five years in prison.

89. Ojeda Reyes, *Vito Marcantonio y Puerto Rico*, 74.

90. *Alma Latina*, July 1964, 15–20, in Norat Martínez, *Historia del Regimiento 65 de Infantería*, 20.

91. The following Nacionalistas were convicted: Tomás López de Victoria, Casimiro Berenguer, Elifaz Escobar, Santiago González, Vicente Morciglio, Leocadio López, Juan Pietri, Guillermo Larrogaiti, and Prudencio Segarra.

92. FDR wrote to Ickes: "I am definitely convinced that the maintenance of Federal authority is the first consideration and that nothing be done until the island thoroughly understands that Federal authority will be unhesitantgly [sic] maintained." See Maldonado, *Luis Muñoz Marín*, 153, citing Watkins, *Righteous Pilgrim: The Life and Times of Harold Ickes*, 526.

93. *Alma Latina*, July 1964, 15–20, in Norat Martínez, *Historia del Regimiento 65 de Infantería*, 20.

94. "The 296th Infantry of the Puerto Rico National Guard is recruiting 34 enlisted men for a service company. 75 applicants were checked up last week of which 9 were found to be members of the Nationalist Party. These will not be accepted as members of the guard." See *Report to Chief National Guard Bureau*, April 27, 1937, CIHPC, Caja 19.

95. In 1936 the National Guard was authorized to expand by assigning the 3rd Battalion from the 295th Infantry Regiment to the reactivated 296th. The War Department authorized the recruitment of enlisted men and officers for a second battalion to complete the 296th. Both regiments would have two active battalions and a third inactive battalion, bringing the National Guard forces

to 99 officers, a warrant officer, and 1,459 enlisted men. The 296th received twice as many applicants as it needed, including several Nationalists. *Report to Chief National Guard Bureau*, April 27, 1937, CIHPC, Caja 19; Marín Román, *El caldero quemaó*, 616–19.

96. See Maldonado, *Luis Muñoz Marín*, 152–57, and Mathews, *La política puertorriqueña y el Nuevo Trato*, 304–9.

97. Marín Román, *El caldero quemaó*, 643, and Ayala and Bernabe, *Puerto Rico in the American Century*, 136–38, 148–50.

98. *Alma Latina*, July 1964, 15–20, in Norat Martínez, *Historia del Regimiento 65 de Infantería*, 20.

99. Ayala and Bernabe, *Puerto Rico in the American Century*, 138–42.

5. Education, Industrialization, and Decolonization

1. The editorial was written in response to an announcement by the War Department that it would drop higher educational qualifications for Puerto Ricans for admittance into the U.S. Army. *Puerto Rico World Journal*, March 29, 1944, filed in 65th U.S. Infantry, Headquarters 2nd Corps, *Report on Monthly Summary of Subversive Activities*, CIHPC, Caja 21. (Hereafter 65th U.S. Infantry Intelligence Report, April 3, 1944, C. 21.) The local selective service units on the island were instructed to require a fourth-grade education for acceptance into the army, which was the standard for continental Americans. In the previous years, natives of the island had been required to have at least an eighth-grade education to be considered for service. In October 1943, the Mayagüez Lions Club initiated the complaint that culminated with the War Department reestablishing the same parameters for Puerto Rican and U.S. recruits. See *El Mundo*, January 13, 1944; filed in 65th U.S. Infantry Intelligence Report, March 1944, CIHPC, C. 21.

2. See House Committees on Insular Affairs, *Providing for the Term of Office of the Governor of Puerto Rico, Election of Governor: Hearings on H. 1032–4*, UMAMC, August 26, 1944, 24–25. (Hereafter H. 1032–4.)

3. Ellsworth was answering questions from Ohio senator Robert A. Taft, a member of the Committee on Insular Affairs and a Republican Party leader between 1938 and 1953. Taft was influential in issues regarding the economy, labor, defense, foreign policy, taxation, and veterans affairs. See *Hearings on S. 725–1*, UMAMC, November–December 1943, 182.

4. H. 1032–4, 30–32.

5. Jesús T. Piñero Jiménez (April 6, 1897–November 16, 1952) distinguished himself first as a Republicano leader and later as a founding member of the Popular Democratic Party. He served as resident commissioner of Puerto Rico in Congress in 1945–46, then he was named governor of the island by President Truman. He served until 1949, when he was replaced by Puerto Rico's first elected governor, Luis Muñoz Marín. See H. 1032–4, 30–32, 35–38.

6. Executive Order 6.726 transferred supervision of Puerto Rican affairs to the Interior Department led by Harold Ickes. The Bureau of Insular Affairs

was abolished by the Reorganization Plan No. II on July 1, 1939, and replaced by the Division of Territories and Island Possessions of the Interior Department, which operated between 1939 and 1950. It was later known as the Office of Territories and still later as the Office of Territorial Affairs. See "Records of the Office of the Secretary of the Interior" NARA, http://www.archives.gov/research/guide-fed-records/groups/350.html; Estades Font, *La presencia militar de Estados Unidos en Puerto Rico*, 120–23.

7. During the war, Albizu Campos's Nacionalistas became a secondary concern for the FBI. The Spanish community, some 5,300 people, especially those who identified with Franco and Spain's Nationalists, became the primary focus of surveillance. The FBI, the Military Intelligence Division, the Office of Naval Intelligence, and the Office of Strategic Services, aided by the Puerto Rican Insular Police, investigated possible Falangista activities and maintained extensive files on the Falange and its sympathizers in Puerto Rico. Founded in October 1933 as an umbrella for traditional and ultraconservative groups in Spain, the Falange Española Tradicionalista y de las Juntas de Ofensiva Nacional Sindicalista promoted Spanish fascism. The Catholic Church was also under surveillance, since the Spanish Church and Rome authorized all appointments to the island. Through social clubs, particularly the Casa España and the Casino Español, and in concert with the Catholic Church and Falangistas in Puerto Rico, the Spanish elite spread fascist propaganda and sent money (with the help of the Catholic Church) to Franco's Nationalists during the Spanish Civil War. The FBI and the War and State Departments feared that the local group of the Falange Exterior would try to aid the Nazis during the war. The Spanish consul in San Juan, the Falangista Mariano de Amuedo, found it proper to declare that after the war, Puerto Rico would "become a dominion of Spain such as Canada was to the United Kingdom," and this did little to ease the fears of federal authorities. See Lefebvre, "Puerto Rico: Quiet Participant," 96–101, 103.

8. Jorge Rodríguez Beruff argues that Muñoz Marín's reconciliation with Washington occurred because of his expressions of support for FDR's domestic and foreign policies, his adherence to social peace and stability in Puerto Rico, his avoidance of the status issue during the war, and his support for military preparedness. The war made sociopolitical change in Puerto Rico essential because of its strategic value. That is the reason that Adm. William D. Leahy was sent to the island to replace the hated Blanton Winship. Leahy's tenure (September 1939 to November 1940) created political changes, which in turn allowed for the creation of conditions that would provide for social and cultural transformations. See Rodríguez Beruff, "La pugna entre dos grandes sistemas," 49, 50; Rodríguez Beruff, *Strategy as Politics*, x–xi, 135–41; and Franqui-Rivera, "Fighting for the Nation," 213–25.

9. State-owned factories (five in total) were not a crucial but an auxiliary component of the economy. Throughout this period the investment in these factories was but $10.7 million, which resulted in the creation of just 992 jobs. During the war, Puerto Rican rum came to dominate the U.S. markets, and

that allowed for a dramatic increase in government revenues. Military expenses and revenue from repatriated rum excise taxes were more than $1 billion. Rum reimbursements and military expenses dominated the period. The Jones Act of 1917 had established that excise taxes paid by exports to the United States were to be returned to the insular government. Bolívar Fresneda, "La economía de Puerto Rico durante la Segunda Guerra Mundial," 208, 211, 219, 229–30, 243–48; Bolívar Fresneda, "Las inversiones y los programas militares," 163–64; and Ayala and Bernabe, *Puerto Rico in the American Century*, 143–44.

10. Rodríguez Beruff, "La pugna entre dos grandes sistemas," 67–68; Ayala and Bernabe, *Puerto Rico in the American Century*, 143–44; Bolivar Fresneda, "Las inversiones y los programas militares," 163–64; and Bolivar Fresneda, "La economía de Puerto Rico," 210.

11. See discussion in chapter 3.

12. Rodríguez Beruff, "La pugna entre dos grandes sistemas," 68.

13. In part due to the Great Depression, which made it difficult to explain military spending in Central and South America to the American public, FDR's administration started a retrenchment from the area while seeking to improve relations with these nations. His administration emphasized cooperation and trade rather than military force to maintain stability in the hemisphere. In his inaugural address on March 4, 1933, Roosevelt stated that "in the field of world policy I would dedicate this nation to the policy of the good neighbor—the neighbor who resolutely respects himself and because he does so, respects the rights of others." In December 1933, Secretary of State Cordell Hull participated in the Montevideo Conference (also known as Pan American or 7th International Conference of American States) and signed the Montevideo Convention on the Rights and Duties of States. Hull declared American opposition to armed intervention in inter-American affairs and backed the main issue of the convention, stating: "No state has the right to intervene in the internal or external affairs of another." Seeking to prove his repudiation of the interventionist policies of past administrations, in 1934 FDR secured the abrogation of the 1903 treaty with Cuba, based on the Platt amendment, which gave the United States the right to intervene to preserve internal stability or independence. See Dallek, *Franklin D. Roosevelt and American Foreign Policy*, 38–39, 62–63, 65, 122–23.

14. See Rosario Natal, *Luis Muñoz Marín y la independencia*, 136. FDR declared in November 1938 that "the United States ought to be prepared to resist any attack on the Western Hemisphere from the North Pole to the South Pole." See García Muñiz, "El Caribe durante la Segunda Guerra Mundial," quoting Conn and Fairchild, *The Framework of Hemispheric Defense*, 3, 7–10, and Conn, Engelman, and Fairchild, *Guarding the United States and Its Outposts*, 10–11, 328, 414. A conference to discuss contingency plans in a possible war against Japan and Germany took place in 1938. Based on the intentions and capabilities of the Axis powers, six possible scenarios were developed. One envisioned a combined Japanese, German, and Italian fleet (supported by a previously defeated

French navy) taking over the Caribbean, from which they would proceed to invade the United States through the Mississippi valley. This was seen as the most viable plan of attack against the Western Hemisphere.

15. Marín Román, *¡A la vuelta de la esquina! El Caribe camino a la Segunda Guerra Mundial*, 37–41.

16. Senate Subcommittee of the Committee on Territories and Insular Affairs, *A Bill to Amend the Organic Act of Puerto Rico Election of Governor: Hearings on S. 1407*, UMAMC, November 16– December 25, 1943, 7–8. (Hereafter S. 1407.) In a "Message from the President of the United States on Progress on Puerto Rico" and included as part of the hearings.

17. The War Department built multiple camps and forts and opened medium and small naval and air facilities throughout the island. Established in 1925 under the name of Fort Miles, this installation became a permanent fixture of the U.S. Army on the island under the name of Fort Buchanan (first commander of the Puerto Rican Regiment of Volunteers). During World War II it served as headquarters of the Department of Puerto Rico and as an induction center. Fort Bundy was built in 1940 to serve as general headquarters for coastal artillery units in eastern Puerto Rico. Camp O'Reilly, in honor of Field Marshall Alejandro O'Reilly, "padre de las milicias Puertorriqueñas," was finished in 1942. Camp Salinas (later renamed Santiago) and Camp Tortuguero opened in 1940 to serve as training centers for the National Guard and Army units on the island. Between 1941 and 1943, at a cost of over $10 million, the War Department built Roosevelt Roads Naval Station, comprising installations in Culebra and Vieques islands and the town of Ceiba on the east coast. This base was intended to provide maritime control over the whole circum-Caribbean area and to host the British government and military in case Great Britain fell to the Germans. Between 1939 and 1943, at a cost of more than $50 million, the War Department built Isla Grande Naval Station (originally intended for naval aviation) near San Juan Bay. This facility housed the 10th Naval District and the Caribbean Sea Frontier headquarters. Protecting the Panama Canal, the Venezuelan oil fields, and trade in the area were the main responsibilities of this naval command. On September 6, 1939, a major air base known as Borinquen Field or Puerto Rico Air Base No. 1 and capable of handling all types of military planes became operational at Punta Borinquen in the northwest city of Aguadilla. This installation provided the United States with a southern air route to Africa and Europe via Brazil. Loosey Field was established on January 1, 1941, east of Ponce in the southern coast. In 1940 and 1941 airports were built in Arecibo and Vega Baja to support Camp Tortuguero and to provide an airbase for antisubmarine warfare. See Negroni, *Historia militar de Puerto Rico*, 415–33; Lefebvre, "Puerto Rico: Quiet Participant," 102; and Marín Román, *¡A la vuelta de la esquina!* 327–28.

18. See Moraza Ortiz, *La masacre de Ponce*, 81–83, and Negroni, *Historia militar de Puerto Rico*, 450–54.

19. Rosario Natal, *Luis Muñoz Marín y la independencia*, 139–40. Leahy later became the White House chief of staff, a fact that illustrates how important Puerto Rico was for FDR's plans.

20. Some of the fraudulent activity included the buying of votes and the "corralling" of rural voters. The latter refers to the practice of luring jíbaros known to sympathize with the opposition into corral-like buildings with the promise of free rum, which then stayed closed until the election was over, precluding them from voting. Leahy was appalled by such practice and ordered the police to set direct lines between the police headquarters and political parties' headquarters with orders to act immediately on any reported cases. Maldonado, *Luis Muñoz Marín*, 176–77. Also see Rodríguez Beruff, *Strategy as Politics*, x, 135–41. FDR asked Leahy to accept the governorship during naval exercises in Puerto Rican waters.

21. The Nationalist Party continued its activities throughout the war period, but they did not attract the numbers they once had, and they limited themselves mostly to rallies and fund-raising. In 1943 they were more concerned with securing the cancellation of Albizu Campos's four-year probation period. To that effect on June 6, 1943, Juan Antonio Corretjer, acting as the party's secretary, ordered political activity to be kept at a minimum in Puerto Rico so as not to jeopardize their leader's pardon. The biggest nationalist rally occurred on August 15, 1943, when some 10,000 people, including more than 1,800 delegates from the island's seventy-seven municipalities and their families, attended a pro-independence congress. However, a "Great Nationalist Meeting" held on June 13, 1943, in Barrio Obrero, Santurce, was attended by only 100 people, and even fewer attended a meeting in Caguas on July 25. Based on the number of people still paying the party's membership dues, the FBI estimated that no more than 500 remained as members of the Nationalist Party in 1943, of which only 150 were known to the public. "Nationalist Party of Puerto Rico," FBI files, 1–13. http://www.pr-secretfiles.net.

22. Bayrón Toro, *Elecciones y partidos políticos de Puerto Rico*, 191–92, and Díaz Soler, *Puerto Rico, sus luchas por alcanzar estabilidad económica, definición política y afirmación cultural*, 258–60.

23. Bayrón Toro, *Elecciones y partidos políticos de Puerto Rico*, 192–93.

24. See Maldonado, *Luis Muñoz Marín*, 182–83, and Rosario Natal, *Luis Muñoz Marín y la independencia*, 125–31.

25. Rodríguez Beruff, "La pugna entre dos grandes sistemas," 50, 56.

26. Rosario Natal, *Luis Muñoz Marín y la independencia*, 128–29, 133–36, 157–59.

27. According to Maldonado, the touring of the country and the endless meetings with jíbaros, workers, and peasants started to convince Muñoz Marín that the Jíbaros' rejection of independence was not "an irrational, mindless, fear of independence . . . nor was it the product of a demeaning cultural defect of Puerto Ricans ashamed of their nationality." Maldonado, *Luis Muñoz Marín*, 180–85, citing Muñoz Marín, *Memorias*, 1:180–86.

28. Though the PPD obtained fewer votes than the Coalición, it secured a majority in the senate (10–9) and a tie in the house of representatives (18–18). In the general elections of November 5, 1940, the Coalición obtained 222,423 votes (134,582 Unión Republicana and 87,841 Socialistas) good for nine senators, eighteen representatives, and thirty-seven municipalities and the office of the resident commissioner in Washington, which went to Bolívar Pagán, new president of the Socialist Party. Unificación Tripartita secured 130,299 votes, three representatives, and eleven municipalities. The Populares amassed 214,857 votes, ten senators, eighteen representatives, and twenty-nine municipalities. Bayrón Toro, *Elecciones y partidos políticos de Puerto Rico*, 194, and Rosario Natal, *Luis Muñoz Marín y la independencia*, 155.

29. Díaz Soler, *Puerto Rico, sus luchas por alcanzar estabilidad económica, definición política y afirmación cultural*, 260–62.

30. As a matter of fact, in 1934 Tugwell had to join Ickes in persuading Roosevelt not to return the Virgin Islands, then under control of the Interior Department, to the Navy Department. Roosevelt's attitude toward ultramarine possessions led Tugwell to believe that "there was an admiral concealed somewhere in Roosevelt." See Tugwell, *The Art of Politics*, 146–51.

31. Rodríguez Beruff, "La pugna entre dos grandes sistemas," 50.

32. José Miguel Gallardo acted as interim governor after Leahy's departure in November 1940 and the brief tenure of Guy J. Swope in 1941. He served again in that fashion before Tugwell replaced Swope.

33. Rexford G. Tugwell, *The Stricken Island*, 148.

34. Rexford G. Tugwell, *The Stricken Island*, 268–69.

35. Rexford G. Tugwell, *The Stricken Island*, 328, 268.

36. Rosario Natal, *Luis Muñoz Marín y la independencia*, 174–75.

37. S.1407, 309–10. The statements were made in a letter dated March 8, 1943, from the president to Secretary of the Interior Harold L. Ickes and included as part of the hearings.

38. The statement was made on September 28, 1943, in a "Message from the President of the United States Transmitting Report on Progress on Puerto Rico" and included as part of the hearings.

39. S.1407, 310. The statement was made in a letter dated March 8, 1943, from Roosevelt to Ickes and included as part of the hearings.

40. S.1407, 218. The statements were made in a letter dated November 20, 1943, from Muñoz Marín to Senator Dennis Chavez and included as part of the hearings.

41. According to the Atlantic Charter of August 14, 1941, the Consent of the Governed Principle established that the signatories believed in "the rights of all people to choose the form of government under which they will live; and they wish to see sovereign rights of self-government restored to those who have been forcibly deprived of them." See Senate Committee on Territorial and Insular Affairs, *A Bill to Provide for the Withdrawal of the Sovereignty of the United States over the Island of Puerto Rico and for the Recognition of*

Its Independence: Hearings on S.952, UMAMC, May, 3, 6, 10, and 11, 1943, 31. (Hereafter S. 952.)

42. H. 1032-4, 30-32.
43. H. 1032-4, 27-29, and S. 1407, 24-25.
44. H. 1032-4, 27-29.
45. Trías Monge, *The Trials of the Oldest Colony*, 103-5.
46. See Tugwell, *The Art of Politics*, 146-51.
47. S. 952, 24-25. See also Trías Monge, *Trials of the Oldest Colony*, 108-9.
48. S. 952, 15-18.
49. S. 952, 10, 15, 17-18.
50. S. 952. The statements were made in a letter dated April 29, 1943, from Muñoz Marín to Senator Millard E. Tydings and included as part of the hearings.
51. Ruby Black sent a letter to Muñoz Marin's wife, Muna Lee, on November 16, 1938. Rodríguez Beruff, "La pugna entre dos grandes sistemas," 50, 56.
52. The Nationalist local leadership had declared on December 14, 1941, that although it recognized that "a state of war existed between totalitarian and democratic powers," the "feasibility of the realization of the ideal of independence of Puerto Rico depends on the survival in the world of the ideals and systems of democratic governments. While these are the only ones that guarantee the right of people to govern themselves according to the principles of free determination," it had still "pending with the United States of North America a solution of the fundamental problem of our political sovereignty, but it holds that the union of its forces with those of said nation in the struggle against the common enemy of the democratic cause, in no way means or implies the renunciation of the ideal of independence for our country." "Nationalist Party of Puerto Rico," FBI files, 1-13, 52.
53. See Rosario Natal, *Luis Muñoz Marín y la independencia*, 125-31.
54. By 1939 the public sector had already become the main source of national income in the island, going from $25 million (14.2 percent of the national income) in 1929 to $63 million (32.1 percent) in 1939. While manufacturing had remained stable and services had doubled their share of the national income, the sugar industry had dwindled from 49.4 percent ($87 million) in 1929 to 30.1 percent ($59 million) in 1939—all that while only employing 19,116 people, compared with the sugar industry, which fully employed a quarter of the workforce. See Dietz, *Economic History of Puerto Rico*, tables 3.1 and 3.12. It was not hard for politicians to realize that a better future for the island was not to be found in the sugar cane fields.
55. Maldonado, *Luis Muñoz Marín*, 180-83, citing Muñoz Marín, *Memorias*, 186-87.
56. This campaign aimed to make Puerto Rico's economy self-sufficient and had high socialist overtones. Economic historian James L. Dietz branded it "state capitalism." According to Dietz, as the private sector in the island did not engage in promoting capital growth, the Puerto Rican government had to become a "collective capitalist, promoter, and entrepreneur." These functions,

Dietz explained, had not been carried out by private capital. The government of Puerto Rico bought and established cement, glass, boxboard, and shoe factories. It also bought the island's electric companies, founded a development bank, and mostly followed a socialist-style approach to the island's socioeconomic problems, including land reform, administrative reorganization, and small-scale public-led industrialization. See Dietz, *Economic History of Puerto Rico*, 185.

57. Bolivar Fresneda, "Las inversiones y los programas militares," 142, and "La economía de Puerto Rico," 208–10.

58. Bolívar Fresneda, "La economía de Puerto Rico," 234.

59. Roosevelt Roads in Ceiba employed 3,474 workers, while the installations in Vieques employed 2,050. Bolívar Fresneda, "La economía de Puerto Rico," 229–31.

60. Bolivar Fresneda, "Las inversiones y los programas militares," 137.

61. Forty-seven percent of all the rum consumed in the United States between 1939 and 1947 was produced in Puerto Rico. As military construction slowed down, revenue from rum excise taxes took its place. In 1944 rum excise taxes rose to $65.8 million, representing 63 percent of the insular government's revenue. Bolívar Fresneda, "La economía de Puerto Rico," 241–48.

62. Bolívar Fresneda. "La economía de Puerto Rico," 208–9, 230.

63. Bolívar Fresneda. "La economía de Puerto Rico," 210, 211, 256, and Ayala and Bernabe, *Puerto Rico in the American Century*, 143–44.

64. Ayala and Bernabe, *Puerto Rico in the American Century*, 149–50, 152.

65. As the United States began the readiness process, Congress approved the voluntary enlistment of 375,000 men and the conscription of another 128,000. Puerto Rico's conscription quota would be 3,600 white and 1,200 black. However, volunteers would not be accepted beyond those required to bring the 65th Infantry to war strength. Military exercises conducted in 1939 and 1940 showed that the National Guard units were in disarray with the exception of the Puerto Rican National Guard, which was rated as superior. However, as Marín Román shows, the War Department did not want to utilize the Puerto Rican units. Marín Román, *¡A la vuelta de la esquina!* 342.

66. *New York Times*, November 11, 1939, CIHPC, Caja 2. On July 1, 1939, the War Department created the, Department of Puerto Rico to coordinate the war effort in the Caribbean.

67. Marín Román, *¡A la vuelta de la esquina!* 349, 371–72.

68. Bolivar Fresneda, "Las inversiones y los programas militares," 158.

69. *Puerto Rico World Journal*, March 29, 1944, filed in 65th U.S. Infantry Intelligence Report, April 3, 1944, CIHPC, Caja 21. The War Department ordered the local selective service unit on the island to reinstate the fourth-grade education requirement for admittance into the army, which was the standard for continental Americans. In July 1942, the War Department had authorized the commanding general of the Puerto Rican Department to require an eighth-grade education from natives of the island in order to be considered for service. The Puerto Rican Department was also authorized to "weed out the most

undesirable men" thought to be "inferior physically, mentally, and in other ways" to continentals. In October 1943 the Mayagüez Lions Club initiated the complaint that culminated with the War Department establishing the same parameters for Puerto Rican and continental recruits. See *El Mundo*, January 13, 1944, CIHPC, Caja 21.

70. War Department, "Puerto Rican Induction Program," April 15, 1945, CIHPC, Caja 17.

71. The 65th was sent to Panama, the southern continental United States, North Africa, Corsica, France, and Germany, and although it underwent chemical, amphibious, and jungle warfare, infiltration, and other intensive training, it remained restricted to security and service missions. See Walthall, *We Can't All Be Heroes*, 24–25; Muratti, *History of the 65th*, 12–14; and Vargas interview, August 6, 2001. The 295th served mostly in the Caribbean, including Panama, Jamaica, and the Dutch Caribbean islands. The 296th trained for war in the Pacific, but the war ended with them awaiting deployment in Hawaii.

72. War Department, "Puerto Rican Induction Program," 1.

73. The Free French, British, and Dutch governments opposed sending Puerto Rican troops to their Caribbean possessions, believing it might stir racial tensions. The presence of Puerto Ricans, who were considered colored troops in these overwhelmingly black colonies, could undermine the racial structure of power and endanger the abysmally small white elite. As a matter of fact, that was the War Department's reason for not sending black continental troops to the Caribbean. At any rate, the War Department did not believe it could spare any white troops, especially for a war theater that had become a secondary concern after the Allied invasions of North Africa and Sicily in 1943. Nonetheless, to placate their European allies, the War Department assured them that only white, highly educated (referring to eight years of schooling), English-speaking Puerto Ricans would be sent to their possessions. See British Joint Staff Mission to Stimson, June 2, 1943; War Department, "Outgoing Classified Message," 18 September 1943; Operations Division WDGS Latin American Theater to Field Marshall Sir John Hill, October 12, 1943, CIHPC, Caja 22.

74. *Puerto Rico World Journal*, March 29, 1944, filed in 65th U.S. Infantry Intelligence Report, April 3 1944, CIHPC, Caja 21.

75. "Puerto Rican Induction Program," 1–3.

76. "Puerto Rican Induction Program," 7–8.

77. "Puerto Rican Induction Program," 6.

78. See my interviews with Vargas, Ortíz, and Mercado Santana, August 6, 2001. All interviews are in my possession.

79. "Puerto Rican Induction Program," 2.

80. Lefebvre, "Puerto Rico: Quiet Participant," 95, and Dietz, *Economic History of Puerto Rico*, 186.

81. Many Puerto Rican career officers tried unsuccessfully to receive combat assignments in Europe or the Pacific theater. See Ulio to Muñoz Marín,

February 2, 1945, Muñoz Marín to Stimson, January 8, 1945, and Muñoz to Muñoz Marin, December 26, 1944, ALMM, Cartapacio 29.

82. Though the Nationalists had remained dormant from late 1938 through 1940, the passing of the Selective Service Law awakened its leaders, who quickly boycotted draft registration. By 1943 forty-five members of the party had been jailed for failure to register for the draft. After serving parts of their sentences for draft dodging, several Nacionalistas were released, and they later accused the officers at the correctional facilities of forcing them to complete registration cards. "Nationalist Party of Puerto Rico," FBI files, 42.

83. "Puerto Rican Induction Program," 4. Some 23,000 Puerto Ricans volunteers were accepted by the War Department, but more than 70,000 volunteered.

84. "Army orders given in Puerto Rico in English and Spanish," *Christian Science Monitor*, April 7, 1942, CIHPC, Caja 21. The comments were not off the mark. Per capita net income had taken a dive in 1931 to $108 from a previous $122, and by 1933 it had hit bottom at $86. Puerto Rico's PCNI was less than a third of the poorest state's PCNI (Alabama with $270) and a sixth of the aggregated PCNI in the continental United States, which was $575. Reconstruction under the New Deal and the coming of the war propelled a slow recovery, and by 1940 PCNI was back to 1930s levels. As land reform and the war effort started to make an impact, PNCI continued to rise: to $184 in 1942, $218 in 1943, $236 in 1944, and $270 by 1945. Underlining the correlation between the war effort and PCNI, after a relatively small increase to $271 in 1946, PCNI again started to decline: to $254 in 1947 and to $252 in 1949. PCNI would not rise to war levels until 1950, when it reached $279. See Dietz, *Economic History of Puerto Rico*, tables 3.2 and 4.1.

85. Marín Román, *¡A la vuelta de la esquina!* 367–69, 377–78.

86. Translated from Spanish: "A la guerra me lleva la necesidad, si tuviera dineros no iría de verdad." See Padrón, *El 65 en revista*, 132–33.

87. Vargas interview. Vargas was not the only one to mention the $21 payment. Antonio E. Padrón stated that "the stipend earned by the lower-class Boricua, and even the middle class, is much lower than that offered by the armed forces." Padrón, *El 65 en revista*, 132.

88. Padrón, *El 65 en revista*, 132–33.

89. Vargas, Ortíz, and Mercado Santana interviews. These veterans cited the poor economic situation of the island as their reason for joining the army. However, all of them mentioned that the respect and the treatment they received when in uniform motivated them to remain in the military.

90. "Army Orders Given in Puerto Rico in English and Spanish," *Christian Science Monitor*, April 7, 1942.

91. The Great Assembly of the Nationalist Party appealed to the Pan-American Convention in Rio, and the Atlantic Charter asked for the withdrawal of all U.S. armed forces from the island, the recognition of national sovereignty, and "the right and privilege of having a military representative in the High Command of Democracies so as to accept equal risks in the war and have the same joy in victory." "Nationalist Party of Puerto Rico," FBI files, 53–54.

92. Bolívar Fresneda, "Las inversiones y los programas militares," 159–62.

93. U.S. Army payment for a private was $21 a month in 1940. In January 1943 a new pay scale went into effect starting at $50 a month for a private. Overseas pay meant an extra $10 a month. Ironically, Puerto Ricans serving in Puerto Rico were entitled to overseas payment while on the island (an overseas possession) but not while training in the United States. The Bureau of the Budget monthly figures included Administration Induction Programs, $5,800; Dependents Benefits: Monthly Benefit of Men Already in the Service, $1,850,000; Initial Payment to Dependents of New Inductees, $118,000 for a total of $1,965,000. Separation Payments: "Mastering out lump sum payment," $80,000; Weekly Readjustment Payment ($20/weekly for 52 weeks), $285,700. The total monthly expenses were thus $2,539,500 for an annual rate of $28,074,000. "Puerto Rican Induction Program," 3–10.

94. "Puerto Rican Induction Program," 12.

95. The *Ley de Salario Mínimo de 1941* set the hourly wage in the island at 25 cents. In theory that meant that a fully employed worker should earn $10 per week. However, the law had so many exemptions that most agricultural and factory workers did not benefit from the minimum hourly wage at all. Dietz, *Economic History of Puerto Rico*, 225–26; see also Wells, "La modernización de Puerto Rico," 87.

96. Muñoz to Muñoz Marín, 1948, ALMM, Cartapacio 29.

97. Bolivar Fresneda, *La economía de Puerto Rico*, 247.

98. By the guidelines of the Service Men's Dependents Allowance Act of 1943, enlisted men and warrant officers deployed overseas earned 20 percent more than those stationed in the continental United States while officers earned 10 percent more. See "Puerto Rican Induction Program," 7.

99. Officials of the Bureau of the Budget went so far as proposing a pay reduction for Puerto Rican soldiers because they believed that it would make sense to treat the Puerto Rican soldiers differently than continentals, since Army regulations did not "take into account the much higher level of living of Continental soldiers' families, nor the much lower cost of living in Puerto Rico." See "Puerto Rican Induction Program," 10. However, the cost of living on the island was higher and wages were much lower than in the continental United States, which had led to the pauperization of the peasantry and extreme poverty of the urban working class, and this situation further deteriorated during the early years of the war. Prices of imported food went up 90 percent between 1941 and 1946 while locally produced food increased 48 percent. Local food production was only increased thanks to the land-reform program carried out by Muñoz Marín and Tugwell. Supported by a federal recognition of the "Law of the 500 Acres," the government bought lands with more than 500 acres and distributed them among landless peasants. This program was credited with bringing the land area devoted to food production from 230,000 acres in 1940 to 300,000 acres by the war's end. Yuca and tubers such as names and batatas, plantains and yautías made up the bulk of the increase in locally produced foods.

All of them were staples of the Puerto Rican peasant's diet. Sugar producers were adamantly opposed to devoting some of their lands to food production, even during the 1941–42 period when the island faced starvation, fearing that they would lose their production quotas. See Dietz, *Economic History of Puerto Rico*, 203–204, and Tugwell, *The Stricken Land*, 215.

100. "Puerto Rican Induction Program," 7, 10.

101. Dietz, *Economic History of Puerto Rico*, 147.

102. There was a very important provision that allowed for veterans ages twenty-five and younger to claim that their studies were interrupted because of military service, which entitled them to a monthly pension of $50 and $75 for single and veterans with dependents, respectively, while they continued their studies. The same applied for veterans over twenty-five, but they had to prove that their studies were in fact interrupted. Another provision set a monthly pension of $80 and $90 for single and married veterans pursuing vocational rehabilitation, $80 to single and married veterans for up to four years. The local government aided in securing documents necessary to claim all these benefits and even created a manual of veterans rights in Spanish. See Servicio Selectivo–Puerto Rico, "Información para veteranos: derechos y beneficios," May 8, 1945, ALMM, Cartapacio 19. Some of the issues studied by the local government were state bonuses to veterans, and they looked at Alaska, Illinois, Massachusetts, Michigan, New Hampshire, Rhode Island, Vermont, Connecticut, Georgia, and North Dakota as guidelines for Puerto Rican veteran bonuses.

103. "Puerto Rican Induction Program," 7, 10.

104. Of those residing on the island in 1947, 13,271 served in World War I and 52,586 in World War II. Veterans Administration Center, "Estimated Veteran Population, Puerto Rico and Virgin Islands," June 9, 1947, AFLMM, Cartapacio 29. The military aide to the governor of Puerto Rico, Teodoro Vidal, prepared a report which stated that between November 20, 1940, and March 31, 1947, 65,034 Puerto Ricans served in the U.S. military, and 368 lost their lives (combat, training, and accidents). More than 12,000 World War II Puerto Rican veterans were not living on the island by 1954. See Vidal, "Participación Puertorriqueña en la Segunda Guerra Mundial y en el Conflicto de Corea," AFLMM, November–December 1954, Cartapacio 7. By the war's end there were more than 67,500 men serving in the Puerto Rican Department. It climaxed at roughly 91,000 (including continental troops) in 1943. See Negroni, *Historia militar de Puerto Rico*, 444–45.

105. The Servicemen's Readjustment Act was finally signed into law by President Roosevelt on June 22, 1944. The Veterans Administration became responsible for carrying out the law's key provisions: education and training, loan guaranty for homes, farms, or businesses, and unemployment pay. Millions of veterans who would have flooded the job market after the war suddenly had the option of attaining college and vocational education. According to the Veterans Administration, in 1947 "veterans accounted for 49 percent of college admissions. By the time the original GI Bill ended on July 25, 1956, 7.8

million of 16 million World War II veterans had participated in an education or training program." Furthermore, between 1944 and 1952, the VA "backed nearly 2.4 million home loans for World War II veterans." More compelling, few veterans "collected on one of the bill's most controversial provisions—the unemployment pay. Less than 20 percent of funds set aside for this was used." See "GI Bill History," http://www.gibill.va.gov/gi_Bill_Info/history.htm.

106. Muñoz to Muñoz Marín, 1948, AFLMM.

107. Muñoz to Muñoz Marín, 1948, AFLMM.

108. See Wells, "La modernización de Puerto Rico," 85, and Pablo Navarro Rivera, *Universidad de Puerto Rico: De control político a crisis permanente*, 86–87.

109. "Todas estas escuelas no serán exclusivamente para los veteranos, pero se le dará preferencia en todo tiempo al veterano que interese asistir a ellas." Muñoz to Muñoz Marín, 1948, AFLMM.

110. Muñoz to Muñoz Marín, 1948, AFLMM.

111. Francisco Collazo, acting commissioner of education, congratulated the adjutant general of the National Guard for conducting a three-day institute on industrialization in June 1950. Another letter from the mayor of Aguadilla lauded the participation of the Puerto Rico National Guard military band in the city's patron saint festivities in 1949. Puerto Rico National Guard, "Annual Report 1949–50," CIHPC, Caja 17.

112. On April 4 the State Guard helped Ponce High School celebrate its field day. The appointment of "Godmothers and Honorary Officers in each town where companies are organized has resulted in greater cooperation from local authorities and prominent citizens. Our aim is to make each community realize that the State Guard company in each town is its own so they will look it up to the limit. The state guard units are no longer considered by the public as something foreign to them, but as organizations of their own." Estevez, "Report on the Puerto Rico State Guard, for the Year 1945–46," CIHPC, Caja 17.

113. A good example of the overlapping military-civilian roles of the Puerto Rican soldier is Miguel A. Muñoz, the director of the Veterans Administration on the island during this period. He was a colonel in the PRNG who served as executive officer of the 295th Regiment as a captain in Camp Las Casas during the war, commander of the Porto Rico American Legion, and vice commander of the National American Legion. He had been the personal secretary of Governor Yager in 1914. After he publicly criticized the tactics of the Insular Police during the Ponce Massacre of March 21, 1937, he had been under pressure from Governor Winship to resign his commission. See *El Imparcial de Puerto Rico: Periódico Ilustrado*, April 1, 1937, clip, filed in *Report to Chief National Guard Bureau*, April 27, 1937, CIHPC, Caja 19. Another example is Col. Juan C. Cordero-Dávila, who served with the 65th Infantry during World War II and then commanded the 296th Regimental Combat Team of the PRNG. Cordero-Davila, who would eventually lead the 65th during the Korean War, was also the director of the Puerto Rican Housing Authority. This government agency built low-income houses as part of the ongoing reconstruction effort. See Villaher-

mosa, *Honor and Fidelity: The 65th Infantry in Korea*, 188–89. During the postwar years, veterans were among those in the best position to buy new houses, some of which first came in the form of housing projects. By 1948 the Insular Housing Authority had built a caserío for 132 veterans and their families in San Juan. The VA estimated that of all new housing, veterans were receiving between 10 and 15 percent. See Muñoz to Muñoz Marín, 1948, AFLMM. The strength of the State Guard (an auxiliary corps to the National Guard activated during World War II) as of June 30, 1946, shows 131 officers and 1,234 enlisted. They included 145 graduates from college, twenty-one engineers, six lawyers, twenty-nine physicians, sixty-eight teachers, eleven accountants, seventeen surgeons, and twenty-five dentists. See Estevez, "Report on the Puerto Rico State Guard, for the Year 1945–46," CIHPC, Caja 17.

114. Of 591,978 votes, the PPD obtained 383,280. Partido Unión Republicana obtained 101,779; Partido Socialista 69,107; Partido Liberal 38,630. The Populares won all district senate seats, three of five seats for senators at large, thirty-four of thirty-five seats in the house of representatives, seventy-three of seventy-seven municipalities, and elected Jesús T. Piñero as resident commissioner in Washington. See Bayrón Toro, *Elecciones y partidos políticos de Puerto Rico*, 202–3.

115. See H.R. 3309, 44–46.

116. S.227, 5–8, 27–29.

117. When Truman became president, he was unaware of the abandonment of the Good Neighbor policy and immediately followed a course that reverted to the former policy. Truman met with Tugwell on August 23, 1945, and informed him that he saw his presidency as no more than an extension of the Roosevelt regime. Therefore Truman was in favor of taking action toward self-government for Puerto Rico and estimated that if he pushed, "it would be done, he would predict, in six months." Tugwell, *The Stricken Island*, xvii–xix.

118. Tugwell, *The Stricken Island*, xix.

119. Trías Monge, *Trials of the Oldest Colony*, 105.

120. Rosario Natal, *Luis Muñoz Marín y la independencia*, 191, quoting Undersecretary of the Interior Abe Fortas: "Perhaps they do not want to sue for divorce, and perhaps we should not propose that the ties between us be dissolved. But there is one thing we can all agree upon: Puerto Rico should have complete home rule."

121. "Special Message to Congress on Puerto Rico," October 16, 1945, TPML, http://www.trumanlibrary.org/hstpaper/presshst.htm. Although Truman repeated this position in his State of the Union address, the proposal of the president with regard to dominion status was indeed vague, and he did not pursue it vigorously. "Message to the Congress on the State of the Union and on the Budget for 1947," January 21, 1946, TPML, http://www.trumanlibrary.org/hstpaper/presshst.htm.

122. The bill has come to be known as the Tydings-Piñero bill, because Piñero and Muñoz Marín talked Tydings into reintroducing it but with statehood and self-government as political options. Trías Monge, *Trials of the Oldest Colony*, 105.

123. H.R. 3309, 15–16, 19.

124. H.R. 3309, 3, 5. According to Article 76 of the UN charter, the United States, as the metropolitan power, had the responsibility to "promote the political, economic, social, and educational advancement of the inhabitants."

125. H.R. 3309, 5–6, 8–9, 10–11, 13.

126. H.R. 3309, 35–36.

127. Reynolds based her arguments on the provisions of the Autonomic Charter of 1897, a position earlier developed by Pedro Albizu Campos, leader of the Nationalists. Title VII, Article 43 guaranteed the veto power of the Puerto Rican parliament over decisions reached by the Cortes of the Kingdom. Moreover, Puerto Rico had over a dozen representatives in the Cortes. Article 2 declared that the "present constitution shall not be amended except by virtue of a special law and upon petition of the insular parliament." Since the military disbanded the insular parliament, and there were no Puerto Rican delegates present to sign the Treaty of Paris of December 10, the passing of sovereignty over Puerto Rico to the United States was a violation of the legal relationship between Spain and Puerto Rico and thus illegal. Representative Fred L. Crawford rebuked Ms. Reynolds and proceeded to discredit her testimony by pointing out the links of her organization and the independence movement with Communists in Puerto Rico and the United States. H.R. 3309, 42–42, 47.

128. H.R. 3309, 15–29.

129. H.R. 3309, 54.

130. H.R. 3309, 55.

131. S. 952, 52–53.

132. By the act of August 5, 1947, the people of Puerto Rico were authorized to elect their own governor. This act also provided that the heads of all executive departments of Puerto Rico were to be appointed by the elected governor of Puerto Rico, including the attorney general and the commissioner of education. As a result of the act, therefore, the people of Puerto Rico assumed direct responsibility and control over the executive branch of the local government. The president of the United States still retained authority to appoint the auditor and the justices of the supreme court of Puerto Rico. See H.R. 3309 and S. 1184. The act providing for the governorship of Puerto Rico by election is Public Law 382, 80th Cong.

133. Trías Monge, *Trials of the Oldest Colony*, 105.

134. "Address upon Arrival at San Juan, P.R.," February 21, 1948, TPML, http://www.trumanlibrary.org/hstpaper/presshst.htm.

135. Of 640,714 votes cast, the PPD obtained 392,386, the Independentistas 65,351; the Estadistas (former Republicanos) 89,441; and the Socialistas 64,396. The former Liberales under the name of Reformistas obtained 29,140. Estadistas, Liberales, and Socialistas formed another coalition. The PPD won all offices and municipalities except the town of San Lorenzo, two senators, and a representative at large—positions which were won by Socialistas and Estadistas. See Bayrón Toro, *Elecciones y partidos políticos puertorriqueños*, 210–11. Once

Muñoz Marín was elected, it became harder for the Independentistas to gain support from anti-American factions in Cuba, Brazil, and Central America, and the United States was able to shield itself from accusations of colonialism. Tugwell, *The Art of Politics*, 64.

136. Norat-Martínez, *Historia del Regimiento 65 de Infantería*, 53.

137. "Report on the Puerto Rico State Guard, for the Year 1945–46."

138. "Soldado Ocasio, ciudadano Ocasio, jíbaro Ocasio, soldados y ciudadanos y jibaros en todos los montes de Puerto Rico y en todos los frentes y campamentos del mundo, la esperanza de Puerto Rico esta en ustedes." Muñoz Marín, "Mensaje en Homenaje al soldado típico, Pedro Ocasio," February 7, 1945, and Muñoz Marín, "Discurso en el Día del Armisticio," November 12, 1945, in *Discursos*, 243–45, 259–62. Cpl. Pedro Ocasio had been featured by the *Daily News* in New York as an example of the model Puerto Rican soldier. "Model Soldier," *Daily News*, AFLMM, subseries 13.1 to 13.33: NY correspondence, 17, ITEM: Pelayo García to Muñoz Marín.

139. *Porto Rico Progress*, July 12, 1918, CPUPRM.

140. An "institutional" link with the metropolis, specifically with the federal government, was hard to miss. For example, the PRERA, PRRA, and WPA and mobilization and postwar veterans' benefits were federal initiatives and federally funded.

141. After pointing out that 35 percent of the island's population was illiterate, the *Christian Science Monitor* argued that "trained Army officers are inculcating in thousands of Puerto Ricans improved ideas of diet, education, and sanitation which they believe will contribute to raising the standards of domestic and community life when the war is over." *Christian Science Monitor*, April 7, 1943. Also see "Army Teaches Our Problem Child," *Daily News*, March 25, 1945, 47, AFLMM, subseries 13.1 to 13.33, Garcia to Muñoz Marín.

6. Fighting for the "Nation"?

1. In Norat Martínez, ed., *Historia del Regimiento 65 de Infantería*, 84–85. I consider José Norat-Martínez's work to be a primary source, since it is a collection of news and documents from the regiment's public relations office and the local press presented in chronological order.

2. In 1946 Muñoz Marín had expelled the Independentistas from the PPD, who wanted him to support another independence bill sponsored by Senator Tydings. The Independentistas responded by forming that same year the Partido Independentista Puertorriqueño, or PIP.

3. Few works hint at the connection between service in Korea and promoting the commonwealth formula. See Álvarez Curbelo, "La bandera en la colina," and Franqui-Rivera, "Glory and Shame."

4. House Committee on Public Lands, *To Provide for the Organization of a Constitutional Government by the People of Puerto Rico: Hearings on H.R. 7674 and S. 3336*, UMAMC, July 12, March 14, May 14, May 16, June 8, 1950, 27.

5. By July 1950 the island had received more than 10,000 professionals, government officials, academics, journalists, and students under the Point Four

training program institutionalized by the Puerto Rican legislature, with the support of Truman and the Interior Department. See Maldonado, *Luis Muñoz Marín*, 285–86, and "Luis Muñoz Marín y Rafael Leónidas Trujillo: Una pugna caribeña," 41.

6. H.R.7674 S.3336, 27, 38, 47, 64. Inés Mendoza Rivera was born on January 10, 1908, in Yabucoa. She was the daughter of an illiterate worker who "had worked himself into economic security." She earned a teaching certificate by age seventeen and a degree from the University of Puerto Rico four years later. Because of her testimony denouncing the Ponce Massacre, she was removed from her teaching position. She was known as a Nationalist when she met Muñoz Marín in 1938. In fact, she had recently broken with the Nationalists after she "heard Albizu comment to his wife, Laura, that it was necessary to kill Americans." Persecuted by the pro-American parties, which won the 1936 elections and who intended to eradicate "independentismo" from Puerto Rico's schools, she had been sacked from her teaching position and sought Muñoz Marín's aid. They quickly became romantically involved. Although they lived together for almost ten years, they had to wait until 1946 to marry because Muñoz Marín's first wife, Muna Lee, would not grant him a divorce. Maldonado, *Luis Muñoz Marín*, 159–67.

7. Of 640,714 votes cast, the PPD obtained 392,386, the Independentistas, 65,351; the Estadistas (former Republicanos) 89,441; and the Socialistas 64,396. The former Liberales under the name of Reformistas obtained 29,140. Estadistas, Liberales, and Socialistas formed another coalition. The PPD won all offices and municipalities except the town of San Lorenzo, two senators, and a representative at large, positions which were won by Socialistas and Estadistas. See Bayrón Toro, *Elecciones y partidos políticos puertorriqueños*, 210–11. Once Muñoz Marín was elected, it became harder for the Independentistas to gain support from anti-U.S. factions in Cuba, Brazil, and Central America, allowing the United States to shield itself from accusations of colonialism. See Tugwell, *The Art of Politics*, 64.

8. A balance account of the public confrontation, mostly through discourses, radio speeches, and commentaries to the press, can be found in Rosario Natal, "Muñoz y Albizu: el choque en la víspera de la insurrección," 309–41.

9. Mathews, *La política puertorriqueña y el Nuevo Trato*, 249, and Maldonado, *Luis Muñoz Marín*, 147–48. On March 5, 1936, Albizu Campos and other seven Nacionalista leaders were arrested and charged with sedition and conspiracy to overthrow the U.S. government The next month a federal grand jury submitted accusations against Albizu Campos and other leaders of the party.

10. Seijo Bruno, *La insurrección nacionalista*, 39, 40, 42–43, citing Albizu Campos, Paredón Records, P-2501.

11. The U.S. Alien Registration Act also required all alien residents in the United States over fourteen years of age to file a comprehensive statement of their personal and occupational status and a record of their political beliefs. Within four months, 4,741,971 aliens had been registered. See Díaz Soler,

Puerto Rico, sus luchas por alcanzar estabilidad económica, definición política y afirmación cultural, 319–23.

12. Negroni, *Historia militar de Puerto Rico*, 455, and Seijo Bruno, *La insurrección nacionalista*, 77.

13. According to Nacionalista Anibal Torres and others interviewed by Seijo Bruno, Albizu Campos himself ordered the riot. The Nacionalistas had contacted at least one of the guards and several inmate leaders who promised weapons and one thousand men to join the insurrection. Seijo Bruno, *La insurreción nacionalista*, 83–87.

14. *Periódico el Mundo*, October 31, 1950; *El Imparcial*, October 31, 1950, CPUPRM.

15. Seijo Bruno, *La insurreción nacionalista*, 53–59, 147. The Nacionalistas claimed that the National Guard summarily executed prisoners in Utuado where five Nacionalistas, a guardsman, and a policeman died, as well as a civilian and a fireman. However, the accounts are contradictory about a group of unarmed Nacionalistas who had just surrendered and were subsequently fired upon. The testimony of some of the Nacionalistas who survived the shooting and several townspeople points to the Nacionalistas being killed and wounded (as well as the National Guardsmen escorting them) after soldiers manning a picket line sometime after midnight saw the approaching column, panicked, and fired on both their fellow national guardsmen and the prisoners.

16. Seijo Bruno, *La insurreción nacionalista*, 127–34.

17. Negroni, *Historia militar de Puerto Rico*, 456.

18. "Insurrection," *New York Times*, November 13, 1950.

19. Truman, November 2, 1952, TPLM, http://www.trumanlibrary.org/hstpaper/presshst.htm.

20. "Revolt Caught U.S. Army Low on Ammo," "4 C-47 Carrying 40,000 Pounds of Cartridges from Panama," "BG Edwin L. Sibert Turned Over His Ammo to PRNG," *Times Herald*, November 3, 1950, CIHPC, Caja 17.

21. More than 140 Nacionalistas took part in the revolt, though it is still believed that probably about the same number were not able to participate and thus evaded capture. Three of the Nacionalistas were women. More than 80 percent were between the ages of fifteen and thirty-four; 14 percent had a college education and 18 percent had finished high school. Only six had no schooling. While 69 percent of the Nacionalistas were described as workers (agricultural 44 percent and nonagricultural 56 percent), the rest were divided equally between professionals, land or business owners, independent, and white-collar workers. See Seijo Bruno, *La insurrection nacionalista*, 233–34, 243–45.

22. As part of Operation Airlift, more than 5,000 Puerto Ricans, many of them loyal PPD supporters, were sent to the sugar beet fields of east-central Michigan in 1950. Once there, they faced harsh conditions and mistreatment. Operation Airlift seemed to be collapsing, threatening the PPD's plans on the eve of the vote that would eventually lead to the creation of the Estado Libre Asociado. Suárez Findlay, *We Are Left without a Father Here*, 48, 163, 165–67, 171.

23. The Estadistas changed their hearts and decided that they could not oppose the passing of P.L. 600 except with the understanding that they did so believing that this step would lead the people of Puerto Rico "to equality within the American citizenry, in fact, a step towards statehood" as announced in a general assembly on August 5, 1951. Only the Independentistas continued to oppose the referendum and to blame the United States for provoking the insurrection. See Bolívar Pagán, *Historia de los Partidos Políticos Puertorriqueños*, 303.

24. Díaz Soler, *Puerto Rico, sus luchas por alcanzar estabilidad económica, definición política y afirmación cultural*, 338.

25. Bolívar Pagán, *Historia de los Partidos Políticos Puertorriqueños*, 300

26. Albizu Campos and several Nacionalistas were charged with violating Law 53, the gag law. He was kept in isolation in the La Princesa jail from November 14, 1950, to May 18, 1951, when he was transferred to a bigger and better ventilated cell. Pedro Albizu declared that he was being bombarded with radioactivity in his cell. The Justice Department argued that he had premature senile dementia. His trial took place between June 30 and August 5, 1951. He was sentenced to twelve to fifty-four years of confinement. As Albizu Campos continued to complain of radiation, a psychiatrist declared him insane, and on September 30, 1953, Muñoz Marín conditionally pardoned him. The government offer stated that he would not try to overthrow the government of Puerto Rico again. He refused the offer but was declared mentally incompetent and set free nonetheless. A year later he would again be sent to jail after Nacionalistas Lolita Lebrón, Andrés Figueroa Cordero, Rafael Cancel Miranda, and Irving Flores opened fire from the gallery of the U.S. House of Representatives, wounding five congressmen. On November 15, 1964, Albizu was again pardoned by Muñoz Marín. He died on April 21, 1965, and was buried in the Old San Juan Cemetery. See Díaz Soler, *Puerto Rico, sus luchas por alcanzar estabilidad económica, definición política y afirmación cultural*, 338–39; and Negroni, *Historia militar de Puerto Rico*, 456–57.

27. Joseph Stalin, the leader of the Soviet Union, supported North Korea's aggression, thinking that "it would benefit the geopolitical position of the USSR in the Far East." In a gross miscalculation, Stalin believed that the United States would not intervene. Immediately after the UN forces crossed the 38th parallel and with Kim Il-sung's regime crumbling, Stalin "dictated a telegram to Mao Zedong [Communist China's leader] advising the Chinese to mobilize five or six divisions to the 38th parallel." On October 25, 1951, the Chinese Communist Forces (CCF) launched their first phase offensive of the Korean War. Intelligence reports, however, disregarded the presence of large numbers of Chinese soldiers in North Korea until the CCF began a large-scale offensive on November 25, 1951. Zubok and Pleshakov, *Inside the Kremlin's Cold War*, 54, 65.

28. Blair, *The Forgotten War*, 88–89.

29. Blair, *The Forgotten War*, 997. Official army documents, however, seem to have overrated the readiness and strength of the four divisions composing

the 8th Army. The 1st Cavalry Division appeared on paper as being 84 percent combat ready, while the 7th, 24th, and 25th Infantry Divisions had 74, 65, and 72 percent ratings, respectively.

30. McGregor, *Integration of the Armed Forces*, 6–7.
31. *Periódico el Mundo*, March 1, 1951, CPUPRM.
32. McGregor, *Integration of the Armed Forces*, 291.
33. Harris, *Puerto Rico's Fighting 65th*, 4–5.
34. Villahermosa, *Honor and Fidelity*, 20–25. Villahermosa also emphasizes the acute lack of manpower and trained personnel as a reason for adding the 65th to the U.S. 3rd Division as it prepared for battle in Korea.
35. Operation Portrex took place on Vieques Island, off the east coast of Puerto Rico, in late February 1950. It was the largest joint amphibious-airborne exercise to that date. The 65th played the role of "Aggressor." Its mission was to defend the island against the liberating forces of the U.S. Army 3rd Infantry Division (reinforced), plus a battalion of the 82nd Airborne Division. To everyone's surprise, by the end of the exercise the soldiers of the 65th still controlled a significant part of Vieques. This exercise helped convince the Army that the 65th was battle worthy. The 198th Fighter Squadron of the Puerto Rico Air National Guard also participated and won accolades. See Puerto Rico National Guard, Annual Report, 1949–50, 15.
36. For a detailed military history of the 65th's experience in Korea, see Villahermosa, *Honor and Fidelity*. Figuroa-Soulet's documentary *The Borinqueneers* focuses on the debacles suffered by the regiment during the autumn of 1952 and the subsequent court-martial of more than a hundred enlisted men and one Puerto Rican officer. A similar narrative is found in Harry Franqui-Rivera, "Glory and Shame."
37. *Periódico el Mundo*, October 12, 1950, CPUPRM.
38. Suárez Findlay, *We Are Left without a Father*, 48.
39. The statements of support for the war effort, especially as the 65th's departure was announced, fall into the lines of earning the trust, being considered apt enough, and following a path to equality. *El Imparcial*, June 1, 1950, and *Periódico el Mundo*, October 12, 1950, CPUPRM.
40. *Periódico el Mundo*, October 31, 1950; *El Imparcial*, October 31, 1950, CPUPRM. The FBI and the Insular Police estimated that the nationalists represented no more than 5 percent of the population.
41. *Periódico el Mundo*, October 12, 1950, CPUPRM; Norat-Martínez, *Historia del Regimiento 65 de Infantería*, 84–85; and Puerto Rico, Constitución del Estado Libre Asociado de Puerto Rico, Preámbulo, in Fernós López-Cepero, *Documentos históricos-constitucionales de Puerto Rico*, 145.
42. *Periódico el Mundo*, August 1, 1950, CPUPRM.
43. The fact that more than 61,000 Puerto Ricans ultimately served with the U.S. forces during the Korean War validates Fernós Isern's claims.
44. Harris, *Puerto Rico's Fighting 65th*, 46–47. Harris commanded the 65th Infantry from 1949 to 1951.

45. Bolívar Fresneda. "La economía de Puerto Rico," 208, 211, 219, 229–30, 243–48; Bolívar Fresneda, "Las inversiones y los programas militares," 163–64; Ayala and Bernabe, *Puerto Rico in the American Century*, 143–44; and Dietz, *Economic History of Puerto Rico*, 204–7.

46. Luis Muñoz Marín, Press and Radio Message, August 14, 1950, AFLMM, Cartapacio 3; *Periódico el Mundo*, August 13, 1950, CPUPRM.

47. *El Imparcial*, June 1, 1950, and *Periódico el Mundo*, October 12, 1950, CPUPRM. Borinqueneers is an English transliteration of *Borinqueños* or the hispanized term colloquially used to refer to those born in Puerto Rico, which itself is a direct reference to the island's Arawak ancestors, who called the island Boriken or Buruquena.

48. *Periódico el Mundo*, October 12, 1950, CPUPRM.

49. *El Imparcial de Puerto Rico*, November 12, 1950, CPUPRM.

50. Muñoz Marín, "Discurso despedida al Regimiento 65 de Infantería," August 26, 1950, AFLMM, Cartapacio 3.

51. *El Imparcial de Puerto Rico*, November 12, 1950, CPUPRM.

52. *Periódico el Mundo*, October 12, 1950, CPUPRM.

53. *Periódico el Mundo*, August 27, 1950, CPUPRM.

54. Throughout most of the Korean War, the quota assigned to Puerto Rico by the Selective Service was filled by volunteers. "The selective service informed that there has not been any recruitment since February 1951, when it was formally authorized to fill Puerto Rico's quota with volunteers." See *Periódico el Mundo*, November 4, 1952, CPUPRM. Another article said that the Department of Defense asked the Selective Service Office (SSO) in Puerto Rico for 1,272 draftees. A spokesman for the SSO responded that although "during most of the last year the Selective Service in Puerto Rico barely had to recruit at all, and the major part of the quota assigned to PR (about 2 percent of the men called to arms) was covered with volunteers, the reserve of volunteers is running low thus it would be necessary to proceed with recruitment." See *El Imparcial de Puerto Rico*, January 21, 1953, CPUPRM. It was not until the court-martial of ninety-four Puerto Ricans became known on the island and the Department of the Army decided to integrate the 65th that the number of volunteers declined. The trials led to the integration of the 65th with continental troops, a policy much resisted on the island. For a detailed account of the events leading to the court-martial and of the trials themselves, see Franqui-Rivera, "Glory and Shame," 62–118, 120–53.

55. The period covered is June 20, 1950, to July 25, 1953. According to the selective service office in Puerto Rico (led by Col. Rafael Jiménez de la Rosa), 10,185 volunteers were rejected in Puerto Rico. The Borinqueneers suffered 3,540 casualties, of which 747 were killed in action (KIA). One out of every 42 U.S. casualties was Puerto Rican. Puerto Rico sustained 1 casualty for every 660 inhabitants, twice as many as the rate for continental troops, which stood at 1 for every 1,125 inhabitants. See Vidal, "Participación Puertorriqueña en la Segunda Guerra Mundial y en el Conflicto de Corea," November–December

1954, AFLMM, Cartapacio 7, and "State-Level Lists of Casualties from the Korean and Vietnam Conflicts" NARA, http://www.nara.gov/nara/electronic/homensx.htm.

56. See *Periódico el Mundo*, November 13, 1952, CPUPRM.

57. *El Imparcial de Puerto Rico*, October 13, 1950, CPUPRM.

58. The concept of Anglo-Saxon and Hispanic cultures' coexistence was soon to be abandoned by the ELA as a decade known as the "six years of Puertorriquenidad" (*sexenio de la puertorriqueñidad*) (1953–59) witnessed a series of state-sponsored cultural policies aimed at stopping further Americanization of Puerto Rican culture. The creation of the Instituto de Cultura Puertorriqueña, several *ateneos*, cultural centers, and folkloric troupes and festivals, sponsored by the commonwealth, displayed this process. See Rodriguez Cancel, *La Guerra Fría y el sexenio de la puertorriqueñidad*, and Dávila, *Sponsored Identities*, xii, 1, 207, 258.

59. Muñoz Marín, "Palabras en la ceremonia para otorgar medalla y diplomas a policías, guardias nacionales y bomberos," May 28, 1951 AFLMM, Cartapacio 4.

60. Apparently 76 percent of the votes were in favor of P.L. 600. See House Committee on Interior and Insular Affairs, *A Joint Resolution Approving the Constitution of the Commonwealth of Puerto Rico: Hearing on H.J. Res. 430*, April 25, 1952, 1–3, UMMC, and Senate Committee on Interior and Insular Affairs, *A Joint Resolution Approving the Constitution of the Commonwealth of Puerto Rico: Hearings on S.J. 151*, April 29, May 6, 1952, 1–3, 13–15, UMMC, *Periódico el Mundo*, June 7, 1951; *El Imparcial de Puerto Rico*, June 7, 1951, CPUPRM.

61. Eighty-one percent voted in favor of the constitution prepared by the convention. See *Hearing on H.J. Res. 430*.

62. Truman, "Special Message to the Congress of the United States," April 22, 1952, TPLM, http://www.trumanlibrary.org/hstpaper/presshst.htm.

63. Truman, "Statement by the President upon Signing Bill Approving the Constitution of the Commonwealth of Puerto Rico," July 3, 1952, TPLM, http://www.trumanlibrary.org/hstpaper/presshst.htm.

64. Tugwell, *The Art of Politics*, 65–66.

65. Truman, "White House Press Release," TPLM, http://www.trumanlibrary.org/hstpaper/presshst.htm.

66. Trías Monge, *Trials of the Oldest Colony*, 120–24. The General Assembly of the United Nations approved Resolution 748 (VIII) to cease the transmission of information on Puerto Rico by a vote of 26–16, with 18 abstentions.

67. Constitución del Estado Libre Asociado de Puerto Rico, Preámbulo, in Fernós López-Cepero, *Documentos históricos-constitucionales de Puerto Rico*, 145.

68. *Pacific Stars & Stripes*, ca. March 1952, Rodríguez Papers.

69. Norat-Martínez, *Historia del Regimiento 65 de Infantería*, 84–85.

70. Norat-Martínez, *Historia del Regimiento 65 de Infantería*, 84–85.

71. *Pacific Stars & Stripes*, ca. August 1953, Rodríguez Papers.

72. Guerra, *Popular Expression and National Identity in Puerto Rico*, 6.

73. Puerto Rican veterans enjoy higher living standards than those of their civilian counterparts both in the mainland and in the island. In fact, the stan-

dard of living of Puerto Rican veterans, including World War II to present conflicts, put them at the same level with the white middle class in the United States. Roughly three-fourths of the World War II and Korean War veterans live on the island. The equation reverses after the Vietnam War, even though the majority of Puerto Rican veterans enlisted in Puerto Rico. See Franqui-Rivera, "Puerto Rican Veterans and Service Members' Well-Being and Place within the Diaspora," 193–96, 199–203.

Conclusion

1. Suárez Findlay, *Imposing Decency*, 2–4, and Julian Go, "Chains of Empire," 335–37.

2. Benedict Anderson has argued that vernacular languages which had been chosen as language-of-states based on unselfconscious inheritance or convenience, became tools to unify (or Russify) ethnically diverse empires. In this regard, German, Russian, and English became "universal-imperial" as well as "particular-national" as the imperial dynasties courted nationalism and national languages while claiming to preside over polyglot peoples. As their empires became global and too big to be ruled by nationals, the metropoles responded by Russifying the educational system to provide an army of indigenous clerks to run the colonies. Anderson, *Imagined Communities*, 86, 109–10.

3. Briggs, *Reproducing Empire*, 198.

4. See discussion in chapter 2.

5. Anderson, *Imagined Communities*, 110, 112–13.

6. After pointing out that 35 percent of the island's population was illiterate, the *Christian Science Monitor* argued that "trained Army officers are inculcating in thousands of Puerto Ricans improved ideas of diet, education, and sanitation which they believe will contribute to raising the standards of domestic and community life when the war is over." *Christian Science Monitor*, April 7, 1943.

7. Bolívar Fresneda, "La economía de Puerto Rico," 208, 211, 219, 229–30, 243–48; Bolívar Fresneda, "Las inversiones y los programas militares," 163–64; and Ayala and Bernabe, *Puerto Rico in the American Century*, 143–44.

8. Anderson, *Imagined Communities*, 139–40.

9. Mallon, *Peasant and Nation*, 4, 6, 9–10.

10. Bayrón Toro, *Elecciones y partidos políticos de Puerto Rico*, 216–17, 225–28, 231–35, 245–52, 261–69.

11. Dávila, *Sponsored Identities*, xii, 1, 207, 258

12. Tugwell, *The Art of Politics*, 66–67.

13. Trías Monge, *Trials of the Oldest Colony*, 120–24.

BIBLIOGRAPHY

Archives/Manuscripts

AFLMM. Archivo Fundación Luís Muñoz Marín, Hato Rey PR. Serie 9: Gobernador de Puerto Rico, 1949–64, Sección V: Artículos, Discursos, Mensajes, Declaraciones.

AGPR. Archivo General de Puerto Rico, San Juan PR. Fondo: Oficina del Gobernador, Serie: Correspondencia General.

CIHPC. Centro de Investigaciones Históricas Proyecto Caribeño, Universidad de Puerto Rico, Río Piedras Campus
- Selected Documents of the Bureau of Insular Affairs
- Selected Documents of the U.S. Department of War
- U.S. Army Intelligence Reports on Subversive Activity in Puerto Rico
- Puerto Rico National Guard Annual Reports

CPUPRM. Colección Puertorriqueña, Universidad de Puerto Rico, Mayagüez Campus
- Microfilm and Rare Books Collection

FBI. Federal Bureau of Investigation. Files on Puerto Rico Project. Nationalist Party of Puerto Rico S.J. 100–3. http://www.pr-secretfiles.net.

LRRP. Luis Raul Rodríguez Papers on 65th U.S. Infantry, Miami FL

NARA. National Archives and Records Administration, Washington DC
- Guide to Federal Records. http://www.archives.gov/research/guide-fed-records/groups/350.htm; Records of the Office of the Secretary of the Interior. Record Group 350
- http://newdeal.feri.org/texts/578.htm: Information Research Section, Facts about Puerto Rico Reconstruction Administration
- Center for Electronic Records. http://www.nara.gov/nara/electronic/homensx.html
- State-Level Lists of Casualties from the Korean and Vietnam Conflicts. Record Group 330
- Modern Military Records Branch, Army-AG

Command Reports, 1949–54. Record Group 407.
Puerto Rico National Guard Museum, San Juan PR
TPML. Truman Presidential Museum and Library, Independence, MO
    Harry S. Truman Papers
    Staff Members and Office Files: White House Press Release Files, 1945–53. http://www.trumanlibrary.org/hstpaper/presshst.htm.
UMAMC. University of Massachusetts, Amherst
    W.E.B. Du Bois Library Microfilm Collection, Bureau of Insular Affairs and Insular Affairs Committee Congressional Hearings

Published Works

Acosta, Ernest. *The Puerto Rican U.S. Army 65th Infantry Regiment*. Montgomery MD: S.1 Regt. Recognition Committee, 1996.

Ai Camp, Roderic. *Generals in the Palacio: The Military in Modern Mexico*. New York: Oxford University Press, 1992.

Álvarez Curbelo, Silvia. "La bandera en la colina: Luis Muñoz Marín en los tiempos de la guerra de Corea." In *Luis Muñoz Marín, perfiles de su gobernación, 1948–1964*, ed. Fernando Picó, 1–19. San Juan: Fundación Luis Muñoz Marín, 2003.

Anderson, Benedict. *Imagined Communities: Reflections on the Origin and Spread of Nationalism*. Rev. ed. London: Verso, 2002.

Anna, Timothy E. *Spain and the Loss of America*. Lincoln: University of Nebraska Press, 1983.

Appleman, Roy B. *U.S. Army in the Korean War: South to the Naktong, North to the Yalu*. Washington DC: Office of the Chief of Military History, 1966.

Ashford, Bailey K. *A Soldier in Science: The Autobiography of Bailey K. Ashford*. 1934. San Juan: Editorial de la Universidad de Puerto Rico, 1998.

Ayala, César J. *American Sugar Kingdom: The Plantation Economy of the Spanish Caribbean, 1898–1934*. Chapel Hill: University of North Carolina Press, 1999.

Ayala, César J., and Rafael Bernabe. *Puerto Rico in the American Century: A History since 1898*. Chapel Hill: University of North Carolina Press, 2007.

Ayala, César J., and José L. Bolívar. *Battleship Vieques: Puerto Rico from World War II to the Korean War*. Princeton NJ: Markus Wiener, 2011.

Baralt, Guillermo A. *Esclavos rebeldes: conspiraciones y sublevaciones de esclavos en Puerto Rico, 1795–1873*. Río Piedras: Ediciones Huracán, 1988.

Barreto, Roberto. "'Appurtenant and belonging . . . but not a part of': ¿Por qué el gobierno de los Estados Unidos le negó a los puertorriqueños el derecho al gobierno propio?" In *1898: Enfoques y perspectivas: Simposio Internacional de Historiadores, Cuba, España, Estados Unidos, Filipinas y Puerto Rico*, ed. Luis E González Vales, 447–63. San Juan: Academia Puertorriqueña de la Historia, First Book Publishing of Puerto Rico, 1997.

Bayrón Toro, Fernando. *Elecciones y partidos políticos de Puerto Rico, 1809–2000.* Rev. ed. Mayagüez: Editorial Isla, 2000.

Bederman, Gail. *Manliness and Civilization: A Cultural History of Gender and Race in the United States, 1880–1917.* (Women in Culture and Society) Chicago: University of Chicago Press, 1996.

Beisner, Robert L. *From the Old Diplomacy to the New, 1865–1900.* 2nd ed. Arlington Heights IL: Harlan Davidson, 1985.

Bergard, Laird W. *Coffee and the Growth of Agrarian Capitalism in Nineteenth-Century Puerto Rico.* Princeton: Princeton University Press, 1983.

———. "Toward Puerto Rico's Grito de Lares: Coffee, Social Stratification, and Class Conflicts, 1828–1868." *Hispanic American Historical Review* 60, no. 4 (November 1980): 617–42.

Bernabe, Rafael. *Respuestas al colonialismo en la política puertorriqueña: 1899–1929.* Río Piedras: Edicciones Huracán, 1996.

Blair, Clay. *The Forgotten War: America in Korea, 1950–1953.* New York: Times Books, 1987.

Bolívar Fresneda, José L. "La economía de Puerto Rico durante la Segunda Guerra Mundial: ¿Capitalismo estatal o economía militar?" *Op.Cit.*, no. 18 (2007–8): 205–57.

———. "Las inversiones y los programas militares: construyendo la infraestructura y los recursos humanos de la posguerra." In *Puerto Rico en la Segunda Guerra Mundial: Baluarte del Caribe*, ed. Jorge Rodríguez Beruff and José L. Bolívar Fresneda, 2nd ed. San Juan: Ediciones Callejón, 2015.

Briggs, Laura. *Reproducing Empire: Race, Sex Science, and U.S. Imperialism in Puerto Rico.* Berkeley: University of California Press, 2002.

Burk, James. "Citizenship Status and Military Service: The Quest for Inclusion by Minorities and Conscientious Objectors." *Armed Forces and Society* 21, no. 4 (1995): 503–29.

Butler, John Sibley. "African Americans in the Military." In *The Oxford Companion to American Military History.* New York: Oxford University Press, 1999.

Campbell, Michael. "Imperialismo sin un imperio colonial": Misioneros protestantes en Puerto Rico, 1898–1914." In *El impacto de 1898 en el oeste puertorriqueño.* Cuadernos del 98 # 12. San Juan: Librería Editorial Ateneo, 1998–99.

Camuñas-Madera, Ricardo. *Desplazamiento y revolución en el Puerto Rico del siglo XIX.* San Juan: Instituto de Cultura Puertorriqueña, 2000.

Carroll, Henry K. *Report on the Island of Puerto Rico.* Washington: Government Printing Office, 1899.

Childs, Matt D. *The 1812 Aponte Rebellion in Cuba and the Struggle against Atlantic Slavery.* Chapel Hill: University of North Carolina Press, 2009.

Chinea, Jorge Luis. *Race and Labor in the Hispanic Caribbean: The West Indian Immigrant Worker Experience in Puerto Rico, 1800–1850.* Gainesville: University Press of Florida, 2005.

Cifre de Loubriel, Estela. *Catalogo de extranjeros residentes en Puerto Rico en el siglo XIX*. Río Piedras: Ediciones de la Universidad de Puerto Rico, 1962.

———. *La inmigración a Puerto Rico durante el siglo XIX*. San Juan: Instituto de Cultura Puertorriqueña, 1964.

Clark, Truman R. *Puerto Rico and the United States, 1917–1933*. Pittsburgh: University of Pittsburgh Press, 1975.

Conn, Stetson, Rose C. Engelman, and Byron Fairchild. *Guarding the United States and Its Outposts*. Washington DC: Center of Military History, U.S. Army, 2000. http://www.army.mil/cmh-pg/books/wwii/Guard-US/index.htm.

Conn, Stetson, and Byron Fairchild. *The Framework of Hemisphere Defense: United States Army in World War II: The Western Hemisphere*. Washington DC: Center of Military History, U.S. Army, 1989. Available from http://www.army.mil/cmh-pg/books/wwii/Framework/index.htm.

Cruz Monclova, Lidio. *El Grito de Lares*. San Juan: Instituto de Cultura Puertorriqueña, 1968.

———, ed. *Obras Completas de Luis Muñoz Rivera, 1890–1900: Introducción, notas y recopilación del Dr. Lidio Cruz Monclova*. San Juan: Instituto de Cultura Puertorriqueña, 1963.

Cubano Iguina, Astrid. "Criollos ante el 98: La cambiante imagen del dominio español durante su crisis y caida en Puerto Rico, 1889–1899." Trabajo escrito para el congreso de LASA, Guadalajara, Mexico (April 17–19, 1997), 2–3.

———. "Política radical y autonomismo en Puerto Rico: conflictos de intereses en la formación del Partido Autonomista Puertorriqueño (1887)." *Anuario de Estudios Americanos* (Tomo 1.1. núm. 2. 1994, 155–73), 155–57.

Dalfiume, Richard M. *Desegregation of the U.S. Forces: Fighting on Two Fronts, 1939–1953*. Columbia: University of Missouri Press, 1969.

Dallek, Robert. *Franklin D. Roosevelt and American Foreign Policy, 1932–1945*. New York: Oxford University Press, 1995.

Darragh, Shaun M. "The Puerto Rican Military Forces." *Military Review* 58 (August 1978): 46–53.

Dávila, Arlene M. *Sponsored Identities: Cultural Politics in Puerto Rico*. Philadelphia: Temple University Press, 1997.

del Moral, Solsiree. *Negotiating Empire: The Cultural Politics of Schools in Puerto Rico, 1898–1952*. Madison: University of Wisconsin Press, 2013.

Departamento de la Guerra: Dirección del Censo de Puerto Rico. *Informe sobre el Censo de Puerto Rico, 1899*. 1899. San Juan: Academia Puertorriqueña de la Historia, 2003.

Díaz Soler, Luis M. *Puerto Rico, sus luchas por alcanzar estabilidad económica, estabilidad política y afirmación cultural, 1898–1996*. Isabela: Isabela Printing, 1998.

Dietz, James L. *Economic History of Puerto Rico: Institutional Change and Development*. Princeton NJ: Princeton University Press, 1986.

Dolcater, Max W., ed. *3rd Infantry Division in Korea*. Tokyo: Toppan Printing, 1953.

Domínguez, Jorge I. *Insurrection or Loyalty: The Breakdown of the Spanish American Empire*. Cambridge: Harvard University Press, 1980.

Dorsey, Joseph C. *Slave Traffic in the Age of Abolition: Puerto Rico, West Africa, and the Non-Hispanic Caribbean, 1815–1859*. Gainesville: University Press of Florida, 2003.

Duffy Burnett, Christina, and Burke Marshall, eds. *Foreign in a Domestic Sense: Puerto Rico American Expansion and the Constitution*. Durham: Duke University Press, 2001.

Eisenhower, John S. D. *Strictly Personal*. Garden City NY: Doubleday, 1974.

Enamorado Cuesta, Jose. *Porto Rico, Past and Present*. 1929. New York: Arno Press, 1975.

Estades Font, María E. *La presencia militar de Estados Unidos en Puerto Rico: 1898–1918*. Río Piedras: Editorial Universitaria, Universidad de Puerto Rico, 1986.

Fernós López-Cepero, Antonio, ed. *Documentos Históricos-Constitucionales de Puerto Rico*. 2nd ed. San Juan: Ediciones Situm, 2005.

Ferrao, Luis Ángel. *Pedro Albizu Campos y el nacionalismo puertorriqueño, 1930–1939*. San Juan: Editorial Cultural, 1990.

Ferrer, Ada. *Insurgent Cuba: Race, Nation, and Revolution, 1868–1898*. Chapel Hill: University of North Carolina Press, c1999.

———. "Rustic Men, Civilized Nation: Race, Culture, and Contention on the Eve of Cuban Independence." *Hispanic American Historical Review* 78, no. 4 (November 1998): 663–86.

Figueroa, Luis A. *Sugar, Slavery, and Freedom in Nineteenth-Century Puerto Rico*. Chapel Hill: University of North Carolina Press, and San Juan: University of Puerto Rico Press, 2005.

Figuroa-Soulet, Noemi. *The Borinqueneers*. Crompond NY: El Pozo, 2008.

Fith, J. Samuel. *The Armed Forces and Democracy in Latin America*. Baltimore: Johns Hopkins University Press, 1998.

Foner, Jack D. *Blacks and the Military in American History*. New York: Praeger, 1974.

Ford, Worthington Chauncey. *The Writings of John Quincy Adams*. New York: Greenwood Press, 1968.

Franqui-Rivera, Harry. "Fighting for the Nation: Military Service, Popular Political Mobilization, and the Creation of Modern Puerto Rican National Identities: 1868–1952." PhD diss., University of Massachusetts, Amherst, 2010.

———. "Glory and Shame: The Ordeal of the Puerto Rican 65th U.S. Infantry Regiment during the Korean War, 1950–1953." Master's thesis, Temple University, 2002.

———. "National Mythologies: U.S. Citizenship for the People of Puerto Rico and Military Service." *Memorias: Revista Digital de Historia y Arqueología desde el Caribe* 10, no. 21 (September–December 2013): 5–21.

———. "'A New Day Has Dawned for Porto Rico's Jíbaro': Manhood, Race, Military Service, and Self-Government during World War I." *Latino Studies* 13, no. 2 (2015): 185–206.

———. "Puerto Rican Veterans and Service Members' Well-Being and Place within the Diaspora." In *Puerto Ricans at the Dawn of the New Millennium*, ed. Edwin Meléndez and Carlos Vargas-Ramos, 182–208. New York: Centro Press, 2014.

Fredrickson, George M. *Racism: A Short History*. Princeton: Princeton University Press, 2002.

García Muñiz, Humberto. "El Caribe durante la Segunda Guerra Mundial: El Mediterráneo Americano." In *Puerto Rico en las relaciones internacionales del Caribe*. Río Piedras: Ediciones Huracán, 1990.

García Ochoa, María Asunción. *La política española en Puerto rico durante el siglo XIX*. Río Piedras: Editorial Universidad de Puerto Rico, 1982.

Gautier Dapena, José A. *Trayectoria del pensamiento liberal puertorriqueño en el siglo XIX*. San Juan: Instituto de Cultura Puertorriqueña, 1975.

Géigel Polanco, Vicente. *El Grito de Lares: gesta de heroísmo y sacrificio*. Río Piedras: Editorial Antillana, 1976.

Gilbert, Martin. *The First World War: A Complete History*. New York: Henry Holt, 1994.

Go, Julian. "Chains of Empire, Projects of State: Political Education and U.S. Colonial Rule in Puerto Rico and the Philippines." *Comparative Studies in Society and History* 42, no. 2 (April 2000): 333–62.

Gould, Lewis L. *The Spanish-American War and President McKinley*. Lawrence: University Press of Kansas, 1982.

Government Printing Office. *Report of the Military Governor of Porto Rico on Civil Affairs*. 1902. San Juan: Academia Puertorriqueña de la Historia, Ediciones Puerto, 2003.

———. *Selective Service Regulations: Selective Service Act of 1917*. https://archive.org/details/cu31924020164152

Graff, Henry F., ed. "American Imperialism and the Philippine Insurrection." In *Testimony of the Times: Selections from Congressional Hearings*. Boston: Little, Brown, 1969.

Gribbin, William. "A Matter of Faith: North America's Religion and South America's Independence." *Americas* 31, no. 4 (April 1975): 470–87.

Guerra, Lilian. *Popular Expression and National Identity in Puerto Rico: The Struggle for Self, Community, and Nation*. Gainesville: University Press of Florida, 1998.

Harris, W. W. *Puerto Rico's Fighting 65th U.S. Infantry: From San Juan to Chorwan*. San Rafael CA: Presidio Press, 1980.

Hawkins, Michael C. *Making Moros: Imperial Historicism and American Military Rule in the Philippines' Muslim South*. DeKalb: Northern Illinois University Press, 2013.

Hermes, Walter G. *U.S. Army in the Korean War: Truce, Tent, and Fighting Front.* Washington DC: Office of the Chief of Military History, 1966.
Herwig, Holger. *Politics of Frustration: The United States in German Naval Planning, 1889–1941.* Boston: Little, Brown, 1976.
Hoganson, Kristin. *Fighting for American Manhood: How Gender Politics Provoked the Spanish-American and Philippine-American Wars.* New Haven CT: Yale University Press, 1998.
Holden, Robert H. *Armies without Nations: Public Violence and State Formation in Central America, 1821–1960.* New York: Oxford University Press, 2004.
Hostos, Eugenio María de. *Los rostros del camino: Antología.* San Juan: Instituto de Cultura Puertorriqueña, Programa de Publicaciones y Grabaciones, 1995.
Jiménez de Wagenheim, Olga. *El grito de Lares, sus causas y sus hombres.* Río Piedras: Ediciones Huracán, 1999.
Johnson, John J. *Latin America in Caricature.* Austin: University of Texas Press, 1980.
Kaplan, Amy. "Black and Blue on San Juan Hill." In *Cultures of United States Imperialism*, ed. Amy Kaplan and D. E. Pease, 219–36. Durham NC: Duke University Press, 1993.
Kinsbruner, Jay. *Independence in Spanish America: Civil Wars, Revolutions, and Underdevelopment.* Albuquerque: University of New Mexico Press, 2000.
———. *Not of Pure Blood: Free People of Color and Racial Prejudices in Nineteenth-Century Puerto Rico.* Durham: Duke University Press, 1996.
Knock, Thomas J. *To End All Wars: Woodrow Wilson and the Quest for a New World Order.* Princeton: Princeton University Press, 1992.
LaFeber, Walter. *The New Empire: An Interpretation of American Expansion, 1860–1898.* Ithaca NY: Cornell University Press, 1963.
Lefebvre, Andrew. "Puerto Rico: Quiet Participant." In *Latin America during World War II.* Lanham MD: Rowman & Littlefield, 2007.
Langley, Lester. *The Banana Wars: An Inner History of American Empire, 1900–1934.* Lexington: University Press of Kentucky, 1983.
———. *The United States and the Caribbean, 1900–1970.* Athens: University of Georgia Press, 1980.
Levy, Teresita. *Puerto Ricans in the Empire: Tobacco Growers and U.S. Colonialism.* New Brunswick NJ: Rutgers University Press, 2014.
Liss, Peggy K. *Atlantic Empires: The Network of Trade and Revolution, 1713–1826.* Baltimore: Johns Hopkins University Press, 1983.
López Alves, Fernando. *State Formation and Democracy in Latin America, 1810–1900.* Durham: Duke University Press, 2000.
López Baralt, José. *The Policy of the United States towards Its Territories with Special Reference to Puerto Rico.* San Juan: Editorial de la Universidad de Puerto Rico, 1999.
Loveman, Brian, and Thomas M. Davies Jr., eds. *The Politics of Antipolitics: The Military in Latin America.* Lincoln: University of Nebraska Press, 1989.

Luque de Sánchez, María D. *La ocupación norteamericana y la ley Fóraker: 1898–1904*. Río Piedras: Edicciones Huracán, 1986.

Lynch, John. *The Spanish-American Revolutions, 1808–1826: A Unified Account of the Revolutions That Swept over South America and Central America in the Early Nineteenth Century*. 2nd ed. New York: W. W. Norton, 1986.

Mahan, Alfred Thayer. *Influence of Sea Power upon History, 1660–1783*. Boston: Little, Brown, 1890.

———. *Lessons of the War with Spain and Other Articles*. Freeport NY: Books for Libraries Press, 1970.

———. *Naval Strategy: Compared and Contrasted with the Principles and Practice of Military Operation on Land. Lectures Delivered at the U.S. Naval War College, Newport, R.I. between the Years 1887 and 1911*. Boston: Little, Brown, 1911.

———. *The Panama Canal and Sea Power in the Pacific: An Original Study in Naval Strategy*. Albuquerque: American Classical College Press, 1911.

———. "The Relations of the United States to Their New Dependencies." In *Lessons of the War with Spain and Other Articles*, by Alfred Thayer Mahan, 245–50. Freeport NY: Books for Libraries Press, 1970.

Maldonado, A. W. *Luis Muñoz Marín: Puerto Rico's Democratic Revolution*. San Juan: La Editorial Universidad de Puerto Rico, 2006.

Mallon, Florencia. *Peasant and Nation: The Making of Postcolonial Mexico and Peru*. Berkeley: University of California Press, 1995.

Manders, Eric I., and Edward S. Milligan. "65th Infantry Regiment, The Borinqueneers." *Military Collector and Historian* 47 (Spring 1995): 38–39.

Marín Román, Héctor R. *¡A la vuelta de la esquina! El Caribe camino a la Segunda Guerra Mundial, 1938 a 1941*. Río Piedras: Publicaciones Gaviota, 2014.

———. *El caldero quemaó: El contexto social-militar estadounidense en Puerto Rico y otros lugares del Caribe durante el periodo Entre-Guerras, 1919–1938*. Río Piedras: Publicaciones Gaviota, 2012.

———. *¡Llegó la gringada! El contexto social-militar estadounidense en Puerto Rico y otros lugares del Caribe hasta 1919*. San Juan: Academia Puertorriqueña de la Historia, 2009.

Martínez Cruzado, Juan C. "The Use of Mitochondrial DNA to Discover Pre-Columbian Migrations to the Caribbean: Results for Puerto Rico and Expectations for the Dominican Republic." *KACIKE: Journal of Caribbean Amerindian History and Anthropology*, 2002.

Marx, Anthony. *Faith in Nation: Exclusionary Origins of Nationalism*. New York: Oxford University Press, 2003.

———. *Making Race and Nation: A Comparison of the United States, South Africa, and Brazil*. Cambridge: Cambridge University Press, 1998.

Mathews, Thomas. *La política puertorriqueña y el Nuevo Trato*. 3rd ed. Translated by Antonio J. Colorado. San Juan: La Editorial Universidad de Puerto Rico, 2007.

McGregor, Morris J. *Integration of the Armed Forces, 1940–1965*. Washington DC: Center of Military History, 1981.

Meléndez, Edgardo. *Movimiento anexionista en Puerto Rico*. Río Piedras: Editorial de la Universidad de Puerto Rico, 1993.

Morales Carrión, Arturo. *Puerto Rico y la lucha por la hegemonía en el Caribe: Colonialismo y contrabando, siglos XVI–XVIII*. Río Piedras: Editorial Universidad de Puerto Rico, Centro de Investigaciones Históricas: Colección Caribeña, 1995.

Moraza Ortíz, Manuel E. *La masacre de Ponce*. Hato Rey: Publicaciones Puertorriqueñas, 2001.

Morris, Nancy. *Puerto Rico: Culture, Politics, and Identity*. Westport CT: Praeger, 1995.

Moskos, Charles. "From Citizens' Army to Social Laboratory." *Wilson Quarterly* 17, no. 1 (1993): 83–94.

Mossman, Billy C. *U.S. Army in the Korean War: Ebb and Flow, November 1950–July 1951*. Washington DC: Center of Military History, 1990.

Moya Pons, Frank. *The Dominican Republic: A National History*. Princeton NJ: Markus Wiener, 1998.

Muñoz Marín, Luis. *Discursos*. Vol. 1: *1934–1948*. San Juan: Fundación Luis Muñoz Marín, 1999.

Muñoz Rivera, Manuel. *¿Hacia donde heroes?* New York: Azteca Press, 1948.

Muratti, Jose A. *History of the 65th Infantry, 1899–1946*. Microfilm. San Juan: U.S. Army Forces Antilles, 1946. U.S Army Military History Institute, Carlisle Barracks, Pennsylvania.

———. *History of the 65th Infantry Regiment: The Borinqueneers*. San Juan: U.S. Army Forces Antilles, 1953. Microfilm. U.S Army Military History Institute, Carlisle Barracks, PA.

Nadal, José R. *Guardia Nacional, sucesora de las milicias puertorriqueñas*. Santurce: Talleres Adria Luisa Monserrate, 1962.

Navarro Rivera, Pablo. *Universidad de Puerto Rico: De control político a crisis permanente, 1903–1952*. Río Piedras: Ediciones Huracán, 2000.

Negrón de Montilla, Aida. *La americanización de Puerto Rico y el sistema de instrucción pública, 1900–1930*. 2nd ed. San Juan: Editorial de la Universidad de Puerto Rico, 1990.

Negroni, Héctor Andrés. *Historia militar de Puerto Rico: en conmemoración del encuentro de dos mundos*. España: Ediciones Siruela S.A., 1992.

———. "Hostos y su pensamiento militar." *Journal of Inter-American Studies* 11, no. 2 (April 1969): 272–85.

Norat Martínez, José, ed. *Historia del Regimiento 65 de Infantería, 1899–1960*. San Juan: La Milagrosa, 1960.

Nye, Robert A. *Masculinity and Male Codes of Honor in Modern France*. Berkeley: University of California Press, 1998.

O'Brien, Philip, and Paul Cammack, eds. *Generals in Retreat: The Crisis of Military Rule in Latin America*. Manchester: Manchester University Press, 1985.

Office of the Chief of Military History. *The Army Lineage Book*. Vol. 2: *Infantry*. Washington DC: Office of the Chief of Military History, 1953.

Ojeda Reyes, Felix. *Vitto Marcantonio y Puerto Rico: Por los trabajadores y por la nación*. Río Piedras: Ediciones Huracán, 1978.
Padrón, Antonio E. *El 65 en revista*. New York: Las Americas, 1961.
Pagán, Bolívar. *Historia de los Partidos Políticos Puertorriqueños (1898–1956)*. Vol. 1. San Juan: Academia Puertorriqueña de la Historia, 1972.
Paralitici, Ché. *No quiero mi cuerpo pa' tambor: El servicio militar obligatorio en Puerto Rico*. San Juan: Ediciones Puerto, 1998.
Pérez, Louis, Jr. *The War of 1898: The United States and Cuba in History and Historiography*. Chapel Hill: University of North Carolina Press, 1998.
Picó, Fernando. *1898: La guerra después de la Guerra*. Río Piedras: Ediciones Huracán, 1987.
Potash, Robert A. *The Army and Politics in Argentina*. Stanford: Stanford University Press, 1969–96.
Raffucci de García, Carmen I. *El gobierno civíl y la ley Fóraker: antecedentes históricos*. Río Piedras: Editorial Universitaria, Universidad de Puerto Rico, 1981.
Ramírez, José A. *To the Line of Fire! Mexican Texans and World War I*. College Station: Texas A&M University Press, 2009.
Rivera Ramos, Efrén. *The Legal Construction of Identity: The Judicial and Social Legacy of American Colonialism in Puerto Rico*. Washington DC: American Psychological Association, 2001.
Rivero, Ángel. *Crónica de la Guerra Hispanoamericana en Puerto Rico por Ángel Rivero, Capitán de Artillería*. Madrid: Imprenta de los sucesores de Rivadeneyra, 1922.
Rodríguez Beruff, Jorge. "El Caribe durante la Segunda Guerra Mundial: El Mediterráneo Americano." In *Puerto Rico en las relaciones internacionales del Caribe*. Río Piedras: Ediciones Huracán, 1990.
———. "La pugna entre dos grandes sistemas: la guerra en el discurso político de Luis Muñoz Marín hasta Pearl Harbor." In *Puerto Rico en la Segunda Guerra Mundial: baluarte del Caribe*, ed. Jorge Rodríguez Beruff, and, José L. Bolívar Fresneda, 49–71. San Juan: Ediciones Callejón, 2012.
———. "Luis Muñoz Marín y Rafael Leónidas Trujillo: Una pugna caribeña (1941–1961)." In *Luis Muñoz Marín, perfiles de su gobernación, 1948–1964*, ed. Fernando Picó, 21–61. San Juan: Fundación Luis Muñoz Marín, 2003.
———. *Strategy as Politics: Puerto Rico on the Eve of the Second World War*. San Juan: La Editorial Universidad de Puerto Rico, 2007.
Rodríguez Cancel, Jaime L. *La Guerra Fría y el sexenio de la puertorriqueñidad: Afirmación nacional y políticas culturales*. San Juan: Ediciones Puerto, 2007.
Rodó, José Enrique. *Ariel: Breviario de la Juventud*. Valencia: Editorial Cervantes, 1920.
Rosa-Vélez, Sonia M. "Acquiring the American Spirit: Americanization through Education and the Puerto Ricans in the U.S. Government Minority Boarding Schools, 1899–1930." Forthcoming.
———. "The Puerto Ricans at Carlisle Indian School: An Experiment in Americanization through Education." Forthcoming.

———. "¿Qué pasó con los becados? La saga de los estudiantes puertorriqueños en la Escuela Industrial para Indios de Carlisle." Forthcoming.
Rosario Natal, Carmelo. *Luis Muñoz Marín y la independencia de Puerto Rico, 1907–1946*. San Juan: Producciones Históricas, 1994.
———. "Muñoz y Albizu: el choque en la víspera de la insurrección." In *Luis Muñoz Marín, perfiles de su gobernación, 1948–1964*, ed. Fernando Picó, 309–41. San Juan: Fundación Luis Muñoz Marín, 2003.
———. *Puerto Rico y la crisis de la Guerra hispanoamericana (1895–1898)*. San Juan: Editorial Edil, 1989.
Ross, Tenny. "El Ejercito en Puerto Rico." In *El Libro de Puerto Rico*, ed. Eugenio Fernández y García. San Juan: El Libro Azul, 1923.Rouquié, Alain. *The Military and the State in Latin America*. Berkeley: University of California Press, 1987.
Santiago Valles, Kelvin A. *"Subject People" and Colonial Discourses: Economic Transformation and Social Disorder in Puerto Rico, 1898–1947*. Albany: State University of New York, 1994.
Scarano, Francisco A. "The Jíbaro Masquerade and the Subaltern Politics of Creole Identity Formation in Puerto Rico, 1745–1823." *American Historical Review* 101, no. 5 (December 1996): 1398–1431.
Seijo Bruno, Miñi. *La insurrección nacionalista en Puerto Rico, 1950*. San Juan: Editorial Edíl, 1997.
Shaw, Albert, ed. "Puerto Rico under Dr. Yager: Citizenship in the New Bill." *American Review of Reviews: An International Magazine* 49, no. 1 (April 1914): 399–400.
Sinha, Mrinalini. *Colonial Masculinity: The 'Manly Englishman' and the 'Effeminate Bengali' in the Late Nineteenth Century*. Manchester University Press, 1995.Stepan, Alfred. *The Military in Politics: Changing Patterns in Brazil*. Princeton: Princeton University Press, 1971.
Stephanson, Anders. *Manifest Destiny: American Expansionism and the Empire of Right*. New York: Hill and Wang, 1995.
Suárez Findlay, Eileen J.. *Imposing Decency: The Politics of Sexuality and Race in Puerto Rico, 1870–1920*. Durham NC: Duke University Press, 2000.
———. *We Are Left without a Father Here: Masculinity, Domesticity, and Migration in Postwar Puerto Rico*. Durham NC: Duke University Press, 2014.
Tischler, Barbara L. "One Hundred Percent Americanism and Music in Boston during World War I." *American Music* 4, no. 2 (Summer 1986): 164–76.
Torres González, Roamé. *Idioma, bilingüismo y nacionalidad: La presencia del inglés en Puerto Rico*. Río Piedras: Editorial de la Universidad de Puerto Rico, 2002.
Trask, David F. *The War with Spain in 1898*. Lincoln: University of Nebraska Press, 1996.
Triandafyllidou, Anna. "National Identity and the 'Other.'" *Ethnic and Racial Studies* 21, no. 4 (July 1998): 593–612.
Trías Monge, José. *Puerto Rico: The Trials of the Oldest Colony in the World*. New Haven: Yale University Press, 1997.

Tugwell, Rexford G. *The Art of Politics as Practiced by Three Great Americans: Franklin Delano Roosevelt, Luis Muñoz Marín, and Fiorello H. La Guardia*. Garden City NY: Doubleday, 1958.

———. *Changing the Colonial Climate*. New York: Arno Press and the New York Times, 1970.

———. *The Stricken Island: The Story of Puerto Rico*. New York: Greenwood, 1968.

U.S. Army Forces Antilles. *The 65th Infantry Regiment, the Puerto Rican Regiment*. San Juan: 1952.

Valle Atiles, Francisco del. *El campesino puertorriqueño, sus condiciones físicas, intelectuales y morales, causas que las determinan y medios para mejorarlas por Francisco del Valle Atiles, Doctor en Medicina y Cirujía*. San Juan: Tipografía de José González Font, 1887.

Vega, Francisco J. "La situación de las Iglesias en Mayagüez en torno a 1898." In *El impacto de 1898 en el oeste puertorriqueño*, ed. Ricardo R. Camuñas Madera, Cuadernos del 98 #12. San Juan: Librería Editorial Ateneo, 1998–99.

Villahermosa, Gilberto N. "From Glory to Disaster and Back." *Army Magazine*, September 2001, 81–84.

———. *Honor and Fidelity: The 65th Infantry in Korea, 1950–1953*. Washington DC: U.S. Army Center for Military History, 2009.

Wagenheim, Kal, and Olga Jiménez de Wagenheim, eds. *The Puerto Ricans: A Documentary History*. Rev. ed. Princeton NJ: Markus Wiener, 2002.

Walthall, Melvin Curtis. *We Can't All Be Heroes: A History of the Separate Infantry Regiments in World War II*. Hicksville NY: Exposition Press, 1975.

Wells, Henry. "La modernización de Puerto Rico: La política y los valores." In *Del cañaveral a la fábrica: cambio social en Puerto Rico*, ed. Eduardo Rivera Medina and Rafael L. Ramírez. Río Piedras: Ediciones Huracán-Academia, 1994.

Wintermute, Bobby A. *Public Health and the U.S. Military: A History of the Army Medical Department, 1818–1917*. New York: Routledge, 2011.

Young, Warren L. *Minorities and the Military: A Cross National Study in World Perspective*. Westport CT: Greenwood Press, 1982.

Zubok, Vladimir, and Constantine Pleshakov. *Inside the Kremlin's Cold War: From Stalin to Khrushchev*. Cambridge MA: Harvard University Press, 1996.

INDEX

Page locators in italics signify photographs.
PR = *Puerto Rico.*

Academia de Infantería, 24–25, 226nn94–96
African Americans, 69, 179; military service barred to, 216n11, 216n15; in Spanish-American War, xviii, 42; in World War I, 83. *See also* racial beliefs and discrimination
El Águila de Puerto Rico, 76, 85, 244n63, 247n114
Aguinaldo, Emilio, Jr., 245n82
Albizu Campos, Pedro, 98, 120, 122, 210; on Carta Autonómica, 103, 273n127; as electoral candidate, 103, 249n7; imprisonment of, 133, 134, 277n26; and Jayuya Uprising, 173–74, 175, 177, 276n13; and Muñoz Marín, xxviii, 173, 277n26; and Nationalist paramilitary units, 107–9; on police killings, 97, 106, 107, 248n1; and Puerto Rican national identity, 96, 99; on Riggs assassination, 112–13; sedition trial of, 114–15, 256n69, 275n9; as Sinn Fein admirer, 98, 254n48; and sugar workers, 104; threats to Insular Police by, 112, 253n37; as veteran, 98, 108, 244n63, 254n45; war against U.S. urged by, 98–99, 107, 204–5, 253n41, 275n6. *See also* Partido Nacionalista Puertorriqueño
Alfonso XII, 27
Alger, Russell A., 37
Alianza, 100, 248n4, 249n5

Alien Registration Act (Smith Act), 174, 275–76n11
Allen, Charles H., 35, 59
Almond, Edmond L., 179
Amadeo I de Saboya, 26
American Civil Liberties Union (ACLU), 114, 118, 258n85
Americanization: education as instrument for, xxiv, 47, 49, 129, 218n35; Hostos on, 54, 94, 203, 237–38n82; Matienzo Cintrón supporting, 94, 238n84; military as tool for, xxii, xxiv–xxvi, 49–50, 58, 60, 61–62, 109, 129; modernization via, 165–66, 203; during U.S. military occupation, 46–47
American League for Puerto Rico's Independence, 163
American Review of Reviews, 68–69, 242n23
Amuedo, Mariano de, 260n7
Anderson, Benedict, xxi, 204–5, 207, 245n76, 281n2
anemia, 50–52, 237n59, 249n10
Anglo Saxon/Hispanic binary, 182, 188, 190, 203, 280n58
annexationism, 61, 152, 209; in early years of U.S. rule, 40–41, 45, 231n20. *See also* statehood
Ante-American heritage, 187–88, 194
Antongiorgi, Ángel Esteban, 120
Aponte rebellion, 219n7
Arielismo, 85, 246n94
Ashford, Bailey K., 60, 61–62, 237n69, 249n12

assimilation, 25, 208; "benevolent," xxvii, 35, 46, 228n2; cultural, xxii, 49, 85, 165–66, 194; via education, 47, 49
Atlantic Charter, 264n41, 268n91
autonomism, xxii, 45; and Commonwealth formula, 158–65, 195; Muñoz Marín turning to, xxix, 161–62, 168; Muñoz Rivera on, 28, 67, 241n19; under Spanish rule, xxiii, 15, 27–29, 201, 223n54; as Unionistas' goal, 46, 85, 90, 94, 203, 234n47, 241n19
Autonomous Charter. *See* Carta Autonómica
Ayala, César, 249n8

Baker, Newton D., 77, 87
Baldorioty de Castro, Román, 27, 223n54
Bandera, Quintín, xix, 216n18
Barceló, Antonio R., 73, 74, 133, 242n36; as independence supporter, 91–92, 100; and Tydings bill, 116–17
Battalion of Porto Rican Volunteers, xx, 55, 238n85
Battle, J. S., 239n97
Beauchamp, Elías, 112, 116, 123
Bederman, Gail, xvii, 216n11
Benejam Álvarez, Pedro, 174–75
"benevolent assimilation," xxvii, 35, 46, 228n2
Bergard, Laird W., 5–6, 219n10, 220n18; on Grito de Lares, 10, 221n32
Bernabe, Rafael, 234n46, 238n84, 241n18; on U.S., 40, 45, 237n78
Betances, Ramón Emeterio, xx, 7, 23, 220n23
Betances Ramírez, Carlos, *191*
Beverly, James A., 103, 163
Bird, Esteban, 251n22
Black, Ruby, 112, 123, 140, 250n16
Blair House attack (1950), 177
Blenk, Jaimes H., 235n57
Bolívar Fresneda, José L., 130, 143, 151
"La Borinqueña," 86, 192, 197
Borinqueneers. *See* 65th Infantry
Borinquen Field, 262n17
Bourne, James R., 252n33
Boyer, Jean-Pierre, 225–26n87
Boy Scouts of America, 109

Briggs, Laura, xx, 200
British colonialism, 43, 44, 136, 267n73
Brookings Institution, 101–2, 248n2
Bureau of Insular Affairs (BIA), 63, 67; creation of, 50, 236n65; DTIP taking over role of, 105, 259–60n6; and World War I mobilization, 76, 80, 81, 244n60
Burges, John, 232n27
El Buscapié, 84–85, 91, 247n114

Cadetes de la República, 107, 108–9, 118, 254n48, 257n82
Caguas PR, *144*, 263n21
Cambon, Jules, 39
Campbell, Philip, 92
Camp Las Casas, 79–80, 84–85, 96
Camp O'Reilly, 145, 174–75, 262n17
Camp Salinas, 262n17
Camp Tortuguero, 145, 262n17
Camuñas-Madera, Ricardo, 221n32
Canales, Blanca, 175
Cancel Miranda, Rafael, 277n26
Cánovas del Castillo, Antonio, 28, 30, 228n120
capitanía general, 16, 224nn56–57
Caribbean Advisory Committee (CAC), 137
Carnegie, Andrew, 228–30n12, 230n16
El Carolina, 86, 246n97
Carta Autonómica (1897), 103, 184, 201; drafting of, 28–29, 227n109; global context of, 29–30; provisions of, 28–29, 250n20, 273n127
Catholic Church, 235n57, 260n7
Catholicism, 41, 46, 109
Cebollero, Manuel, 8, 9
Ceiba PR, 262n17, 266n59
Celso Barbosa, José, 28, 83
Cervera y Topete, Pascual, 38–39
Chamber of Delegates, 44, 45, 57, 63, 71
Chardón, Carlos, 105–6, 257n77
Chavez, Dennis, 138
Chinea, Jorge Luis, 12
cholera, 89
Christian Science Monitor, 150, 274n141, 281n6
Cifre de Loubriel, Estela, 11, 222n42
citizenship, U.S.: Foraker Act on, 44; Jones Act granting of, xxvii, 63–64,

296   *Index*

66, 68–71, 93, 94, 203–4, 242n32; pre-1917 consideration of, 66–67; statutory, 242n32
Clark, Victor S., 249n10
Cleveland, Grover, 30, 227n116
Club Damas de Puerto Rico, *147*
coffee, 4, 6, 10, 16, 57, 101
cold war, 164, 170–71
Collazo, Oscar, 177
Collins, James Lawton, 150–51
Coll y Toste, Cayetano, 54, 89–90, 223n52; on Albizu Camps, 248n3; and Puerto Rico self-rule, 91, 247n113
colonialism: "benevolent," 43, 228–29n2; British, 43, 44, 136, 267n73; Dutch, 136, 267n73; French, 19, 267n73; power relations under, xx–xxi, 200; rationalizations for, 41–44, 53; Spanish, xxiii–xxiv, 1–34, 200–201; U.S., 39, 46, 212, 215n2, 230n17
Colton, George, 67, 77, 240–41n15
Comité Revolucionario de Puerto Rico, 7, 220n21
Commonwealth formula: and Korean War participation, 180, 188; and Muñoz Marín, 170, 171, 189, 207–8; Puerto Rican soldier as embodiment of, xxvi, 157, 170, 196; support for, xv, xxv, 187. *See also* Estado Libre Asociado de Puerto Rico
"compassionate uplifting," xxvii, 35–36
conscription: during Korean War, 279n54; during World War I, 69–70, 72; during World War II, 145, 266n65, 268n82
conservatives, 5, 22, 23, 227nn109–10; electoral participation of, 26, 27, 29, 227n114; opposition to independence from Spain, 12–13
Constitution of Cadiz (1812), 21–22
Constitution of the Commonwealth of Puerto Rico, 188–90, 212
Cordero Dávila, Juan César, 169, 190, *192*, 194, 271–72n113
Córdova Dávila, Félix, 74, 81, 91, 92, 249n5; and Puerto Rico military units, 77, 79, 80, 244n73

Corozal PR, xiv, 215n3
La Correspondencia, 241n19
Corretjer, Juan Antonio, 10, 221n37, 256n69, 263n21
Cortes, Spanish, 23, 26, 227n102
Craig, Clayton C., *192*
Crawford, Fred L., 163, 273n127
Creel, George, 243nn56–57
criollization, xxiv–xxv, 206, 208; of nation building, 199–200, 204
criollos: and autonomism, 15, 223n54; class interests of, 4, 6, 10, 32, 219n10; and Grito de Lares, 10, 221n32; *peninsulares*' relationship with, xxiii, 2, 4, 33, 218n32, 219n10, 219–20n13; and Spanish cultural legacy, 15, 223n52; struggle against *peninsulares* by, 6, 13–14, 221n32; as term, 217–18n31; and U.S. occupation, 34, 336
Cuba: final independence war in, xviii, 13, 30, 42–43, 216n18, 223n50, 228n120, 230n18; and race, xviii, xix, 13, 42–43, 223n50; Ten Years' War and Little War in, 7, 13; U.S. policy toward, 30–31, 227–28n116, 228n121, 230n50
Cubano Iguina, Astrid, 218n31, 223n52, 223n54
Cuerpo de Voluntarios Distinguidos, 21, 22
Culebra, 132, 262n17
cunerismo, 26, 27

Dabán, Juan, 224n66
Dasher, Charles L., *192*
Daughan, Donald A., 114
Dávila, Arlene, 11, 211, 212
Davis, George W., 54, 55, 58
decolonization, 95, 127–31; and Korean War participation, xv, 168, 180–82, 184, 188–90, 194–96, 211; and Muñoz Marín, xxv, 124, 125, 145, 160–61, 164, 189, 212–13; reports to United Nations on, 189, 212–13; Truman support for, 164, 170–71
Degetau, Federico, 227n109
de Haas, Louis J., 229n5
del Moral, Solsiree, 49, 65, 218n35, 247n119
La Democracia, 101

Index 297

Department of Education, 49, 155–56
Department of the Interior, 115; Puerto Rico placed under control of, 50, 105, 128, 259–60n6; support for Puerto Rico home rule by, 161, 164, 272n120
Dewey, George, 38–39
Dickinson, Jacob McGavock, 240n13
Diego, José de, 74, 91, 119, 241n22
Dietz, James L., 10, 221n32, 221n35, 265–66n56
El Diluvio, 82–83, 88, 89, 247n106
Division of Territories and Island Possessions (DTIP), 105, 252n31, 259–60n6
Domenech, Manuel V., 243n53
Dominican rebellion of 1861, 22–23, 225–26n87
Dorsey, Joseph C., 12, 222n43
Downes v. Bidwell, 233n41
Du Bois, W. E. B., 83
Dulaney, Rovert L., *192*
Dutch colonialism, 136, 267n73

economy: during Great Depression, 95, 97, 101–2, 249–50n14, 268n84; during Korean War, 183; and salary of soldiers, 151; under Spanish colonialism, 4, 16; and state-owned factories, 143, 260–61n9, 265n54; women in, 249–50n14; during World War II, 130, 141–43, 260–61n9, 265n54
education: English as language of instruction in, 47, 49, 234n44, 235n59; military, 24–25, 226nn94–96; public, xxiv, 49, 60–61, 202, 218n33, 235n58; as vehicle for Americanization, xxiv, 47, 49, 129, 218n35; vocational training, 95, *154*, 155–57, 203, 270n102
Ejército Libertador, 107, 108–9, 111; and Jayuya Uprising, 173, 174–75
Ejército Revolucionario, 8–9
elections: of 1871, 26, 226n99; of 1872, 26; of 1876, 27; of 1891, 227n106; of 1898, 29, 227n114; of 1914, 241n17; of 1917, 73–74, 243n53; of 1924, 100, 248n4; of 1928, 103, 249n5, 250n18; of 1932, 249n7; of 1936, 117, 257n81; of 1940, 135, 264n28; of 1944, 158, 272n114; of 1948, 172, 273n135, 275n7

electores pudientes, 22
Ellsworth, Elmer, 128, 138, 259n3
Enamorado Cuesta, José, 107, 253n42
English language, instruction in, 47, 49, 173, 234n44, 235n59
Escabí, Norberto, 88
Estades Font, María, 44, 52
Estadistas. *See* Partido Estadista (Statehood Party)
Estado Libre Asociado de Puerto Rico, 170, 197, 213; 1922 bill calling for, 92; formal creation of, 189, 209; Korean War mobilization as key to, xiv–xv, xxix, 168, 190. *See also* Commonwealth formula
Esteves, Luis Raúl, 80, 96, 179, 247n120
Executive Order 6.726, 105, 236n65, 259n6
Executive Order 9981, 179

facultades omnimodas, 22, 26, 27
Falange Española Tradicionalista y de las Juntas de Ofensiva Nacional Sindicalista, 260n7
fascism, 254n48, 260n7
Federación de Trabajadores de Puerto Rico, 241n18
Federación Libre de Trabajadores (FLT), 45, 104
Federal Bureau of Investigation (FBI), 104, 109, 114, 174, 255n58, 260n7
Federal Emergency Relief Administration, 105
Federal Party, 45, 234nn45–46, 248n4
Fernández, Enrique R., 195
Fernández García, Rafael, 106, 257n77
Fernando VII, 20, 22
Fernós Isern, Antonio, 162, 171, 182–83
Ferrao, Luis A., 254n44
Ferré, Luis A., 11
Ferrer, Ada, xix, 216nn18–19
Figueroa Cordero, Andrés, 277n26
Fijo (Batallón de Veteranos), 18, 20, 25, 225n78
Fiske, John, 232n27
Flores, Irving, 277n26
Foraker, Joseph B., 44
Foraker Act: amendments to, 57, 240n3;

provisions of, 44–45, 70, 233n41, 234n44
Fortas, Abe, 138, 272n120
Fort Buchanan, 145
Fort Miles, 262n17
Franklin, Jay, 248n2
Fredrickson, George M., 234n55
French colonialism, 19, 267n73
French Revolution, 19

gag law (*Ley de la mordaza*), 174, 277n26
Gallardo Santiago, Juan, 256n69
García, Calixto, 230n18
García Méndez, Manuel A., 133, 249n7
gender narratives, xvii, 41–42, 53, 232n29
GI Bill (Servicemen's Readjustment Act), 128, 155–56, 183, 270–71n105
Gil, Pedro, 156
Glorious Revolution (Spain), 7, 22, 23, 220n20
Go, Julian, xxi, 199
Gomez Brioso, José, 227n109
Gómez Pulido, Ramón, 26
Gompers, Samuel, 241n18
González, Manuel María, 7
González de Linares, Francisco, 21
Good Neighbor policy, 124, 131, 160, 170–71, 261n13, 272n117
Gore, Robert H., 103, 250–51n21, 251n24, 252n31
Governor bills, 127, 137–39, 161; congressional approval of, 164, 273n132
Great Depression, 95, 97, 102, 249–50n14, 268n84
Grito de Baire, 30
Grito de Lares, 23, 201; account of events, 6–9; aftermath of, 13–15; class conflict as cause of, 10, 221n32; dismantling of militias following, xxiii, 1, 14; national mythology around, 10–11; Republic of Puerto Rico formed during, 8, 220–21n26; significance of, 9–13; and slaves, 8, 13, 220n25, 223n48
Grito de Yara, 7, 23
Gruening, Ernest, 105, 115, 250n16, 257n77; and Muñoz Marín, 116, 123
Guardia Civil, 21, 24, 27, 32, 226n91
Guerra, Lilian, 64–65, 196, 215n1, 217n30

Guerra, Miguel, 90–91
Gurnes, Myron E., 251n27

Haiti, 171, 225–26n87; revolution in, 12, 20
Hanson, Parker, 257n77
Harding, Warren H., 91–92
Harris, William W., 183
Hawkins, Michael C., xiv, 215n2
Hays, Arthur Garfield, 258n85
hegemony, xxi, 208–9, 211; and national identity, xxix, 194, 195, 200, 209
Hendrickson, C., 88–89
Henry, Guy V., 54, 236n66, 239n97
Hernandez de Rivera, Hilda Alicia, *191*
hijos de este país, 92, 96, 172; access to US military institutions for, 60, 201; colonial militias manned by, xxiii, 1, 18, 19, 20; officer corps opened to, 94, 204; Spanish demobilization of, 14, 32, 225n78
Hispanic legacy: and Anglo Saxon/Hispanic binary, 188, 190, 280n58; Nationalists on, 109, 121–22, 205
Hoganson, Kristin L., xvi, 232n29
Hollander bill (1901), 249n8
hookworm, 50, 249n12
Hopkins, Harry, 252n32
Hostos, Eugenio María de: on Americanization, 54, 94, 203, 237–38n82; on military training, xx, 54–55, 237n80
Hull, Cordell, 261n13
Hurricane San Ciprián, 102
Hurricane San Ciriaco, 50, 236nn66–67
Hurricane San Felipe, 101
Hurricane San Narciso, 6
Huyke, Juan B., 91

Ibarra, Eusebio, 8, 9
Ickes, Harold, 120, 136, 137; and Muñoz Marín, 135; supervision of Puerto Rican affairs by, 105, 252n31; and Tydings bill, 115, 116
Iglesias Pantín, Santiago, 73, 133, 234n46, 247n116, 249n7, 252n31; assassination attempt against, 117, 255n64; and criticism of the police, 253n37, 255n57; as Socialist Party leader, 45, 241n18

illiteracy, 53, 66, 207–8, 247n119; of peasantry, 65, 223n54; rate, 237n75, 240n8, 274n141
immigration, to Puerto Rico, 11–12, 222n42
El Imparcial, 118, 185, 187
Incondicional Español, 27, 227n110
independence bills. *See* Tydings bills
independence goal: of Barceló, 91–92, 100; and Liberal Party, 100–101; and Muñoz Marín, xxv, 99, 135, 140–41, 143, 196, 207, 211–12, 263n27; and Nationalists, 103, 104; and Unionistas, 67, 91–92, 242n36; U.S. opposition to, 160, 164
independence movement, 181, 211, 273n127; legal arguments of, 231n18; Nationalist violence impact on, 112, 122, 123; under Spanish rule, 6–15. *See also* Albizu Campos, Pedro; Partido Independentista Puertorriqueño; Partido Nacionalista Puertorriqueño
industrialization, 121, 125, 142, 155, 157, 166, 205; infrastructure for, 130, 143
Instituto de Voluntarios, 21, 23–24, 27, 32, 33
Insular House Project, *159*
Insular Police: Albizu Campos threat against, 112, 253n37; creation of, 239n97; intelligence activities of, 109, 174; militarization of, 104, 251n27; and Ponce massacre, 118–19, 258n85; and UPR gun battle, 106–7, 248n1; in war with Nationalists, xxviii, 97–98, 106–7, 112, 113, 116, 117–19
Intendentes de Ejército y Provincia, 16
Internal Security Unit, 174
Ireland, 97–98, 248n2
Irizarry, Luis A., 120, 123
Isabel II, 22, 226n87
Isla Grande Naval Station, 262n17

Jayuya Uprising (1950), 174–78, 188, 276n13, 276n21
jíbaro figure: contradictory meanings of, 64, 217n22, 224n59; as icon, 64, 197, 224n59; laments of extinction of, xiv, 215n4; military remaking of, xiii, 16, 64, 65, 76, 84–86, 95, 96, 246n92; modernization of, 76, 203; and national identity, 64–65, 196, 215n1; and new jíbaro, 84–86, 95
Jiménez de Wagenheim, Olga, 223n54
Johnson, Jack, 216n11
Jones Act, 66, 68–71, 94, 240n11, 242n32; Puerto Ricans' welcoming of, 71, 242n36
Junta Informativa de Reformas de Ultramar, 4–5
Junta Suprema y Gubernativa de España e India, 19
Justicia, 82

Kaplan, Amy, xviii
King, William, 92
Kinsbruner, Jay, 222n46
Kochner, Harvey F., *191*
Korean War: beginning of, 178–79, 277n27; Corozal monument to, xiv, 215n3; and decolonization of Puerto Rico, xv, 168, 180–82, 184, 188–90, 194–96, 211; mobilization of Puerto Ricans for, 180–86, 209, 211; and Muñoz Marín, 183–84, 185, 186, 187, 188; Nationalist Party stance toward, 181; number of Puerto Ricans serving in, xv, 186, 278n43; press support for participation in, 184–85; Puerto Rican casualties in, 186, 279n55; and Puerto Rican flag, 190, *191*, *192*, *193*, 194, 197; and Puerto Ricans' patriotism, 183, 185, 187; returning veterans from, xiii–xv, 196–97, 281n73; 65th Infantry during, xv, 179–80, 184–87, 190, 278n34, 278n36, 279n47, 279nn54–55; Stalin on, 277n27; United Nations in, 172, 185, 211; U.S. unpreparedness for, 179–80, 277–78n29
Krug, J. A., 162

labor movement, 45, 104, 233n40, 251n22
Labra, Rafael María de, 27, 227n106
language, vernacular, 281n2
Lares PR, 7–8, 58, 239n93. *See also* Grito de Lares
las Casas, Bartolomé de, 79–80
Lastra, Manuel, 90

Leahy, William D., 133, 135–36, 260n8, 263n19, 263n20
Lebrón, Lolita, 277n26
Ley de Reclutamiento y Reemplazo del Ejercito (1878), 228n124
Ley Electoral Maura (1892), 227n106
liberals: in Spain, 4–5, 19, 21–22, 23; under Spanish colonialism, 25–26, 27. *See also* Partido Liberal Puertorriqueño
Libre Asociación concept, 94, 203, 234n47. *See also* autonomism; Commonwealth formula; Estado Libre Asociado de Puerto Rico; self-government
libreta de jornaleros (passbook system), 5–6, 8
Lloréns Torres, Luis, 74
Long, John D., 38
Loosey Field, 262n17
López-Alves, Fernando, 2

Maceo, Antonio, 228n120
Macías y Casado, Manuel, 38
Mahan, Alfred T.: on benevolent colonialism, 43, 228–29n2; imperialist perspective of, 39, 132, 229–30n12; on naval power, 233n38; racial views of, 43; and Spanish-American War, 38, 230n13
Maine, 31
Maldonado, A. W., 263n27
Mallon, Florencia, xxi, 1, 208–9, 211, 217n25
manhood, 53–54, 149; and military service, xvi–xxii, xix–xx, 42, 65, 180
manifest destiny, 41, 231–32n27
Marcantonio, Vito, 248n2
Marchessi, José María, 23
María Cristina de Borbón, 22
Marín Román, Héctor, 108, 110, 255n65
Martí, José, 223n50
Martínez de la Rosa, Francisco, 22
Martínez Nadal, Rafael, 133, 249n7, 257n78
Martínez Plowes, Juan, 27
Matienzo Cintrón, Rosendo, 94, 203, 227n109, 238n84
Mayaguez Lions Club, 146, 267n69
McCloy, John J., 139–40
McIntyre, Frank, 72, 73, 75, 76, 78–79, 243n45

McKinley, William, 43, 59; and "benevolent assimilation," 46, 228n2; and Cuba, 30, 227n116; and Puerto Rico, 39
Medina Ramírez, Rafael, 120
Meléndez, Edgardo, 231n20
Meléndez, Salvador, 19, 20, 21
Méndez, Aurelio, 220–21n26
Mendoza Rivera, Inés, 172, 275n6
Menéndez Ramos, Rafael, 106
Meneses, Laura, 98
metropolitan-colonial power relations, xx–xxi, 200
Michigan affair (1950), 178, 276n22
Miles, Nelson, 36–38, 53
Milicia Disciplinada, 17–18, 21, 224n66; elimination of, 24, 25, 32
Milicia Irregular Urbana, 17, 224n62
Milicia Urbana, 17–18, 19, 20, 224n62; demobilization of, 21, 25, 225n81
military bases, 132, 262n17
military intelligence, 109–10, 113, 254–55n52
military service: of African Americans, xviii, 42, 69, 83, 179, 216n11, 216n15; and Americanization, xxii, xxiv–xxvi, 49–50, 58, 60, 61–62, 109, 129; and dependents' benefits, 152–53; economic reasons for, 149–51, 268n89; educational requirements for, 146, 259n1, 266–67n69; and jíbaro figure, xiii, 16, 64, 65, 76, 84–86, 95, 96, 246n92; in Korean War, xxv, 180–86, 209, 211; and manhood, xvi–xxii, xix–xx, 42, 65, 180; modernization through, 60, 62, 129, 167, 169, 203, 205–6, 274n141; and national identity, xv, xxi, xxii, 3, 167, 184, 187–88, 194, 200–201, 205–6; and nation building, xxi, xxii–xxiv, 65, 94, 157–58, 195, 208; Puerto Rican officers in, 58, 72, 76, 77, 80–81, 94, 148, 239nn94–95, 243n49, 245n74; Puerto Ricans deemed unfit for, xviii, xx, 43, 146, 148, 149; racialized view of, xvii–xix, 42, 69, 146, 148, 179, 180, 216n12; salary from, 151, 152, 269n93, 269nn98–99; and self-government, xv, xvi, 53; Spain's exclusion of Puerto

military service (*cont.*)
  Ricans from, xxiii, 1, 14, 15, 20–21, 23–25, 32–33, 201, 225n78; in Spanish-American War, 37–38, 42, 229n10; under Spanish rule, xxiii, 1, 8–9, 17–18, 19, 20, 24–25, 228n124; as technicians and technocrats, xxv–xxvi, 62, 157, 196; transformative nature of, xiv, 64, 77–80, 96, 180, 201–2; under U.S. occupation, 48, 52, 54, 55–60, 63, 201, 202; in World War I, 75, 87, 94–95, 108, 202–3, 244n58; in World War II, xxv, 127, 130, 145–53
military training, xxv–xxvi, 167; Hostos on, xx, 54–55, 237n80; as road to modernization, xx, 205–6, 281n6; under Spanish rule, 24–25, 226nn94–96; during World War I, 76, 77–79, 84–85, 244n73
militias, Spanish colonial: *hijos de este país* in, xxiii, 1, 18, 19, 20; Lares rebellion fought by, 8–9; reformation of, xxiii, 17–18; size of, 17; Spain's demobilization of, xxiii, 1, 14, 15, 20–21, 23–25, 32, 225n78
Millán, Clemente, 220n26
modernization, 35, 199; and Americanization, 165–66, 203; military service as isntrument for, 60, 62, 129, 167, 169, 203, 205–6, 274n141
Monroe Doctrine, 70, 230n17
Montevideo Convention on the Rights and Duties of States, 261n13
Morales Lemus, José, 5
Morris, Nancy, xxi–xxii
Moya y Ojanguren, Miguel, 227n106
El Mundo, 118, 185, 187
Muñoz, Miguel A., 118–19, 151–52, 258n87, 271n113
Muñoz Marín, Luis: and Albizu Campos, xxviii, 173, 277n26; adopting autonomism, xxix, 161–62, 168; on Brookings Institution report, 248n2; and commonwealth formula, 170, 171, 189, 207–8; as first elected Puerto Rico governor, 165; and Gore, 104, 251n24; and Governor Bill, 138, 139; independence perspective abandoned by, xxv, 135, 140–41, 143, 196, 207, 211–12;

263n27; industrialization promoted by, 143, 157; on Jayuya Uprising, 177, 188; and Korean War, 183–84, 185, 186, 187, 188; and Liberal Party, 100–101, 116–17; popular sectors' support of, 166, 210; and PPD formation, 117, 133; and PRRA, 106, 124; and Puerto Rican national identity, 96, 99; and Puerto Rico decolonization, xxv, 124, 125, 145, 160–61, 164, 189, 212–13; returning to political prominence, 123–25; and Riggs assassination, 116, 123; and Roosevelt administration, 103, 122, 134, 135, 142, 250n16, 260n8; socio-economic focus of, xxv, xxix, 102, 134, 141, 158, 167, 169, 250n15; split with independentistas by, 158, 274n2; and Tydings bills, 116–17, 140, 160; U.S. military fears of, 255–56n65; and veterans benefits, 155; and World War II, 129–30, 134, 149, 165, 206. *See also* Partido Popular Democrático
Muñoz Rivera, Luis, 68, 71, 223n54, 241n17; and autonomy, 28, 67, 241n19; and Carta Autonómica, 28, 227n108; and Federals, 234nn45–46
Mussolini, Benito, 254n48

Nadal, Jaime, 239n94
national identity: Albizu Campos and Nationalists on, 96, 99, 109, 151, 210; Anglo Saxon/Hispanic binary, 182, 188, 190, 280n58; complexity of, xxix, 86, 188, 195, 196; contested nature of, xxii, 60, 202, 211–12; developing under Spain, xxiii–xxiv, 6–7, 13–15, 33, 47, 201; discernible Other needed for, 4, 234–35n55; double, xxii, xxix, 85, 94, 182, 187, 190, 194–95, 203, 210–11; as flexible and broad, xxii, xxvi, 200; hegemonic, xxix, 194, 195, 200, 209; as Hispanic, 109, 121–22, 188, 190, 205, 280n58; and jíbaro figure, 64–65, 196, 215n1; military's role in forging, xv, xxi, xxii, 3, 167, 184, 187–88, 194, 200–201, 205–6; Muñoz Marín on, 96, 99; mythology and iconography of, 10–11, 64, 134, 197; and *puertorriqueñi-*

dad, xxvi, 173, 196, 211, 280n58; and racial divide, 12–13; and racial triad, 188, 212; subaltern groups' creation of, xxi, 208–9, 217n25; and U.S. institutions, 61, 202
nationalism, 6–7, 217n25; Anderson on, xxi, 207, 281n2; symbols of Puerto Rican, 196, 211–12, 217n30
Nationalist Party. *See* Partido Nacionalista Puertorriqueño
nation building: criollization of, 199–200, 204; military's role in, xxi, xxii–xxiv, 65, 94, 157–58, 195, 208; and state building, 199; under U.S. colonial rule, 35, 46, 49; during World War I, 167, 206
Navy, 132, 160, 233n38, 262n17; in Spanish-American War, 38–39, 230n13
Negrón de Montilla, Aida, 218n33
Negroni, Héctor Andrés, 16, 17, 22, 24, 225n78
New Americanism, 85, 90–91, 94, 203
New Deal, 135–36, 142, 143
New York Times, 116
94th Infantry Division, 75, 244n58
Norat-Martínez, José, 274n1
Norzagaray, Fernando de, 21
Núñez de Cáceres, José, 225n87

O'Daly, Demetrio, 22
O'Donnell, Leopoldo, 226n87
officers, Puerto Rican, 58, 239nn94–95; during World War I, 72, 76, 77, 80–81, 94, 148, 243n49, 245n74; during World War II, 148
O'Mahoney, Joseph C., 171
100 percent Americanism, 74–76, 94, 203, 209, 243nn56–57
Operation Bootstrap, 142, 166
Operation Portrex, 180, 278n34
Orbeta, Enrique, 110, 118
O'Reilly, Alejandro, 17–18
Ortiz, Silvestre, *192*
Ortiz Pacheco, Rafael, 256n69

Pacific Stars & Stripes, 195
Padín, José, 257n77
Padrón, Antonio E., 268n87
Pagán, Bolívar, 257n81, 264n28

Palacios, Romualdo, 27
Panama Canal, 87, 132, 262n17
Pan-American Convention, 261n13, 268n91
Parks, G. B., 160
Partido Autonomista Histórico (Ortodoxo), 28, 227n114
Partido Autonomista Puertorriqueño (PAP), 31, 228n120; election results for, 29, 227n106, 227n114; goals of, 27–28
Partido Comunista Puertorriqueño, 250n19
Partido Constitucional Histórico, 100, 248n4
Partido de Izquierda Progresista Incondicional, 227n110, 227n114
Partido de la Independencia (founded 1912), 67, 238n84, 241n19
Partido Estadista (Statehood Party), 172, 181, 273n135, 275n7
Partido Independentista (founded 1934), 250n19
Partido Independentista Puertorriqueño (PIP) (founded 1946), 163, 172, 181; election results for, 273n135, 275n7; formation of, 162, 274n2
Partido Laborista Puro, 133
Partido Liberal Fusionista Puertorriqueño, 28
Partido Liberal Puertorriqueño (PLP): election results for, 117, 249n7, 257n81, 272n114; formation of, 100–101; and Muñoz Marín, 101, 117; Nationalist attacks on, 113, 117, 255n64; split in, 116–17, 122
Partido Liberal Reformista, 25–26
Partido Nacionalista Puertorriqueño: Albizu Campos joining of, 98; assassination attempts by, 119–20, 255n59, 255n64, 258n91; attacks within U.S. by, 177, 277n26; bombings by, 106; dissension within, 118, 120–21, 257n82; economic and social ideology of, 104, 251n23; election results of, 103, 248n4, 249n7, 250n18; electoral activity abandoned by, 103–4; government and military surveillance of, 110, 114, 260n7;

Partido Nacionalista Puertorriqueño (*cont.*) and Grito de Lares, 10–11; and Hispanic legacy, 109, 121–22, 205; Insular Police at war with, xxviii, 97–98, 106–7, 112, 113, 116, 117–19; and Jayuya Uprising, 174–75, 177–78, 188, 276n13, 276n21; on Korean War participation, 181; loss of support for, 117–18, 120–21, 133, 181–82, 205, 260n7, 263n21, 278n40; membership of, 111, 255n58, 263n21; and national identity, 109, 151, 210; paramilitary units of, 99, 107–8, 205; and Ponce massacre, 117–19; and Riggs assassination, 112–16; sedition trial against, 114–15, 256n69, 256n72, 275n9; stance during World War II of, 140, 265n52, 268n82, 268n91; and sugar workers, 104; war plans of, 106–9, 110–11. *See also* Albizu Campos, Pedro

Partido Obrero Socialista, 45

Partido Oportunista, 227n110, 227n114

Partido Popular Democrático (PPD): creation of, 117, 133; electoral participation of, 133–34, 135, 158, 206, 264n28, 272n114, 273n135, 275n7; independentista wing of, 134, 139, 158, 162, 274n2; insignia and iconography of, 134, 197; and Korean War, 182, 188; and Michigan affair, 178, 276n22; national discourse of, 210, 211, 216n7; popular support for, 124–25, 135, 169, 196; and socioeconomic reform, 141–42, 158; and Tydings-Piñero bill, 162; and veterans benefits, 153, 155. *See also* Muñoz Marín, Luis

Partido Reformista Puertorriquéno, 275n7

Partido Republicano, 46, 85, 102, 242n36; election results for, 100, 103, 243n53, 248n4, 250n18; and Federals, 45, 234n46; 100 percent Americanism supported by, 74, 76, 94; pro-statehood position of, 74, 240n8, 257n78

Partido Socialista, 74, 92, 102, 242n36, 257n78; about, 241n18; election results for, 100, 243n53, 248n4, 249n7, 257n81, 264n28, 272n144, 273n135, 275n7; and Korean War participation, 181

Partido Unión de Puerto Rico, 67, 100, 241n18; autonomist-separatist split in, 76–77, 85, 91–92; and autonomy goal, 46, 85, 90, 94, 203, 234n47, 241n19; election results for, 57, 73–74, 241n17, 243n53; formation of, 45, 46; and independence goal, 67, 242n36; and U.S. citizenship, 68, 241n22

Partido Unión Republicana, 100; election results for, 249n7, 257n81, 264n28, 272n144

Partido Unión Republicana Progresista, 133

passbooks. *See libreta de jornaleros*

Pavía, Julián Juan, 7

Pavía, Manuel, 227n102

peasantry: illiteracy among, 65, 223n54; landless, 5–6, 8, 269–70n99; proletarianization of, 101–2, 249n8; U.S. military relationship with, 52. *See also* jíbaro figure

peninsulares, 3, 4, 25, 219n5, 220n18, 336; *criollos*' relationship with, xxiii, 2, 4, 33, 218n32, 219n10, 219–20n13; *criollos*' struggle with, 6, 13–14, 221n32

Pérez, Louis, 30

Pezuela y Ceballos, Juan de la, 225n81

Philippines, 115, 215n2; anti-U.S. insurgency in, xiv, xviii, 53; during Spanish-American War, 38–39; and Taft, 57–58, 238n92

Picó, Fernando, 229n10

Piñero Jiménez, Jesús T., 128, 138, 162, 164, 174, 259n5, 272n114

Platt Amendment, 228n122, 261n13

Point Four, 171, 274–75n5

Pol, Bernabé, 220–21n26

political enfranchisement, xvi–xvii, 2, 36, 47, 58

political violence: during 1930s, 97, 98, 99, 104–5, 106–9, 121, 122, 128, 207; during Jayuya Uprising, 174–78, 188, 276n13, 276n21; Muñoz Marín and, 99, 123–24, 173; Puerto Ricans' rejection of, 120, 123

Ponce massacre, 119–21, 258n85

Popular Democratic Party. *See* Partido Popular Democrático (PPD)

popularization, xxv, 47, 208, 212
population, of Puerto Rico, 4, 11, 12–13, 219n8, 222n46
Portilla, Segundo de la, 27
Porto Rican Commission (PRC), 37
Porto Rican Scouts (PRS), 38
Porto Rico and Its Problems (Brookings Institution), 101–2, 249n10
Porto Rico Progress, 63, 85, 86, 89, 239n1
Porto Rico Regiment of Infantry, 56, 80, 87, 246–47n102–3
Porto Rico Regiment United States Volunteers, 55, 57, 59, 238n88
Power y Giralt, Ramón, 25–26
Public Law 600, 171–72; independentista opposition to, 173, 277n23; referendum on, 172, 178, 186, 188, 280n60; signed into law, 181
Puerto Rican docility myth, xx, 43, 148, 217n22
Puerto Rican flag, 117, 165, 255n64; in Korean War, 185, 190, *191*, *192*, *193*, *194*, 197; origins of, 253n37
Puerto Rican Induction Program, 145–53
Puerto Rico Emergency Relief Administration (PRERA), 105, 124, 166, 252n32
Puerto Rico National Guard: and community-building projects, 157–58, 271n112; creation of, 77, 87, 93, 95, 204, 247n120; expansion of, 122, 258–59n95; and Jayuya Uprising, 175, *176*, 177, 276n15; and Nationalist Party, 110, 111–12, 258n94; nation building by, 190; in Operation Portrex, 180, 278n34; 295th and 296th regiments of, 87–88, 145, 267n71
Puerto Rico Reconstruction Administration (PRRA), 121, 142, 166, 257n77; creation of, 105–6, 252–53n33; Muñoz Marín role in, 116, 124
Puerto Rico status: Commonwealth formula, 170, 171, 180, 188, 189, 207–8; Estado Libre Asociado formal creation, 189, 209; Foraker Act on, 44–45, 70, 233n41, 234n44; Governor bills on, 127, 137–39, 161, 164, 273n132; Jones Act on, 66, 68–71, 94, 240n11, 242n32; Muñoz Marín on, xxv, 124, 125, 135, 140–41, 143, 145, 160–61, 164, 171, 189, 196, 207–8, 211–13, 263n27; P.L. 600 on, 171–72, 181; referendums on, 172, 178, 186, 188, 189, 280n60; sovereignty transfer to U.S., xxvii, 40–41, 201–2; under Spanish rule, 1–34; Supreme Court on, 233n41; Truman on, 160, 161, 164–65, 170–71, 189, 272n117, 272n121; Tydings bills on, 115–17, 139–40, 158, 160, 161–63, 257nn77–78, 272n122; under U.S. occupation, 35–62. *See also* Estado Libre Asociado de Puerto Rico
Puerto Rico strategic importance: during cold war, 164; U.S. Navy on, 160; and U.S. seizure from Spain, 39, 163; and World War II, 132–33, 136, 262n17
Puerto Rico World Journal, 127, 259n1
puertorriqueñidad, xxvi, 173, 196, 211, 280n58

Los Quijotes, 108
Quintero Rivera, Ángel, 46

racial beliefs and discrimination: and African Americans, xviii, 42, 69, 83, 179, 216n11, 216n15; and Caribbean population, 12–13, 267n73; and colonialism rationalizations, 41–43, 53; and Cuba, xviii, xix, xxix, 13, 42–43, 223n50; and military service, xvii–xix, 42, 69, 146, 148, 179, 180; and skin pigmentation, 234n55; Social Darwinism, 41, 232n27; during World War I, 82–84
racial triad, 188, 212
Ramírez, Francisco, 220n26
Real Cédula (1540), 224n61
Real Cédula de Gracias (1815), 11, 12
referendums, on Puerto Rico status, 172, 178, 186, 188, 189, 280n60
Reglamento Especial de Jornaleros (1849), 225n81
Reily, E. Montgomery, 92, 247n116, 252n31
Reina, Félix, 88–89
Republicanos Puros, 100
Republicans. *See* Partido Republicano

Republic of Puerto Rico, 8, 220–21n26
Reynolds, Ruth M., 163, 273n127
Riggs, Elisha Francis, 104, 106–7, 110, 248n1; assassination of, 112–15
Riva Agüero, Fernando de la, 18
Rivera, Ángel J., *191*
Rivero Méndez, Ángel, 231n19
Rodil, F. G., 88–89
Rodó, José Enrique, 246n94
Rodríguez Beruff, Jorge, 129, 130, 135, 260n8
Rojas, Manuel, 8
Roosevelt, Franklin Delano, 102–3, 129, 134, 136, 160, 258n92; and elective Puerto Rico governor, 137–38, 139; and Good Neighbor policy, 124, 131, 160, 261n13, 272n117; hemispheric defense policy of, 131–32, 261–62n14; and Interior Department supervision of Puerto Rico, 50, 105, 128; and Muñoz Marín, 103, 135; New Deal programs of, 141, 142; and Tydings bill, 115; and Winship, 104, 133, 260n8
Roosevelt, Theodore, xviii, 39, 59, 66
Roosevelt Roads Naval Station, 262n17
Root, Elihu, 44, 59, 67
Rosado, Hiram, 112, 116, 123
Rosado Ortiz, Pablo, 256n69
Rosario Natal, Carmelo, 235n59
Rossy, Manuel F., 90–91, 100
Ruiz Belvis, Segundo, 23
rum excise taxes, 130, 152, 261n9, 266n61

Sagasta, Práxedes Mateo, 28
Salinas, Francisco, 150
Saltari, Domingo, 255n64
Sampson, William T., 39
San Sebastian del Pepino, 8–9
Sanz, José Laureano, 13, 14, 23, 24, 27, 223n51
Scarano, Francisco, 64, 217n22, 224n59
Schwan, Theodore, 38
Selective Service Act (1917), 69–70, 72
Selective Service Law (1940), 268n82
self-determination: as distinct from self-government, 240n4; the need for, 63, 65, 70–71, 89–90, 91
self-government, 41, 63, 129, 171; Atlantic Charter on, 138, 264n41; and citizenship, 68–69, 71; darker races seen as unworthy of, xviii, 42, 43, 69; Interior Department support for, 161, 272n120; and military service, xv, xvi, 53; P.L. 600 on, 171–72; self-determination as distinct from, 240n4; Truman support for, 160, 161, 162, 164–65, 272n121; Unionistas' support for, 67, 76–78, 89, 90; Wilson call for, 70–71; Yager support for, 68, 74. *See also* autonomism; Commonwealth formula; Estado Libre Asociado de Puerto Rico
shoes, 78, 84, 102, 249n12
Sibert, Edwin L., 177
Sinn Fein, 98, 254n48
Situado Mexicano, 4, 219n6
65th Infantry: creation of, 87, 95; injustices suffered by, 180, 276n36, 279n54; intelligence section of, 109–10, 113–14, 254–55n52; in Korean War, xv, 179–80, 184–87, 190, 278n34, 278n36, 279n47, 279nn54–55; as national hero and icon, xv, 165, 186–87; as nation-building instrument, 190; recruitment into, 183; training of Boy Scouts by, 109; during World War II, 145, 165, 179, 267n71
slavery, 12, 26, 222n43
slaves: in independence struggle, 8, 220n25, 223n48; population of, 219n8, 222n46; rebellions by, 4, 219n7
social Darwinism, 41, 232n27
Socialists. *See* Partido Socialista
Soldevilla, Guillermo, 118
Soto Vélez, Clemente, 256n69
Spain, 1–34; absolutist power of, 20–23, 27; Carta Autonómica issued by, 28–29, 227n109; colonial elites under, 6, 15, 34, 200–201, 221n32, 223n52, 223n54; Constitution of Cadiz in, 21–22; Cortes of, 22, 23; declining empire of, 3–4; demobilization of Puerto Ricans by, xxiii, 1, 3, 14, 15, 20–21, 23–25, 32, 33, 225n81; federal republic in, 26–27, 227n102; Glorious Revolution in, 7, 220n20; independence struggle from, 6–15; Junta Informativa de Reformas de Ultramar

of, 4–5; liberalism in, 4–5, 19, 21–22, 23; military budget of, 16; in Napoleonic Wars, 19–20; passbook system of, 5–6, 8; Puerto Rican national identity under, xxiii–xxiv, 6–7, 13–15, 33, 47, 201; Puerto Rico as military colony of, 15–16
Spanish-American War: African American soldiers in, xviii, 42; lead-up to, 30–31, 227–28n116; naval actions in, 38–39, 230n13; occupation of Puerto Rico during, 36–38, 229n5; in Philippines, 38–39; Puerto Rican troops in, 37–38, 42, 229n10; Treaty of Paris ending, 31; U.S. troops' conduct during, 40, 231n19
Stalin, Joseph, 277n27
state capitalism, 265–66n56
statehood: as annexationist goal, 40–41; Republicans' support for, 74, 240n8, 257n78; support in U.S. for, 163–64, 212. *See also* annexationism; Partido Estadista
Stimson, Henry L., 240n13
Strong, Josiah, 231–32n27
Suárez Findlay, Eileen, xxi, 178, 216n7
sugar cane workers: general strike by, 104, 251n22; wages of, 142, 151
sugar industry, 4, 102, 225n81, 250n15

Taft, Robert A., 139–40, 259n3
Taft, William Howard, 67, 240n15; and Bureau of Insular Affairs, 63, 236n65, 240n3; and Philippines, 57–58, 238n92; Puerto Rico put under War Department by, 57, 236n65
Teller Amendment, 31, 40, 228n122
Tercer alzamiento de artilleros (1867), 23
Thompson, Edgar K., 251n27
375th Porto Rican Colored Regiment, 82–83
Tischler, Barbara L., 243n56
Tomás de Córdoba, Don Pedro, 225n78
Tormos Diego, José, 118
Torreforte, Juan de Mata, 8
Torres, Anibal, 276n13
Torresola, Griselio, 177
Travieso, Martín, 91, 243n53
Treaty of Paris (1898), 31, 40, 230–31n18, 250n20, 273n127

Triandafyllidou, Anna, 235n55
Truman, Harry S.: armed forces executive order by, 179; assassination attempt on, 177, 182; and Puerto Rico self-government, 160, 161, 164–65, 170–71, 189, 272n117, 272n121
Tugwell, Rexford G., 142, 145, 212, 264n30; as Puerto Rico governor, 135–37; and Truman, 160, 272n117
Turbas Republicanas, 234n46
Turner, Frederick Jackson, 232n27
Tydings, Millard, 104, 115, 139, 163, 252n31, 274n2
Tydings bills: of 1934 (Tydings-McDuffie), 115–17, 257nn77–78; of 1943, 139–40; of January 1945, 158, 160, 162; of May 1945 (Tydings-Piñero), 161–63, 272n122

unemployment, 76, 106, 183, 252n32; benefits for, 151–52, 166, 271n105; and military mobilization, 145, 206; statistics on, 149
Unificación Puertorriqueña Tripartita, 133, 264n28
Unionistas. *See* Partido Unión de Puerto Rico
Unión Republicana. *See* Partido Unión Republicana
United Nations: charter of, 162, 171, 273n124; and Korean War, 172, 185, 211; and Puerto Rico decolonization, 189, 212–13
United States Naval Academy, 81, 245n82
U.S. troops in Puerto Rico: as avenue of socioeconomic advancement, 122; bases of in Puerto Rico, 132, 262n17; Puerto Rican forces within, *48*, 54, 59–60, 63, 201; and Puerto Rico population, 50–52, 202; return of to U.S., 55, 58, 238n89; sanitary and relief campaigns by, 35, 47, 50–52, 202; during Spanish-American War, 36–38, 229n5
University of Puerto Rico: enrollment in, 156, 157; Nationalist Party at, 106–7, 110–11
"uplifting benevolence," 43
Utuado PR, 51, 255n59; and Jayuya Uprising, 175, 276n15

Vagas, Victor, 150
Valencia, Federico, 220–21n26
Valle Atiles, Francisco del, 16, 84–85
Velázquez, Erasmo, 256n69
Velázquez, Julio H., 256n69
Velázquez, Luis F., 115, 256n69
veterans: benefits paid to, 151–52, 166, 270n102; housing for, 271–72n113; from Korean War, xiii–xv, 196–97, 281n73; living standard of, 280–81n73; as returning jíbaro-soldiers, 196–97; vocational programs for, *154*, 155–57, 203, 270n102; from World War I, 88–89; from World War II, 129, 153–58, 270n104
Veterans Administration, 151, 155, 156–57, 270n105
Vidal, Teodoro, 270n104
Vieques, 180, 262n17, 278n34
Villahermosa, Gilberto N., 278n34
Vivario, George, *192*
vocational training, 95; for veterans, *154*, 155–57, 203, 270n102
voter fraud, 133, 263n20
voters, registered, 45, 234n49
voting rights and restrictions, 26, 45–46, 226n89, 257n81; Jones Act on, 68, 71, 241n21, 242n38

wages: of soldiers, 151, 152, 269n93, 269–70n99; of workers, 102, 142, 151, 251n22, 269n95
War Department, 53, 258n95, 262n17; Bureau of Insular Affairs of, 50, 57, 236n65; control of Puerto Rico by, 50, 57, 63, 66, 75, 93, 236n65; having low opinion of Puerto Rican soldiers, 43, 148, 266n65, 267n73; Interior Department's taking of control from, 50, 105, 128, 259–60n6; Military Intelligence Division of, 104, 254–55n52; and World War I, 70, 75, 77–78, 79; and World War II, 145, 146–47, 148–49, 150, 152, 153, 183, 259n1, 266n69
Washington Post, 77–78
Wells, Henry, 156
Weyler, Valeriano, 30, 230n18
White, Edward D., 233n41
white supremacy, xvii, 216n11

Wilson, Woodrow: and granting of U.S. citizenship, 67, 71, 242n35; and Jones Act, 68, 70–71; 100 percent Americanism discourse of, 75–76, 94, 203; and Selective Service Act, 72; self-determination rhetoric of, 70, 71, 89, 90, 91
Winship, Blanton, 104, 118, 119–20, 133, 260n8
women: economic activity of, 249–50n14; and right to vote, 249n6
Wood, Frank C., 83
Works Projects Administration (WPA), 142, 153, 166
World War I, xxvii–xxviii; demobilization of Puerto Ricans following, 86–88, 94; ending of, 86, 246n99; mobilization of Puerto Ricans for, 77–79, 80–81, 93–94, 244n73; 100 percent Americanism campaign during, 74–75, 76, 243nn56–57; onset of, 66; Puerto Rican troops during, 75, 87, 94–95, 108, 202–3, 244n58; racial divide during, 82–84; and self-determination question, 63, 65, 70–71, 89–90, 91; U.S. citizenship granted during, 66–71; U.S. entry into, 71–74
World War II, xxviii, 205–9; as catalyst for change, 128–29; and Muñoz Marín, 129–30, 134, 149, 165, 206; Nationalist Party stance toward, 140, 265n52, 268n82, 268n91; New Deal brought to Puerto Rico by, 135–36; Puerto Rican economy during, 130, 141–43, 260–61n9, 265n54; Puerto Rican military mobilization during, 127, 130, 145–53; Puerto Rican troops serving in, 145, 165, 179, 206, 267n71; Puerto Rico's strategic importance in, 132–33, 136, 139; returning veterans from, 153–58; and U.S. hemispheric defense strategy, 131–32, 261–62n14; U.S. preparations for, 145, 266n54

Yager, Arthur, 72–73, 74, 80, 81, 245n80; biographical information, 241n16; pro-segregationist views of, 82; on Puerto Ricans' military training, 78–79; and Puerto Rico National Guard, 77, 87; and U.S. citizenship, 67, 68–69

Studies in War, Society, and the Military

Military Migration and State Formation: The British Military Community in Seventeenth-Century Sweden
Mary Elizabeth Ailes

The State at War in South Asia
Pradeep P. Barua

Death at the Edges of Empire: Fallen Soldiers, Cultural Memory, and the Making of an American Nation, 1863–1921
Shannon Bontrager

An American Soldier in World War I
George Browne
Edited by David L. Snead

Beneficial Bombing: The Progressive Foundations of American Air Power, 1917–1945
Mark Clodfelter

Fu-go: The Curious History of Japan's Balloon Bomb Attack on America
Ross Coen

Imagining the Unimaginable: World War, Modern Art, and the Politics of Public Culture in Russia, 1914–1917
Aaron J. Cohen

The Rise of the National Guard: The Evolution of the American Militia, 1865–1920
Jerry Cooper

The Thirty Years' War and German Memory in the Nineteenth Century
Kevin Cramer

Political Indoctrination in the U.S. Army from World War II to the Vietnam War
Christopher S. DeRosa

In the Service of the Emperor: Essays on the Imperial Japanese Army
Edward J. Drea

American Journalists in the Great War: Rewriting the Rules of Reporting
Chris Dubbs

America's U-Boats: Terror Trophies of World War I
Chris Dubbs

The Age of the Ship of the Line: The British and French Navies, 1650–1815
Jonathan R. Dull

American Naval History, 1607–1865: Overcoming the Colonial Legacy
Jonathan R. Dull

Soldiers of the Nation: Military Service and Modern Puerto Rico, 1868–1952
Harry Franqui-Rivera

You Can't Fight Tanks with Bayonets: Psychological Warfare against the Japanese Army in the Southwest Pacific
Allison B. Gilmore

A Strange and Formidable Weapon: British Responses to World War I Poison Gas
Marion Girard

Civilians in the Path of War
Edited by Mark Grimsley and Clifford J. Rogers

A Scientific Way of War: Antebellum Military Science, West Point, and the Origins of American Military Thought
Ian C. Hope

Picture This: World War I Posters and Visual Culture
Edited and with an introduction by Pearl James

Indian Soldiers in World War I: Race and Representation in an Imperial War
Andrew T. Jarboe

Death Zones and Darling Spies: Seven Years of Vietnam War Reporting
Beverly Deepe Keever

For Home and Country: World War I Propaganda on the Home Front
Celia Malone Kingsbury

I Die with My Country: Perspectives on the Paraguayan War, 1864–1870
Edited by Hendrik Kraay and Thomas L. Whigham

North American Indians in the Great War
Susan Applegate Krouse
Photographs and original documentation by Joseph K. Dixon

Remembering World War I in America
Kimberly J. Lamay Licursi

Citizens More than Soldiers: The Kentucky Militia and Society in the Early Republic
Harry S. Laver

Soldiers as Citizens: Former Wehrmacht Officers in the Federal Republic of Germany, 1945–1955
Jay Lockenour

Deterrence through Strength: British Naval Power and Foreign Policy under Pax Britannica
Rebecca Berens Matzke

Army and Empire: British Soldiers on the American Frontier, 1758–1775
Michael N. McConnell

*Of Duty Well and Faithfully Done: A History of the
Regular Army in the Civil War*
Clayton R. Newell and Charles R. Shrader
With a foreword by Edward M. Coffman

*The Militarization of Culture in the Dominican Republic, from the
Captains General to General Trujillo*
Valentina Peguero

Arabs at War: Military Effectiveness, 1948–1991
Kenneth M. Pollack

*The Politics of Air Power: From Confrontation to Cooperation in
Army Aviation Civil-Military Relations*
Rondall R. Rice

Andean Tragedy: Fighting the War of the Pacific, 1879–1884
William F. Sater

The Grand Illusion: The Prussianization of the Chilean Army
William F. Sater and Holger H. Herwig

Sex Crimes under the Wehrmacht
David Raub Snyder

In the School of War
Roger J. Spiller
Foreword by John W. Shy

*On the Trail of the Yellow Tiger: War, Trauma, and Social Dislocation in
Southwest China during the Ming-Qing Transition*
Kenneth M. Swope

Friendly Enemies: Soldier Fraternization throughout the American Civil War
Lauren K. Thompson

The Paraguayan War, Volume 1: Causes and Early Conduct
Thomas L. Whigham

*Policing Sex and Marriage in the American Military: The Court-Martial and the
Construction of Gender and Sexual Deviance, 1950–2000*
Kellie Wilson-Buford

The Challenge of Change: Military Institutions and New Realities, 1918–1941
Edited by Harold R. Winton and David R. Mets

To order or obtain more information on these or other University of Nebraska Press titles, visit nebraskapress.unl.edu.